Madam
Prime
Minister

Madam Prime Minister

A Life in Power and Politics

GRO HARLEM BRUNDTLAND

Farrar, Straus and Giroux
New York

Farrar, Straus and Giroux
19 Union Square West, New York 10003

Distributed in Canada by Douglas & McIntyre Ltd.
Printed in the United States of America
Originally published in two volumes in 1997 and 1998, respectively,
by Gyldendal Norsk Forlag, Norway, as Mitt Liv and Dramatiske År
Published in the United States by Farrar, Straus and Giroux
First American edition, 2002

Grateful acknowledgment is made to Scanpix Norway and Bergens Tidende for permission to
reproduce photographs of Gro Harlem Brundtland.

Library of Congress Cataloging-in-Publication Data
Brundtland, Gro Harlem.
     [Mitt liv 1939–1986. English]
     Madam Prime Minister : a life in power and politics / Gro Harlem Brundtland.—
1st American ed.
        p.   cm.
     Originally published as: Mitt liv 1939–1986 and Dramatiske år 1986–1996.
Norway : Gyldendal Norsk, c1997 and c1998.
     ISBN 0-374-16716-8 (hc : alk. paper)
     1. Brundtland, Gro Harlem.   2. Prime ministers—Norway—Biography.   3. Norway—
Politics and government—1945–   I. Brundtland, Gro Harlem. Dramatiske år
1986–1996. English.   II. Title.
DL535.B78 B7913 2002
948.104'092—dc21
    [B]
                                                                    2002019925

Designed by Patrice Sheridan

www.fsgbooks.com

10 9 8 7 6 5 4 3 2 1

Contents

Preface

Since I left Norwegian politics with nearly a quarter-century's experience in its top positions, and assumed new, global responsibilities as Director General of the World Health Organization, many people in a variety of positions worldwide have expressed interest in reading my memoirs.

Writing this book has given me the invaluable opportunity to put my private, professional, and political life in perspective and to reflect on many of the central issues of our time, both national and international.

I have lived a most interesting and productive professional life. I was born into a family of medicine and politics, and I chose an education in public health from the University of Oslo and Harvard University. I worked as a physician and then at the age of thirty-five was catapulted into politics at the national level as Minister of the Environment. I became the first female Prime Minister of my country six years later, serving as leader of the biggest political party of Norway, the Labor Party, for twelve years, and ten as Prime Minister. I formed and led the U.N. World Commission on Environment and Development. Its 1987 report, "Our

Common Future," helped establish the concept of sustainable development.

During my time in public office, Norway has experienced dramatic changes. Care for the environment has been ensured. We have made revolutionary progress toward gender equality. My second cabinet included eight women Ministers among the eighteen posts, a world record. We modernized the Labor Party and gave renewed meaning to "social democracy" long before the "New Labor" concept became fashionable in other countries. And Norway is now internationally known for its efforts to bring about peace, reconciliation, disaster relief, public health aid, and development around the world.

I now have the privilege of making a difference in global health and development through the World Health Organization. Mobilizing for health, bringing the awareness of health to the highest levels of decision making in every country, has always been my aim. We badly need health reform in many countries and particularly those where billions of human beings are still living on a bare minimum unserved by the last century's enormous advancements in health and standards of living. I see much of this work as a contribution to the formation of a global public sector amid the tremendous changes brought about by globalization.

I offer this English-language version of my memoirs as my contribution to the analysis of our common problems as I see them and as testimony to the possibility of their solution through democratic government.

—Gro Harlem Brundtland

Madam Prime Minister

Love, War, Childhood 1

The Sailing Trip

Inga Brynolf is twenty years old, blue-eyed and dark-haired. The young Swede is hiking her way from Stockholm to Oslo. It's July 1938. She and her boyfriend, who is leader of the Swedish chapter of Clarté, an international association of socialist intellectuals, are going to spend the summer sailing off the coast of Norway.

She is a radical, a socialist who dreams of a coming era of justice and equality. Her mother, the Stockholm lawyer Margareta Sandberg, is also a politically active radical and was for a time part of the group that formed around Alexandra Kollontai, the Soviet ambassador to Sweden. Like a real-life Nora in Henrik Ibsen's *A Doll's House,* Margareta left her husband, the barrister Ivar Brynolf, after five years of marriage. Her two small children, Inga and Lennart, were four and two. Margareta was twenty-four. She wanted to be a lawyer herself. In the early 1930s she became the first female solicitor ever to hold public office in Stockholm.

In Oslo Inga and her boyfriend are met by Gudmund Harlem, known to his friends as Gubbe, a young medical student and leader of the Norwegian chapter of Clarté. Gubbe's girlfriend has suddenly taken ill and can't come sailing. But Gubbe feels an obligation to go. Ola Evensen, a friend from Clarté, joins them.

During the day, there is hectic activity on board the sailboat. The twenty-four-foot boat has one cabin and four berths for the three men and one woman. The quiet evenings are spent discussing socialism and visions of the new era dawning. Two pairs of eyes soon establish a powerful contact, just looking, intensely interested in each other.

I was conceived later that thrilling summer. And Inga would stay in Norway. She decided to study law at the University of Oslo. She and Gubbe got married in Stockholm in the autumn. "Hurray! We're getting married today!" read Gubbe's telegraph to a friend in Oslo.

I was born on the night of April 20, 1939. At the maternity ward Mamma was referred to as "the dark Swede who screamed so terribly." Her labor was long and difficult. When my proud father came home that evening to tell his friends of the great event, the radio was on. Air Marshal Hermann Goering was speaking in Berlin on the occasion of Adolf Hitler's fiftieth birthday. My life surely started at a most intense moment of history, just four months before war broke out in Europe.

In the summer of 1938 Pappa turned twenty-one and assumed control of a small inheritance from his father, who died when Pappa was an infant. One hundred thousand Kroner (about $11,000) was a lot of money in the late 1930s. Twenty-five thousand Kroner went to the moving spirits behind a workers' encyclopedia, so they could realize their dream. Gubbe provided the capital and even joined the writing team. But he also bought an apartment at Camilla Collett's Way No. 2, "CC2," just behind the Royal Palace. The architect had designed the seventh floor especially for Aase Bye, the most prominent actress at the time, but when the Harlems moved in, it was put to an entirely different use. The large living room was divided to provide an extra bedroom and the dining room was divided in two. Thus the elegant apartment became a seven-bedroom collective.

The Coming War

By Easter 1940, Mamma was pregnant again. But Pappa, determined to show his sporty Swedish wife the beauty of the Norwegian mountains, took her on a holiday to the Jotunheimen. I remained at home in the care of Grandma Margareta, who had traveled from Stockholm to look after me. But the idyll was short-lived.

The German strategic surprise attack on Norway started in the early hours of April 9. One of the women who lived with us in CC2, another new mother, had been a volunteer against Franco in the Spanish Civil War. She decided that her child should be spared future air raids spent in the cellar. As she recalls it, "I try to get the young couple we are living with to dry the baby's diapers, but a future Defense Minister [Pappa] refuses to take the matter seriously. The next morning we dispatch my baby and the young mother [Mamma] with her baby to a cabin outside of Lillehammer in a delivery truck. That other baby, the future Prime Minister, has to travel with a suitcase full of wet diapers."

At the cabin, Mamma was determined to find out what had happened to Pappa. The following day she made the long trip down to Lillehammer and back again. The Germans had already occupied the town and there were soldiers in the streets. She discovered that Pappa was with the Director General of Public Health, Dr. Karl Evang. They were with members of the government as the Norwegian defense campaign began to emerge. The improvised Norwegian defense managed to resist for two months and even gave the Germans their first tactical defeat of the war at Narvik. Mamma decided to go to Stockholm and hand me over for safekeeping to her mother. Shortly afterward she traveled north through Sweden and Finland to join Pappa, who was now already in Tromsø.

At the border she ran into problems—no one could quite make out the purpose of her journey. She had to call Dr. Evang in Tromsø. Once he confirmed her identity, she was allowed to pass.

On June 7 King Haakon and his government were forced to leave Norway. Largely by chance, Mamma and Pappa did not travel with the convoy to England. At the last moment Dr. Evang decided that they should return to Oslo and work for the Resistance at the University.

Several weeks passed while I was left in the care of my grandmother; I even learned to walk. When Mamma opened the door to find me playing on the floor, I rose and ran to greet her. But I did not easily forgive the separation: It took months before I would allow Mamma out of my sight again.

For the first two years of the war, daily life continued in more or less normal fashion, but food was in short supply, and heating proved problematic in the severe winters. My parents continued their studies even as they became involved in illegal activities. Mamma worked on the publication of the newspaper *Free Trade Union*. At all hours the smell of correcting fluid wafted from one of the two rooms that made up the original dining room in CC2. The typewriter had to be kept hidden. My parents did not even know the names of those to whom they delivered the paper. All precautions were taken to minimize the risk of the networks being exposed.

We froze that winter. The temperature indoors was often as low as 50 degrees Fahrenheit. My father sewed sleeping bags for me and my little brother, Erik. Made out of old wool blankets, the sleeping bags itched. After the war they remained on a shelf down in one of the basement lockers for many years. You never know, after all.

Arrest and Flight

In 1942 the occupying forces were tightening their grip. Several of the students active in the CC2 group were instructed to assist a group of Norwegian Jews who needed to go into hiding to avoid being transported to Germany. CC2 was a dangerous address to have. People came and went. Strangers often stayed overnight with us.

In autumn 1943 relations between the Nazi authorities and the University deteriorated and on the night of October 15 the police arrested fifty students and ten professors. This action would have serious repercussions for the CC2 student group.

The Norwegian Nazi police came in the early hours of the morning. They had warrants for the arrest of two of the students. Both were taken. They did not discover my father sleeping in the same room. Nor did they ask for him by name, so presumably his name was on a different list. He at once made his way down the narrow fire escape.

Half an hour later the German police, the Gestapo, came. This time they wanted Gudmund Harlem—a bigger catch than the first two. They failed to find him, so they took his young wife. She protested loudly when they tried to check another room where her sister-in-law Gegga lay sleeping: "She's just a schoolgirl!"

Ola Evensen went out to look for Pappa and by some miracle found him in a nearby side street. Ola told him that Mamma had been arrested, and Pappa's first reaction was that perhaps he ought to turn himself in. Ola disagreed. Pappa was the one they really wanted for his activities as an organizer of illegal resistance work among the students.

Pappa went into hiding in Ola's mother's house. A few hours later my mother was released. She had Swedish parents, and the Germans set store by their good relationship with the Swedish authorities; it was not the first time the accident of my mother's birthright had come to my parents' assistance.

Now they had to make their way to Sweden as quickly as possible.

Earlier that year, my Grandma Margareta had managed to get a diplomat's passport and travel papers that enabled her to retrieve Erik and me and take us on the train from Norway back to Stockholm.

Grandma had her work as a solicitor to take care of, so Erik and I were sent to a children's home just outside the city. We stayed there for almost five months. Erik was just three years old; I was four.

Mamma and Pappa remained in hiding during those cold autumn weeks and had to keep on the move all the time, equipping themselves with forged papers. At one point Pappa's sister Gegga received a message to meet them and bring a backpack with a few of their clothes. As Mamma and Pappa were cycling, they were stopped by a German patrol because Pappa was wearing the backpack. Incredibly, he was not taken in for questioning. A few days later, they were finally able to board the train to Rena, a village close to the Norwegian–Swedish border. Tension was high. Would they be stopped? They were ostensibly going northeast to cut timber.

On the last section of their journey, their guide left them; in the first snowfall of the winter he was afraid the escape route would be discovered. Early in the morning they reached what they assumed to be Sweden and knocked on the door of a little house on the edge of the forest. As the door was opened Pappa whispered, "No, this is still Norway!" Tin cans were being used for flowerpots; this couldn't be Sweden. My parents held their breath, then realized that the people inside were just as afraid as they were. They were given directions and soon they were across the border.

A few days later they arrived at the home to pick us up. Erik ran toward them with a beaming smile; I, however, was rooted to the spot where I stood, profoundly skeptical after having been "abandoned" for a second time. Mamma could never forget it.

Mamma and Pappa rented an apartment outside the center of Stockholm. Mamma worked in the office for refugees; Pappa was the camp doctor for the Norwegian police units, which were recruited by Norwegian refugees and allowed by Swedish authorities to be stationed outside Stockholm. There were many Norwegian families in Stockholm during the war, including the novelist Johan Borgen. Among the non-Norwegians I recall was Willy Brandt, who later became mayor of West Berlin, Prime Minister of West Germany, and chairman of the German Social Democratic Party. Another was Bruno Kreisky, who became Prime Minister of Austria. Mamma can remember how unhappy Willy Brandt's wife was. She and Mamma went for long walks to talk about her marital problems.

In spite of everything, those war years in Stockholm were good and safe. Money was tight, but then it was tight for everyone. We went to a nursery school full of the children of Norwegian refugees. Erik and I were inseparable.

Childhood Streets

May 1945: I can remember the excitement and joy, Mamma's keen anticipation—our train was bound for Norway! I waited impatiently, my nose pressed against the compartment window, looking for the exact moment when we would cross from Sweden into Norway. There were no houses, just trees and woods the whole way. And there had been no marker in the forest when suddenly someone exclaimed, "Now we're in Norway!"

Gradually many of the old CC2 circle returned to join us. There were always many adults at home, and lively discussions at which I was allowed to sit and listen and soak up impressions. From an early age I had strong opinions and a large vocabulary.

My first year at school was exciting. But I was really not a very good little girl. Unlike some of my classmates, I was allowed to bring friends home with me. I was so proud and happy to be able to show off my new baby brother, Lars, a child of peacetime born in February 1946. And I had even more to offer: using my father's medical textbooks in gynecology and obstetrics, I would explain to the other girls how the whole business worked!

I was full of ideas and energy and would enlist Erik in all sorts of downright mischief. We tormented the old ladies who lived in our building, hiding and teasing. I remember once in particular, not long after we came home from Sweden, Erik and I stood on the first-floor landing and shouted down to an elderly lady who had scolded us, "You silly old bag!"

I was always the ringleader.

When we lived in Sweden I had a friend named Sølvi. Now her family had moved into one of the new apartment buildings in central east Oslo. Sølvi's father was the caretaker at the Labor House in Oslo. Eventually most communities had such a house consisting of offices and meeting facilities for the movement.

During that first year we visited each other almost every Sunday, riding the trolley across town. It was very exciting to travel by ourselves. That fall we both began at Progress Group, a Labor-inspired organization for children, with branches all over the country. I enjoyed myself in Progress Group's central branch, not least because of our Sunday rambles in forests east and south of Oslo. Prime Minister Einar Gerhardsen and his wife, Werna, lived on a nearby block, and he would sometimes join us.

Their daughter was my group leader; she was a couple of years older than me. Their son and I were the same age and were sweet on each other. Werna was a woman who commanded respect and we children were a little afraid of her. She was an energetic leader with a ready smile, but she was strict. I heard her discussing politics, too, and I understood that she really meant what she said. She had no doubts. Werna was on the Oslo school board, as was my father.

At the National Hospital

Pappa and I climbed the dark, broad stairway to the children's clinic at the National Hospital. Mamma and Pappa had explained that I had to go to the hospital for a few days so they could try to find out what was wrong with my stomach.

It was autumn. I was six and a half years old.

I carried a grown-up briefcase with books, paper, and colored pencils. We entered a large room with big windows and many beds. Halfway along the long wall was a separate room, completely enclosed in glass. Inside was one single bed. That was where I was to be. In isolation.

Pappa escorted me in. A nice nurse welcomed us and talked to me when Pappa left.

I remember needles and blood samples. Someone came and squeezed my stomach, just as Pappa had done many times. I had a stomachache, sharp and painful under my ribs.

Two days later I was home again. It had been a special experience for me. I was small but brave in that big glass case. My books had helped me to behave myself.

Mamma's experience was completely different. She wasn't told why they had to carry out a major examination at the children's clinic. All Pappa would say was that he didn't know what it was but that he thought it ought to be checked. But he was unable to protect her from the pain of fear, for never before had she seen him in the state he was in during those days I was away. He was silent and would lie awake for hours in the middle of the night, staring at the ceiling.

Leukemia was always a fatal diagnosis in those days. No one survived. My liver and spleen were enlarged, and the blood tests looked bad. But the more experienced members of the clinical staff thought I looked too healthy to have cancer of the blood. Once they had examined me my father permitted himself to start hoping again. Might it, after all, be something else?

Mononucleosis, an illness familiar to us today, was almost unknown in those days. Someone in the clinic thought it might be one possibility. The symptoms in children were very similar. That was what I had.

Relief and joy replaced dark forebodings. I knew nothing of what was going on and was never afraid. Pappa had managed to hide his fears from me.

Friends

Inger lived in a large apartment on the fifth floor. She had two sisters. Big sister Borghild was bossy, so we often slipped away if she was there. Inger's mother was always at home. She spent most of her time in the kitchen, baking bread and making sure nothing got wasted. Inger's father read newspapers and chatted with us children. We sat quiet as mice when he told us his stories. He was a relative of the legendary arctic explorer and humanitarian Fridtjof Nansen, as well as of the radical historians and pioneering oceanographers, Ernst and Georg Sars.

Inger's parents were older than mine. Her apartment became a second home to me.

We had another friend, Liv, who lived right next to our school, but we didn't often go to her home. There wasn't much room. She had several brothers and sisters, both older and younger. Her eldest sister was grown up and married and lived there too, with her husband and children.

One day the "teacher on duty" knocked on our classroom door and asked that Liv come to the headmaster's office. We all wondered why. At recess Liv wouldn't say anything, and we understood that we shouldn't ask anymore.

A few days later Liv was wearing a pretty new coat. Then our teacher told us that she had gotten this coat from the school's welfare budget. We were to act as though we knew nothing.

There were big class differences in our class and in the school. We noticed it. We could see that it wasn't right that Liv should have to wear old clothes when children from the wealthier areas got whatever they wanted.

An episode at my friend Eva's made a deep impression on me. After school we often did our homework at her kitchen table. Eva's mother didn't go out to work like mine; she was a full-time housewife.

One day there was a math problem we just couldn't figure out. "Ask your mother," I suggested. Eva hesitated, but she did it. Her mother puzzled over the problem and said, "I don't know."

Eva wasn't surprised, but I certainly was. We were nine or ten years old. I had never known what it was like to ask a grownup a question and hear that he or she didn't know the answer. It was an important lesson.

"Why is your father in the Labor Party?"

It didn't take long for me to realize how lucky I was to have young parents who knew a lot and would have an answer when something puzzled me. Mamma was the one most often at home, and so it was easiest to ask her. She listened and explained. I asked and asked, curious and persistent, but Mamma never gave the impression that whatever was bothering me was not important. She often impressed on me her deep concern about all the injustice in the world.

There was always a group of grownups around at our place—and always in discussion. It was exciting for me, gathering up so many different impressions of the world in this way. They talked about Prime Minister Einar Gerhardsen, about the Labor Party and the government. At an early age I understood from what I overheard that it was important to defend the Labor Party.

At Progress Group we began handing out election leaflets and putting up posters. Our parents considered it only natural. Our newfound righteousness was exciting.

Early on, I developed a sort of perverse pride when schoolmates or other children made sarcastic remarks about the Prime Minister or the Labor Party. It happened a lot. With great gusto I defended the government and the Labor Party and the Progress Groups as well. The political struggle was harsh, almost hateful, in the first postwar years, and the antagonism percolated down to us children. We had our debates, too, and I know I was always considered provocative. I just wouldn't give up. Why should some people earn so much more than others? Could anyone explain that to me?

One day on the way home from school my friend Cecilie suddenly stopped, looked straight at me, and said, "Why is your father Labor Party, when he's a doctor? I mean, he's not a worker, is he? He pays higher taxes with the Labor Party." We had a real argument about what was right and wrong, about how things ought to be. I remember thinking as I stood there, I'm proud of my father for voting Labor because it's right, even though he doesn't benefit from it.

My Own Person

I leapt out of bed. It was spring! The sun shone in through the bedroom windows; I stepped out onto the balcony and the streets were dry. There was still a little snow left on the grass, but no matter: I could wear short socks to school today! Winter was finally over.

At school the others stared at me in disbelief: "Gro's wearing short socks! Can you believe they let her!" Shock was mingled with envy.

I liked it. I was proud of having a father who let me decide for myself: "It's up to you to make sure you're warm enough, Gro. It's your responsibility." I used the freedom that my parents gave me.

Another spring morning when I was almost ten, I got up at 5:00 a.m. I'd suddenly had an idea: Yeah, I've got time to make myself a skirt before school. I hunted around, but there wasn't enough material. So I cut two different bits of cloth, one blue and one floral-patterned, sewed them together, and put an elastic band round the waist. A skirt!

I'd never seen anything like it before, but so what? I liked to obey my impulses, and I wasn't afraid of others' opinions. I had a lot of energy to use up, a lot of limits to test.

The summer of 1947 was the hottest in living memory. The six thousand children at the Progress Camp just about doubled the population of Gjøvik. Erik and one-year-old Lars were there, too.

Mamma and Pappa helped run the camp, and Pappa was the camp doctor.

Boiling-hot days that burned the grass brown. I wore just a little pair of cotton shorts. The camp had its own "towns" and "roads," and handsome gateways erected by the various Progress Groups. There was a competition for the best gate.

One day a suntanned man with curly blond hair drove by our gate in an open jeep. "That's Haakon Lie!" someone said. The news spread like wildfire. I caught a glimpse of his strong face, open expression, and blue eyes. Lie was the formidable Secretary General of the Labor Party. I'd heard talk of him at home.

"Sssssh, Pappa's sleeping!"

Ruseløkka was regarded as a progressive school. The headmaster was intelligent, hardworking, and modern. We had a swimming pool and the first kiln in town. We were proud of our school.

The boys didn't have cooking lessons, and they had more math classes than we did. I wondered about that. Was it right? Why shouldn't boys learn how to make dinner, bake bread, budget for the housekeeping? Why just mothers and girls? Certainly it was wrong to give us fewer math classes than boys got, but it was inexcusable to believe that boys had no place in the kitchen.

Needlework and woodworking were also segregated activities. That's just the way things were. I was disappointed that we girls weren't offered woodworking, but the poor boys needed to learn to sew and knit just as much as we did. My father had taught himself to sew, and he'd made anorak jackets for himself and my mother for their Easter trip to the mountains in 1942. I saw them in our basement, with their French seams, ties, and tie-guides. They were splendid.

There was certainly more of a balance at home than at school. Pappa worked, and for him his job was the most important thing. The rule in our house was the same as in many others: "Sssh— Pappa's sleeping!" Mamma was in charge of the house, and after my little brother Lars was born, she was home a lot of the time. But she was also a law student and had a job at the Labor Party's offices.

In everything connected with leisure time, the holiday homes, and open-air life, I noticed that Mamma and Pappa shared the work equally. Mamma sharpened tools, painted and varnished, carried water. She thought it the most natural thing in the world to carry a yoke with a three-gallon bucket of water hanging from each end. She taught herself to drive the car; she carried her own backpack in the mountains when we went hiking from one hostel to another; and she participated actively in all conversations about politics and social questions. Gender equality was simply the norm in many areas of my life. Mamma knew her own mind and knew what she wanted. All the same, she did the most work in our house, conscientiously looking after the home and performing all the little chores of daily life.

To America

In August 1949, Mamma, Erik, Lars, and I boarded the *Gripsholm*, a huge Swedish ship. We were on our way out into the wide world, to see America and stay there for a whole year! I had been looking forward to it for what seemed like ages.

CC2 was rented out to some Americans. We would live off my father's Rockefeller scholarship money while he did advanced studies in medical rehabilitation. We soon noticed that Mamma and Pappa were very worried about whether we would be able to manage. We children were certainly not spoiled with pocket money. We took our entire savings with us, thinking it might be all we had to live on for the whole year.

Pappa had made the crossing a few weeks before us. He met us when we docked in New York and installed us in a hotel room right next to the Norwegian Seaman's Church. Then off he went to a lecture.

We went out for a walk, my mother escorting three curious and slightly impatient children who were beginning to feel hungry.

"Mamma, can we have something to eat?"

"No, Pappa will be here soon. Then we'll see."

In one shop we saw some enormous blue plums. "Mamma, can't we have one of those?" Mamma gave in, probably hungry herself. Just one plum each. Big, sweet, and juicy.

When Pappa came back, he saw the four big plum stones in the ashtray. "What are these?" he exclaimed. There was a bit of an argument between the grownups. "We can't afford it," he said.

"Yes, but the children have to eat something," said Mamma.

In Pappa's opinion, the plums were a luxury. Bread and margarine would have been fine. I understood that we would have to be cooperative and careful if we wanted this trip to work out well.

We found an affordable apartment on 11th Street in Brooklyn, close to Prospect Park; the rent was $75 a month. Even so, it ate up most of Pappa's scholarship money. Fortunately, we also had the money from the rent of our apartment back home. In December a dark-haired, dark-eyed man named Rafael came over from the Seaman's Church with a sack of frozen potatoes, a welcome addition to the household. We got used to the fact that they tasted sweet.

Elaine, our next-door neighbor on 11th Street, was Irish. Her father was a lawyer, but I don't think they had much money. She had two younger brothers, too. We were together every day, both in school and afterward.

Down on the corner on the way to school was a big drugstore, which had a few small tables at one end. A sign in the window read, "Special Treat." Three scoops of ice cream, strawberry and chocolate sauce, with a creamy topping. This concoction cost 15 cents.

We'd never seen anything like it back home in Norway. Elaine and I saved up for several weeks. On the big day we had our brothers in tow. They hadn't saved up. It spoiled our joy a bit to see them staring through the window at us, but we gritted our teeth and ate our special treats.

The deepest impression we had from that year in the United States came from all the things you could buy, all those unfamiliar vegetables and fruits, and berries ten times the size they were at home! Also, the colorful street life and all the cars. On Sundays we went walking in the parks—it wasn't much like walking in the great forests back home around Oslo.

One Sunday we drove out to a skiing area in upstate New York and rented skis. I remember the signs in the woods along the sides of the road: "No Trespassing." "Private Property." This wasn't like home, where nature was for everyone and you could just fasten your skis and set off in any direction you liked.

The great divisions in American society were very evident. We lived in a lower-middle-class area, and by a narrow majority most of the students at school were white. A few streets away it was another situation entirely. Everyone knew about these divisions. In the classroom and the playground we scarcely noticed it, but we knew it was different for the adults.

I was strongly influenced by my mother's attitudes. She drummed into us that we were all equal—and that went for all peoples of all colors. She often worked to persuade me that black skin was more beautiful than white. Couldn't I see that? Dark-skinned people were more beautiful; we were just pale and gray.

I could of course see for myself that people were different from one another. Some dark-skinned people were more beautiful than other dark-skinned people. But I didn't have the heart to contradict her. For her it was a vitally important ethical question. In general my mother held very strong ideals and attitudes.

That year at school was educational, too. I particularly enjoyed American history and geography. But one thing was really odd—we stayed inside during recess! At home it was on with your jacket and outside with you, no matter what the weather. I preferred our way. It made you a bit sluggish to be indoors all the time.

At the beginning of May we traveled home on the *Oslofjord*, a magnificent new transatlantic liner. It was like a fairy tale. One early morning I was standing on deck alone amid a multitude of islands and skerries bathed in sunlight, and everywhere a blue, blue sea and sky. As we sailed into the city of Bergen, love and pride for my home country welled up in me. The national anthem was played on the quayside, and the tears came flooding. I sang along with all my heart.

Independence

One day in sixth-grade social studies we discussed the different forms of government. Norway was a kingdom ruled by a lifelong king, while countries such as Finland, Germany, and the United States had a president elected as head of state to serve for a limited period, with various possibilities for being reelected.

Then the teacher asked: "Which do you think is best?" Everybody shouted in unison: "A king! A king!" Our King Haakon was a very popular monarch.

The teacher noticed that I hadn't put up my hand and said: "Well then, Gro, what do you think?"

"President, because that way you can choose, and if you don't like it you can change it." Everyone looked at me, almost annoyed. Why take that line, when King Haakon was such a wonderful king? I thought he was, too, but we were discussing a matter of principle.

I suppose the reason I remember that incident so clearly is that I found myself in a minority of one. This happened more than once, and it was something I discovered I was able to live with. It was more important for me to dare to think independently than to be one of the crowd. I was very sociable and had many friends, but when the subject we were discussing was important to me, I dared to stand alone.

In the sixth and seventh grades I had time and energy for everything, both what Mamma suggested and what I wanted. Every weeknight I did something, and on the weekends there was Progress Group or the family cottage. Some days I attended two classes after school. I did sewing, pottery, English, and woodworking. I remember the English course particularly, because I had learned so much during my year in America. And then there was dance class.

Mamma thought dance class was a good idea for all three of us. My brothers weren't so enthusiastic, but I liked going. I had one dress for my dancing class, which Pappa had brought back with him from a trip to England. It was meant for Mamma but it didn't fit her. It was bright green wool with a red and green tartan taffeta border round the neckline. Perhaps the pride with which I wore it, more than anything, made it mine.

Orienteering

When I was twelve years old I went on to summer camp below Gaustad Peak, but it was a hike through the wilderness of Vassfaret in south central Norway that made the most powerful impression on me. Rolf Hansen, who would later be an important partner in politics, walked ahead of me. He was the leader, a man in whom I felt complete trust. It's curious, how significant other adults besides one's parents and teachers can be. Werna Gerhardsen and Rolf Hansen were probably the most important adult role models for me. I remember how I took longer strides than a girl of five feet four naturally would, because I was proud to follow in Rolf's footsteps.

We came across several deserted small farms with open doors. Everything told a tale of an era long vanished. For economic and other reasons people had moved away from such wild places to seek work and an easier life closer to "civilization." For several days we didn't see a single human being. We were in a wilderness.

Our great dream was to see the tracks of a bear. Some on our expedition thought bears had become extinct, or if not, so few bears were left that the chances of finding tracks were slim. In fact, we never found them, but a mystical, enchanted mood remained with us throughout the whole adventure. At Vassfar Place we finally met people. The isolation we had experienced was broken. Some Boy Scouts had made the climb from the other side, and our paths had now crossed.

Twenty-five years later, as Minister of the Environment, I was deeply involved in the conservation of Vassfaret. I and my department studied research on the size of the bear population, debated logging, and considered the formulation of a system of rules that would ensure the survival of our traditions and the conservation of our natural places. I felt quite at home: My position had its roots in intimate, personal experience.

In My Teens

The big question the spring I turned thirteen was whether I should apply to the Oslo Cathedral School, the oldest and most prestigious high school in Norway. My grades were good enough, but I worried that it might be a bit snobbish. And going there meant leaving behind some of my best friends.

In the end I chose the neighborhood school, Hegdehaugen. No one forced me; the choice was mine. I enjoyed myself there, but I grew a bit more stubborn, more restless in class. With puberty came an interest in boys and competition for them. Truls Gerhardsen, the son of Prime Minister Einar Gerhardsen, was in my class. He and I had been friends in Progress Group since 1945, and we had always had crushes on one another. Flirtation, for us, meant disrupting classes, throwing paper darts at each other, and teasing one another. Together we distracted everyone. There was a bit of insecurity in this behavior and a certain amount of showing off in a new environment.

We all liked and trusted our headmaster, a scruffily dressed good sport with a ready smile. He epitomized the open, progressive atmosphere in the school. One of our teachers read us short stories by Ernest Hemingway and Mark Twain. We were fascinated by both the reader and what he was reading. Our school gave me a lasting appetite for good literature and for the company of adults who believed in something and wanted to pass on that belief.

Our religion teacher was Mr. Lilleøien. We'd been told by older students that he seldom gave tests and that we needn't take the subject too seriously. During the few tests we did have, we all used our books quite openly.

One day during a test, all the students were sitting with their books open, some on top of the desk, others underneath. Suddenly the usually mild-tempered Lilleøien stopped by my desk and said sharply, "What do you think you're doing, Gro?"

I looked at him, surprised, then looked around at the other desks. All books had been cleared from them. I knew that his tests had been conducted the same way for years, and we had been permitted use of our books in an exam earlier that schoolyear. I knew that he knew it. Why then this sudden attack on me? No one came to my defense, and I didn't want to defend myself by telling on the others. That would have been too embarrassing. I felt strongly that it was unreasonable, even immoral, for him to make an example of me on a whim. I stood up, looked him in the eye, and in a loud, clear voice I cried, "You shit!"

My heart was beating like thunder. But it was what I felt I had to do; I had no choice in the matter. Then I walked or, more accurately, marched out of the classroom. As I took hold of the doorknob I saw that Lilleøien was coming after me! I ran down the corridor and down a flight of stairs, Lilleøien hot on my heels as I burst into the schoolyard and out into the streets.

How had we wound up in such a tense, fraught situation? I felt offended, and afraid, too. Afraid of what I had done, afraid of what he might do.

I brought the matter up with the headmaster myself, describing to him everything that had happened, and I accepted responsibility for having used bad language. My parents were never involved at all. Shortly afterward the headmaster suggested I transfer to another class, in which I might find much more to stimulate me. It was a blessing for me, as it certainly must have been for others around me.

The Struggle over Lipstick

Poor Mamma had the task of keeping up with a teenage daughter. She had always been the outdoors type, wearing no makeup and dressing simply. As a rule she didn't even wear lipstick. In my teens I began making friends with girls from other backgrounds and we would try all sorts of things, curling and cutting our hair, experimenting with lipstick, and buying earrings. In short, we played at being little women.

My parents disapproved of lipstick almost as much as the silk and taffeta I wanted to wear to dancing school. I could and did wear lipstick whenever I liked, but my ballgown had to be made of cotton—they said it was prettier. The fact that it was cheaper must have been entirely coincidental.

Eventually I realized that my mother genuinely thought cotton was prettier. It was obvious that she had two aims in mind: to make her position clear and to try to guide me toward a similar one. My friends were all wearing taffeta with no apparent protest from their parents. I wore the cotton dress and envied the other girls. But a voice inside me whispered, Maybe Mamma was right after all.

Later I made my own dresses and chose the material myself—taffeta and tulle, as it just *had* to be in those days, the top strapless, the skirt full. This feminine phase lasted two or three years, and then it was away with the lipstick and bring on the outdoor look for open-air Gro, rambling and hiking Gro, skiing Gro. I took this so far that one day when I was visiting my aunt Gegga, she said, "Look at you, Gro, you're dressed like a domestic missionary!"

Hegdehaugen was a stimulating place. I was only fifteen when one of the older students asked me to take over as editor of the school magazine, *Lightning*. I was taken aback. Surely that was something one of the older students should do! I spoke to my new classmates Lars and Even, and we agreed to give it a try. We worked late into the night at Lars's father's office in the Directorate of Prices and used the photocopy machine. We had a lot of fun and learned that working together, we could achieve a lot more than we imagined.

Lars and Even were knowledgeable, and increasingly the three of us spent time together both in and out of school. We read books and discussed them. Lars was very interested in Nietzsche. The discussions about Hegel and Kant continued round the dinner table at home with Pappa.

We went sailing. Lars was skipper on board his father's boat; they used to sail in regattas together. Gradually I became more interested in Even than in the boat. We walked home through the streets, chatting away as we wheeled our bikes along. We went walking in the forests together, just the two of us. We were sweethearts. I had turned sixteen. But my friendship with Lars survived being in love with Even.

Wanted

One Sunday morning in the late autumn my friend Else and I were sitting at the breakfast table at home in CC2 discussing where to go on our hike. We decided on the tourist hostel at Løvlia, fifteen miles up north; we would stay overnight since Monday was a holiday. We were a bit late starting to make such a long distance on foot. We were also a lot slower than usual because Else had an upset stomach and had to keep stopping to answer the call of nature.

It began to get dark, but I felt pretty sure that it would be quicker to go on than turn back, and I knew there was a phone at Løvlia where we could call home. Soon it was pitch-dark and we were faced with a choice of several different routes. We had no flashlight and had to go right up to the signs and try to read them with our fingers.

We arrived sometime between ten and ten-thirty. This was November, so it had been dark for over five hours. We were worn out but glad to get there at last. We told the manager at Løvlia that we had to call home at once. He said that was not possible, unfortunately; the phone was out of order. In that case, I said, we would have to walk on to the nearest village, because the people at home didn't know where we were. He said that the next village was a long way away and we would just have to wait until daylight.

I remember how uneasy I felt. It didn't seem right. But the advice was offered by a friendly and experienced adult, and Else and I were both dead tired. I had no inkling that the man had a car, and that there was a road to the village!

It was eleven o'clock when the first announcement about us was made on the radio, but Else and I had gone to bed five minutes before. The radio was on, and later the manager said he hadn't heard it.

It was a dreadful experience to reach the village the next day and hear that we had been reported missing, and that the police and a lot of volunteers were still out looking for us in the forest. The temperature had fallen below freezing in the night. Our parents and the police were afraid that we might have had an accident and had frozen to death. Our teachers and classmates also organized search parties for us.

Tuesday at school wasn't a pleasant experience. I felt I was to blame. We ought to have turned back in time, but since we didn't, we ought at least to have ignored the manager's advice. So you certainly can't always trust adults, and you can never relinquish responsibility, not when you're sixteen years old!

When I was asked to stand for election as president of our school society, I was every bit as surprised as I had been the year before when I was asked to take over as editor of the school magazine. Still, I said yes.

We worked out an interesting program for the autumn of 1955, beginning with a political debate. There were local elections that year, so I invited both the Conservative and the Labor Parties to provide speakers. I must admit that the conservative who stressed individual freedom was more elegant than the socialist with whom we mostly agreed.

Later that autumn I managed to get the most controversial author of that time, Agnar Mykle, to attend a debate about his book, *The Song of the Red Ruby*. I can't remember a better-attended meeting at Hegdehaugen. Freedom of speech and morality were the red-hot subjects of discussion at that time. Mykle had even been taken to court for having written an obscene book. The prosecuting attorney in the case was Mr. Dorenfeldt, who lived on the fourth floor in CC2. I remember asking him in the elevator one day just how the law operated in such cases. He ducked the issue.

One of the president's obligations was to arrange the Christmas ball and invite the headmaster to dinner. I also had to give the main speech of the evening. I had plenty to say. But when I stood up at the dinner table to deliver the speech, I noticed that a rash had appeared on my chest. Well, there was nothing I could do about it, so I continued. And when I sat down some seven or eight minutes later, the rash had disappeared. It had only been the result of nervous anticipation.

My experiences editing the school magazine proved very useful when I began coediting *We Students,* the organ of the School Socialist Society, which I cofounded with other radical students from various Oslo schools. Quite a few of them were the children of former members of the "Dawning of the Day" movement (from the times of socialist intellectuals' activism in the 1930s), so I wasn't the only one with a well-known father. Throughout my childhood the workers' movement and the ideals of social democracy had influenced me. On the bookshelves at home classics like Marx stood next to Karl Evang's *Sexual Education* and the *Workers' Lexicon.* There were history books, polemical tracts, party literature. I started reading early and I read a lot, borrowing and being given children's and young people's books with socially conscious themes. Founding the School Socialist Society was a natural continuation of the process that had begun in my childhood, and was at the same time something fresh and exciting.

Graduation was approaching, and I made myself a dress of white cotton with a flared skirt and jacket. A Simplicity pattern, Mamma's sewing machine, Singer thread. It had a decorated pattern round the neckline and arms and on the collar and down at the wrists of the jacket. I chose a blue blazer, not the customary red one. Blue would be more useful for later. I was getting 50 Kroner a month in pocket money at this time, and that was supposed to cover everything except my winter coat.

The graduation celebration in those days ran from early in the morning of our National Day, May 17, until the middle of June. While many of the most popular celebrations were going on, Even and I were far away, walking in the forest.

When you have a boyfriend, there isn't really room or time for many other people. So it was only after Even moved away to Trondheim to study that I began to meet a new crowd.

Before Even left we had become engaged to be married and had exchanged rings. As time passed, though, the distance between Oslo and Trondheim had its impact. And so did the fact that we were very busy in different circles, Even in his world of engineering and me among medical professionals and people with political interests. The second year, when Even had come to Oslo to spend the Christmas holidays, I was at a party with my medical student colleagues. We were having a good time. Some wicked boys had even put pure liquor in our beer. When Even arrived and asked me to leave with him, I declined his invitation. I knew instantaneously that I had made a decision with far-reaching personal consequences; I had broken up with him. It was a moment of truth, a sad one.

I had chosen what to study at university the summer I turned eighteen. Law, economics, and engineering were attractive to me, but medicine had never been far from my thoughts since I was a little girl and had found out about illness, poverty, and the groundbreaking strike among the matchstickmakers in Christiania in 1887. All of them were women who had been exploited and had suffered from terrible health problems. But perhaps I should think about being a dentist, since I also wanted to marry and have children, and dentistry would give me more control over my own time.

It was a very difficult choice to make. I had put considerable pressure on Pappa to tell me what he thought. In a letter from London he concluded, "So I think, Gro, in the end, the best thing for you would be dentistry."

Then I was ready to choose.

Why medicine? It was not out of a willful desire to do the opposite of what Pappa had advised. It was probably because, reading between the lines, I realized that the advice he gave me was based on a logical, sensible deduction, not an idea of what he thought I would find most challenging and rewarding.

A New World

I encountered much more than knowledge and learning at the university. In my fellow students I met Norway the way it was.

I came across a great deal that was new to me—new dialects, new attitudes, new cultures, religious fundamentalism. We got to know each other better in the chemistry lab than at the lectures. As a city girl I had read and learned a great deal, but firsthand experience was something quite different.

Now I made friends with people who had lived away from home since they were fourteen, who had gone to secondary schools in the country, whose whole cultural attitude was formed by these experiences. This was a world in which equality between boys and girls was not taken for granted, a world in which sons rather than daughters were sent on to be further educated. Religion and the church played a much more influential role for many of the students than I had experienced.

We had heated discussions about sex education, sexual equality, and abortion; about Christianity and religion; about religious fundamentalism and hell. I was always an active participant, curious to discover the strength and variety of other people's views. But unlike me, none of the other medical students frequented the Student Union or belonged to student political organizations.

The first two and a half years we saw plenty of Bunsen burners, as well as gases and powders under the microscope, but not a single human body.

There was a lot of theory to digest, and much memorization of the names of all the bones, muscles, and nerves. Our teachers were all highly respected and excellent instructors. And what excitement when we finally began at the clinic! At last we would know what it felt like to be a real doctor. We were based at the Municipal Hospital, Department Eight, internal medicine. Here we learned about people, about case histories, about fate. Here we began to study the limits of medicine.

I will never forget one particular patient, a young girl of nineteen who had been born with a chronic heart condition. We listened as she told us how her condition gradually deteriorated, how she had difficulty climbing the stairs, difficulty even standing up. She had coughing fits from which she turned blue and passed out. She had Fallots tetralogy, four classical major faults in the structure of the heart.

In those days such patients were not operated on until they were adults, if it was at all possible to wait. But now an operation to try to correct some of the faults was imperative or else this girl was unlikely to live much longer. We were told that the operation involved a considerable risk, but that there was no real alternative.

As young students, standing on the threshold of our adult lives, it was easy for us to identify with that girl. Our hearts were in our throats at the thought of what she must endure, and of the great risk involved.

She was taken into surgery. The days went by. We heard that the operation had proved difficult. And then one morning came the shock: Complications had arisen and she had died during the night. We stood there, boys and girls, and wept. How brutal life and this world of medicine could be.

Why did it go wrong? What sort of complications were there? Could things have been done differently? A discussion ensued. Why indeed had her operation been carried out here at Oslo Municipal Hospital? The team at the National Hospital had operated on several similar cases over the years; they had more experience and more results on which to base their procedures. There the mortality rate both during and after such operations was markedly lower.

The situation presented some difficult questions. Shouldn't any patient with a rare and complex diagnosis be offered only the best treatment? Medically and socially, wasn't this their right? One could argue that the municipal hospital too must somehow acquire the competence to handle these cases; its surgeons must also learn. I remember concluding that, no, the surgeons must learn from and with the team that has the greatest experience.

It is a prickly issue in the world of medicine. How many of our hospitals should have specialist departments and offer specialist treatment? To increase and distribute the number of specialists means that competence and knowledge in the area advances less. The patient first and always—that must be our credo. The patient's desire to be treated close to home, when the condition may be life-threatening, cannot be entertained.

No one would deny the need for specialization within medicine. It is not the issue on which to raise a cry of protest against centralization. When an individual needs a difficult operation or a special course of treatment, an expert in the particular field should take charge.

No Substitute for Experience

I remember one summer early in my medical career. Pappa and I were talking about the tough daily routines of the young American hospital interns. I thought it would be practically impossible for any mother with young children to deal with such routines. The situation was almost feudal, with the interns on call day and night for a period of two years.

It was not simply a question of convenience. I had personally experienced some very trying work routines, including working a shift in a hospital every weekday, every second night, and every second weekend. And these watches were not inactive. Generally speaking we were up and working at least half the time, including the night. But it was fun, and I never complained.

We discussed the American system. Pappa explained, "This is how they learn as much as possible in the two-year period. They are only ready to assume the responsibilities of being a doctor once they have acquired experience of the greatest possible variety of cases. There is no substitute for experience. Less learning time means fewer patients and worse doctors. Practice breeds perfection."

No social considerations such as working conditions and hours can be weighed against that reality. And in the health sector, people's lives and futures are at issue all the time.

The Student Union Unites

I was used to inspired debates about politics and social issues from my time at Hegdehaugen. I was very surprised at the lack of interest among my fellow students at the medical school.

I was a curiosity because I spoke about political matters, followed issues in the newspapers, and always tried to apply what we were learning as students to a wider social perspective.

The Student Union brought me into a broader community of students. And the Student Socialist Society, of course, had interesting and intense political debates.

One day a theology student approached me in the reading room at the university library. He wanted me to put my name forward as a member of the radical team in the Student Union elections. Again, I was surprised to be asked, but again I said yes. And again we won.

Through the Labor Party's student group I got to know several people from the Institute of Political Science. One was a certain Arne Olav Brundtland.

"Is your boyfriend a Conservative?"

I have often wondered about the role chance plays in our lives. Would I have been so intensely curious about who Olav was and what he was like, had it not been for my medical school friend Marit? One Monday she told me that when she was eating her dinner the day before in a nearby restaurant, she had been sitting near two other students, Olav and Pål Caspersen, his friend from Drammen. She told me that the two of them had sent their food back to the kitchen because it was cold.

Marit and I would never have dared to do such a thing. We were both speechless at the behavior of such cheeky boys—and rather impressed. I guess my curiosity was aroused.

Over the years we've had many a laugh about that episode, with Olav insisting that I had been completely misled—it was Pål who had been the active party, Pål the bold one who had made the big impression on Marit, and on me.

There was something charming about Olav's eyes that attracted me, something in his look. He had a bold, open way about him that I liked. Later I heard that his sergeant in the army had written of him, "He isn't one to hide his light under a bushel." He certainly wasn't afraid of me.

But what was it about his eyes? Later on I realized what it was I had seen: Olav has an unusual little fold over the corner of his eye, right by the root of his nose. Inuits and Asians have it. Many years later, I was trying to explain to my Swedish aunt what I meant. Finally she understood and said with a big smile, "Oh, you mean the Mongolian fold?" Yes, that's what it was, all right. A dominant gene. Our four children and eight first grandchildren all have it, too!

Olav was the editor of *Minerva*, the Conservative student magazine. My male Labor Party friends were not at all pleased, even though they liked Olav. Was I crossing the divide? And what a fuss when I met Werna Gerhardsen, the wife of the Prime Minister, in the street one day that winter of 1960: "What's this I hear, Gro? Are you going out with a Conservative?"

"Yes, but I don't know whether it'll last," I mumbled. Werna was a powerful authority figure. And Olav and I had only been together for a couple of months.

The rumors ran ahead of me. If Werna knew, then obviously many others must know, too.

I felt a growing sense of defiance. This wasn't right. I was a free woman, after all. The Labor Party didn't own me. I was still Gro, and Olav was Olav. That was equality, if you like—and this was life in a free, modern country.

I immediately regretted that I had vacillated when I met Werna. Surely I could stand by whatever I did, in this as in any other matter. All the same I felt a certain ambivalence. The values and ideals associated with social democracy were central to my life and attitudes. Wasn't it a little odd that I should fall for someone with other values and traditions? I could understand Werna and the others. All the same, it was my choice.

Engagement

In the spring while we were visiting his family in Drammen, Olav proposed in traditional style, hardly to be believed today. He solemnly knelt down and expressed his wish. It felt beautiful and not at all comic.

At home my father was standing in the kitchen by the bread board holding a knife in his hand when we came in and I told him the news: "We're engaged to be married."

"Damn!" he said as the knife fell from his hand.

How much of his reaction was due to differing political viewpoints, and how much to the fact that this was new, that it had happened so quickly, and that his only daughter, young, but still his oldest child, was about to leave the nest, I don't know. He had asked me down to his office one day in February or March, and we talked about Olav. I ought to think deeply about whether I was making the right choice, he said.

"Yes," I said. "I ought to." And then we didn't talk about it anymore. He probably sensed the ties loosening, bit by bit.

The Bride's Father

One image from our wedding is stamped indelibly on my memory. On the wedding day, December 9, at home at CC2 where I grew up, the table is set for fifteen (the same table that we have today at our summer holiday home at Helleskilen). Pappa rises to give his speech. The opening words of welcome are second nature to him. Then he comes to a full stop. I hear the lump in his throat, the sob in his voice—"Now, now that Gro is leaving us . . ."

He is crying.

My heart sinks. First of all, I'm not leaving anyone. Secondly, I have never seen Pappa this way before.

It makes such a lasting impression on me, to behold this secure, well-balanced, and rational man reacting in such an emotional way. Strong feelings well up inside me too. Tears come to my eyes. I feel the strength of our bond, all the love. It goes both ways. In the years since, I have often thought about my father at my wedding. Especially when I have noticed how hard it is for me when I speak straight from the heart, at funerals and remembrance ceremonies in particular. No doubt our genetic heritage also includes much of our own psychosocial and biological mechanisms.

The Trip to Yugoslavia

In 1960 I traveled to Tito's Yugoslavia—to the part that is now Croatia—with my school friend Marit. We paid a visit to a birthing clinic in Split on the Adriatic coast, a lovely town with its ancient Mediterranean culture and Diocletian's palace. We spent long days on the sunny beaches and didn't work too much. We were not really given a chance to.

We two young medical students were allowed to eat with the doctors, who were all men. In their small black bowls were meat, potatoes, and vegetables. Our two bowls held just potatoes and vegetables. I remember thinking, Haven't I been through something like this before? Yes—in nineteenth-century literature! Some of our colleagues elected to share meat with us, no doubt finding such open discrimination embarrassing.

We saw our first birth. It was impossible to forget. The mother was expecting her seventh child. Her body showed her long life of struggle and hard work. We kept a discreet distance as the drama that is every birth unfolded before us. Suddenly the baby shot out like a projectile and ended up between the mother's feet. She smiled in relief, saw the shock in our faces, and laughed.

I can still see it now: The experienced mother and the quick, expert midwife, the power of nature, the mother's pride and joy over her newborn child.

The standards at the hospital were those of a relatively poor country. We noticed also that women had a considerably lower status than in our own country. The equal treatment of men and women was not considered a natural thing, nor was anyone especially interested in pursuing it. The kind of attention we received in Yugoslavia was largely due to the fact that we were nice young women, and had little to do with professional consideration or the sharing of medical knowledge. It was another lesson to me, in the practice of discrimination between men and women.

How Does She Dare?

It is my week on duty in the surgical ward at the Municipal Hospital. New patients arrive in the course of the afternoon and evening. A pleasant but anxious woman of about sixty has been admitted. In his referral her doctor writes that he has felt a small lump in her right breast. She says that she too believes she can feel it.

I examine her thoroughly, both breasts, and describe my findings: "There is a tumor about the size of a hazelnut in the right breast, to the right and beneath the nipple." I feel for her. She may have cancer. I show her record to the assistant doctor on duty that evening and he promises to take a look at her.

The next day all the doctors are gathered in the auditorium for clinic, with the professor on the first row. One patient after another is wheeled in. Each doctor describes his patient's condition and suggests treatment. Heads nod. Now and then someone asks a question. We students sit tightly packed together in tiers. Finally my patient is brought in.

"She has been admitted with a suspected tumor," says her doctor. "I can find no tumor, and I suggest she be discharged."

I go hot and cold. What am I to do? Is he going to let her go, just like that? My heart is pounding. Am I really prepared to have this on my conscience? He does not even say that I, the student, have written up in my practice report what I have observed.

I stand up. "Professor, I felt that tumor."

All heads turn. Nothing like this has ever happened before. What did she just say, that young Harlem girl? How does she dare challenge the doctor? Alarm and astonishment are written across every face. The young doctor in front of the blackboard is clearly irritated.

The professor stands up. "Come down here," he says. We go out into the corridor where the woman is lying. He draws up a chair for me. "Sit down. Show me what you found."

Then it's his turn. He examines the woman, hesitates, then says, "We'd better take her into the operating room." I feel relieved. Now matters are in good hands. A person with a possibly fatal condition will be properly treated, not ignored and sent away.

A few weeks pass. In the corridor one afternoon I meet the chief anesthesiologist. She comes straight up to me. "Congratulations."

This is the early summer of 1960. I look down at my hand: Does she know I have just got engaged?

"Oh, you saw it in the newspaper," I say, a little surprised.

"Newspaper? No, I'm talking about the clinic that morning. A sample of frozen tissue was examined. You were right. There was cancer of the right breast. She was given a mastectomy."

Only then did the anesthesiologist congratulate me on my engagement. I sensed in the whole encounter a sort of sisterly solidarity. She was glad that the woman had been given the treatment she needed, and she was proud because I had stood up in front of all those people. She wanted to express her support and admiration.

I had learned how to observe properly. And, furthermore, I had learned to be sensitive to the dangers of overconfidence, but also to take people seriously, to be precise.

Mother, Doctor, Rebel, Researcher

The Firstborn

Nothing can compare with the moment when your first child passes through you and separates from you. The sense of wonder when you can feel the shape, the shoulders, and even the arms along the sides of the little body.

Knut was born after a long and stressful labor. He was delivered thirty-six hours after the first contractions became rhythmic, ten to twelve minutes apart, hour after hour, prolonged enough to prevent any real sleep.

His head was forced out, all on its own. We had to wait for another contraction; what seemed like an eternity was probably only a matter of seconds. He cried out, loud and clear, while the rest of his body was still inside me. I don't know how often that happens, but it brought me enormous relief to know that he—or she—was fine.

I say *I*, because I was alone, with only a wonderful midwife as helper. Her face is etched in my memory. She was wise, supportive, and expert in her work. Her help was incalculable. In those days there was never any question of the father being present, except in the Red Cross' private clinic, where that practice had just begun. I gave birth in the maternity ward of the National Hospital.

Knut was special in more ways than one. He was born three weeks old. He was clearly "overdue." He was a little too thin, and his skin was rather dry and slack. Had he been born earlier he would probably have been a bit chubbier, more like my next three children.

The midwife laid my son in a little cot at the side of my bed. He looked at me with clear, direct eyes. We saw each other then. We made contact. The first bond between us was established with our eyes, which is unusual, though I didn't know that then. I shall never forget it.

He smiled on day eight—about three weeks earlier than normal. It's strange to think that the maturing of the nervous system and the growth of receptiveness to human, external, and social stimuli had continued during those three weeks in the womb.

When my future pregnancies showed the same tendency to go long, my doctors made more effort to speed up the procedure. Things can sometimes go wrong in long pregnancies—the placenta begins to degenerate and the whole system slows down, with an attendant risk of damage or possibly stillbirth.

I was a student, with two more years of medical studies ahead of me. In five weeks the autumn semester would begin. But Knut had a serious attack of jaundice and I had to stay in the hospital for another eight or nine days. The doctors were almost on the point of giving a blood transfusion. I was uneasy and hoped that we could avoid that. Then the illness peaked and over a period of weeks slowly receded.

Mother and Student

Those first years as a young mother and student were good but intense. I concluded my studies on time. My mother and Olav made it possible. During the early autumn, when I was nursing Knut and studying for my exams, Mamma took a few weeks of unpaid leave from her work in Parliament. She wheeled Knut down to the National Hospital where I sat studying in the reading room, sometimes twice a day. I nursed him in the ladies' cloakroom.

When we took the second part of our exams, I remember how my breasts erupted and dripped as I sat there writing in Engineering Hall, Mamma waiting patiently with Knut down in the basement. Olav was working on his Master's dissertation in political science. I'm sure Mamma knew that she was helping us both, and she was delighted with her first grandchild. Ever since then the relationship between her and Knut has been very special.

Knut thrived, and Olav and I both felt privileged to have interesting jobs and studies. We had moved from our first one-room apartment in the "Student Village" into new quarters for married couples. The apartment was small but big enough for the three of us. We had a combination living room/kitchen and a bedroom. We bought a used Volkswagen and were able to bring Knut to nursery school when he became one year old.

The third part of my exam was in the spring of 1963. By then I was seven months pregnant again. We planned our family carefully, not wanting too great an age difference between our children.

Kaja was born in September. I was doing my internship at a neighboring hospital and was off work for only two weeks. I had hoped, if possible, to complete my six-month training in the medical department without a break. All went well. We hired a young girl named Berit from inland Norway to look after Knut and Kaja. I breast-fed Kaja and we lived close to the hospital, so I could take her with me on the night shifts. We were lucky to be healthy and strong.

Neighbors and passers-by would meet Berit, a happy, ebullient girl wheeling a carriage and singing her heart out. Knut sang too. He was very helpful with baby Kaja. If she cried as we changed her diaper or fed her, he would position himself formally beside her crib. Whether he sang to her or "read" without a mistake from all the children's books he knew by heart, the result was instant silence. We had two changing tables so we could work on both of them together—and avoid passing bacteria back and forth between the children.

Knut and Berit were an incredible pair. At times being a working mother was simplicity itself. I was on duty every third night, and with patients and breast-feeding I didn't manage much sleep. But I recall that year as full of joy, exciting and important for my future.

Night Duty

That was an important year for teamwork and for establishing the father's role in our family. Olav was a research assistant at the Institute of Political Science at the University of Oslo, and he would take Knut back and forth to the students' nursery just behind the university library. I was happy, but a little jealous, too, when I saw what fun Olav and Knut had together during the spring evenings when I sat in the reading room. At nine o'clock I stopped for the day, because I simply had to see Knut before he went to bed.

During my internship this "equal-father-principle" remained almost but not entirely in place. Olav started at the Norwegian Institute of International Affairs, known by its Norwegian acronym, NUPI, and began working more than he had the previous year. Berit could assume daytime duties, until Olav came home for dinner at about four-thirty—at least on those days when I was on duty.

But what about the parental night shift? As students we had always shared this. We had had just the one bedroom with Knut in a cot beside us, so we never missed a thing.

By the following year Olav had acquired an extraordinary ability to not hear the children at night. It is a talent he has preserved. It is one of several reasons that I can truthfully claim to have done most of the work of raising the children between 1963 and 1967, when Kaja, Ivar, and Jørgen were born.

I was worried. Olav seemed to hear nothing at all at night; not even when there was a lot of activity in the children's room. What about the three nights a week I was away on night duty? To this day

Olav insists that his ears did work perfectly—as long as I wasn't there! "No accident on my watch" became his slogan.

We had a disruptive period with Knut when he was about one and had fallen into the habit of waking up several times each night and demanding his bottle. I knew we had to cure him of this. One night I looked at him very gravely and said sternly, "Knut, you can't have your bottle at night. All you're getting is one bottle just before bed. This is the last time. After this, no more bottles."

It was terrible. He woke up crying at ten o'clock, as usual. I reminded him of what I had said, and I left. It broke my heart. He didn't stop crying until after one o'clock, by which time we had our neighbors at the door wondering if everything was all right. Perhaps we ought to have forewarned them, but it never occurred to us that he would show such persistence!

We dreaded the next night, which began similarly. When he woke up at ten, I told him he couldn't have any more bottles. He carried on for about ten minutes, then quieted down. No more disturbed nights after that.

The following year it was Kaja's turn to cause problems. By then we were in Boston doing our studies at Harvard. Berit said that Kaja was hardly eating during the day. She was hot, and it turned out that she had a fever. I examined her throat. Swollen. She was given penicillin and recovered within a few days. But she continued to refuse most food and grew thinner and thinner, and in the following weeks she still ate very little. Under such circumstances you end up giving a child exactly what she wants—cake, chocolate milk, jam. Something had to change.

"Berit, from now on, just water and vitamins. It's time she ate normal food again!" I finally said. It hurt me to demand it. It took more than three days for Kaja to eat anything, and she was so thin already. And then at breakfast one morning she asked for bread. Our sorrows were at an end. She then ate everything—eggs, fish, vegetables—everything she had been shaking her head at for the past few weeks. But I had been dreadfully worried. Had I done the right thing?

Public Health Doctor

I don't know whether every young mother shares this constant fear that something awful is going to befall her child. In my case such unease was a frequent part of my daily life. Olav and Pappa tried to calm my worries. They said I was too afraid, too pessimistic. But I remember thinking, I must do whatever I can to minimize the risks, to prevent dangerous situations from arising.

Mamma probably had a better understanding of my maternal anxieties, having experienced them herself. She and I were the wagging fingers of warning in our families. Children are such impulsive beings: Suppose one suddenly darted out into the road? I lived with this fear constantly inside me. the worst must not be allowed to happen.

I read a great deal about physical and mental development in children, always searching for knowledge, both as a mother and as a doctor. I was preoccupied by medicine's role in society, by the need to educate people, by how best to improve public health, safety, equality, and dignity of treatment in the broadest sense. Social unrest, such as the strike of the female matchstick workers in Christiania in 1887, the first working-class women to organize in Norway, served as a lasting inspiration. The battle against tuberculosis, the people's sickness, the struggle for legislation that would better protect children—these matters had preoccupied me since I was a young girl. I wanted to be part of the search for new knowledge, to spread the sort of knowledge that everyone had a right to, and to ensure that everyone was free to exercise that right. I wanted to pass on to others the attitudes and knowledge that I had been fortunate enough to acquire myself. I wanted to work in public health.

Elise Ottesen Jensen was my heroine. She had been a real pioneer, traveling through Sweden and Norway in the 1920s and

1930s, spreading the word about women's rights to protect themselves and to plan their reproductive lives. Even in the 1950s and
1960s these things were by no means taken for granted. The political debate about sexual education in schools was in full swing.
Later, in 1967, when I became a part-time school doctor, I entered
the fray, educating public health nurses, working together with the
most enlightened teachers. I made appearances in classes, gave lectures, wrote articles.

The years following my time on hospital duty were completely
devoted to being Gro, doctor in public health. From the start I lived
according to my principles and my passions.

I also had very clear ideas of what I wanted as a mother. I wanted
to breast-feed, being convinced of its biological and psychological
importance for both mother and child, for good connection, self-
confidence, and future health.

Kaja was still nursing when Olav and I had the opportunity to
spend a year studying in America. When Pappa heard about it, he
made a suggestion: If Olav and I wanted, he and Mamma would
happily look after Knut and Kaja for the year we were away. I was
stunned. It was of course absolutely out of the question! I don't
think he had discussed it with Mamma beforehand, because she
certainly would have known how I would react.

To Harvard

It had been fourteen years since I had last traveled to the United
States. This time we flew, but by the cheapest route possible, via
Iceland. Olav had accepted an offer to be a visiting scholar with
Henry Kissinger at the Harvard Center for International Affairs. I
had to decide whether I too would study at Harvard. Doctors could
receive special training in public health at Harvard, and other Norwegians had done so. It was tempting. I sought advice and received
firm encouragement, not least from the superintendent of hygiene
at the National Directorate of Health, Dr. Fredrik Mellbye. This was

the area of medicine that interested me most, as it had interested Mellbye; Karl Evang, the influential Director General of Public Health; and my own father. To influence society in such a way that sickness and suffering could be prevented and the general level of public health raised was, for me, the vocational heart of the medical profession.

Fortunately I was accepted by the Harvard School of Public Health and was offered a tuition waiver. I also got an award of $1,500 from the American Women's Club of Oslo. This enabled us to make the trip and live on Olav's salary from NUPI and his stipend from the Norwegian Council on Arms Control. It also meant that we could afford to bring the children, as well as Berit, of whom the children were so fond and whom we fully trusted.

We moved into a cosmopolitan environment, both at the International House where we lived and at Harvard. The standards were high, and I had to take a number of demanding examinations that year, in English. I don't think I have ever read so much or experienced so much in such a short period of time—and that's no small claim, considering that the years since 1974 have not exactly been characterized by routine jobs and light reading!

Being at Harvard gave us a chance to get to know New England. Early in the autumn we were invited by one of the teachers, William Forbes, to Cape Cod, where his family had a country home. He was a member of one of the original English Puritan families that landed in Boston in the seventeenth century. His speech, style, and manners were British, but his generous hospitality was American. That particular quality was in evidence throughout our year there. Americans open their arms, they open their hearts, and they are easy to get to know. We felt wonderfully welcome.

Money proved not to be any particular problem. Food was cheaper, shopping simpler. Supermarkets made things easier. Once a week, usually on a Thursday, we would all pile into our venerable Rambler and do all the shopping.

Along with other students living in International House we organized a nursery school in the basement. For four or five hours each day Berit helped out there while she looked after Knut and Kaja, who thoroughly enjoyed themselves. In fact, we all really enjoyed ourselves. Berit learned English, made new friends, and had new experiences, and in addition she received certification of her work in the nursery. I gave her my warmest recommendations the following autumn when she successfully applied to enter a child-care school in Norway.

Olav and I stuck rigidly to a timetable: Dinner at six o'clock, then time with the children, reading and playing, then from eight o'clock at least two hours in the reading room in the basement.

The most important part of our trip was the inspiration we received from all the new people we met, both teachers and fellow students. The trip brought the whole world, not just the United States, into focus. The teaching was international, and each day we learned about the poverty, population trends, food resources, and health problems that affected different parts of the world.

My whole political stance was strengthened by the impressions I picked up. My fellow students came from all corners of the globe, including several African countries, Islamic countries in the Middle East, India, Japan, and Korea. The American students were socially committed and several of them had been in the Peace Corps in Africa.

The days were filled with new experiences and new colleagues. Many became our friends. David from the Peace Corps, Jacques from Canada, George from Nigeria—he was at least fifteen years older than I. For many of my colleagues, this was education many years after they had completed their formal studies. They were technically experienced, and also worldly-wise. Stephanie, perhaps twenty years older than I, was a pediatrician from Israel. She was a fantastic friend as well as an excellent professional inspiration. I have kept in close touch with her ever since.

And then there was Al-Awadi from Kuwait, who was Health Minister in his own country for a number of years in the 1970s and 1980s. I remember a car trip with him and his brother down to Williamsburg, Virginia; the three of us had been chosen to attend a student conference. I asked them a lot of questions about the Middle East, the Arab-Israeli conflict, and the Palestinians.

Their answers really made me sit up. Here were two well-educated, pleasant colleagues, and what were they telling me? We should throw the Israelis into the sea. They had no right to be there. The land belonged to the Palestinians and the Arabs. They must be talking metaphorically, I told them; they couldn't really mean that. But they looked at me with hard eyes. They did indeed mean it.

One day in September 1993, almost thirty years later, I recalled these powerful impressions as I gave a speech at a dinner held at the residence of the Israeli ambassador to the United Nations in New York. It was just after the signing of the groundbreaking Oslo peace agreement on the Israeli-Palestinian conflict. Now there was real hope, and I was sitting between Foreign Minister Shimon Peres of Israel and Foreign Minister Johan Jørgen Holst of my own Norwegian cabinet. It was as though a great burden had been lifted from my chest. The Oslo accord enthused and surprised the world. A new era was in the making. The assassination of Yitzak Rabin and new terrorism to come was unthinkable.

A Visit from the Defense Minister

Pappa came out to Boston to see us in November. He had been Norway's Defense Minister since 1961, so he was an official guest of his American colleague, Robert McNamara. Many years later, after I had been active in Norwegian politics for a long time, I realized how important such a contact was, with its friendship and the confidence it inspired. McNamara developed a deep insight into Norwegian foreign affairs and security matters. He and Pappa discussed the "Nordic balance," the need to keep the level of tension in northern Europe low, and how Norway's policy—not allowing foreign forces to be based or nuclear weapons to be stored in Norway in peacetime—contributed to the security of the NATO alliance. The two of them spent a whole weekend talking.

It was not until the 1980s that this insight and mutual understanding died out in the Pentagon, in the era of the Reagan administration, with its high-profile politics and its hawks on the offensive against the "Evil Empire" in the east.

My little sister Hanne, truly a late addition to the family, had been born a few days before Pappa arrived in Boston. Mamma had turned forty-six and had almost given up the hope of renewed motherhood. Twenty-five years younger than I, this little girl turned out to be appointed Minister of Justice thirty-five years and four months later, at exactly the same age her older sister was when she had become Minister of the Environment in 1974. Strange coincidence!

Pappa came with us to a Thanksgiving dinner with some distant relatives of Olav's who had immigrated to the United States. They were an ordinary working family living just outside Boston, and they got quite a shock when a limousine and a security guard turned up outside their front door.

Pappa had given us a couple of weeks' warning of his arrival and the teachers at the school asked if he might be willing to give a talk to the students. He said yes. Poor man, he wanted to know what I thought would interest them most. I was so full of all the new things I had been learning about, and now Pappa and I had a profession in common as well as a political viewpoint. To me he was still the doctor who led the Ministry of Social Affairs and Health, more than the Defense Minister. I began talking with great enthusiasm about ecology, about how important it was to work toward a condition in which people lived in harmony with nature. I assumed he too would have insight into such a profoundly important subject. Of course, I wasn't fazed by the fact that this autumn at Harvard was the first time I had ever learned anything about the subject myself. At the age of twenty-five I was still wedded to the idea that a parent would know more than I did about practically any subject, in any field.

Pappa heard me out without saying much, but in his first lecture he did not talk about ecology. There were enough other issues to preoccupy a Norwegian politician with a background in medicine. He had considerable experience on the international stage, too, both with the World Health Organization and as a U.N. expert on rehabilitation medicine in Egypt in the 1950s. As early as the 1940s he had been an international delegate for the Young Socialists.

I was twenty-two years younger and my head was filled with new ideas. I could not understand why ecology was not universally viewed as a crucial issue. The problem of the environment did slowly make its way onto the political agenda, but that was several years after I came back from Harvard. By that time I was well prepared. Ecology was something I had studied, as well as sociology, statistics, and epidemiology. We frequently discussed Ralph Nader's book *Unsafe at Any Speed*. Traffic, pollution, road accidents, and the need for lifesaving protective equipment were already all-important parts of the public health education of young doctors.

The Importance of Breast-feeding

For my main subject at Harvard I chose prophylactic medicine for mothers and children, but most of my time was still spent studying general research methodology and the key tools of public health: statistics, epidemiology, research methodology. I lapped it all up. I chose to write my thesis on the importance of breast-feeding for both mother and child.

My point of departure was the disquieting fact that in Norway and other countries the practice had become much less widespread in recent years. What would be the effect of this? Might it be harmful to both mother and child? For hours, days, weeks, I sat in the large medical library and plowed my way through international literature and the results of recent studies.

The report I submitted analyzed the incidence of breast-feeding in various countries, its frequency and duration, and its evolution over time. I wrote about social class and education, and the effect these factors have; about such special factors as the professionally employed mother; and about the general observations that can be made about the role of genetic heritage. I examined the psychological aspects of nursing, too, the attitudes of mothers toward breast-feeding, the attitudes among medical professionals, and professionals' influence on the practice at different hospitals.

Historically speaking, it had been a privilege for the upper-class woman to forgo breast-feeding by employing a wet nurse. This in itself may have reduced the status of breast-feeding, by associating it with the middle and lower classes. When alternative methods and milk substitutes appeared on the market, it was once again the upper class that determined the fashion. In former times, a considerably higher proportion of patients in public clinics practiced breast-feeding than in private hospitals. Now, however, this was in the process of changing. Women in the clinics were copying the wealthy and turning to the new alternatives. At the same time there was a movement in the opposite direction: Many of the private patients and those with the highest education were returning to breast-feeding, probably in response to an awareness that it might be instrumental in creating a bond between mother and child.

I determined that the decline in breast-feeding created dangers for infants in the many developing countries that presently began to imitate the "Western way." Mothers who took inspiration from U.S. television advertisements for using the milk bottle increased their risk of infection and of infant deaths because of poor hygienic conditions in such countries. This seemed most evident during a winter study trip we took to Puerto Rico. In my report I quoted the head of the pediatric clinic in San Juan, who told us that among the hundreds of cases of serious diarrhea among infants in the previous year, not one had involved a child who had been breast-fed.

It was an arduous task to unearth and evaluate all the scientific data. This was the first sizable and systematic piece of professional research I had undertaken, and I was aware both of its importance for me and of how alone and frustrated I felt during this period. It was not the first time I would experience a conflict between the desire to contribute to the store of scientific knowledge and the more pragmatic intention to get down to practical work with the knowledge we already possess.

The American System

At all hours of the day and night, we talked politics, society, and public health. I was very critical of the American system, which offered its citizens no broadly based program of national health. On the other hand, I was proud of Norway and of what social-democratic action had achieved in this field both before and after

World War Two. In 1964 Prime Minister Einar Gerhardsen of the Labor Party and Director General of Public Health Karl Evang were already establishing a system that offered health insurance for every resident of Norway.

I would become angry and upset, arguing fiercely with my American colleagues over the definition of a truly just society. When I recall those days I am reminded of what my father's fellow medical students wrote in their graduation book about Pappa: "Evang the means, Evang the way—we heard all about it all night and all day." That leitmotif was apparently destined to be passed from generation to generation!

One evening shortly after our arrival in Cambridge we were visited by Olav's "Aunt" Evelyn, a second-generation immigrant from Norway. Evelyn was mother and foster-mother to a number of children and a warm and committed person. It was good to know that we had family not too far away.

Berit was on her way out. "So long," she said, "I'm just going to walk down to Sears." Evelyn was alarmed and asked, "Where is she going?" Then she taught Olav and me a bit of a lesson. "Under no circumstances should a young woman go out alone after dark. Nor should anyone else for that matter. You must always be at least two."

Crime was a reality in the Boston area. Such warnings had never been necessary in Oslo. But today Aunt Evelyn would, unfortunately, probably feel the same way about many parts of Norway's capital city.

Another incident remains unforgettable. One evening I was crossing the lawn opposite Park Drive, where we lived, with a colleague. We were on our way home after a day of lectures. We heard a loud bang close by and realized at once what had happened: A car had crashed headlong into a tree just down the road. I could see someone doubled over the steering wheel, seriously injured. I began to run toward the car, but my colleague grabbed me by the arm and held me back. "Stop, Gro, you mustn't!"

I looked at him, speechless. What on earth was he saying? Our doctor's oath was clear: to help where you can. He shook his head, sad and at the same time a little embarrassed. "That's the way it should be. But in this country it's dangerous to get involved in a situation like that—even for doctors. You risk years of lawsuits, you could lose everything you own." I was shocked, and continued toward the injured person. Just then the police and an ambulance arrived, and we were both relieved from our dilemma.

For me, as a young Norwegian doctor, it was highly disturbing that such a state of affairs had been allowed to develop. It must never be allowed to happen in Norway, I thought. And it hasn't. We have a public health service. The majority of our doctors are hospital employees, or in some other way earn their wages from the state. *They* are the focus of our system, not a gang of lawyers and insurance companies squabbling over treatment, rights, and compensation.

And yet even our situation has also changed slightly in recent years. Judicial provision for the rights of patients and compensation for incorrect treatment have become relevant concepts in our own social discussion. But it is crucial that we not let ourselves drift into a situation in which doctors and other medical personnel are more concerned about protecting themselves from potential criticism than about offering help where it is needed.

A Physician's Refined Feminism

There was another aspect of the American system that I found terribly upsetting. From medical literature and from personal experience I discovered that doctors often induced births on particular dates. Sometimes it was at the request of the mothers. But primarily it was as a convenience to themselves, so that several babies could be delivered in the clinic the same day or the same evening. Thus it was quite normal to be attended by one's own doctor during the birth. Many women felt it offered them both security and familiarity.

I was critical of the practice. Far too many cesarean births resulted and far more frequent use was made of the tongs and the suction cup than in other places, such as Norway. In the United States, apparently, natural birth was regarded as an old-fashioned, näive, romantic notion. That it was safer and caused fewer injuries was mostly ignored. One argument I heard was that some mothers preferred to have a cesarean because that way the vagina isn't stretched! And it avoided compressing the baby's head. But what about the increased risk to the mother?

I was convinced that the artificial means to promote the onset of labor increased the risks for both mother and child. In Norway, the child was born when the time came, and doctors and midwives were in attendance day and night, offering support and assistance. I was proud when I found out that our infant mortality rate was the lowest in the Nordic countries, which have a lower rate than that of any other region of the world.

One of the major concerns of our studies was to compare and contrast various state health services and social systems, to consider nutrition, water quality, food production, and social conditions in an international context. For me this year had been of crucial importance. I not only achieved a clearer perspective on the connections between health, environment, and social conditions in my own part of the world; I also saw that such matters transcended national, regional, and continental borders. Poverty and inequality were the root of many evils. I became increasingly convinced that the values and experiences on which we were building Norwegian society were applicable to other countries where inequality, sickness, and need were the daily reality.

That year at Harvard also deepened and refined my views on gender equality. I had grown up with a basic belief in the equality between men and women, but I also understood the necessity of avoiding the wrong-headed notion that men and women were the same, and that this sameness must be endlessly cultivated. The importance of breast-feeding is a case in point. Here there could be no absolute equality between men and women that would not also be harmful to the child. The effects of the advertising campaigns for powdered milk were dangerous, and not just in the developing countries. Men and women were of equal value, yes, but the roles we perform must also harmonize with the conditions imposed upon us by nature.

One might say that I returned home in 1965 with the seeds of several elements of what would later be called new feminism. Not everything in society should be dictated by what the boys thought. There were other values worth promoting and praising.

Four Little Bedrooms

Our son Ivar wasn't planned, he just happened. But even on our honeymoon I had said to Olav that I wanted four children. I had seen the trouble my mother had in fulfilling her wish for a late addition to the family. Mamma had her first miscarriage when she was thirty-eight and I was seventeen. After this I was always asking myself: Can I have children? That was what caused my impatience once Olav and I were engaged. I'm sure my subconscious desires played a part in the conception of Knut. That I still had three years of studies to go was of secondary importance.

Soon after we returned from America, we were lucky enough to be offered a house at Bygdøy peninsula in Oslo. I had begun work at the Department of Hygiene in the National Directorate of Public Health. We sat in the real estate agent's office as he called the bank: "I've got a young couple here. They're wondering how much of a loan they can count on, and how much they can put down themselves. She's a doctor. Let's say that together they have a net income of 100,000 Kroner."

I gave a start. He had guessed, and guessed wrong. Olav earned 40,000, and I earned 30,000. Could we manage it? I said nothing. Neither did Olav. The house cost 300,000 Kroner. It was a lot of money.

We went back home and did the math. "No, it won't work," said Olav. "We can't manage it even with the 20,000 Kroner that my parents are offering us." But I wasn't going to give up so easily. Soon we'd have three children, then there was the new nanny. We needed the four little bedrooms. "If we rent out two of the rooms, we can afford the house," I offered.

We turned the dining room into a bedroom for Olav and me. The nanny had the innermost room, the one meant for the parents. All three children shared one small room. The other two bedrooms we rented out to students.

Five years later the family would finally occupy all the rooms, and when Knut was nine we would build a basement under the outdoor terrace.

A Mother Like Me

We wanted to lay natural stone slabs across the terrace, but financially we weren't ready. I wanted the stones, though, so I decided that I would start work as a mobile first-aid doctor in addition to my regular work. It was to prove an interesting, exhausting, but valuable experience.

I drove all over Oslo and encountered every sort of social condition, environment, and family situation. I learned a lot about the city, rather as I had when I was a Progress girl meeting friends from these parts of Oslo. I soon became aware of deficiencies in the after-care and follow-up treatment of the patients I had seen during the evening and the night. I got involved in after-care, working during the day in my capacity as deputy superintendent of school health of Oslo, a position I began in 1971. Child-care, contagious diseases, psychiatry, internal medicine: There was much to learn and much to do.

My worst experience from that time was a home visit I made late one evening somewhere in central Oslo. The woman was in utter despair. "Rita said she'd be home at eleven," she repeated over and over again, clinging desperately to what her daughter had said when she had left home at nine o'clock the previous evening.

The tragic fact was that the woman's only daughter had been killed in a traffic accident that evening. She was a passenger in a car with a young driver that crashed on the highway. The mother had lost touch with reality. I had to call out the duty psychiatrist. I have never forgotten that room, that distraught mother, and the headlines I read in the newspaper early the next morning, after I came off duty: "Fatal accident on highway." Nothing could be worse than to lose a child.

Ivar

Ivar was born on December 9, on our fifth wedding anniversary. The first eight days of his life were fine. We drove home from the clinic in our gray Volkswagen, proud of the latest addition to our family. My youngest brother, Lars, was there. He suggested the name Ivar, after my grandfather. I remember repeating the name exactly where the road swings left toward the fields at Gaustad.

On the ninth day Ivar began to nurse in a new way, taking in a lot of air and losing the knack of emptying the breast efficiently. Ivar and I struggled as I had never struggled with any of my children before or since to get the breast-feeding to work. For several months I didn't sleep much at night. I wasn't one to give up easily.

Three and a half months after the birth, at Easter, we took a walk up on Holmenkollen, the site of the famous ski jump. As we sat down to eat our sandwiches, I could feel that something was wrong. I had dull and then sharp pains in my lower stomach. I had to go to the emergency room, where I was treated with antibiotics and confined to bed.

I had an infection of the womb. It hung on and on. After another course of antibiotics I was hospitalized well into the summer. Mamma's nanny looked after Ivar at Helleskilen. I remember holding that sweet little six-month-old boy in my arms. I didn't want to let go of him, but I had to.

This was the first time that I had been put out of commission as a mother, and I discovered that being fit and well isn't something to take for granted. I continued to suffer pain and discomfort whenever I moved. It lasted right up until I got pregnant with Jørgen that same autumn.

I had been terrified that I might not be able to have children again. Such was often the result of the kind of infection I had had. I had no peace, I had to know. That's why Ivar and Jørgen are just eighteen months apart. When I got pregnant again, all my pains disappeared!

But I had learned something: Strength and physical well-being were not limitless. You could get sick. And you had to take proper care of your children. I made up my mind to cut back on my full-time job, and the next summer, when Jørgen was one year old, I took a job at a municipal health center, which meant I could come home at about three in the afternoon, put Jørgen in the carriage, and go for a walk with the other children.

Ivar grew to be an easy child. Often after he woke up from his midday nap he would lie in his carriage and look up at the trees and the sky. He rarely cried. He clearly had a technical cast of mind, dismantling whatever he could get his hands on and then reassembling it. To the surprise and envy of his older brother and sister he could add and do his two times table by the age of four.

On top of that he was a real little worker. We spent all of one Sunday afternoon filling with sand an enormous flower box at the front of the terrace. Olav and Ivar each had a wheelbarrow. We thought Ivar would soon get tired of it, but for four whole hours he went back and forth to the big pile of sand with Olav. He was almost three. To this day Ivar displays unusual powers of endurance and determination.

Since 1961 we had had a new child once every other year. Those were years with several new nannies as well. Most stayed a year, two at the most. Once Jørgen was eight, we stopped having nannies. Olav couldn't take it anymore, he said. Looking after the children was soon to be largely his responsibility, and he didn't want to administer a fifth child!

I had given some thought to the role of the nannies. Mending, ironing, and cleaning were to be done when the children were out in the park, at the nursery, or in school. All the children spent time outside the house; once they were no longer infants I didn't want to leave them solely in the care of young girls. What they needed then was the company of grown, experienced adults—and playmates their own age.

It wasn't cheap, but I felt it was worth it. Private nursery fees for three and a paid worker in the house—it really added up.

Eventually, Olav took over, and he talked the children into accepting responsibility for the different jobs that have to be done in order to keep a reasonably tidy house. He brought along a little bit of organization from his military service. And the money we had previously paid the nanny we now paid the children for the work they did. Our household had the appearance of a joint stock company, and the system worked to some degree. For instance, Olav changed the chore of ironing by putting up two boards so the work could be done in company. Sometimes men can improve routines in what has traditionally been the women's arena!

Generations

When I was thirteen or fourteen my father and I had a fierce argument at the breakfast table. That afternoon Pappa called me at home to concede that I had been right. On reflection he thought he had not listened closely enough to what I was trying to say and had then used his authority as an adult to ride roughshod over me and my opinions—which I had every right to even if they were not the same as his. He apologized for his behavior and thereby greatly increased my confidence in him. I can't remember the subject of our debate now; what mattered was his attitude afterward.

For most of my youth and young adulthood, I tended to defer to Pappa. I simply assumed that in both medical and family matters he knew best. Then, when Ivar was three years old, Pappa and I had another reckoning. His authority as a father and doctor was posed against mine as a mother and doctor.

Ivar had been ill with a fever. He had developed spots around his mouth and was pretty testy. At the table he pushed away a piece of bread and cheese I had given him and pointed instead at the jam. So I gave him a new piece of bread, with jam. Pappa exploded. "What do you think you're doing, Ivar? You've already been given one piece of bread!"

I defended Ivar. I was the one who had given him what he asked for. He had eaten little the previous week, and in this instance his calories counted for more than his upbringing. I would see to that later. That exchange marked the end of Pappa's reign as the ultimate authority in family matters. It was perhaps a long-overdue rebellion. From then on there was more equality between generations, and the life of the extended family resumed in a fine, balanced atmosphere.

The Ph.D.

After a few years at the Oslo Board of Health, I wanted to take a sabbatical year to do research on girls' development and maturation. In 1952 a study had examined the age at which girls attending Oslo schools experienced their first menstruation. Now it was 1972. Had there been any further lowering of the age? Most researchers seemed to assume so. But I made some surprising discoveries.

With my friend and colleague Lars Walløe I published an original article in the prestigious journal *Nature* under the title "Halt in the Trend Toward Earlier Maturation." With leave from the Municipal Board of Health, a research scholarship, and an office at the National Hospital, I was now able to get my doctoral thesis under way. Once again I was alone with my papers and data. I had written more than half of my dissertation, as well as several articles, by the day the Prime Minister called.

Women's Right to Choose

My experiences as a doctor had made me passionate about the issue of abortion. It was a subject that aroused strong feelings at all levels of society.

My first personal experience with abortion was in the surgical department at the Municipal Hospital in 1968. An apathetic nineteen-year-old girl was admitted to the emergency room. She was eleven weeks pregnant, and someone had helped her start the bleeding. She needed immediate medical attention. I felt that she had cut herself off from everything and didn't want to say much. All the same I sensed her relief when she realized that a young woman was going to examine her.

At that time there was no guarantee that a young girl like her would be allowed to have an abortion if she turned to a family doctor or a health clinic. This girl hadn't even tried. She had so little confidence, she didn't think doctors would help her. So she'd elected to call a friend who knew someone, who had an address.

Opinion was divided among my student colleagues, but most of us felt that the situation was undignified and potentially dangerous. Public debate on the matter came some years later.

When we were learning about medicine and society in our course on social medicine, Pappa told me that as Minister of Social Affairs and Health he had tried to keep the framework of the abortion law flexible. He wanted to allow doctors the proper exercise of responsibility toward their patients. Later, in 1969, opposing demands for a tightening of the abortion law and for a relaxation that would allow women to choose for themselves were raised at the Labor Party National Congress. A large majority voted for women's right to choose.

The Abortion Committee

I was an active participant in the battle over abortion that had now gotten under way. As a state-employed doctor, through my work at the Municipal Health Center for Mother and Child, and as a member of the abortion committee at another municipal hospital, I saw how unsatisfactory the current system was.

This was an area, like so many others, in which those with the fewest resources found it most difficult to tell their stories and to explain their point of view. Our hospital's two-doctor committee was in effect a court of judgment. We decided the fate of women and of families. On several occasions my medical colleague, a gynecologist who was the head of his department, recommended against abortion. Under the existing rules, this could lead to an appeal.

In several instances the committee of appeal supported my opposing point of view. After a year or two I found I still had not turned down a single application. I had not encountered one concrete situation in which I felt it right to say to the woman involved: You are wrong, you must give birth to this child against your wishes; my colleague and I know better.

We were dealing with people who were enduring a crisis in their lives over a period of many weeks, people in doubt and distress, often in need of advice and support. It takes a lot to make such a decision, and to face the ensuing critical questioning. There were, however, a few cases in which the women had not thought through their decision very thoroughly, and later changed their minds.

I was determined that no one should be forced into having an abortion under direct or indirect pressure from others. Our job was to support the pregnant woman against any such attempts to influence her choice. Yet sometimes I personally worked toward having a woman withdraw her application when I sensed her doubts.

With my colleague and neighbor Dr. Berthold Grünfeld, I wrote a series of articles based on my personal experiences as a doctor. Some attracted considerable attention. I wrote about real cases I had dealt with on the abortion committee, changing the names and a few of the details but presenting real-life situations. In general the abortion debate was being conducted over the heads of most people; it lacked a recognizable human dimension. To arrive at an informed opinion one had to know about the individual cases that we on the committee regularly encountered. We soon found ourselves in the middle of a highly charged emotional debate, which continued not only in the daily papers but also in the pages of our medical journals.

I felt I had a duty to fight for women. The "judges" on the abortion committee were usually men. But women, not men, experienced the effects of lacking or failed contraception. Should anyone be placed in judgment over other independent, grown individuals?

Of course we knew that the technology and the will to carry out illegal abortions were there. No one could stop anyone from doing
what he or she really wanted to do. But we could prevent dangerous situations by establishing a woman's basic right to have the final
say.

There was an observable paradox at the heart of the whole debate. Those who were most agitated by our position were often
lukewarm or even directly opposed to improvements in sex education, contraception, and family planning. I was all for the notion
that the way forward was to make it easier to prevent the incidence
of unplanned pregnancy, because I had the greatest respect for the
view that emerging life has a right to protection. Yet I knew that
society could not practice this protection against the mother's
strongest wishes and convictions. Once a child has come into the
world we can all take responsibility for it, but the fetus is wholly
dependent on the mother's body.

During these years of struggle I myself had become a mother four
times. I had experienced how strongly affected a woman is by what
grows inside her, how all her thoughts and feelings were concentrated on what is going to happen. I knew that I personally would
have had great difficulty giving any of this away. Some of our children arrived at less than convenient times, but our joy increased
with each week of pregnancy that passed, even before we reached
the three-month stage.

For many of the women I worked with, each passing day
brought new fears, new uncertainties for the future. No one else
could take away their burdens: the pain of being left by a husband,
the exhausting experience of already caring for a sickly or handicapped child, or the difficulty of life with an unemployed or alco-
holic husband.

I remember one woman in particular, whose application seemed
thin. She was married, had a child already, a girl of six. Her application stated that she "couldn't face having another child." It
seemed odd. She was about thirty; there was no reference to illness
or other difficulty, even financial. I wanted a long talk with her. Had

she really thought this through? Didn't she want her daughter to have a brother or sister? Was there something behind it all, something she hadn't mentioned? Perhaps I could persuade her that a second child was worth it. Might this be a case where I should be on the lookout for signs of undue influence or pressure?

I asked her about her first pregnancy, how she had experienced that, how the birth had been. Then it all came out. The whole thing had been a nightmare from beginning to end. She hadn't wanted that child either. By the time she had been denied an abortion, it was too late to get one illegally. She hated being pregnant, could not bear the thought of giving birth again. What left me with the deepest impression of all was the black look in her eyes when she said of the child she already had: "I can't bear her. I can't stand being a mother. I don't want her."

Deep psychological conflicts were involved here. We agreed that the abortion should be performed. On paper, the case had suggested a "no."

Free Contraception?

As a young doctor on the Municipal Board of Health I was given the task of formulating a proposal for how best to prevent unwanted pregnancies. A group was set up and we discussed numerous aspects of sex education in schools and afterward.

I thought we needed free contraception. It was a radical proposal, but it seemed to me the logical conclusion to all our discussions. We wanted to prevent abortion and unwanted pregnancy. That required knowledge, and it required access to contraception for all young people. It seemed to me that the very least we could do as a society was to extend to all this ability to choose.

I felt that the Municipal Health Center for Mother and Child where I worked for a year should be able to provide help free of charge in a situation where expense was a hindrance. I remember one young woman who screwed up her courage to come and see us. After I had examined her, chatted with her, and given her the advice she sought, she asked, "What does it cost?"

It wasn't much, but she said, "Then I'll have to wait until next week."

It was Friday. I thought, I'd better make sure nothing goes wrong this weekend. I told her she could have what she needed from me. Later I broached the subject with the head nurse. We needed to put ourselves in a position to help individuals in a difficult situation.

"No, we can't do that," she said. "We've never done it before."

"Really? Then perhaps it's time for a change," I said.

So several times after that I paid out of my own pocket rather than run the risk of unwanted pregnancy in girls who had come to us for help, until I could start working more comprehensively on the whole issue.

Involvement and Care

For a number of years before and after 1970 I worked one evening a week at a hostel for homeless men, a place anyone could stay for the night and get hot food and a bath. Many of the residents were alcoholics. With great enthusiasm, I approached the task of trying to help such people escape from their unhappy situations.

Several of us younger doctors often discussed these difficulties. How should the social security system be developed? Should everyone have the right to a minimum wage? I wasn't certain. The most important thing for these men was help to get back on track, and to reclaim their dignity. Wouldn't money alone be a kind of pseudo-help? Were we as a society really offering what was needed? Moreover—and just as important—we had to consider how such a solution might serve to increase the number of people who ended up living this kind of life.

With time I grew ever more convinced that in such matters we had to work constructively toward prevention. It was essential that we think through the long-term effects of the political solutions we chose. Offering the young who found themselves on the scrap heap the money to continue to be there was not a good idea.

As a school doctor I had many encounters with youngsters from problem homes. One must get involved, show that you care.

I remember a fifteen-year-old girl who came to me, two and a half months pregnant. She came from a large family in which alcoholism was a problem. She had already been in touch with a social-service agency, and on account of her age they had recommended an abortion. Then she had changed her mind. We of course had to respect her decision in such a serious matter, and give her all the support we could.

I was unconvinced and found myself wondering whether someone at home was putting pressure on her. She denied it. Still, she wanted to get away from home. If she had the child she would be given financial aid and other support during her pregnancy, and afterward she would be given help finding an apartment. She would have money to buy cigarettes and clothes and pay her train fare, she explained to me. Someone had told her she would receive maternity benefits.

There's a lot one could say about such a situation. To me this was confirmation that the frameworks we establish have an effect on the way people choose their own futures. It emerged in the course of our conversation that the girl had deliberately gotten herself pregnant so that she could leave home and be financially independent. As a society we ought to have had a better alternative than that to offer a fifteen-year-old girl!

The Oil Crisis and Imagination

Of all the Easters we spent at Grandfather's holiday home in the mountains at Geilo, I remember the one in 1972 best. Olav and I were both in our early thirties and in good shape. We had been taking long ski trips all through the winter. In order to ski a good distance each day we would have to pull four-year-old Jørgen and six-year-old Ivar behind us, we reasoned. We dictated the pace, for it was a question of how slow we were prepared to go. The kids kept going, laughing and chatting as we pulled them along. I had been worried that we might have problems with our youngest's coordination and stamina, but no.

Ivar and Jørgen had body hooks at the end of the towing rope, which they could unhook to whizz downhill by themselves. The first day we skied ten miles. The promise of a little cafe serving soda and potato cakes and a lot of other goodies kept the children's spirits up.

Our fears about retarding the boys' development as skiers were groundless. I have never seen such progress made in the course of a mere nine days. Spirits were high. We competed with ourselves, each day taking longer trips and setting ourselves ever more daring challenges.

The experience proved invaluable during the following year's oil crisis, when the Minister of Energy appeared in his wool sweater on television and drew diagrams and explained about ration cards and emergency measures, such as the weekend ban on all cars. During those weeks we not only experienced quiet, car-free streets, but also learned how to look for imaginative solutions.

Our winter routine was to drive up to Lake Mylla every weekend if possible. What were we to do now? Taking the train would eat up most of the time we had. We decided to ski from Oslo, all six of us, those twenty miles.

The children thought it was a great thrill being allowed to ski on ahead of the adults, with our promise to give them a tow when required. Several weekends in succession we had splendid fun doing this and it was good exercise for Olav and me. Out Saturday. Back Sunday. The feeling of freedom, of overcoming difficulties, was very special. And after such long trips it was rare for either of the two little ones to ask for help from the tow ropes. They became experts and kept up a good steady pace behind the two eldest.

A Krone for the Bus Home

From our earliest days with Ivar and Jørgen, Easter at Geilo had become a family tradition. When Knut and Kaja were seven or eight they were allowed to go with Mamma and Pappa, skiing from hostel to hostel in the mountains. They kept my little sister Hanne company, and Pappa was able to pass on the traditions he had taught us to another generation.

It was a four-hour drive to Geilo if there was no traffic. Knut and Kaja were often "returned" by their grandparents Thursday or Friday of Easter week, so we had four kids in the backseat going home. Mostly the children showed discipline, but it wasn't always easy.

There was one dreadfully noisy journey home from the mountains. Ten- or eleven-year-old Knut was responsible for a chaotic fracas. Finally I asked Olav to stop, just by a streetcar station in Oslo. "If you don't stop at once, Knut," I said, "you can get out." No sooner said than done. "You'll have to take the streetcar to downtown and the bus the rest of the way home." It hurt as much as when I listened to him crying for his milk as a one-year-old.

He still had the chance to say he would stop all his nonsense. But he took the money I held out to him and went off in silence to the station. The other three howled, "Knut!" In truth, I was uneasy until he got home. The incident was not forgotten, by any of us. That was the point.

The New Minister of the Environment

In late August 1974 while in my office in a research institute at the National Hospital I received a message. The Prime Minister wanted me in his office at twelve o'clock. I didn't know why—could it have something to do with the abortion issue?

Prime Minister Trygve Bratteli headed the minority Labor Party government. He asked me to sit down.

"I want you to join my cabinet." It came like a bolt from the blue. I was stunned. I knew that he had lost his Minister of Social Affairs and Health during the summer. The Prime Minister, who is responsible for finding a suitable candidate, is not obliged to pick from the Parliamentary Group (those Members of Parliament who share a party affiliation). I later learned that another Minister had suggested my name to the Prime Minister after seeing me on TV defending the Labor Party position on abortion.

"I want you to be Minister of the Environment," the Prime Minister continued.

"Social Affairs and Health would be easier," I said.

"No, I am convinced that it is not a good idea to be

a politician in an area in which you already have professional competence."

I made two calls immediately, to Olav and Pappa. Both advised me to say yes. I had only a few hours to think it over. Could I do the job? And if so, could Olav and I continue to care for our children in the best possible way?

This latter point was the major topic of my conversation with Olav. He was then working at NUPI, the Norwegian Institute of International Affairs. I knew that I would now have to either share or relinquish my leading role in the children's lives.

We had a modern marriage, living our lives together in the spirit of equality and the new feminism. Olav had always been more progressive than most men, even when we first met. His parents were college teachers; Olav's mother had been his math teacher, an unusual profession for a woman at that time. He understood and accepted the demands of our life together. We were equals. The work had to be shared, at home as well. But how would the theory translate into the realities of everyday life?

Of the two of us, I had the stronger opinions. I was primarily the one who decided what we would do and eat, what was common sense and what was right. The arrival of children did not change this. I was not only a mother; I was a doctor. It was I who felt the greatest responsibility for the home and the children. This was not something I regretted. It was simply the reality of the situation. I think both of us felt it had developed naturally.

Now a new situation had arisen. Was he willing to take a greater share of responsibility for the children? Olav had the presence of mind to make his demand on the spot: "In that case, it will be on my terms."

I could no longer take it for granted that I would be the boss.

After ten years as a cabinet Minister, Pappa had left politics and returned to medicine. But he told me, "Yes, you can do it. Accept the challenge." And he offered some advice. On relations with Parliament he said, "Remember not to say any more than you're willing and able to stand by. You have the right to remain silent. Remember also, whenever you put aside the proposals that come into your office, it means others will have to wait for your response and the overall efficiency of the Ministry suffers."

I have passed this good advice on to colleagues and fellow workers. It often requires two or three hours of work every evening after office hours to keep your head above water as a political and ministerial leader.

His third piece of advice was no less important: "Make sure you have political allies, so that others are involved in your thinking and decision-making. In difficult cases you will need their support."

And that has been the way I have worked—and inspired others to work. In all the roles that I successively filled—as Deputy Leader, as Prime Minister, Party Leader, and Parliamentary Group Leader— the process of inclusion naturally became an ever more important focus for my effort, energies, and commitment.

I had one important question for the Prime Minister: How should I relate to those civil servants and others who perhaps held very different political views from my own? Wasn't it difficult to navigate the lines between politics, bureaucracy, and administration?

"No," said Bratteli. "In my experience it is straightforward. Treat everyone as an intimate and trusted colleague, as part of the team. You will find this is appreciated. Be yourself, be open about what you think and what you want."

I have never regretted following that advice. It is a fundamentally sound attitude toward running a ministry. And that's the way things were done in my Ministry of the Environment.

It was an incredible time of challenge and inspiration, one which I spent in the company of talented and committed people. Together we formed an unstoppable team, which succeeded in bringing our field right into the center of the political debate. Only two years old, the Ministry had already had four leaders. Our total staff was about one hundred. Only Fisheries and Communications had smaller workforces. The Ministry of the Environment was multidisciplinary, focused on long-range planning, and was scientifically grounded in a fusion of biology, physics, ecology, and economy. It also required us to adopt an international perspective, for many of the problems and projects demanded solution or realization at the international level.

As a government Minister you are dropped straight into a role. Indeed, within a matter of days (if not hours), you *are* the role. You are consumed with responsibilities and obligations. On my first day in office, I had to deal with a proposal for governmental regulations to the law on sewage duties. The outgoing Minister told me everything was okay and that I could let it go to the King in Council that first Friday for final approval. The King in Council is the government, more or less: the council of Ministers who act "on behalf" of the King in Norway's constitutional monarchy. I felt uneasy about having only the most superficial knowledge of the proposal, but I did not want to show a lack of respect and confidence in my predecessor, who had now taken over as Minister of Social Affairs and Health. I decided to see how much I could read and understand in the twenty-four hours at my disposal.

It's strange to recall the deep impression this very first issue made on me. It wasn't because it was my first as a government Minister, nor because King Olav asked me a question about the proposal in the Royal Palace that day—I had good cause to be glad I had made the effort to do the homework—but rather because on many occasions in the years to come I faced fierce opposition on these very rules and regulations. The Social Democrats in the Oslo municipality refused to accept that the polluter should be held financially responsible for the pollution, even though this principle was enshrined in the law. Their view was that the degree of financial responsibility should be proportional to income. I had to insist upon the letter of the law. Nor was it permissible under the law to levy more in water and sewage charges than the real cost of supplying these services. A number of local politicians did not like this limitation very much.

This first experience illuminated a fundamental issue: The endless debate about how central and local government should divide legislative and regulatory responsibilities is in large measure what characterizes everyday political life in society.

A few days after I became a Minister, I was asked to address a large demonstration on the abortion issue. I spoke from the heart. I was angry and dismayed at the arguments used by some of my medical colleagues in the course of the public debate.

The following day the Prime Minister asked me to contribute to the parliamentary debate on the new white paper on the family. I listened to a number of speakers who gave no sign of understanding women's experiences and the great variety of family lives. A number of contributions were, to put it mildly, lacking in subtlety. I had to present my experiences so that the doctors who were being used as "expert witnesses" would not go unchallenged. Indignation colored all my words. I concluded: "We cannot deny the fact that a law that gives women the final say is at the same time a law that will prevent doctors from exercising an authority to which they have become used over the years. There will never be clear lines of legality in these cases as long as doctors and others deprive women of a responsibility which in reality cannot be shared with anyone else. Women in our country have been incredibly patient, for an incredibly long time."

A leading commentator in the liberal Oslo tabloid, *Dagbladet*, wrote, "She threw away her apron." Well, I certainly did that! In one of his later books, the then President of the Parliament wrote about the young Minister who hit the rostrum with her pen. In politics, passion is an important ingredient. I learned on that occasion how powerful a message can be when it comes from the heart and is backed by sound practical insight. I also noticed that you win not just friends but also enemies by speaking out!

Have We a Feminist in the Cabinet?

Rereading an interview from the same period with a female reporter from *Dagbladet*, I am now struck by how candidly I expressed myself.

The journalist began by introducing her readers to this "sharp," forthright, and professionally respected doctor with an advanced degree from Harvard University.

"Do the Norwegian people have a new feminist in their government?" the journalist asks.

Brief silence. Brundtland carefully lowers her knife and fork and, lifting her pleasant blue eyes and smiling with her whole body, says, "Yes. I came late to a realization of the status of women in society. Early on I thought that if women were good enough then there was no problem about competing on equal terms with men. At home my brothers and I had the same upbringing, and it never occurred to me to stand at the back of the line just because I was a girl. I got myself a proper education and married a man who was used to cleaning the house on Saturdays because both his parents worked. At home there was no struggle for equal rights, and at work I have achieved professional success in a field dominated by men. Perhaps that is why I remained blind for such a long time to the situation of so many other women."

The journalist follows with a sarcastic little jab: "Can we say that interested parties who want the support of the Environment Minister for their group can apply to the Minister's office? Mark your envelope: Brainy newcomer with a lot of self-confidence. Aren't you worried you might find your letterbox empty?"

In a situation like that you have to hide your feelings. You have to learn to remain calm and smile. I said, "I'm really not all that self-confident. In fact, I was over thirty before I dared to stand up and say something at a public meeting where I wasn't actually one of the speakers invited in a professional capacity."

This comment must have surprised the journalist, but she included it in her article.

My first few weeks as ministerial "boss" and a member of the government brought a whirlwind of impressions and a steep learning curve. In cabinet meetings, I listened. I was a junior member. But I always read all cabinet briefing notes and benefited from the discussions. I was never merely the technical head of my Ministry. The work of the Ministry of the Environment was inextricably involved with almost every other Ministry. I became "Finance Minister" for issues pertaining to nature and the environment, pleaded the case for conservation interests and defended a number of "soft" values that might otherwise have been brushed aside by powerful interests and traditions. I was also involved in the whole broad spectrum of social-democratic ideas, including gender equality, education, children and family life, housing policy, and local affairs.

The importance of regional politics was soon impressed upon me as well. Local government bodies were to be responsible for planning the use of land in industrial and residential developments, and these plans were from now on to be ratified by the Ministry of the Environment.

Behind the King's Door

A new Minister's first cabinet meeting is at the Royal Palace. A chauffeur of the government car drops you off, and you go up the stairs to the left of the palace gate. Two minutes to eleven. Ministers go in and line up at our designated places and chairs, our backs to the windows, our faces turned toward the King's door. Monday, September 9, 1974, at eleven on the dot, the small, highly polished brass door handle is turned downward, and the King enters. He greets each of us individually. We are seated according to seniority so that, from the King's point of view I am furthest away, on the long left-hand side of the table. I move up just three weeks later when the new Minister of Trade comes along. The Prime Minister sits near the head of the table, on the King's right; the Foreign Minister on the King's left.

The fall session of Parliament opens in the office of the Vice President of Parliament along a similar format. There is an individual greeting from the King, then the cabinet follows him in and stands on his left before the civil servants' box, remaining on their feet throughout the whole session. At the opening of the Parliament in the fall 1974, I had been asked to deliver the "account of the state of the nation." This is always given in Norway's second language, "rural Norwegian," and is traditionally delivered by the newest or

youngest minister. I offered up a silent prayer of thanks to my excellent Norwegian teacher, who taught us respect for rural Norwegian and the regional dialects, and I delivered the address with a
due sense of honor.

In my first cabinet meeting the Prime Minister suggested as the
first order of business that a committee be established to create a
listing of all regulations. The statute book is in need of simplifica-
tion and editing, he says. We also discuss the low proportion of
women in the public sector, and both the Prime Minister and the
Minister of Consumer Affairs stress the need for change. Rather encouraging, considering both are men!

The Prime Minister also brings up the issue of fishing boundaries, and he requests a briefing before the matter is brought before Parliament's Foreign Relations Committee. We had then the
opportunity to negotiate a considerable extension of our fishing
grounds. This was an important issue for Norway, involving the
Foreign Minister, the Minister of Trade, and the Fisheries Minister.

Soon we would have a difficult piece of business on the agenda.
It concerned the organization set up by the Western democracies after the oil crisis of 1973 to coordinate energy policies, the International Energy Agency (IEA). The question was whether Norway
should be a member. A recommendation was on the table, along
with a minority statement. The Prime Minister was looking for a
"statement that cannot be interpreted as vacillation in our attitude
toward Western cooperation."

We discussed the obligations we would take on if Norway were
to join. This wasn't just a sensitive issue for our party and the
unions, but also for the Parliament, and there had been much discussion of the fact that Norway would have only 4 of 160 IEA
votes. We were still aware of the popular reluctance against joining
any supranational organization, which had been so clearly demonstrated by the 1972 referendum rejecting membership in the European Economic Community (now the European Union).

Finally, we did arrange for Norway to join the IEA, with special status as an oil-producing country. We could decide for ourselves whether or not to participate in any action decided by the other members. Such a delicate balancing act was required to safeguard our common interests and still secure broad popular support.

King in Council

Matters to be concluded with the King in Council on Fridays were always discussed at the "Preparatory Council" on Thursdays, with the Prime Minister assuming the role of the King.

A Minister would say, for example, "I have three matters to put forward: number one, white paper on regional policy." The King would say yes, signaling that the matter had been dealt with. As the turn came to each Minister, he or she would rise and deliver the list of questions for consideration personally to the King. If, as some- times happens, the Crown Prince was present, two such lists were prepared, one for each of them. This father-and-son convention cre- ated a sense of tradition and continuity. Then it was King Olav and Crown Prince Harald; now King Harald comes with Crown Prince Haakon.

At the conclusion of the Friday meetings in the Royal Palace, the King would turn to the Prime Minister: "Are there any more matters to be discussed?"

"No, there are none, Your Majesty." And with that the King would rise, nod, thank his cabinet, and leave the room, with the Ministers all on their feet and facing in his direction. The King's role has become mostly *pro forma*. But it is of the greatest legal and po- litical importance that matters be passed through "King in Council."

The ministers then return to the government building, two or three to a car, and have lunch. It is a good way to end the week, providing an opportunity for conversation, reflection, and a joke or two. These get-togethers serve to develop friendships and a sense of joint responsibility. Several times over the years it has been sug- gested to me that we should have secretarial staff present at these lunches, because an issue may reach its real political resolution there without anyone having taken a formal note. Yet I have always said no, in the belief that formalizing such meetings might harm the mood of relaxed comradeship, which is so vital to their function.

Ministers of the Environment in Paris

I had been a Minister for only a few short weeks when I was appointed to lead a conference of environment ministers in Paris. This was the first such conference ever sponsored by the Organization for Economic Cooperation and Development. I decided to arrive a day early and get to know the most important people in its secretariat. After months and years of preparation in our respective governments, we now needed international political agreement; after all, issues of the environment know no borders.

Agreed-upon texts had been negotiated and prepared. But there was also some vehement dissent about key policies. I immediately set about coming to grips with it all.

A guiding policy was that the polluter shall always pay for cleanup and restoration. A number of countries, notably Spain and Portugal, had expressed reservations about this well-founded principle. I decided to approach the ministers involved directly. I went to work at the opening-night reception and had meetings the next morning with representatives from a couple of the countries. I was grateful for the English I had learned as a child! My conversations paid off. Positions shifted slightly.

In the course of the conference we shoehorned quite a few bits of business into place, often by means of open appeal during the final round of discussions. It was thrilling to get things done and to see how effective the powers of persuasion could be.

In the years since then I have had a number of similar experiences. Civil servants always warn against raising sensitive issues in international meetings. But for a politician it is often a pleasant surprise to have a common issue presented with enthusiasm by a fellow politician from another country. Yes—why not? Maybe we can risk going a little further here! Shouldn't I show that I have the guts to suggest a new course of action here? Politicians meeting one another across national borders often find the experience inspiring, and enjoy the feeling of mutual support. They are meeting colleagues with a common interest.

The Woman's Year 4

Having women in the government made a difference. One day when a cabinet briefing note on nutritional policy was discussed, only the three female Ministers had observations to make. This happened several times, not always in cases involving typically female or familial matters.

Early in 1975, the Minister of Justice showed me her draft for Norway's inaugural lecture for the International Year of the Woman and invited me to comment. Such gestures of trust and solidarity increased our sense of cooperation and the pleasure we took in our work.

I became ever more aware of how much my background and experiences as a doctor had influenced my attitudes toward issues involving gender equality. And I felt increasing sympathy for the ideas of the new feminism.

I said to my colleague that there were greater differences between girls and boys—from the moment of birth onward—than was implied in the draft of her speech. Her main point was of course very important: The fact that we are treated differently and encounter different experiences in life serves only to reinforce the differences. For this reason it was critical that parents and teachers offer the same opportunities to both girls and boys, and make the same demands of them. This is the only way we can promote equality between the sexes. But over the years I had kept abreast of research into child development, both before and after birth, and it was clear that from the very start there is a great deal that divides the two sexes when we compare large groups of girls and boys. The "politically correct" position my colleague had chosen was that such differences only come into being gradually because as adults we operate with stereotypes and our behavior is conditioned by the sex of the child with whom we are dealing. Biology and nature, however, are not that simple. A great deal of our potential and our tastes are with us even before the external environment starts to affect us. A combination of genetic heritage and environment is involved, and in general terms there are also congenital differences between boys and girls that go beyond the purely visual and external.

I was not concerned that this research contradicted what I had been brought up to believe, for to me it simply clarified the nature of real gender equality—equality of opportunity for the development of all the qualities and talents we each possess. Neither men nor women should be reduced to uniformity, and the most typically "womanly" impulses and passions should be granted the same status as the "manly."

If the Women Said No—The Party Congress of 1975

After being appointed Minister, in less time than a pregnancy is brought to term I was elected Deputy Leader of the Labor Party. It was quite a surprise when I was called up one evening a few days before the Party Congress by the Minister of Education, who was a member of the nominating committee: "Gro, you must stand as candidate to be Deputy Leader of the party." Since I had served as a Minister for such a short time and had held only local positions in the party previously, this was very unusual. As Deputy Leader I would be part of the central leadership and would be considered a future candidate for Party Leader and Prime Minister.

I worried that I couldn't manage this in addition to all my responsibilities as Minister of the Environment. My colleague tried to reassure me: "There will be only one major difference from what you do now. You will have to be at the meetings of the Party Central Executive Board every Monday evening."

The caller was clearly not going to take no for an answer, but what he said was a little misleading. Obviously the post would radically change the nature of my political responsibilities and would begin a major, long-term commitment.

A few days later the Women's Secretariat of the party also urged me to take the post, and that clinched my decision. I couldn't say no. How could we hope to achieve equality if the women said no?

And there was more to come. In 1977 I agreed to run for Parliament as a representative from Oslo. Our system is that while a representative is serving as a cabinet Minister, an alternate is called in to take the seat until the actually elected representative steps down from the cabinet position and can begin service as an MP.

The Stamp of Political Leadership

One day I received a written statement from the Ministry of Industry which was highly critical of the draft proposal from my Ministry of the Environment on a new law regulating the quality of consumer goods. The Minister of Industry had signed the critical statement himself. I had been a member of the government for less than a year, but I knew that something was fundamentally wrong here. The Labor Party had gone before the electorate with a ten-point strategy for reforms. A law on product control was one of them. Could I, as Deputy Party Leader, accommodate my colleague's opposition?

No. Instead I gave him a call: "Have you read the letter you just signed, the one that flies in the face of both the party's program and the government's?" His answer was inconclusive; but by the end of our conversation we had agreed that his letter would be returned to him. The ministerial statement on the issue then took a different form.

Ever since, I have observed a basic rule: I never sign anything I have not read myself. It costs me time and energy, but the practice sends an important signal. It also leads to an improvement in the quality of my department's work.

In politics and administration, conclusions are important, but the foundations, the premises on which those conclusions are expressed, are often just as important. An item of legislation intended for a democratic, rights-based society must survive rigorous scrutiny—or be repealed.

Today it is truer than ever that wording is golden. Issues have to make their way within a media-dominated society. Newspapers now devote less space to issues, which makes the politician's task as communicator even more difficult, since the fundamentals behind the catchphrases must remain equally firm.

In East Germany

An invitation to visit East Germany gave Norway the opportunity to try to influence an important Eastern Bloc country about the harmful effects of acid rain and to develop a broad political dialogue with the countries behind the Iron Curtain.

It was in East Germany that I experienced what it's like to arrive at an airport far from home—without one's luggage. The four men in my delegation all had their suitcases—but what did they need them for? They wore suits and looked the same whatever they put on. Well, such is life. My hosts assured me that my suitcase would surely turn up later in the day. For the next four days I heard all manner of soothing and encouraging words about it. Our hosts took my white cotton blouse and my underwear and had them washed every evening.

On our visit to Dresden we saw the tragic effects of the bombing of 1945. In 1977, much of the city still looked just as it did after the air raids. The following day we visited Eisenhüttenstadt, an iron-foundry town, which featured huge areas of ancient, antiquated heavy industry, terrible working conditions, and not a hint of green anywhere. Fifteen years later, after the fall of the Iron Curtain, we would see the same conditions magnified a thousand times. The pollutant technology had terrible effects on the health of the workers and of the children who lived in the vicinity.

In Berlin our program included a visit to the opera, where my casual woolen suit would not have been appropriate. The ambassador thought it might be possible to make a quick trip to West Berlin to shop for clothes, but our hosts would definitely not have approved. No, I thought to myself, there's no need to offend them. Let's just buy something locally. So a visit to a room in the basement of the largest department store in East Berlin was hastily arranged.

There a remarkable exhibition of outfits from various departments had been assembled. The selection bore witness to a lack of raw materials, and there was precious little about it to remind one of what was fashionable in Western Europe at that time. I ended up with a bottle-green patterned dress that was a size too big for me, a problem solved with a black patent leather belt. I bought black evening shoes with heels of a type I hadn't seen since the 1950s. These were two sizes too large. I wedged newspaper into the toes and managed to walk along without betraying just how nervous I was that my stocking feet would stride right out of them.

Our female translator kept us under constant observation. On our last evening she managed to prevent us from leaving our locked guesthouse in its locked garden. She offered all sorts of explanations. I felt sorry for her; we were not in a free country and she was not a free person. I didn't want to add to the difficulties of her life. The following day I gave her the black shoes. Her eyes shone with a pleasure she could not disguise.

Our discussions with the East German Minister of the Environment revealed that in their own opinion, the East Germans had no problem with pollution, nor with the acidity in their water supply and on their farms. The Minister also claimed that there was no scientific proof that sulfuric emissions from East Germany had any significant effect on the quality of the environment in Norway. Yet they were willing to send their experts to Norway and to cooperate on the Norwegian suggestion for a European convention against cross-border pollution.

Just like Margaret Thatcher, the East German authorities were eventually obliged to recognize the damage that airborne pollution caused across great distances. And even in 1975 they had to concede that they had a considerable problem with local pollution. Lignite was their most important fuel, and they anticipated that this would remain the case until the year 2000. The continued use of lignite, they understood, would vastly increase the pollution in their country.

On Home Ground

At home, Olav and I had agreed to dismiss our nanny, which made for big changes in our household. Knut, Kaja, Ivar, and Jørgen no longer came home from school to a house with an adult. There was less order and structure, but they had one another—so there was never a question of an empty house. Knut was fourteen by now, Kaja twelve, Ivar nine, and Jørgen eight. Olav got home at five, as did I whenever possible.

I often called home at about four-thirty just to check in, and not infrequently Olav would say: "Gro, you finish what you're doing, come home a bit later, before the kids have gone to bed. Everything's going so smoothly now; we're just about to have dinner." I think Olav often felt it was best to stick to his routines and his way of being with the children without having a competing adult around.

I traveled a great deal; I was probably away until very late or on overnight trips on two or three out of every five weekdays—and on quite a few Saturdays and Sundays as well. Breakfast was our most structured time. The whole family sat down together to a properly laid table with tea and thick slices of bread, cheese, and cold meat. I regularly helped the children with their school lunches by packing their sandwiches, which they, like all schoolchildren in Norway, carried from home. The tradition of hot school lunches is alien to us. And of course our family still made our regular visits to the holiday homes in summer and on winter weekends, as well as our trips to the mountains at Easter. We also always took off the week between Christmas and New Year's. This helped to give our family life a degree of stability in the midst of the chaos created by my job.

In 1975 the family presented me with a large blue scrapbook. When I opened it I saw in a child's handwriting: "Christmas 1975—to Mamma from Jørgen, Ivar, Kaja, Knut, and Pappa." Under that, there was a lovely photo of all six of us, Jørgen having just lost one upper tooth, Kaja holding Snoopy, the guinea pig, in her arms. The scrapbook's pages were full.

The five of them had worked out a secret plan, collecting newspaper clippings, pictures, and articles, and pasting them in the book with captions. It was valuable for several reasons. They were doing something together, they were reading and learning, and they understood something about what Mamma did at work. Wonderfully done, Olav!

The Sunny Side of the Street

My feelings about women's rights were exposed to the world in a father–daughter interview in the Labor Party's main organ, the Oslo daily Arbeiderbladet. Addressing my father, I describe our disagreement over the speed at which the equal-rights movement should advance: "You were worried that if it happened too quickly it might harm the women's cause. Through my work as a doctor I have seen that the relative progress made so far largely involves educated women. Many other women still haven't been part of the process at all. I, with my background and my education, can fight my way up. I have even joined your doctor's club. But I realize that in order to help the struggle forward, it's not useful for women to fight on men's terms."

Another interview ran during the summer of 1975 with the headline: "Minister from the Sunny Side of the Street." The journalist's tone was challenging, rather jocular: "Do you really need a medical degree? As soon as these Harlems reach thirty-something,

they get drafted into government, always as the youngest member."
Today the journalist could have further supported his case by
pointing out that my sister Hanne joined the Labor Party cabinet of
Jens Stoltenberg in March 2000 as Minister of Justice.

My son Knut thinks that his grandmother is very special, because
her husband was cabinet Minister for ten years and she had two
daughters who also became cabinet Ministers, one after the other.
In Norway, the constitution forbids close family to serve as cabinet
Ministers at the same time. My brothers never showed any sign of
wishing to go into politics, but my youngest brother, Lars, was a
trade union leader for several years, heading the Union of Engineers. My brother Erik has always been in private business; he runs
his own firm, Harlem Food.

I answered the interviewer: "Social and political factors alone
dictated my choice to study medicine. In my opinion, I am using
my education much more effectively as a government Minister than
I could have as a doctor. I have more challenges than ever before,
and I could hardly be doing a more important job than the one I'm
doing now."

He then writes, "This very first answer bears all the hallmarks of
the Environment Minister's style. There is little room left for further
discussion, and the answer is delivered in such a declamatory and
self-assured manner that it is almost irritating—but the hint of a
permanent smile lurking at the corners of her mouth charms you
instead."

The journalist's real point comes with the next question: "A university degree is at the very least an original route to take to reach
the top of the Labor Party. You must have had an exemplary education in the Progress Group and the youth organization of the Labor
Party, the Young Labor, to circumvent the party's widespread skepticism toward academics?"

I replied, "I said yes when Prime Minister Bratteli asked me to
do a job. Why should I apologize for having had the kind of education that Labor wants to make available to as many people as
possible?"

Dirty Tricks in the Election

As early as three months after I took government office, I was exposed to political underhandedness. *Norwegian Trade and Shipping News* and the conservative Oslo morning paper, *Aftenposten*, both printed big articles with more or less open accusations of political hypocrisy. My father had transferred shares in his modest summer holiday home at Helleskilen to his children, in the form of family ownership. This act was the subject of repeated comment in the press, and was later used by the Conservatives in their campaign literature. We were accused of having tried to circumvent a natural resources law that the Labor Party supported. It was an attack on our integrity, our ethics, and our morality.

The political advice I got was of the order of "Don't pay any attention to it." It pained me not to defend myself, because no one was writing about the actual facts of the matter. Early in the election campaign, the Right used the story at their meetings and rallies. But I was never confronted with it. It would not have been politically savvy for them to give me the chance to demolish the rumors and the accusations.

Toward the end of the campaign we held a press conference in Labor House. One journalist in particular fired a number of unpleasant and insistent questions on this issue, and I experienced something that became familiar over time: You are asked a question, and you answer. But your answers are not what the journalists want, so they are plainly not accepted; sometimes they are even ignored.

I repeated, "Several years before the new law became an issue, Pappa raised this question of family ownership with a lawyer in Fredrikstad." My point was that his action had predated the law in question. The journalist suspected that either Pappa or I was bluffing and asked for the name of the lawyer.

A few days later, to his great credit, the journalist did report the truth to his readers. Unfortunately, readers all too rarely get the help they need to supplement, clarify, or completely revise a thoroughly false picture.

After revealing that the winter home at Lake Mylla had also become family property, the article continued, "Harlem's property dealings started back in 1969. We have approached Dr. Gudmund Harlem in order to establish the type of property involved and the motives behind this latest transaction, and his information reinforces our earlier picture of a prudent father—and this time we intend no irony.

"Even though the actual transfer of property within the Harlem family seems like a political gift to the Conservative campaign because it occurred in the period of time between the passage of the natural resources law and its subsequent implementation, one must nevertheless in the name of decency make the basic facts of the matter clear."

The whole episode was rich in lessons. Journalistic standards of accuracy are not always the highest, and once attacked, you find yourself in a situation in which, however you choose to respond, some of the dirt always sticks.

I learned, too, that regardless of how helpless you feel, you absolutely must take such attacks seriously. If necessary, you should even write an article giving the facts of the matter, which can afterward be used for reference. It does not suffice simply to stand and answer questions; if you expect that your answers will be printed, you will soon find yourself disappointed.

Where Did I Stand Within the Labor Party?

At the National Congress of the party in 1975, the big question was who would become the new Party Leader and the next Prime Minister. Bratteli had announced that he wanted to step down from the party leadership. After months of division within the party between two main contenders, Einar Gerhardsen designed the Solomonic verdict: Odvar Nordli was elected to be the new Prime Minister when Bratteli stepped down, while Reiulf Steen, who had been Deputy Leader of the party since 1965, was elected Leader.

I considered myself left of center within the party on a number of issues, but I was solidly in favor of continuing our NATO membership and had voted for Norwegian membership in the European

Common Market in 1972. But more important, I was young and remained curious about the real content of the various issues. I noticed at that time that party members often spoke to me openly because I was not regarded as belonging to any particular wing. I entered the political debate on the new issues with an open mind.

Despite my yes vote, I generally shared many of the viewpoints of those who had voted no to European Common Market membership. I was also skeptical of a too-rapid expansion northward of the Norwegian oil fields because of the effects on fish stocks and the dangers of pollution. I was critical of the nuclear power lobby. I came to enjoy support in many different camps.

Having been elected Deputy Leader, I wanted to help create a new and less divisive party platform open to new approaches to old issues. In my view there was a need for new thinking and a critical attitude toward many established "truths." Our platform must have as its basis a yes to NATO, as before, but with a critical, balanced viewpoint that stressed the special nature of Norway's role within the alliance, including our low military profile in the north and our concern for stability and low tension in the Nordic area.

In the best of Young Labor I saw many good and highly necessary allies who were also searching for the best solutions. The most radical of the Young Labor group no doubt considered me too much of a party loyalist, too aware of my responsibilities to the party. Yet at the same time I was not sufficiently traditional about environmental protection and gender equality for many of the old guard—especially for those who believed that the obligations pertaining to our membership in NATO meant that Norway should follow all signals from Washington without asking questions, particularly when it came to nuclear weapons.

As Deputy Leader of the Labor Party, I was able to take part in the general assessments made when new candidates for government posts were to be chosen. My attitude was firm. It was about time the protection of the environment was taken seriously. At the very least, the Ministry of the Environment had to be accorded equal status with other important Ministries. So I balked at suggestions that I should move on to other, potentially "more important" Ministries. I stayed in my post for five years, exerting my power as Deputy Leader.

I wanted ours to be a "green party," and not to shirk the difficult decisions. There should be no need for someone interested in environmental issues to resort to voting for a party other than Labor. Looking back, I think my attitude was more than a little annoying for some. These were the days of struggle over how to preserve the Hardangervidda wilderness, the law on product control, and the laws on pollution control, as we were planning the use of real estate and natural resources. Not everyone was happy to see the Deputy Leader taking a leading role in such controversial issues in which powerful interests were involved, including trade unions.

And yet I believe I had vital support. Many union and party members—especially the young—did not want to see the Labor Party identified exclusively with what they saw as "electric power socialism, because of insensitivity to nature." We were in favor of job creation, strong export industries, and the right to work for all, but we did not believe these goals should be achieved at the expense of the long-term effects on nature, people, and the environment. I include people, because if the damage to people inherent in a loss of biological diversity cannot be ignored, neither can the toxic effects of chemical pollution of our air, our waters, and our soil.

I think we did Norwegian business a great favor by accentuating our environmental profile in these vital years. Our industry was then in much better shape to face the demands that arose as shortages of resources and energy began to take effect in other countries. We saw it after the international oil crisis of 1973, in the effort that was made to introduce new and more ecologically friendly technologies. This proved to be an economically useful investment for those forms of industry that had already been compelled to seek for new solutions.

Policy Must Be Based on Facts

The battle against acid rain was a main concern in 1976–77. It was then that the pollution related to the burning of fossil fuels was shown to transcend national boundaries. But some critics cast doubt on the whole basis for our campaign to protect Norwegian nature—and not only industrial magnates and politicians from abroad.

One critic was Ivan Rosenquist, a professor of geology at the University of Oslo. He dismissed the whole thing as a load of nonsense. Acid rain would be neutralized by the topsoil, he argued. Neither water nor trees would be affected. I was accused of interfering in the field of research. The fact is that government members are obliged to base their policies on the results of research. But it was hard going. More than once I wished other researchers had used a little of their time to put the professor in his place.

The debate about Professor Rosenquist's criticism came to a climax in the wake of my choice of words at a press conference: "*Koepenikiade!*" (Ludicrous swindle.)

But Professor Rosenquist said he was no swindler; he was a serious researcher. Rosenquist was a combative personality, and I wasn't exactly the opposite.

In order to get the acid rain project going we needed a new leader of the research board, someone who had thus far not been involved in the strife between government and the researchers. My old friend Lars Walløe was chosen. He had become a highly respected scientist. He succeeded in getting the dialogue back along constructive lines.

This period of intensive debate was both dramatic and decisive for me. I realized that I could not sit back passively without risking a weakening of the environmental effort at both national and international levels, an effort that had taken so much hard work and so many human resources, to get off the ground. Nature could not afford any indifference.

I spent a lot of time acquiring a basic knowledge of the scientific background to the conflict. Only then did I feel certain that we could proceed in our political task of securing a broader acceptance of the measures necessary to combat the effects of acid rainfall. In the end I was even successful in convincing Professor Rosenquist in a personal conversation in my office that many of his scientific arguments were not valid.

Looking back on the whole affair, it strikes me that it strengthened both my approach and my range of possible reactions when a great disaster struck at the end of April—in the form of a blowout from one of the oil platforms in the North Sea.

Challenges Offshore and Inland

Is There a Blowout?

It was Friday, April 22, 1977, and we were at the wedding of two of Olav's friends from the institute. The atmosphere on this early-spring evening was warm and joyful, but the mood was soon spoiled: telephone for Gro, from the Ministry of the Environment. The time was 11:55 p.m. Two thoughts crossed my mind: This must be something serious, and I hoped it had nothing to do with the children or the family.

My fears were well founded. Oil was pouring out of drilling platform "Bravo" in the Ekofisk field in the Norwegian continental shelf. Was it a blowout? We had no precise details yet about the extent of the disaster. What we did know was that the Rescue Services Headquarters had been alerted and that Hans Christian Bugge, our new director of the State Body for Pollution Control, was already on his way southwest to Sola airport in Stavanger.

Any decisions to be made immediately? No, emergency procedures had already been set in motion.

Bugge and the chief of police in Stavanger would report to me at the earliest opportunity.

I went straight home, confident that the matter was in good hands. I was concentrating so intently I no longer felt the glow of the red wine from the wedding. I recognized the feeling from my days as a doctor when I could be awoken in the middle of the night to deal with a serious accident or a patient suddenly entering crisis.

My thoughts were focused. Who should be informed, and in what order? Did the Prime Minister know? I wasn't sure, although I did know that the Minister of Industry had been informed. I'd wait to act until I had a little more information.

At home Knut was up, very concerned about the drama that was unfolding. He was the one who took the message that the Ministry of the Environment urgently needed to get in touch with his mother. I had left the wedding alone, but I was glad that my fifteen-year-old was awake. I told him the little I knew, and recalled the discussions we had had around our dinner table about the dangers of being an oil-producing nation.

"Let's go to bed, Knut, there are sure to be more phone calls and disturbances tonight." But quite a few thoughts occupied my mind before I finally managed to fall asleep.

I was thankful for all the work we'd done over the past two years to analyze the risks of major oil pollution from the continental shelf. Local and state emergency procedures had been drafted and were in the process of being implemented. The cabinet had discussed the delegation of responsibilities during pollution crises.

Safety is first and foremost the responsibility of the oil companies. We have strict laws allowing us to impose injunctions, carry out inspections, and follow them up. The responsibility for formulating actual preventative and emergency measures belonged to the Ministry of the Environment as of January 1, 1975. New injunctions and demands had been presented to the companies. The final deadline for compliance, however, was not yet upon us.

I thought of the drama the spring before when the government had debated whether to permit drilling north of the 62nd parallel, a difficult question for me as Minister and as Deputy Leader. Our own analysis in the Ministry indicated that, with the equipment available in 1977, safety measures were not yet adequate. Within the oil industry and in broad political circles, there was a decided push to extend activities northward as soon as possible. The majority of union leaders and the population in northern Norway agreed. I had my doubts, to put it mildly.

It was difficult for others to gainsay my arguments from a technical point of view. New equipment would have to be developed to deal with the extreme weather conditions in the north. The existing equipment was inadequate even for the North Sea. Equipment designed to meet the special needs of the open sea simply did not exist anywhere in the world before the Norwegian environmental authorities set in motion a research and development program oriented toward this goal. The program could not offer enough useful results in such a short time. My advice to the government was clear: It was not advisable to begin drilling in the north in 1977.

I shudder to think where we would have been had my cautions not prevailed. The counterarguments had been based on the assumption that the risks involved were minimal. Blowout was considered a very remote possibility, and proponents argued that it shouldn't be factored into our calculations regarding security measures.

And now here we were. The possibility was no more remote than this!

An Eventful Night

Two a.m. Bugge calls with an update. An uncontrolled blowout is indeed taking place. All 112 men on board the platform have been evacuated. The fire ship *Seaway Falcon* is on hand, dousing the oil with water to reduce the risk of fire. We have set up an Action Leadership Group, agreeing that the law on oil pollution must form the basis for our actions. The scope and depth of the involvement of the Norwegian authorities will become clear, particularly to

Phillips Petroleum, which owns the rights to the Ekofisk field and is responsible for the drilling there.

Four a.m. I have my next conversation with Bugge. The members of the Action Leadership Group have met, and they have drafted a press release based on the information so far received from Ekofisk.

"Right," I say, "then you take over." The traditional oil authorities would of course be part of the whole action. I was convinced that we should put a young, efficient, and well-prepared "pollution boss" in charge. And with that I asserted my Ministry's leadership role and gave formal authority to the Action Leadership Group, with Bugge as its head. The next twenty-four hours would be tense; at a time like this the command structure must be crystal clear. I knew I was taking a political risk, not having consulted the Minister of Industry and the Prime Minister.

Five a.m. I call the Prime Minister. I give him an overall picture of the catastrophe. A blowout; the actual size is as yet unclear. Experts from the United States have been contacted. We don't know yet how quickly the platform can be shut down. The environmental damage might be considerable.

Five-thirty a.m. I call the Minister of Industry. He has the same information as I do, and he refers to mechanical faults that have arisen during maintenance work on the well.

Seven-thirty a.m. The Ekofisk report comes in: A helicopter from the Oil Directorate has returned with new observations. The size of the leak is provisionally put at 4,000 tons of oil per twenty-four hours. Black, uncontrolled, but luckily many miles off the coast. We might be able to avoid a major environmental disaster.

Less than two hours sleep tonight.

Morning comes for the children, except for Knut, who has been involved in some of the night's activities and is now sleeping like a log. Kaja, Ivar, and Jørgen listen to the radio news with me. Olav sleeps. I tell them in more detail what a blowout is, and how it can be stopped, with a little bit of luck. Kaja is most concerned for the seabirds and the fish. Environmental awareness is high among young people, and my own children are no exception.

I close the door to the basement, where I have an extra telephone line. The children's voices fade away. The Defense Minister calls. He confirms that the KNM *Stavanger* has been ordered to the area, in addition to two surveillance vessels from maritime defense.

The Foreign Minister is on the line. The Foreign Ministry is at work on the management of information to other countries bordering the North Sea. Rescue services in Sweden, Denmark, and Great Britain have already been informed of events, and all the other North Sea states are officially informed of the disaster, as required by the terms of the Bonn agreement on security and cooperation.

The atmosphere in my Ministry is tense. Everyone is determined. We will do our utmost to minimize the damage.

At two o'clock in the afternoon, the Prime Minister, the Minister of Industry, and I fly to Stavanger. The Action Leadership Group at Sola is officially put in charge after they have briefed us. We are all impressed by what has been done.

This was a time when it was essential for the environmental powers to display their authority and to secure greater influence on the process of corporate decision making. The sequence of events during the Ekofisk disaster played an important part in the gradual strengthening of the role of the environmental protection authorities.

Oil Shock

Saturday evening we make key decisions. Phillips put its faith in so-called "capping," believing that it was possible to close off the blowout mechanically, to literally put a lid on it. I support the demand made by the State Body for Pollution Control that in addition to this measure, drilling rigs must be brought to the scene in order to bore a relief shaft—in case the capping operation fails. This costs money, and the company hesitates, but complies.

I return to the hotel just after midnight. I still haven't eaten dinner; I have no pyjamas and no change of clothes.

Sunday is a full working day. Central to the day's discussions is the possible use of chemicals to break down the oil. We are very skeptical, because of the chemicals' damage to the environment. The Action Leadership Group is encouraged to take a restrictive line.

Later in the day, the Ministry of the Environment reports on its efforts to organize regional backup. My Danish counterpart has expressed concern about the possible use of chemicals. We could ease his mind; all available mechanical means of cleaning up were mobilized.

The notable experience of the day was the helicopter trip with members of the Oil Directorate to the disaster area. Space was found for a TV team to come along so that the public could see what was going on.

At the back of my mind were the discussions about the relief shaft; in a worst-case scenario this blowout could last for months. The weather was overcast and windy, and visibility was poor.

We glimpsed Ekofisk on the horizon. Everything looked normal from a distance. But as we neared, we saw the pitch-black plume of oil jetting into the air. On the surrounding sea it looked brownish, glistening on the waves. It couldn't have been easy to get mechanical booms working efficiently in high seas like this, but workers were trying. Come what may, this would be valuable experience for the future.

Back on land, a great crowd of journalists was waiting for us. All of them would have liked to make the trip with us. I answered questions from both Norwegian and foreign journalists, investing time to explain technical aspects of what was going on and to correct misunderstandings. I was reminded again how important my job was, and how essential that the information be put in the right perspective.

Yes, Norway is an oil-producing nation. What was going on out there was pioneering stuff. The government has made firm safety demands. And in the field of emergency response procedures, as well as in our efforts to develop new technological solutions to environmental problems, we had set the highest standards.

I knew a bit about how much further ahead we were than, for example, the British. That was helpful. The Norwegian authorities had chosen to invest in the field of oil exploration safety. Many times over, I gave technical answers to questions roughly along the lines of, "How could you let such a thing happen?"

The last press conference was at 11:00 p.m. There was one last meeting after that before I went back to the hotel. I washed my underwear and stockings, rolled them in towels, and put them on a chair in front of a radiator. Only as I dropped off to sleep did I notice that I felt hungry. When was my last meal?

I took the earliest flight out from Sola the next morning.

At the Rostrum of Parliament

Work on a speech to Parliament was the main business on Monday. Hans Christian Bugge returned from Stavanger.

Nine a.m. Tuesday. A meeting of the Labor Party's Parliamentary Group Board, followed by an extraordinary meeting of the cabinet at which the rules and regulations governing the conduct of the Action Leadership Group were formalized. Then it was back to the Ministry for a few last touches to the speech before leaving for Parliament. I ran up the stairs. The Minister of Industry was already speaking.

I felt I was on safe ground. I gave a thorough account of the facts of the situation. I described the equipment that had been assembled at Ekofisk, where the overall capacity for oil absorption was 300 tons per hour. Under favorable conditions it would be possible to remove considerable quantities of oil. The current prognosis was that it was very unlikely that any of the oil that had so far leaked would reach the coast.

For the rest of the evening it was interviews, interviews, interviews. The defense of Norway's honor remained a major concern. I managed to wash my hair before watching the evening news program and going straight to bed. How lovely that was after so many days with so little sleep!

Disaster Management

Eight-thirty Wednesday morning. Action Leadership Group meeting. The section for the conservation of nature goes through its listing of areas of outstanding importance along the coastline. We need to know which areas are to receive priority treatment if worse comes to worst.

One p.m. Phone call from Bugge. Phillips is again suggesting the combined use of chemical and mechanical means to clean up the oil slick. We are faced with a difficult decision. If our rejection of chemicals leads to serious damage to the coastline, the responsibility will be ours.

We decide to summon a meeting of experts. I will participate personally. Experts from Sweden are present at the 8:00 p.m. meeting, and for the next four hours we discuss various aspects of the question. Finally we draw our conclusion: We will proceed with a more intensive use of the mechanical booms, floating barriers designed to contain spills, in order to avoid the use of chemicals. A statement to the press follows.

NRK Radio News calls before seven the next morning. They ask about the poor success rate with the booms. I stress that this is the first time that such equipment has been tried on the open sea. Philips is responsible for the operation, with the participation, advice, and leadership of the State Body for Pollution Control.

Later in the day a warning arrives from Sola. The press is not happy with the information coming from Phillips, especially the foreign journalists. I agree to return to Stavanger in the afternoon, after the cabinet meeting.

Meeting the World's Press in Stavanger

Five-thirty p.m. More than a hundred journalists are waiting. The
news conference is in English. The Norwegians accept this, and I
thank my lucky stars for my English. The questions range widely,
covering not just oil and safety, booms, high seas, and chemicals,
but also Norwegian politics and the role of the state in this disaster.

It seems to go well. A senior reporter who is usually critical of
the Labor Party sings my praises in his report but reveals his male
bias: "Look at her as she takes her place before the cameras, completely at ease and relaxed, lovely as a jewel, nerves and brain cells
under complete control. She speaks concisely, always to the point,
seriously, but unsentimentally, and yet with a tough optimism that
many of her male colleagues from the world of politics might envy
her, instead of indulging themselves in a mixture of hysteria and
opportunist point-scoring."

Certainly I was serious, eager to establish full control. From the
time I started in politics my instinct has always been to stick to the
facts and avoid being too emotional. The arguments for environmental protection, to give one example, are strong enough to stand
by themselves.

I attend meetings at Sola that evening and the 10:00 p.m. press
conference, at which the head of Philips Norwegian operations is
grilled. There are delays with the rig for the relief shaft. The Action
Leadership Group repeats its injunction and sets a time limit.

Taming the Well

Eight a.m. Friday, Rescue Headquarters. I give a series of interviews
on foreign television. Afterward I meet with the Action Leadership
Group. At the press conference the Oil Directorate describes how a
faulty valve has hampered the operation to cap the well.

Then the two well-tamers, Red Adair and Boots Hansen, arrive
from Houston. The Norwegian press wants to know if I will personally meet the legendary Red Adair. But, although I am curious
about him, I feel such a meeting would have no practical use. I

withdraw into the background, as there is a rush for the window. I catch a glimpse of a small, stocky, powerful-looking man, and on the television screens hear him express great optimism. "We'll manage it, you'll see." I hope he's right.

Late that evening Olav told me that someone at NUPI wondered whether it was true that Red Adair had remarked to the Norwegian Minister of the Environment, "Don't worry, baby. I'll fix it." Could well have been! I thought.

I ate a late lunch with Ron Apple, the London correspondent for *The New York Times*. It's rare for star reporters like him to show interest in government ministers from a small country. We talked about all sorts of things, not just oil and safety measures. And with the exception of two breakfasts at home, I ate my first proper meal of the whole week—in fact, the first since the wedding dinner!

Flight home late in the afternoon. The press was waiting at Fornebu airport, as well as a staffer with a list of telephone messages and requests. At last I make it home with my family. Then I suddenly remember that we have to prepare for May First. If the situation in the North Sea persisted, it would not be much of a celebration.

Saturday morning there is a First of May preparatory meeting at the Prime Minister's office. What to do? How to address the nation? We are interrupted by a call from Sola. The well-tamers have succeeded! They have managed to stanch the flow of oil by mechanical means. The blowout is capped; the drama is over.

After the constant tension, it feels strange. After the relief comes a sort of empty feeling.

We still did not know whether the marine environment had suffered serious damage, even though the oil was rapidly broken down in the water. Researchers would later establish that the damage was small, far smaller than expected.

Sun Over Bergen

The following day was May First. I was to give my speech in Bergen on the West coast. I was optimistic and relieved. We had saved the nation's honor. The journalists who had streamed into Stavanger expecting to see a catastrophe had instead witnessed the way an advanced country successfully deals with a national crisis. It was good publicity. The new oil-producing nation of Norway had risen to the challenge.

Clear skies. As if the day itself were saying, Yes, now celebrate and enjoy yourselves. And that turned out to be the mood of the May Day crowds.

I have often experienced warm receptions, both at home and abroad. Even so, that day stands out in my memory. A blue outfit, rather loose and comfortable after the weight loss (six pounds!) of the preceding week. Norwegian flags. Happy party members, happy citizens of Bergen.

There was applause for the procession, something I had never experienced before. The town square was jam-packed. The public listened attentively. I spoke about quality of life, about our environment and our children, about the Hardangervidda wilderness, to thunderous applause. This was about more than our own oil crisis.

As we stood waiting for the rest of the marchers to enter the square, I heard some rhythmic, repetitive shouting coming from a few streets away. What was it? Monotonously, again and again: "Down with everything! Down with everything!" Someone identified the protesters as the Marxist-Leninists.

The moment assumed a symbolic significance for me. I was trying to build something, create something, and make something work. I believed in the power and the will of human beings to shape our own development, to look after ourselves and each other in the name of an active democracy. What was it that made these shouters take such a derogatory stance? It made such a dramatic contrast to the joy and sense of togetherness and solidarity that the rest of us shared at that moment.

The Struggle to Create a National Park

The high mountain plateau covering a sizable part of inland southern Norway goes under the name Hardangervidda. It is the largest continuous high mountain plain area in Europe. The question of whether the wilderness should be turned into a national park had been under discussion for some time before I became Minister of the Environment. Also under consideration was whether the two rivers running down from the "Vidda" should be included. The one flowing west is called Veig; the one flowing east, Dagali.

A 1974 report of the Special Committee on Hardangervidda indicated that the government faced some very difficult choices. The biggest stumbling block proved to be the major financial interests in the development of hydroelectric power. Thus far, all major conflicts involving hydroelectric development or protection of rivers had ended in defeat for the environmental lobby. But there were also other powerful economic interests involved. The Farmers Union, numerous property-owning groups, and local political leaders all contributed to the debate. The parties on the Right would have great difficulty accepting the perpetual conservation of land not owned by the state.

There were also opposing interests within the government. The Minister of Industry was my chief opponent. From the very beginning there was probably a slight public majority for conservation, and this faction gradually grew, picking up a great deal of support among the young, among women, and at the grass-roots levels of Labor. I did all I could to advance the conservation line.

In the Ministry of the Environment we focused on many of the controversial issues. We were deeply involved in the debate on electric power, and on how to economize on our use of energy. If we could reduce our need for electricity, our conservation attempts would be much more effective. The Minister of Finance supported this analysis, not only because he was sympathetic toward the cause of environmental politics but also because he believed it was good economic policy to invest less in the power industry.

As Deputy Leader I was already working to ensure that the program committee opt for the clearest possible profile on this issue in the draft program to be presented to the Party Congress in May 1977. And a majority, including the Party Leader, the Party Secretary, and the leader of Young Labor, expressed in very clear terms the belief that Dagali and Veig should be protected. On March 29, a few weeks before the Party Congress, I gave a public lecture in which I made my own position very clear. The lecture attracted widespread newspaper coverage. I said: "I have no doubt that there is no other area in southern Norway which is in greater need of our protection than the Hardangervidda wilderness."

Several turbulent weeks followed. Powerful interests had to be combated. The Oslo branch of the party, the women's movement, and Young Labor fought for conservation. In other branches of the party, out in the country, the division between opposing sides was extreme.

Two weeks later, Party Leader Reiulf Steen delivered an influential speech calling Hardangervidda "one of the great testing issues in Norwegian politics, because here is an opportunity to demonstrate that what we say in our programs and speeches about conservation is more than mere rhetoric."

The Party Congress of 1977 voted that a national park should be established on the Vidda, but the formulation was not crystal clear. The Party Leader exhibited some "personal problems" that attracted media attention and also colored events. He had given incoherent comments to the press, and the secret of his serious alcohol problem now started to spread. In order to show solidarity, the congress avoided any strong confrontation over the Hardangervidda question.

The day after the congress ended, I wrote a cabinet briefing note which was discussed at the cabinet meeting on May 16. In it I discussed the two possible alternative ways of treating the question of the Vidda: as a conservation issue to be resolved under the terms of our laws on environmental protection, which was my preference, or as a matter for the laws governing the use of natural resources.

The Minister of Industry still maintained that the latter was the correct procedure, and to the surprise of many he no longer enjoyed the support of the Minister of Trade, who now said he was for conservation. The Trade Minister was an elected member of Parliament from Hordaland, the county through which Veig runs. His position illustrates the delicate balancing act many politicians must perform, in a case where such strong feelings are involved and so much is at stake.

Two Rivers

That spring the parties of the Middle and the Conservatives declare their willingness to form a coalition with the intent of creating a new government. Labor's election campaign focuses on our willingness to plan and manage resources properly, and opposes the Center-Right. One newspaper notes that in certain quarters a national park is regarded as an unwarranted imposition of socialist ideology. "Well," I reply, "words can be used and abused. In our view, controlled planning in such matters is necessary for the common good. In any environmental issue, good caretaking and a respect for nature will often involve a diminution of private property rights." I had on many occasions noticed that all the parties on the Right, not just the Conservatives, were so preoccupied with the protection of the right to own property privately that in questions involving environmental protection they simply could not be trusted.

The struggle within the ranks of the Labor Party Parliamentary Group intensifies. A few days before the decisive meeting, former Prime Minister Bratteli, who is now our Parliamentary Leader, tells me, "Be careful. The Hardanger wilderness is a very complex issue for the parliamentary party."

I say, "I don't have a choice. The issue is too important. For the sake of the party, I cannot in all conscience do anything but go all the way with this."

The Secretariat of the Trade Union Council (TUC) makes a surprise move. It suggests a new compromise: the development of Veig and the conservation of Dagali. But the Labor Party Central Executive Board advises the government and the parliamentary party to support the conservation of both Veig and Dagali.

The meeting of the Labor Party Parliamentary Group turned out to be one of the most tense I would ever attend as Minister of the Environment. It lasted nearly five hours. Many of the heavyweights spoke in favor of development. It was not until the end of the meeting, when a vote was called, that it emerged that I had the support of the group, by a margin of only 31 to 30.

The government still had not made a formal position statement because it was waiting for the outcome of the group meeting; only then did the Prime Minister insist that it do so. The government was in favor of conservation. The Central Executive Board was in favor of conservation. The Party Leader, the Deputy Leader, and the Party Secretary all supported this line.

The political editor of the right-of-center Oslo tabloid *Verdens Gang*, *VG* for short, asked me, dramatically, whether it would have been possible to continue as Minister of the Environment had the vote gone the other way. Answering would risk reopening wounds, and I declined. "Do you consider this a personal victory?" he continued.

"*No*, I think the right decision was reached. It was not mine alone, it was an issue that concerned us all." That a party crisis arising out of such an issue would have involved something much more fundamental than the fate of a single individual was my line, although I knew I had taken a really big risk.

The Weather Is Wrong: The Soviet Union

In 1978 I visited the Soviet Union. In the pan-European perspective, Moscow was an important center. In the spirit of the Helsinki Agreement, we hoped to ensure the close scientific and technical cooperation of Soviet experts and administrators to get their support for a convention on air pollution and on other agreements that benefited the environment. We wanted to build bridges between East and West.

In Moscow I talked about the damage to the Norwegian environment that we had registered since the early 1970s. The United States and Canada had been experiencing similar environmental problems. A week earlier I had been in the United States to discuss the problems, and rather recently the East German Minister of the Environment had paid a return visit to Norway. I told the Soviets that Norway was extremely concerned about airborne pollution, that practically every Norwegian knew about acid rain.

Some ten years later I went back to Russia as leader of the World Commission on Environment and Development and as Norwegian Prime Minister, this time just after the terrifying accident at Chernobyl in the spring of 1986. Again uppermost in our minds was the fear of serious damage to health. During our talks, the Soviets pointed to other European nations, such as Belgium and West Germany, that opposed the steps the Nordic countries were proposing because of the great costs that would be involved in shifting to a more environmentally sound method of fuel production.

On my 1978 trip, Olav came to the Soviet Union with me. This was a treat, since usually one of us had to stay home with the children. And during the years I spent in the Ministry there were more working trips and few official state visits, which generally include spouses.

Early on the morning of September 21, we sat waiting for the Aeroflot departure from Helsinki. Luckily, one of the ministerial advisers spoke Russian. He knew the country, too, and he cautioned Olav and me, "If there is anything you need, toiletries, for example, you'd better get them while we're here. You'll not believe how difficult it can be to get hold of even the simplest things over there." Toiletries? We had them with us. After all, we were only going to be away a few days.

How I came to regret my casual attitude! From the days in Leningrad and later in Kiev there are two problems I remember with particular vividness. First, we were miserably cold. The dark and gloomy hotel was freezing. That first evening we said nothing and went to bed fully clothed. You don't get much sleep under such circumstances. I experienced the same thing later, as recently as 1996, in Lithuania, where the temperature in the bedroom of the guesthouse was 40 degrees Fahrenheit. In Leningrad it was only 38 degrees. The worst thing is that the air you breathe is so cold. Clothes and blankets don't help.

The icy temperatures prevailed wherever we went. And nothing could be done about it. It was September 22 and, according to the relevant directives, the heating could not be turned on until October first. "There is nothing wrong with the directive," one of the Soviet hosts told us. "It is the weather that is wrong." I was reminded of the war years I spent as a child, of how we froze then.

That morning we're due to attend several meetings. We are cordially received and shown to a cloakroom where we can hang up our coats. I have chosen a dark blue woolen dress with brass buttons, two underskirts, and an extra blouse under the dress. On top of all that I'm wearing the jacket from a woolen suit—and still my teeth are almost chattering. I refuse to take off my coat. My hosts give me some rather curious looks, and I choose to tell them straight out, with a smile, "I'm rather cold." I'm sure they were freezing, too, but it just wasn't admitted there.

In the afternoon a second problem arises. I haven't packed sanitary napkins. I was to find out just how relevant they were, our young adviser's cautionary words. I contact the female escort in the Soviet Foreign Office's protocol group and tell her what I need. At first she doesn't seem to understand, but after all it isn't too hard to explain what I mean. Everything seems fine, and she asks me to accompany her to a pharmacy.

She speaks Russian to the pharmacy staff. Much head shaking. We come away with several small square packets. These turn out to be bandages, what we call compresses, a little over an inch square, with very little absorption. This wasn't going to be easy! Several others are put on the case—still no luck. What did the Russians do?

I can imagine it. That first summer Knut was born we washed a lot of diapers. That was the way it always used to be done.

A Red Flag

It was a little warmer in Kiev, and the traditions in the Ukraine were slightly different. In various ways they made it clear to us that we were in another country altogether. After a visit to a museum, we ate lunch somewhere out of town. Both wine and vodka helped to warm us during the meal; there were lots of toasts, speeches, and a good atmosphere. I thanked our hosts for their hospitality and drank a toast to cooperation between our two countries. Olav risked a toast to Shevchenko, the Ukrainian freedom fighter, and mentioned Kirishenko, the Soviet ambassador in Oslo, who had expressed pleasure that we were to visit his homeland, the Ukraine.

This caused a certain amount of discomfort around the table. Kirishenko's father had been party chief in the Ukraine until 1960, when he was removed from office by Khrushchev. You simply did not mention his name, as you made no mention of any sign of Ukrainian nationalism. A Soviet official found it necessary to remind us all that the ambassador in Norway was the Soviet ambassador, not the Ukrainian ambassador.

On the way back to Kiev we drove along mile after mile of flat wheat fields while we sang. It turned out that my female colleague, the Minister of the Environment in the Ukraine, liked singing as much as I did. As we sang our way through socialist battle hymns of the nineteenth and twentieth centuries, our common heritage as Europeans emerged. We sang for each other, songs from our own respective traditions.

I sang, "When I see a red flag flapping, on a clear fresh day in spring," and she joined in. She knew the tune; she could sing along in her own language. There was no interpreter with us in the car, just our two husbands, so I don't know whether the words of the song were also identical.

It's tragic the way the ideas and the inspiration behind the fight for freedom and against exploitation could have gone as badly astray as they did in the wake of the Russian Revolution. I met my colleague on other occasions, both before and after this. She was still a member of Soviet delegations, right up to the end of the 1980s, but I don't know what happened to her after the breakup of the Soviet Union and the coming of the new era.

During the visit I established good working contacts in research institutions and even in the centralized bureaucracy in Moscow. I especially remember the sharp but matter-of-fact encounter with the chairman of the State Committee on Science and Technology. He behaved like a self-confident boss. He primarily represented the interests of those who lived according to Lenin's words, seeing the foundation for the future in "socialism and electricity." But gradually the Soviets would come along in the European discourse on transboundary air pollution.

Sidelined

The late 1970s and early 1980s proved to be tough years for the Labor Party. However, we did useful work at the Ministry of the Environment, and my efforts to modernize the party were met with understanding, even if they were opposed within the party and by trade union interests. We were under outside pressure from the conservative wave, both nationally and internationally. In the 1970s the government had used considerable sums of money to stimulate the economy and to protect our level of high employment. According to *The Economist* of London, Norway was odd man out in Europe by using public money to uphold ailing industries. We could not continue in this way. It was too expensive, and we were not getting the necessary modernization of our economy while we were losing in competitive power. Under pressure from the marketplace we had to trim public spending. We had to find new solutions. The Labor Party had chosen as an ideal "social democracy." But the party was deeply split over a variety of major issues: tax reform, crime prevention, elimination of grades on school report cards, and the environment. It was a time of struggle between opposing traditions, between old and young. We had another very difficult matter to contend with as well: the nuclear weapons question in NATO, known as the dual-track decision of 1979, under which NATO would both modernize its nuclear weapons with missiles based in Europe and negotiate arms control agreements with the USSR, which had greatly improved its military capabilities.

The municipal election campaign of 1979 got off to a bad start, on a train journey through the Gudbrandsdalen Valley to Trondheim. I was sitting beside the Minister of Finance when a radio reporter appeared and asked for an interview about our tax policy. The Finance Minister's answers made the next radio news bulletin, and the Labor Party's internal strife on taxation policy made big headlines. The election campaign was derailed before it had even started.

Too little sleep and a couple of drinks too many instantly made their mark on the Leader of the party and the government, making things worse. The reporters observed their unconvincing performance the following day. I myself had needed the help of the conductor to keep several troublesome men away from the corridor where I had my sleeping cabin that night.

On the day of the election I made my way to the party's offices to await the results with my colleagues in the usual fashion. I had many forebodings. I had had good experiences during the campaign, speaking to packed houses, meeting people, signing autographs for children. And yet our campaign had generally not gone well.

Party Leader Reiulf Steen hadn't arrived, and the journalists were beginning to ask for comments. Where was he? He had gotten back rather late from Sweden after election night there, I was told. Time dragged, and the Party Secretary fielded the first interviews. Then the pressure increased for the leadership to say something. The results weren't good: 7 percent below the last general election two years earlier. The Party Secretary and I had to make a decision: In Reiulf's absence I would speak. I had by now heard that he was in a hotel room out at Fornebu Airport, that he was in very poor shape after his flight, and that his back was bad. It was a tough night. We simply said that Reiulf was unwell. But rumors circulated, and journalists knew, of course.

In the week that followed, Reiulf never appeared in public, not even at the postelection meeting of the Central Executive Board. I chaired the meeting. The press referred to me as "Acting Leader." But a Deputy Leader can hardly avoid acting as Leader when the elected Leader is not present. I felt it was extremely unfair when some news reports accused me of usurping the leadership when I was simply doing what was obviously my duty.

A negative image of the party emerged over the next weeks. The press reported: "The Conservative success in the local elections will lead to changes in the Labor Party. It is now obvious that a thorough reshuffling of Prime Minister Odvar Nordli's cabinet is imminent. And the ongoing discussion about the leadership of the party will intensify . . . After yesterday's catastrophic election results, both Prime Minister Nordli and Deputy Leader Brundtland concede the need for a period of profound self-analysis."

According to another paper, this is "the Labor Party's worst local election result for more than forty years." Late that night I say to the paper, "All we can do is roll up our sleeves and start working toward a better result in the Parliamentary election in 1981."

That prompts a bold question: "Are you prepared to play a more important role in the party than being Deputy Leader and Minister of the Environment?"

"I choose to regard that question as unasked," I reply.

The day after the election, a lead article reports, "Labor's grassroots unhappy with the leadership." The reporters have spoken to a number of local leaders around the country and summarize the comments thus: "Important political questions were flagged during the election before they had been discussed and decided upon internally. There was a complete lack of coordination between government and party in the election campaign."

Up from the Couch

As early as September 19, the day the Central Executive Board met, VG had an interview with Reiulf Steen. The journalist asked: "When it was announced on TV that your absence from the debate on the party leadership was due to a bad back, several passengers and members of the public who had been at Fornebu Airport rang VG and said that you were visibly drunk when you arrived."

"I don't find it strange that people who saw me thought I was drunk," replied Steen. "I was in great pain, and I had taken pain-killers before I hobbled off the plane at Fornebu."

The media continued to report on Labor's leadership question. "Unreasonable" was how Steen described the extensive discussion of personalities that was now taking place within the Labor Party, in the wake of the thumping electoral defeat the week before. Under the headline "Reiulf Up from the Couch," a junior reporter wrote that "on television on Saturday, Reiulf Steen maintained firmly that he has a mandate from the Party Congress and proposes to continue on that basis."

The New Team

The Trade Union Council leader Tor Halvorsen had asked for a meeting the day after the election. Only the Party Secretary and I were present when Tor said, quite unequivocally, "This won't do anymore. Someone else must take over as Leader. Odvar and Reiulf aren't up to the job." From then on, Reiulf Steen, who later recovered and returned to his office, was always cool and dismissive toward me.

Today it is my belief that Reiulf had contacted Tor and Odvar and that the three of them—possibly also including the Party Secretary—discussed the whole situation. Plans were made for the future without my being invited to attend any of the meetings. I was simply pushed aside. This was something the boys wanted to do on their own.

Some days later Prime Minister Nordli informed me that I was to leave the cabinet and enter Parliament. I had to prepare myself for the inevitable day when I would become Party Leader and Prime Minister, he said. This seemed a little odd. I had not been present at any meetings about the composition of the reshuffled government. Reiulf also had regular meetings with the Party Secretary, from which I, the Deputy Leader, was excluded. Such conduct was contrary to standard procedure.

At a meeting of the National Executive Board just before the opening of Parliament, Prime Minister Nordli presented the new government. Party Leader Steen was to become the new Minister of Trade. I, who had been an elected Member of Parliament since 1977, was to take my seat there, while the Defense Minister took over at the Ministry of the Environment. My departure from the government was presented to the public as the inevitable consequence of the fact that the Party Leader was now joining it.

I believe that both the Prime Minister and the Party Leader felt pressured by the poor electoral showing. Neither felt strong enough on his own.

I had no doubt by now that Reiulf saw me as a serious rival and that he was extremely happy to see me moved out onto the periphery. All the same, it seems to me now that he found the political struggle between development and conservation burdensome. The Minister of Industry, who was also skeptical about the environmental policies that I was executing on behalf of the party, was close to Odvar. Both of them thought of me as tough, someone who knew her stuff a little too well for comfort. I had become a heavyweight opponent.

It would not have done much good—and it certainly wouldn't have been wise—to have attacked me openly. I would just have to take it all with good grace and explain how logical it actually was for me, as Deputy Party Leader, to acquire some parliamentary experience. Any signs of criticism or visible unhappiness from me would automatically have created a political storm, which would have weakened the party. Being angry about having to serve as a Member of Parliament would simply make no sense, in particular to all those who already were serving or whose strong wish it was to obtain such a position.

The political observers offered a variety of interpretations, from "Gro Goes to Prime Minister's School" to "Gro Sidelined." I decided to make the best of things where I was.

The first months in Parliament turn out to be an extraordinarily active and productive time. Friendships develop in "the House," both within the party groups and between them. One also gets to know leading figures from the other parties when one sits on the Finance Committee, as I did. You get to know the way they think and the way they like to present themselves—two things that are sometimes quite contradictory!

My First Trip to China

Working with the Finance Committee also provided me with more international experience. In 1980 the committee traveled to Singapore, Hong Kong, and the People's Republic of China. Beijing and especially Shanghai were very different then. You saw the effect of centralized control on a whole society, the lack of spontaneity and freedom.

The protocol was very strange. It proved impossible for the Norwegian Embassy to make it understood that I was there simply as a regular committee member, and that Gunnar Berge, later my Finance Minister, was the committee's leader and should be treated accordingly. The Chinese nevertheless insisted that I was the Deputy Leader of the Labor Party. We managed—just barely—to abide by our own sense of fitness and decorum. I had to keep a sharp lookout for the seating arrangements at meetings and lunches, and when the keys to the hotel rooms were handed out I trotted along after Gunnar and insisted on seeing his room before I would take possession of my own. He didn't care in the slightest who had the biggest room, but I did. On more than one occasion we swapped keys.

In 1995, fifteen years later, I visited China for the fourth time. Shanghai was completely changed. There were still bicycles everywhere, but also bridges, multilane highways, heavy traffic, skyscrapers—and major pollution. There's no time to lose here. China must now move toward a more sustainable form of growth.

The "Dual-Track Decision"

On October 31, 1979, Foreign Minister Knut Frydenlund informed the Labor Party Parliamentary Group of the so-called "dual-track decision" to be taken by NATO in December 1979. NATO wanted to restore parity in medium-range missiles in Europe in the wake of the Soviet Union's recent weapons buildup. The new plan was for more nuclear weapons within range of the Soviet Union combined with an offer to the Soviets about balanced reductions. "No matter how you do your sums, the inescapable conclusion is that the Soviet Union is involved in an arms buildup," Frydenlund said. The problem was first raised in Europe by the Chancellor of West Germany, Helmut Schmidt, from the Social Democratic Party, who insisted that the West had to respond to the Soviets. Frydenlund described the debate among the Social Democrats in West Germany, who were chief architects of détente with the East and who felt a strong need for both increased security and continued détente: "West Germany, Holland, Belgium, Italy, and the U.K., which are candidate countries for eventual deployment of the new missiles, will ask for our support," Frydenlund explained. "I think we will find it incredibly difficult to refuse. They too have domestic differences of opinion to deal with."

It proved difficult to offer our support. All over the place, people were asking, "Why arm in order to disarm?"

Frydenlund replied, "Our role must be to support those who are most likely to achieve a real offer of arms negotiation," referring to Brezhnev's recent offer of talks.

There was considerable irritation in the Parliamentary Group over the fact that this difficult problem had not been aired before the Labor Party earlier. It was certainly completely new to me.

It seems likely that the government and the party leadership had preferred to postpone the discussion rather than face a potential problem.

In conclusion, Frydenlund commented on how the Conservatives would exploit the opposition within the Labor Party. And he was right. But—and this was the main thing—we had a problem ourselves. And within weeks it would get worse. In a foreign affairs debate in November, I discussed the various dilemmas we faced. There was the danger of a modernization that did not include a real disarmament; we might have to accept a resolution for rearmament in order to acquire the credibility that would enable us to disarm.

The matter is to be discussed at a meeting of the National Executive Board on November 27. The day before there is a meeting of the Central Executive Board, at which the Foreign Minister tells us that there is a majority in the Danish parliamentary party group of Social Democrats against the government's line, and that a proposal for a six-month postponement of NATO's decision has been aired.

The National Executive Board turned out to be divided down the middle. It was a difficult situation for the government. We did something quite extraordinary. We decided that Party Leader Reiulf Steen should go to Moscow and Prime Minister Odvar Nordli to Washington to stress our strong desire for a solution through negotiation with the Soviet Union. I was sent to the West German Labor Party Congress in Berlin. Chancellor Schmidt, Party Leader Willy Brandt, and Defense Minister Hans Apel did not expect Norway to show any enthusiasm for the upcoming decision, but they took for granted that Norway would not block it.

I came to the conclusion that we should plan a follow-up meeting in NATO in a couple of years' time at which we could respond to the results of the negotiations. Then we could take up a final position on deployment. A new appraisal of the question of deployment at some future point in time would increase the likelihood of real results and create a degree of pressure that could prove helpful.

War Behind the Scenes

Political work in the party and in Parliament took all the time at my disposal. So it was painful to realize that there was a war going on, in which I was an object but not a participant. The newspaper article that made the strongest impression on me during this difficult period for the Labor Party appeared in *VG* on February 15, 1980. There were big headlines about the widespread leadership crisis accompanied by large photos. It was not a pleasant overall picture.

The newspaper reported that active moles in the party and the movement were trying to undermine Prime Minister Nordli, Deputy Leader Brundtland, and TUC boss Tor Halvorsen. The only leader whose position seemed sound was, incredible as it might seem, the Party Leader, Reiulf Steen.

On the same page: "Powerful forces within the party and the unions are now working to put forward Cabinet Minister Sissel Rønbeck as an alternative to Gro Harlem Brundtland at the next Labor Party National Congress in the spring of 1981."

Leaks to the Media and Slander

For several years a series of articles had appeared in the press, apparently based on systematic leaks. Summaries of what was said at Labor Party Central Executive Board meetings and other, smaller meetings appeared in a word-perfect and yet highly selective form. A serious act of disloyalty was involved here, and we could all see who escaped attack. So there was a distinct feeling that the Party Leader—or a very close associate—was the source. At about this time Prime Minister Odvar Nordli told TUC boss Tor Halvorsen, the Party Secretary, and me that he knew of the existence of tapes with the Party Leader's voice, in which he expressed himself very openly and negatively on the subject of, among others, the Prime Minister. The press had obtained copies. "I have them here," said the Prime Minister. "But I refuse to listen to them. I can't bear the thought; it's just too incredible, just too unbelievable." It turned out later that there were many such tapes.

Ten years would pass before all this became public knowledge, so it is no wonder that both party colleagues and others had difficulties in understanding the reason for the leadership problems during these turbulent years. The use of leaks through tapes took place over and over again, right up until the revelations of 1989.

The article in *VG* about my position in the party surprised me. It was inaccurate and malicious. It did not analyze my position carefully or discuss the party's confidence in me. It pretended to be a political analysis, but in fact it was put together from fairly limited sources.

There was much indignation in Parliament that day. People were shocked. "Where did the paper get this from?" "What are you going to do, Gro?" To this question I had my answer ready: "Nothing!" What could I do, confronted by a completely anonymous personal attack like this? I could hardly claim that the reporter had not spoken to anyone. The party and the trade unions combined had about a million members!

The paper wrote: "*VG* has been told that Brundtland's position within the party and the TUC has weakened considerably. The most serious accusation leveled against her is that her fierce ambitions are out of all proportion to her political qualifications. Today she is said to have little influence on the Parliamentary Group and on other central organs, although all recognize the strength of her position out in the country . . . She has however experienced greater difficulties in making her mark than in the days when she was a minister."

I was an active participant in the major debates in the House. I did not long to get back into government office. I felt that I was learning a great deal about the way Parliament worked and about relationships with the other party groupings. All the same, it was hurtful to experience these attempts to waltz me to the wall through anonymous attacks in the country's largest newspaper. I bottled it all up, while my mother said: "Why do you put up with all this, Gro?"

I did not want to be forced out. And it was my view even then that one shouldn't allow oneself to become, economically or personally, dependent on one's political job. There is no job security in politics; there is always another election.

But this was slander. Mamma's suggestion to give up was dismissed. I knew what my responsibilities were. And I was determined not to let the bullying break me. I had great confidence in the National Congress, and it was up to the National Congress to elect its officials.

It was through a book written by two journalists in 1989 that the whole story of tapes and leaks to the media became public knowledge. In *Spider: The Story of a Furniture Dealer*, they quote and confirm almost word for word what *VG* had been writing in 1980. The book includes transcripts from many conversations, each prearranged to be recorded and distributed to select reporters by furniture shop owner Arvid Engen along with a close colleague of mine, Reiulf Steen, whom I was foolish not to suspect at the time. Finally, but much too late, there was proof. For nearly fifteen years journalists who had known had kept this scandal a secret. I was the one to suffer the most.

My Creed

Had I not possessed the peace of mind that came from knowing that I had behaved honorably and correctly—showing respect for the position with which I had been entrusted—I would never have survived these difficult years. But it was hard—very, very hard.

Olav and my parents were essential supports for me. Mamma sometimes became so indignant on my behalf that I worked hard to steel myself: Don't break. Hold on and hold out. And at other times she had the opposite reaction: "Gro, how can you be bothered? Why not just wave it all good-bye? Why should you put up with such crude and unfair treatment?" That too helped me to draw the line: No, I could not let such methods succeed. Politics—or at least the politics of the labor movement—should have as its foundation a basic ethics and integrity, a respect for cooperation, for true participation in open debate.

This conviction, this creed, has been a driving factor in my work and has helped me face the hard times. I think many people have come to understand and respect this fundamental belief of mine. Others evidently view it as rather naïve. They see it as a sign that I lack the interest, ability, or will to practice politics as they believe politics has always been and ought to be practiced: an arena in which strategic ploys, including personal attacks, are considered an everyday part of achieving the desired results.

My Contribution to Modernize

It is a difficult objective to make party activists understand that we can't do everything at once and that the essence of politics is choosing which of several directions we should take, which values to promote. In an address to the National Executive Board in February 1980 I discussed the problems we were faced with. I spoke about the current political debate and the lack of clarity in our political standpoints. I said, "Another general election approaches. What was the song of the Right at the last crossroads? Freedom or socialism. Social democracy as a threat to democracy. It was about politics and issues. The others attacked what we stood for—in unison. But what looms ahead of us now? A debate on our very ability to create our policies, our ability to govern. This is something new."

I concluded, "We—all of us—have to be able to say no. To say that not everything can be done at once, to say that every good intention cannot always harmonize with every other good intention. We have to be ready to live with the fact that not everything we do will be popular. This is firm government, demanding real debate and openness, which in turn enables the creation of a united political front. If we cannot create such an image of ourselves for the outside world, well, then, gradually the right-wing press will work away at our party's and our unions' influence and prestige and confidence—in short, our ability to run Norwegian society."

During the debate one MP remarked, "I am in favor of discipline, but what we need is greater discipline at the very top. Party members are very upset by the behavior of the leadership in the party and the government. What's lacking in the Labor Party is a unified leadership. We need one man or woman to lead both party and government."

Social Democracy Under Fire

"At the moment we are seeing a sustained conservative attack across a broad front on the welfare policies of the Labor Party. We don't want social control for the sake of social control but for the sake of the people. Activity in the social sector is not in itself a goal but rather a means to the end that we are determined upon."

With these words I opened my speech on our party's principles and intentions March 15, 1980. I felt the need to stress this point following the assaults on social democracy from a strengthening Right in the country. Catchphrases such as "For you—against the Guardian State" proliferated. Self-interest was appealed to rather than solidarity, and the people were advised to "take a break" from social reforms.

There was no reason to doubt the basic vision and ideals that our movement stands for. I assured my audience that faith, enthusiasm, and the will to work together had always been our strengths. I paraphrased the famous Danish humorist Piet Hein's words about pessimists. They believe in the opposite of what they hope. While the optimists upon whom life depends are the ones who dare to hope for what they believe in.

A preoccupation of mine at this time was the right to work, including the rights of women to work. Jobs for all was closely related to other goals to which our party gave high priority: equality of living standards, zero tolerance for gender discrimination, personal growth, and security. As late as 1979, the debate over the role of women in society was greeted with skepticism or eloquent silence in the Conservative Party.

The Freedom to Choose

In a Labor speech early in 1981 my subjects were the election and
our party principles: "It is not enough to know what we want. We
must also know why we want it. And we must be able to tell the
voters. So an important test of the validity of our policies is whether
they are formulated clearly enough, whether they can be defended
in a convincing and logical way."

I discussed the concepts of freedom and equality, and under-
scored why inequality among people is the important starting point
for the ideal of equality. The least advantaged had to receive the
most help in order to equalize the standard of living. A policy of active differential treatment had to be employed. For example, we had
to expend more resources on the children who were in need of special help in their formative years.

I argued for freedom of choice as an important human need.
Could we achieve this at the community level, at the family level, at
the individual level? Yes. But our task then would be to find the
best areas in which deregulation and individuation are most advantageous.

A key political aim of the workers' movement is to achieve the
greatest possible equality in living standards. To attain that ideal
should not necessitate a meddlesome government, an overly detailed comparison of every aspect of people's standards of living. It
was important to strike a balance in order to enable variety and
freedom of choice to flourish. Decentralization's greatest challenge
is that it creates inequality.

"If the power to influence our own decisions is increased, then
the aim of equality in detail must decrease," read our working document on party principles.

I think one important reason for the 1980s swing to the right
was that the people were cautioning us against unnecessary limitation of individual growth and self-expression. And one must simply
accept that there is an unavoidable conflict between freedom of the
individual and society's need for solidarity and security. In response
to the rightward trend, I declared that the Labor Party ought not to

regard any talk of "individuals" and the "need for personal growth" as a reactionary point of departure for the formation of ideological principles. Greater freedom of choice is an important aspect of the struggle to achieve a higher quality of life. And I think we must dare to say so.

I then offered a statement of intention that empowered us through many of the years that followed, and helped us reach many of our aims. "For a great many people today, a higher standard of living will bring a greater freedom of choice. One can, for example, choose shorter working hours and a lower wage." I maintained that the differing needs of families and children at various stages of life could be allowed for. Greater flexibility, more choice, not least in working life, would be our watchwords for the 1980s. I spoke too of the need for flexibility in retirement and pensions. We would have to avoid making a mold into which all must fit. Greater freedom of choice in some of life's most important areas would improve the quality of our lives.

Solidarity: What Is That?

My concerns at the turn of the decade formed the basis for the reforms carried out by the Labor Party government in the 1980s and 1990s—changes in working hours, maternity leave, optional retirement.

During the 1980s, the word "solidarity" sounded worn and outmoded to many young people. But by the beginning of the 1990s it was much easier to promote the word as something positive. Indeed, we were even able to successfully introduce a term like "the solidarity alternative." The fight against unemployment had to be a combined effort. People understood that, not least the young. The notion of solidarity once again began to appeal.

Socialism is about solidarity and equality, about moving together, about protecting and looking after the weak. But that does not mean we can't make demands of our fellow human beings. These ideas have always seemed absolutely central to me, and never contradictory. Unless such thinking lies visibly behind what we say and do, we cannot hope to persuade a majority to join us in promoting our ideals in the form of practical politics.

Young people find it difficult to accept the lack of clarity in our attitude to property ownership. I still believe that the ownership of private property by an individual in the name of his or her family is quite natural and acceptable. In the early 1980s, however, it was by no means clear that the Labor Party and the unions were fully committed to protecting an individual's right to private property. In rural areas, people owned their own houses, heavily subsidized by loans from the State Housing Bank that had been given in the years of the postwar reconstruction. But in towns the situation was different. We could not persuade people who lived in a housing association apartment that they would enjoy the same security if they had to move or switch jobs, for there was always the fear that they would not be able to get something similar in another town as long as the housing association gave preference for seniority of membership and length of residence in the specific community.

In my view, we did not need to entertain doubts about our fundamental social-democratic principles. This was not where our problems lay. Our ability to apportion our resources, to provide job security, income security, to meet the challenges of international diplomacy, would depend on our proven principles. Our only viable way forward was to become ever more conscious of these issues.

A Party at War with Itself

Reiulf Steen in his added capacity as Minister of Trade said, "The balance of payments is important, but it can never be a goal." This came at a time when one of the government's most difficult tasks was to create an understanding of the vital importance of good economic housekeeping. So a statement like this from the Party Leader and a cabinet member was not exactly helpful to the Prime Minister and the Minister of Finance. But it would undoubtedly be popular in certain strategically important circles, in, for instance, the trade unions.

To Steen I responded, "A policy of retrenchment is politically demanding, both inside the party and beyond. It creates disquiet, discontent, resistance, and ill will. But this is precisely what makes even greater the demand for working together and sharing the responsibility." No, the balance of payments couldn't be a goal, but it was one index among many of our capability to practice a responsible and defensible overall economic policy.

I'd begun to argue that the Labor Party minority government should secure sufficient support in Parliament. It was the government's job to propose measures, but, I stressed, once that was done we could not change our opinion until those measures were implemented, even if it proved necessary to draw the support of the Conservatives!

This is something that crops up again and again in Norwegian political life. A minority government such as the Labor government, which had been losing its overall majority since 1961, could not behave as if it had a majority mandate. A policy that enjoys support, even shared support among rival parties, should not be deemed a political problem for the party of government. And yet time and time again, the fear in the Labor Party of being supported by the Conservatives has been detrimental. We would work extra hard, resorting to unnecessary compromises, to establish coalition support among the centrist parties, the Center Party and the Christian People's Party, and from the Socialist Left Party, which was left of Labor.

Disarmament and Dissent

So 1980 turned out to be another turbulent year, the year before the next election, and the newspapers returned over and over again to the theme of difficulties within the Labor Party. It was a year largely characterized by unrest surrounding important aspects of foreign policy and national security. The debate within the party generated widespread interest and involvement. The establishment of the committee on disarmament was in itself a symbol of this increased attention. It was a tool and a responsibility that had been handed to me.

At the meeting of the National Executive Board on December 1, the party's position on the question of stockpiling weapons for a U.S. Marine brigade was also discussed. After a very difficult time, coming on top of the problems we had faced with NATO's dual-track decision, we had finally arrived at a decision that most people felt they could live with. The sites proposed as a compromise location for the weapons were in central Norway, just north of Trondheim, not the location believed to be preferred by the military, which was in northern Norway, where the bulk of Norwegian forces were stationed.

The final form of the agreement reached with the Americans on the stockpiling of weapons had been discussed in the party's newly established disarmament committee, in our international committee, and numerous times in our Central Executive Board. We had been assured that our policy on bases and nuclear weapons was respected. Nevertheless, five of the nine members of the disarmament committee voted against the compromise, including Thorbjørn Jagland, leader of Young Labor.

The disarmament committee included some people who wanted to avoid any stockpiling of weapons, as they maintained that this could easily be seen as Cold War escalation. One of the most skeptical committee members later wrote, "The question was raised whether the stockpiled weapons were intended for the defense of Norway alone, or for the defense of the whole alliance [NATO]. In reply it was said that the weapons could not be used outside the country, and that the stockpile would at all times be under full Norwegian control and military command. In any hypothetical conflict that might arise, each individual country had the right to decide for itself the extent of its contribution to the defense effort."

Skeptics wondered whether Norway would find itself dragged into a nuclear war in the event of war in Europe, and the question was raised whether our area would indeed remain nuclear-free in the event of a war.

My Fortieth Birthday

Just a year earlier, in the spring of 1979, the climate of cooperation between the party and the government leadership had been progressing nicely. When I turned forty on April 20, we arranged a party including family, friends, and key political colleagues from both the party and the government.

There were several speakers that evening, among them the Minister of Justice. She referred to me as the natural next Prime Minister of Norway. I felt instantly uneasy. What if some in the room believed that the idea had been promoted by me? Nothing could have been further from the case. In the end I put it down to the enthusiasm born of a woman's desire for equality. There wasn't much that could be done about it. Fifty people were listening—and at least five must have been sitting there thinking: Not if I can help it.

Celebrated and Under Attack

First-Time Prime Minister

One evening in late autumn of 1980, I met a former
Member of Parliament and old friend of the family
wandering the corridors of the Parliament Building.
He said at once that he came with a message for me.
He implied it was from party headquarters and the
Trade Union Council. It was time for a change at the
top. He knew that many people felt that I should be
the next Prime Minister.

"But you have plenty of time, Gro," he told me. "It
would be better if it's your turn next time around. Let
me know whom you prefer, the Minister of Energy or
the Minister of the Environment?"

I didn't doubt that he was serious. I told him that I
thought this kind of backroom deal-making was
wrong. Shouldn't other party members have more of a
chance to influence events? I added that I did not
think the party members at large would consider either of his candidates a natural successor to Prime
Minister Odvar Nordli. I said I could not help him.
My responsibility as Deputy Leader was to do what I

thought was right for the party and to safeguard its right of choice.

"By God, you're tough, Gro," my friend said before he left, his mission unfulfilled. But the atmosphere was one of respect.

With hindsight I can now see that this encounter was part of a continuous process in certain party circles and in the trade unions, that had been ongoing since 1979. The struggle for the future leadership of government and the party was a preoccupation for many individuals in the TUC and in party headquarters. But I was not among them.

Nordli Resigns

On the afternoon of Thursday, January 29, 1981, a journalist called to ask if I had heard that the Prime Minister was ill, had taken sick leave, and was about to resign. At a meeting in the Labor House, I had heard Nordli say that he would be retiring for health reasons. Nordli was suffering from severe headaches and something was wrong with his eyes. He needed rest and treatment. He said that the Minister of the Environment, Rolf Hansen, was his choice of successor, and that he believed Hansen was agreeable. There were no objections raised, and it was agreed that the whole matter would be discussed in more detail at a later meeting.

Later that evening, a press release was issued saying that Odvar Nordli was going to resign on grounds of ill health. The newspapers responded with banner headlines and speculations that Rolf Hansen was the most likely new Prime Minister. Rolf and I talked. It became clear that Nordli had not asked him. He wondered if I had been contacted in person and whether my opinion had been solicited. My answer was no. He was clearly shaken by this and said that such behavior was both incomprehensible and unacceptable— I was, after all, the party's Deputy Leader!

That afternoon there was a meeting of the Central Executive Board. My diary entry for January 30 reads: "Production law. On the line at two o'clock: TUC/Party." For Sunday, February 1, it says: "seven o'clock. TUC/Party, Ullevaalsveien 58 [the home of Trygve Bratteli]."

Banner headlines once again in the papers on Saturday. In *VG*: "Rolf Hansen Now." But according to *Dagbladet*, it was going to be Gro.

A Conversation with Rolf Hansen

Throughout the weekend there was a stream of conflicting messages and rumors on both radio and television. At party conferences and branch meetings all over the country, people said what they thought. It was clear that I enjoyed the support of the party at large.

Personally I had great respect for Rolf Hansen and believed him capable of doing a good job. But he was a member of neither the Central Executive Board nor the National Executive Board, nor had he been for the last ten years.

As Deputy Leader it seemed to me the whole thing was being handled poorly, without even a single meeting of the party's elected leadership. Clearly, our Party Leader, Reiulf Steen, did not want any dialogue.

I made up my mind to accept whatever might come at Trygve Bratteli's on Sunday. This would be the first time that Rolf was present and able to give his own assessment of the situation. That afternoon, a few hours before the meeting, Rolf called me at home. He asked if the two of us could talk before the meeting. He was at his office close to the Akershus Castle, in Myntgata, where I had spent five years myself as Minister of the Environment.

Rolf said that several people had spoken to him about taking over after Nordli, but that he had not so far responded. His impression was that this had all been done behind my back, which he did not think was good for the party. He also expressed his great concern over the lack of leadership and the general conduct of the Party Leader. He felt that this was where the party's problem really lay. He thought it natural now that I should take over the responsibility, and he said that he was going to suggest this.

Rolf responded to a phone ringing in the reception room. He soon returned: "That was Reiulf. He wanted to know if I was prepared to take over as Prime Minister. I told him my views."

At Trygve Bratteli's House

Trygve Bratteli's wife, Randi, welcomed us with coffee and cake in their pleasant home. Earlier in the day Trygve had received a phone call from Gunnar Berge, who then was Deputy Leader of the Labor Party Parliamentary Group, telling him that there was widespread support for me as the new Prime Minister. Berge asked Bratteli to communicate this feeling to the meeting of the coordinating committee. The rest of us knew nothing about this, and Trygve did not mention it.

Odvar began. He soon suggested Rolf Hansen as his successor. Then Rolf spoke. He said that he had never expressed the wish to be Prime Minister, and that it seemed natural to him that the job go to the party's Deputy Leader. That was his suggestion.

There were at least three very surprised faces round the table: Odvar, TUC boss Tor Halvorsen, and Trygve Bratteli. For a brief moment there was complete silence.

Odvar Nordli then vocalized his astonishment at Rolf's answer. He had thought that everything was settled. Moreover, if Rolf was chosen, that would leave the party free to choose a new Leader at the Party Congress scheduled for May. Rolf repeated his answer, but added that this was the next question that would have to be discussed. Now was the time to sort out once and for all the problems surrounding the future leadership of the party.

Intuitively I felt that this was more than the meeting was equipped to deal with on the spot. I wanted to stress that party leadership was altogether a different matter, and that the next Party Congress must be able to independently choose, so I said that there was no reason why I could not continue as Deputy Leader even if I were to become Prime Minister. From now on things should be done by the rules. Party members and delegates to the Party Congress should be the ones to make this absolutely central choice.

Reiulf Steen concluded: "Gro will be our next Prime Minister." He was cornered. He had no other choice.

Certainly we made Norwegian political history that evening. I would be the first woman Prime Minister, and the youngest. I honestly felt that I was as capable as any of the men with whom I had been working in national politics. Olav remarked when I came home that I looked surprisingly composed.

Prime Minister in Fact

I came home a little late that Sunday evening, but Kaja, Ivar, and Jørgen had not yet gone to sleep. (Knut was away working on an oil rig.) The telephone had rung continuously since Saturday, after the newspapers had reported there would be a change of Prime Minister soon. Happy voices brought congratulations from all over the country. My children wanted to know what was going on. I had not told them anything about the possibility of being the next Prime Minister, only that I had been to a meeting at Trygve Bratteli's home. But now I could tell them.

Olav and I knew what we needed to do first of all. The burden of popular enthusiasm this weekend left us in no doubt. We would have to get an unlisted telephone number!

Both of us understood that life from now on would be different. For six years my family and I had been in the public spotlight. We realized that we would have even less calm and privacy now. I had already seen the first signs that the children were suffering from my being under public scrutiny. It wasn't just that I had less time for them. Photographers and journalists caused considerable strain during weekdays—also at home. They were frequently on the telephone or at the front door. They even showed up at our holiday home in Helleskilen during summer vacation.

The children did not complain. They were loyal. Kaja was the least enthusiastic about having a mother in the public eye, but she did not say much. Neither did Jørgen, who I felt experienced the pressure acutely. They both said more later, as grown-ups.

Today Kaja says that she was particularly happy that we usually managed to have a normal May 17 (the anniversary of the signing of the Norwegian constitution) at home. Neither the Prime Minister nor the cabinet ministers have any special functions on the national day; it belongs to the people, the King, and the elected representatives of Parliament. For our family, it was the children's day. We participated in the program at our local school in Bygdøy. The children were active in the brass band and in the Folklore Museum's dancing group.

The year 1975 was an exception for me. I had been invited to deliver a speech at Eidsvoll, located thirty miles north of Oslo, where the constitution had been signed on May 17, 1814. The children did not want to come along. They wanted to stay home with their friends. Olav agreed with my decision and had to be tough to enforce his will. Olav's father, who taught history and Norwegian language and who wanted very much to come along to this historic place, could not cope with the resistance of his grandchildren and went back home to Drammen. He and my mother-in-law were usually with us on May 17. That was one of our family's traditions.

During the Sunday night on which I was actually made Prime Minister, I wrote notes and made plans for the coming days. I needed concentration and a fresh spirit and went to bed relatively early. But I didn't sleep very well.

I received nice letters and declarations of support from many of my fellow citizens. People were enthusiastic about having the first female Prime Minister in the history of Norway. There had been very few female heads of government in the world at that time. Margaret Thatcher of Great Britain was a most recent appointment, although India, Israel, and Sri Lanka had all been headed by women. Word of my appointment spread around the globe, and everyone wanted to interview me. I felt that both my father, who had served ten years as cabinet minister, and my mother were very supportive. Whether they were proud, I can't say. We did not customarily show too much emotion in our family. We were more likely to be matter-of-fact in our attitudes. But I remember my father giving a long and very positive radio interview about me when I formally had taken over.

Four Women in the Cabinet

Prime Minister Nordli gave me a rundown of his cabinet. He told me who had been asked to change ministries or would be happy if allowed to step down. In a meeting with the party leadership I said that I thought it best not to have a major reshuffling. We'd had enough of uneasiness and infighting.

A female Prime Minister by definition strengthened the position of women. I nonetheless felt it important to go a bit further. Since 1979, when I had been forced to leave the cabinet, the rest of the party leadership had not given the gender issue much attention and only two women had become cabinet members. The boys had not thought it was particularly important, but I knew this could not be the model of the future. Under my leadership we added two women for a total of four in the cabinet of eighteen, one woman more than in the Bratteli cabinet and one more than Odvar Nordli had had at any time.

My Minister of Justice was the first without a formal legal professional background. I thought it was important to break the hegemony of lawyers in the ministry. I remembered Trygve Bratteli's advice against having a physician as Minister of Health and Social Affairs. Later in my administration, we did pick a Minister of Justice who was a lawyer and a Health Minister who was a medical doctor; after all, there was no reason to exercise an iron rule. I only wanted to establish that the positions should not be reserved for the people with the relevant formal education.

To the King

"His Majesty wishes Gro Harlem Brundtland to come for a conversation." The message came from the Royal Palace. Mamma, who served as my secretary, was calm when she gave me the message. She had worked for the Labor Party Parliamentary Group for decades and had advanced to become the secretary of the Parliamentary Leader. Our professional relationship worked very well. Some journalists dubbed her "Gro's secret weapon." Both she and I knew the importance of keeping the meeting with the King confidential until it had taken place. The press was on alert but did not know what time I would be going to the palace. In those days we did not inform the press about such things.

Some saw me leaving the Parliament building for the short ride up Karl Johan Street to the Royal Palace. I felt very alone on the way to the King, filled with the responsibility of and respect for the task. His Majesty plays an important role in our constitution and in particular when a change of government takes place.

A few spectators had assembled outside the Royal Palace, some mothers with children. They waved and I waved back, but I doubted that they could see me. You have to roll down the tinted window of the official car, but I hadn't figured that out yet.

A representative of the royal staff greeted me. I was shown up the stairs to the second floor. A broad corridor leads into what is called the Birds Chamber because it is lavishly decorated with wall paintings of birds. It is adjacent to the King's working chamber. The room also has doors with knobs of solid brass. I heard the clocks strike and the officer in service say: "Your Majesty, Member of Parliament Gro Harlem Brundtland is here."

The King gets up from his chair and comes around his desk to greet me. His smile and friendly face elicit trust. I'm glad I know him not only from cabinet meetings but also from less formal arrangements and social occasions. I remember a lecture I once gave with His Majesty present. A reception had followed. According to tradition no one leaves such a party before His Majesty, but he knew that I had a long trip to make the following day and told me to feel free to go while he stayed on.

"I will ask you to form a new cabinet," the King says now. He tells me that he had received this advice from Prime Minister Nordli, and says that he had not been surprised. Our conversation is short. There is not much to say but a lot to do. I take leave of the King and go back to put the new cabinet together. The formal change of cabinet will take place at the Royal Palace the next day.

A new cabinet is always met with curiosity and enthusiasm. This time, however, the reception was quite exceptional. Outside the

Royal Palace many hundreds had assembled, adults and children, young and old. Lots of flowers and happy faces. Lions Hill, which forms the entrance to Parliament, and carries its name due to the presence of two enormous stone lions, was also full of people, more women than men. Some of the children held Norwegian flags.

The spirits were high in the Labor Party Parliamentary Group, and the Prime Minister's office at the top of the government building was also filled with friendly faces. Journalists from across the world covered the event. There were flowers everywhere. Outgoing Prime Minister Odvar Nordli was smiling and joking. A big burden had been lifted from his shoulders.

When the keys were transferred and the celebration was over, I sat down on the sofa with Nordli. He wanted to tell me a few things confidentially. One was highly sensitive. The Surveillance Police were looking for an agent spying for the Soviet Union. Only the Prime Minister, the Foreign Minister, and the Minister of Justice had been informed. The person was thought to be highly placed in the civil service or somewhere in the political apparatus. The police were keeping their eyes on more than one person. What did the new government need to do, I asked. "Nothing for the moment," Nordli said. The police had been given the authority to search for the suspect. It would be better to refrain from speculation about names. It was important that nobody should notice anything out of the ordinary. Therefore I was not informed about the concrete suspicion which already at that time was focused on Arne Treholt, who had been State Secretary for the Minister of the Law of the Sea. Treholt was arrested for espionage in 1984, and later convicted and sentenced to many years in prison.

"This will all be fun, Martin"

My State Secretary for public relations, Wiktor Martinsen, "Martin" among friends, describes the afternoon of February 5, 1981: "Gro was something completely new at the Prime Minister's office. It was not only that she is a woman. She was glowing with a fighting spirit and willingness to work. It seemed that there could be no task so difficult that it would scare her away from taking it on right away with the conviction that she would find a solution.

"The new style at the Prime Minister's office was evident from the first moment. Right after having received the keys and sitting down in her new chair, Gro called in her coworkers. I entered a bright, well-ordered office. The sun came in through the large windows to lavishly light the ocean of flowers that spread a carpet of color all over the room.

"The heavy atmosphere had been lifted. Behind the desk sat Gro, smiling with her whole body. She put out her arms and exclaimed: 'This will all be fun, Martin.' "

Yes, I was full of energy and conviction. Together we could do a good job. And I knew it was important to create an atmosphere of optimism and fighting spirit, particularly in the cabinet itself. We could do a much better job if team spirit and togetherness became the order of the day, and if the belief that we could make a difference became second nature to us all.

In the cabinet meeting room I experienced an atmosphere of welcome. I went in with a spirit of openness, looking for a common analysis of difficult problems and a team that could stand together. Lack of clarity and double messages will always backfire sooner or later. Attempting to be everybody's friend by not being clear about where you stand on an issue is a short-lived strategy.

From the very beginning I worked very hard. It was necessary in order to get a grip on the many issues over which there was discord. The unnecessary lack of clarity in the party, cabinet, and parliamentary group had to be dispelled. It wasn't easy to find calm time for systematic work at the office. The media continued to ask for interviews. And from all over the world came a stream of requests for interviews, visits, and more information about the new Prime Minister.

Wiktor Martinsen notes: "We knew little what the day would bring before we could turn off the lights and call it a day. And as a rule, Gro still sat working in her office. She must have worked from fourteen to sixteen hours a day. She did not demand the same long hours from her coworkers, but she demanded the same concentration during regular office hours."

What I have to call my "social-democratic soul" dominated my attitudes about what was right to ask from other people, especially my coworkers. I could not demand that they put in twelve hours a day. During my second period as Prime Minister, from 1986 to 1989, we accepted that one person alone with the responsibility for my anteroom could not match my working hours, so we hired an "afternoon watch." The staff would not accept my proposition that I could be left without an assistant at four o'clock.

An episode from the Ministry of the Environment came to my attention. One of the bright young lawyers working there had the courage to admit that he had to leave the Ministry at four to pick up his children from nursery school. Good. Of course, people need to be able to pick up their children from school. But I felt a little ashamed that he had been in a situation in which he felt the need to speak out. I should have known myself and should have remembered that some of my colleagues had such obligations.

Fortunately, Wiktor Martinsen was exaggerating about the length of my normal working day. But my workload did demand more time in the late 1980s when international duties and the work of the World Commission on Environment and Development took more time, concentration, and dedication. Then I had to maintain an exceptional pace, which I believe I would not have been able to keep up throughout my whole political life.

"She will call the boys to order"

What did our political opponents say?

The leader of the Conservative Party characterized Nordli's stepping down as an expression of a dangerous discord within our party. Labor might give the appearance of unity and vigor in the months subsequent to the change of leadership, but this would not be enough, he said. But he added that the inner problems of the Labor Party were greater than those within the parties to the right of

Labor, which, incidentally, hoped to form a non-socialist government after the September 1981 election.

One of the more curious comments came from my son Knut.
Asked by the press to characterize his mother, he replies that I am
strict but fair. And as a politician? "Well, I do not trust her any more
than I trust the others. They all promise a lot, but do not necessarily deliver." Who needs enemies when you have such friends! Knut
lacks nothing in outspokenness and independence. He added
somewhere else: "She will call the boys to order!"

The *International Herald Tribune* carried this headline: "Brundtland, Strong NATO Supporter, Named Norway's First Woman
Premier."

The American press had picked up the news during the night between Sunday and Monday. Olav had shocked the reporter from
The Washington Post who called for an interview at four o'clock in
the morning, by turning the interview down right away. "She is
sleeping," he said.

"But this is *The Washington Post*," the reporter said.

Olav replied, "Does not matter, she is still sleeping." I am happy
to have a husband who can draw a line!

Apart from the Bravo blowout in the North Sea, Norway had not
seen so much international coverage since the Nazi invasion on
April 9, 1940.

The Trade Unions

The trade unions are important in the Norwegian political system,
and in particular for the Labor Party. Through their membership in
the Trade Union Council, the unions have a special relationship to
our party. As I have mentioned in previous chapters, every Monday,
union and party leaders meet in the so-called Committee of Coordination.

The deputy chairman of the Union of Iron and Metal Workers

was reported to have said that his union supported me wholeheart-edly. "But has she demonstrated sufficient will to listen?" the media asked him.

"It is the future that matters," he answered. "It is obvious that the Minister of the Environment has had to play a special role, leading her to step on some of the interests of the industrial trade unions. But one cannot point at any general lack of willingness to listen," he added.

Point well taken. As Deputy Leader I cared very much for party–trade union cooperation. But sometimes one has to make a choice. To both protect and develop the same river does not work. *VG* wrote: "It might be pleasant enough to be lifted up to the fifteenth floor of the government building to the Prime Minister's office on a wave of popular support, but it might be a heavy burden to operate in an environment where there is fear she will attain too much power." I must say I was suspicious of this sort of reportage.

Dagbladet, however, offered a more analytical outlook: "What does she symbolize? She has turned the environment into a political reality and become the symbol for the soft sides of politics in a so-ciety dedicated to economic growth. She might attract new voters, and Labor needs them dearly."

The press did not need to worry; I certainly knew how important it was to take care of the traditional close relations between the La-bor Party and the trade union movement. But I wanted more women and young voters to feel at home in the party—and in the unions. Both institutions were still male bastions.

Labor vs. Conservative—Round One

Our most important competitor for political power was the Conser-vative Party. It wanted to form a non-socialist government with the support of the Center Party and the Christian People's Party, which we often referred to as the "parties of the Middle," which occasion-ally also included the minuscule Liberal Party. The economy and national security were the most controversial issues.

Soon I had to debate the Conservative Leader, Kåre Willoch. Our first radio encounter would not be the last. I had experienced Willoch as sharp, ironic, icy, and self-confident. He could be condescending, like a schoolmaster teaching a schoolgirl. My tactic: Pretend to ignore it. This was not easy. I learned only later to more fully control my temper, body language, and facial expressions.

Willoch attacks. He says Labor has no policy for taming our current bout of inflation and points at the idea of a fifth week of vacation, which is being supported by Labor. "We cannot afford it," he says.

I answer his claim and press forward. "Let us take a look at whether Mr. Willoch really thinks that the three non-socialist parties have a common, clear, and distinct position on income policy and collective bargaining. The Conservative Party seems to me much more reluctant than the two other parties, the Christians and the Center, with regard to coordinated bargaining in which the government also has a role."

We were now discussing a central area of conflict between the Conservatives and Labor: the idea of a tripartite cooperation between employers, employees, and the government regarding the national economy and possible reforms. My line on such a cooperation was a concept we called the "solidarity alternative." That policy had produced good results for Norway. But Labor could not have sustained it alone. We needed the support of one or both of the political parties of the Middle to carry the majority in Parliament.

Willoch asked, "Will the Prime Minister accept a Nordic nuclear-free zone that does not include parts of the Soviet Union?"

My answer was clear if somewhat complicated: "No, not if by the word 'include' you mean that the rules regulating nuclear weapons would not be applicable for the Warsaw Pact countries and the Soviet Union. It is fully clear that any unilateral declaration of the Nordic countries—Iceland, Denmark, Norway, Sweden, and Finland—as a nuclear-free zone will not be my policy." In spite of this no, which I thought would satisfy him, he never stopped harping on this very complicated question.

Some thought that confronting such sharp attacks could help the Labor leadership to distinguish itself from the Socialist Left Party and other parties on the Left. But others were at least as occupied with keeping the insecurity and doubt on the agenda in order to weaken the Labor Party. Willoch belonged to this latter category.

The River Alta and the Same People

The fact that I had previously been Minister of the Environment emboldened protesters against hydroelectric development to pursue their cause. The most controversial project was the hydroelectric power station on the River Alta in the northernmost county of Finnmark. Central to the protest was the argument that living conditions for the Same (pronounced SAH-mee) would be destroyed. The Same were an indigenous northern minority population traditionally living from reindeer herding. So when the new cabinet left the Royal Palace for the first time on February 5, with the TV cameras capturing everything, we had demonstrations.

Some women in traditional colorful Same dresses asked to be received to argue their case. I invited them to come to my office the next Friday morning. They came in numbers far exceeding what we had expected. The atmosphere was friendly and open. The conference room just across the corridor from my office filled with Same women of all ages, along with some children. They did not say much, but one of them spoke about her concerns regarding reindeer herding and nature.

I gave them the background for the Parliament's decision. I looked into stern faces. They were not convinced.

It was close to eleven. I had to leave for the royal cabinet meeting with His Majesty. Nobody arrives late. Leaving the Royal Palace, I was informed that the women had refused to leave the meeting room. My staff thought we could give them some time and take it easy. The press seemed to have been informed ahead of time. The visitors had from the outset wanted to "occupy" the Prime Minister's office.

We did not want confrontation. I asked about the children. They must have felt claustrophobic in the small meeting room. Food and drinks were brought to the occupiers. They were not willing to leave until the next morning. We did not wish to use any force. From the outside it was made to look dramatic. Radio and TV followed the incident very attentively. Some start for my premiership!

Alta was the most demanding of problems. People were deeply entrenched in their attitudes. People's action committees were established against Alta construction and for protection of waterfalls and the Same population. "Let the river live" was one of the slogans.

With my background in the Ministry of the Environment I could not disregard the possibility that new information might shed new light on this problem. Some of the arguments from the minority were important and relevant. There were differences of opinion within Labor as well. A clear majority, however, was in support of moderate development.

We had to take this issue seriously. The Environment Minister discovered that both the Norwegian Water and Electricity Authority (NVE), and the Tromsø Museum were to blame for incomplete and superficial handling of the case. The cabinet concluded that an investigation had to be conducted according to the 1978 law on the protection of cultural heritage.

Alta was special, but not so special that the law should not be applied. From my fight over acid rain and the Bravo blowout I had learned to take the longer perspective. It does not pay to cut corners. You have to be conscientious in applying laws and regulations when you are representing public authorities. The minority has rights.

A culture and tradition in which such thoughts were disregarded had for too long dominated decision-making agencies such as NVE. It had become necessary to take the so-called "soft values" more seriously. We also had to be sure that local authorities were heard, so we could avoid new conflicts. We postponed the project to give us time to handle the situation properly, but the construction that Parliament had supported was ultimately completed in the following years. The disagreement on whether it was the right thing to do, however, will not stop.

Gender Quotas

The atmosphere was one of radical change. We soon agreed that the principle of gender quotas should be applicable for the individual branches in the administration and not only as an overall principle. Otherwise, there would simply be many women in the lower echelons. For junior positions we decided to apply radical gender quotas. Women should be selected if they were qualified. For top positions, however, we decided to be a little more careful. Women should be selected only if they were as equally qualified as the male applicants.

Later we examined how to change the whole law to further strengthen the position of women, so that women would be represented on all committees, boards, and councils. The new law said that there must be equal participation of women and men, and that there should be at least two members of each sex in every entity.

Gro-Fever and Gro-Day

In the spring I visited the politically radical Telemark County in the south. Its radicalism stems from traditions of sharp confrontations in the many heavy industries in the area. I spoke to packed houses. Lecture halls in retirement homes were filled to such an extent that on one occasion a man fainted and fell to the floor. VG dramatized the event, reporting that Dr. Gro immediately rushed to the patient, took his pulse, and pronounced him out of immediate danger.

When an old gentleman asked for a hug, I ended up on his lap, and the picture made the papers all over the country!

Some days later Olav gave a foreign policy lecture to a meeting of the local Conservative Party. The chairman of the branch was very happy indeed. Never before had so many people turned out to one of his meetings. When he told one of his colleagues, a seasoned journalist and onetime MP for the New Liberal Party, about the high turnout, the response was: "They must have come only in order to meet Gro's husband!" When Henry Kissinger visited Oslo in 1981,

Olav participated as an expert for Willoch. A much surprised
Kissinger said about this strange relationship between husband and
wife in two different political parties: "This would not work in the
United States. The press would tear it apart."

The demand for a fifth week of paid vacation continued. But the
economy was in bad shape. I talked it over with the TUC boss, who
was inclined to pursue the matter on principle. What about a gradual introduction? He pressed for two days, while I felt that our
economy could support only one extra day. One day it was. Many
were surprised—some happy, some disappointed. But most important, "Gro-day" demonstrated that the party and TUC had regained
the ability to govern in tandem. "Gro-day" became a symbol of our
success.

To Lead Labor

Two months after I took over as Prime Minister, the National Congress of the Labor Party began. I had recently said to the media that
I felt we should have a unified leadership of government and party.
The same person should be Party Leader and Prime Minister. Even
though I felt sure that I had a big majority of the party supporting
me, I traveled to the session with premonitions of conflict. I was
convinced that the incumbent Party Leader, Reiulf Steen, would do
whatever he could to make difficulties for me.

Reiulf, in turn, charged that the Labor Party was becoming a corporation, a big, anonymous business concern. Yet I had all along
called for openness in the organization, emphasized participation in
the branches and at the county level, and insisted that the party's
operation amount to more than declarations issued from the rostrum.

On a sheet of paper I jotted down some of my pre-congress
thoughts about what it was that Steen and his cronies wanted to
convey but dared not say openly:

- She is not genuine Labor.
- She is a pragmatist, not a visionary.
- She is moderate—with right-wing leanings.
- She is pro-NATO.

But I could not react to veiled attacks. I would have to speak about ideas and about our policies.

Reiulf's opening statement sounded much like the one he had delivered at Young Labor a few days before. I did not recognize myself in his veiled characterizations of me. His words conveyed bitterness. The speech did not establish a constructive atmosphere among the delegates to the congress. And he declared in conclusion that for the sake of the party, he would refrain from being a candidate for reelection. It was a betrayal of me and the party to play on personal pity, and it reduced the possibility of a straight and open fight based on political attitudes and principles.

In 1975, leadership problems had led to Steen being chosen as Party Leader and Nordli as our next Prime Minister candidate. Based on that experience, I now thought it would be better and more democratic if the National Congress were given an opportunity to make a real choice. It would have enhanced my confidence and strength as Party Leader if my appointment had survived a vote. I was fully prepared to stand for an open election, even if the nominating committee brought a split recommendation, some supporting Steen, others me.

The Interview That Was Not Printed

Einar Gerhardsen, Leader of the Labor Party from 1945 to 1965 and the longest-serving Prime Minister in democratic Norway, had been to every Party Congress since 1918. Now he was sick in bed at the National Hospital. But he remained a keen observer. From his sickbed he told the editor-in-chief of *Arbeiderbladet* that it was natural to elect Gro the Leader.

Gerhardsen argued that Reiulf Steen should step down. He felt that during Steen's tenure, cooperation within the leadership of the labor movement had not been satisfactory. The Party Leader had to take responsibility for this, even if he alone was not to blame.

Gerhardsen concluded that there was no natural solution other than to make Brundtland both Prime Minister and Party Leader. "During the short time of her premiership she has demonstrated the strength and ability to lead and to make use of her coworkers. It suffices to mention her handling of the protests against the power dam at Alta, her management of the capsized offshore platform, *Alexander Kielland,* and the solution she found concerning the fifth week of vacation."

The interview was never printed. It later became apparent that Reiulf Steen had forced the editor of *Arbeiderbladet* not to print the interview with Gerhardsen. The editor had wanted to show consideration for Reiulf and informed him of the interview; then he had refrained from printing it when Reiulf stated to him that he would step down.

I knew nothing about the drama behind the suppression of this historic interview, which would have made a lot of difference to me as a new Party Leader. I did not even know that the interview existed.

After Steen's opening speech I had to keep up appearances as best as I could. Smile courageously, Gro!

In an interview given while the congress was taking place, Steen said, "I don't see why my decision not to seek reelection has been construed as an attack on Gro Harlem Brundtland." The atmosphere was very negative. It wasn't easy, but I forced myself to appear unfazed. I did not want my personal feelings to get in the way of a political debate. To conclude the congress, I spoke as the newly elected leader, making it a point to thank Reiulf Steen in all sincerity for his services to the party.

In his 1988 memoir, *Deadline,* the editor of *Arbeiderbladet* writes of influences that sought to discredit him and spin the whole story of that congress. Normal reputable sources had deliberately sought to plant in competing newspapers stories contrary to the correct one. *VG*, for instance, had deliberately been misinformed.

The editor also writes that it was his distinct impression that Gerhardsen would have preferred to have his interview printed without its having been shown to Steen, and that both the TUC boss and a coeditor had thought that the paper could not refrain from publishing such an interview.

When I read *Deadline*, I realized that the evil day we had lived through could have been avoided if only Gerhardsen had been allowed to make his views known.

Could Women Show Their Toughness?

Unfortunately, certain stereotypes about women in politics seem hard to avoid. The prominent Danish social-democratic politician Ritt Bjerregaard visited Oslo, and a male reporter asked the two of us, "Is it only men who describe you as rock-hard, strong-willed, and obstinate?"

"I seldom see 'rock-hard' used to describe male politicians," I responded. "You cannot be active in political work if you have no will. You used another ugly word: 'obstinate.' A Swedish newspaper once wrote that, as Minister of the Environment, I had lost all my battles. Fortunately this was not true. But I wouldn't have won any if I had not been what you call obstinate. I would prefer 'dedicated to producing results.' You cannot lead a full bureaucracy into action if you are obstinate. This holds for both Ritt and myself."

Occasionally it felt good to speak out against myths and slander and outright discrimination in the male-dominated press. The double interview with Ritt provided an opportunity to give readers a different perspective. It's the only way to fight myths.

The Loneliness of Leadership

It is difficult to describe your own style of leadership, so let me refer to Wiktor Martinsen, my State Secretary for public relations, who wrote about his initial impressions of my administration. He wrote about my will to go deep and never give up before all aspects of complex and controversial problems were examined, and about my commitment to sitting down with the relevant ministers right away to work toward a solution. My first advice from Pappa was to remember that when a problem lay on my table, others would be waiting. Tempo is important in politics. But it must be linked with respect for facts and quality. Otherwise society loses time and strength, and resources are wasted.

Wiktor describes the way I sat down at the age of forty with leaders from the ministries and politics, with people who were used to getting their way after long service. "Already during my first appointment under Gro, as secretary for the party's ad hoc committee on energy, she impressed them with her straight talk and complete lack of veneration for 'the older wise gentlemen.' It was true that I had learned the central importance of clear and unambiguous communication. She managed to inspire her coworkers to give their best. Some of us, to our own surprise, were able to excel more than we thought possible."

When you become a leader, you have to reach out. You must listen to all aspects of a problem and try to comprehend as well as any of the experts the totality of the case. That is the role of the leader. There's no point in being scared. You must put the experts to work for you, respect their expertise, but never forget that any problem worthy of your time is neither simple nor unequivocal. You must ask the critical questions. Nobody else takes that role if you as a leader do not.

In politics this is bound to create conflicts. Not everybody likes to be questioned. And of course, as a politician you also use feeling and intuition. But if that is all you rely on, you will frequently go astray. The law often gives room for maneuvering and political considerations, and in many cases it is legitimate to show creativity— but never to go outside of the limits of the law. If the law stops you, it is advisable to ask whether the law should be changed and if so to take the initiative to make that happen.

Decisions based on momentary intuition can lead to poor long-term policy. What will be the result of your decisions a year from now? In two or three years? Will you cause new problems you might be overlooking at the moment?

Gunnar Berge, who became my Minister of Finance in 1986, often said that many are surprised to realize that I show the patience of an angel. He is partly right. I have patience when it serves the solution of the problem. But I am no angel!

Grandma Stays the Course

In 1981 Mamma's mother, my Swedish grandmother, turned eighty-four; her partner was ninety. She had fallen ill in the midst of her intense work on a doctoral dissertation in economics and was now in a rest home. It was time to go and see her, over in Sweden. *Dagbladet* came along as an interested observer.

Grandma had a sharp tongue. She spoke very freely. The journalist reported that it was the first time he had observed Gro Harlem Brundtland sitting speechless for long periods of time. A relative was required to keep her silent, the reporter wrote. Perhaps. With your grandmother you continue to be the little girl you once were. Besides, what would the journalist have written if I had argued with my forthright grandmother?

Vulnerable and Invulnerable

At the end of May 1981, I paid my first official visit to President Mauno Koivisto of Finland. The Ministry of Foreign Affairs and the office of the Prime Minister took care of the practical arrangements. I concentrated on the political preparations. No one asked me if, when, and how we should fly.

However, there were a number of problems that I needed to discuss with the State Secretary in the Ministry of Foreign Affairs, who was working on propositions for a Nordic nuclear-free zone and on some NATO questions. These problems were not appropriate for discussion on a commercial flight. Instead we had our meeting on the way to Finland in a small Falcon Jet operated by the Royal Norwegian Air Force. This was not an unusual or particularly expensive mode of transportation, and it was nothing new. It had been used between forty and fifty times by Prime Ministers, Foreign Ministers, and Ministers of Defense, as well as by top-ranking military officers. But critics pointed out that the trip would have taken no longer on a commercial flight. I later learned that someone in the Ministry had phoned the media and given a twisted version of events. There was an election coming up.

The episode became the starting point for a year-long discussion about politicians' travel expenses. I felt exposed and helpless.

Wiktor Martinsen advised me to remain silent in order not to prolong the discussion. But I think I would have been better off politically if I had spoken up. I believe I could have prevented some of the ridiculous falsehoods that dominated the atmosphere that summer and fall as elections were approaching.

Conservative forces made a bumper sticker: "Get rid of her!"

The media attack contributed in no small measure to this seeming like a reasonable demand. But both in form and in content this was really discrimination against a female politician.

Of course I was vulnerable. A young woman in leadership was something new in politics. And such a novelty had its price. Intuitively I felt that it was important to be strong and to show it. Not to be blinded by praise and expectations. Not to be paralyzed by criticism and unjustified attacks. That would be a way to break a woman.

The attacks came on many fronts: clothing, hairstyle, speech, gait, manner of leadership. Everything about me was examined, mostly without particular substantiation and often in an indirect way, in critical articles, headlines, and ways of presenting photographs. Women leaders are criticized more, and differently, than their male counterparts. You cannot defend yourself against such tactics. Your only option is to try to look past them.

But there is reason for real concern. Media attacks legitimate further attacks. It is dangerous. Politicians nowadays are attacked in a way that represents a threat to the functions of democracy. It also becomes difficult for a leader's spouse and children.

In 1981 I did not understand that it was not enough only to maintain a stiff upper lip even if I felt deeply offended. I could pull myself together and fight for what I believed in, for the party, for democracy, for women to be treated as men's equals. But I did not realize how painful these attacks were for my children. Children become associated with the public image of their parents, which means it is a great burden being the child of a top politician. My children imitated my own behavior and tried to protect me by not telling me how they felt. They refrained from sharing their experiences and the cruel kinds of casual remarks they had to abide. In the end, my strategy of forced invulnerability helped me more than it helped my children.

Fresh or Processed Debate

Sometimes being a politician is very satisfying. I attended the 1981 Congress of the Norwegian Union of Food-Processing Workers. The final summing-up is always fun on such occasions. You can respond, react, and reflect upon the input that dominated the debate, observing the parallels among a number of the different speakers. You can give concrete answers to questions, bringing forward your own view and the attitude of the party or the cabinet if it differs from what has been said from the rostrum. And you can explain your vision.

More than one speaker had discussed a demand from Labor's women's organization for a six-hour workday. Some were enthusiastic; others were deeply skeptical and suggested lowering the retirement age or lengthening yearly vacations as better alternatives.

I said that more effectively combining work, family, and child-care was a priority, but that we were not in a position to put through such a great reform in short order. I pointed to our recent negotiations for "Gro-day," an achievement joined by other important initiatives in Norwegian politics.

Fortunately, some of the participants had also expressed concern about the high increase in prices, and I could point out that we would not be able to bring prices down without a long-term, sober, and responsible attitude. It is self-evident that to simultaneously establish a step-by-step lowering of retirement age, introduce a fifth week of vacation, and initiate the six-hour day was impossible. But all the aims were important in the long term, I said.

"It does not make sense to begin with the illusion that the state could simply distribute money to schools, day care, the health sector, private consumption, and all other things on everyone's list of good wishes," I said. "It's easy to write such lists. It is dismaying how many of them we have at any given time in Government House."

This drew spontaneous applause. Sometimes it's rewarding to speak out. With a twinkle in your eyes you can hit back.

We would go on to prepare a reform for a more flexible combination of welfare payment and actual wages while acknowledging the right to a shorter work week for those who could document special needs. Gradually we would enter into more flexible working arrangements, so that families and others with temporary difficulty managing a normal workday could better adapt their jobs to the other phases of life.

These ideas have required quite some time to anchor, and it's a pleasure to observe that the trade unions continued to argue for them even after I left office. They now promote a flexible work hours system, a program already built into the rules for flexible parental leave.

The Right-Wing Wave

The change of Prime Minister infused new optimism in the rank and file. Nevertheless, we could not stop the conservative wave that summer and early fall. We experienced inflation and stifled economic growth. Labor had been in government for eight years, the last three of which were characterized by politically demanding cuts in public expenditures. We faced an international right-wing movement. No easy test.

The cabinet had introduced a price freeze in order to remove the threat of an extra round of collective bargaining in the fall. For the first time since the Second World War, employees in average income brackets accepted a small reduction in wages. Our income policy worked. The government helped by means of an economic package including tax reductions, which had come out of our discussions with the TUC.

Given the price freeze, the media asked me about the future of collective bargaining. I replied, "We are in an economic and political situation in which cooperation between the state, labor, and industry is a necessity. We have to think anew to sort out a future platform with less confrontation in the labor market." This model of cooperation helped to strengthen the national economy in the years from 1986 to 1996. The unions retained their independence and their full right to bargain with employers, who likewise guarded their independence. The state, however, played an important role as a third party.

One day in August 1981 I speak in the Student Park in Central Oslo during our campaign. Like all the other parties Labor has an election kiosk there. I have a microphone and walk around without a script. A young woman is sitting against one of the large trees. She is listening intently but does not ask any questions. As I finish, she comes cautiously forward to greet me. She wanted to see me in action because she felt she knew me, she says. She is one of my father's graduate students. He was newly appointed professor of "workplace conditions" at the Norwegian Institute of Technology in Trondheim. Only seldom did I get any direct impression of his work up there. On weekends, he comes home. We see each other at holidays, but we are all so preoccupied with the political situation that we rarely take time to discuss his new job.

The young woman is enthusiastic about her professor, her field of study, and me. She has joined one of the branches of the Labor

Party in Trondheim and has participated locally in the campaign. Now she wanted to see me in person, because my father and I have made her want to join the party.

Small encounters could sometimes give me the biggest pleasures!

Gro-Kåre: New Rounds

The 1981 campaign was dominated by the Labor-Conservative debate. The Conservatives had obtained a stronger position on the non-socialist side since the last municipal elections. Kåre Willoch was the unchallenged leader of the Conservatives, and he was also treated as a natural candidate for Prime Minister if Labor lost. The Conservatives, Christians, and members of the Center Party each had different programs, but in order to gain credibility among voters as an alternative to Labor, they did what they could to iron out their disagreements.

The Labor platform stressed achieving full employment, securing the welfare state, and developing an oil policy with a strong role for the state. We warned that Conservative policies amounted to promises of tax cuts and a weakening of the welfare state. We held up Reagan and Thatcher as examples of the adverse effects of the conservative wave.

TV appearances were so significant. I had long ago learned that I, more than most, had to come across as calm and relaxed and to conceal my true reactions to whatever I found unreasonable or provocative.

A *Dagbladet* reporter pointed to the popular change of heart after one of my latest TV encounters with Kåre Willoch. Polls showed that Labor would receive 37 percent of the vote were the election held now. Less than we had hoped for, but more than we had feared. The reporter wrote, "Even if Gro managed to increase the support from its bottomed-out level before she took over, it is now clear that the change of Prime Minister in itself was not enough.

The party had for a long time been dallying in the political land-scape. And when TUC showed little loyalty during the campaign, the battle was lost."

Yes, some in the trade unions protested the price freeze and the tax package. Little was heard about active TUC support for solutions to the problems. It is only when you stand for something and fight for something that you succeed. The party and the government could have used more support.

The outcome of the election was clear. The Conservatives had increased their support substantially. Together with the Christians and the Center Party, they made up a majority in Parliament. When the newly elected Parliament assembled in October, the leader of the biggest non-socialist party, the Conservatives, would be the next Prime Minister. This was a triumph for the Conservaties. With the exception of three weeks in the 1960s, that party had had no Prime Minister since the 1920s.

For Labor it was time to pick up the pieces and work together. This I felt very strongly. Kåre Willoch left the TV studio on election night in 1981 with his arms filled with flowers. I walked behind him and knew that the political battle would go on. We would have to make a social-democratic impact from another position, namely from the benches of the opposition.

Playing the Chair Game

The change of government is a solemn and a touching act. I expressed my thanks to all for excellent cooperation and explained to my successor, Kåre Willoch, how superb the permanent staff at the Prime Minister's office is. I wished him good luck and gave him the key to his office.

The press asks for the traditional picture. The incoming Prime Minister sits, the outgoing stands by. But Willoch refused outright. He wants me to sit. It becomes embarrassing. He points to the fact that this is the first time a female Prime Minister leaves and says, "I cannot sit while she stands." I am younger; I feel this as a sign of lack of acknowledgment of equality between man and woman. When we had to change again, four and a half years later, I chose to use his principle. I did not sit down. If that's the way it is, that's the way it is. Equal.

To *Arbeiderbladet* I say after having been again elected a parliamentary leader, "We look forward to the job." I felt that I had done my best during the few months since I was appointed Prime Minister and elected Party Leader. We had progressed, but not sufficiently to keep our position as the party of government.

There is one point of light. For eight years the Conservatives had criticized us. They had built up enormous expectations. We would soon see how well they could fulfill them.

Nuclear Arms and 8
Security—The Big Test

On a fine summer weekend in 1980 the telephone rang at home. I was still serving as a Member of Parliament before my short first stint as Prime Minister. Prime Minister Odvar Nordli told me that the Prime Minister of Sweden, Olof Palme, wanted a Norwegian member for his commission, an independent commission with members from all over the world, East and West, working together to analyze security and disarmament.

Former U.S. Secretary of State Cyrus Vance was a participant and so was former British Foreign Minister David Owen. The West German politician and former Party Secretary Egon Bahr, and the director of the Soviet "America Institute" Georgi Arbatov, who would become a close counselor to Gorbachev, were invited as well.

Serving on this commission was one of the most important assignments in my political career. I made new acquaintances and gained insight into a central field of world affairs. I learned about the tug-of-war between strong-willed personalities. I saw both the genuine and the pro forma fury of the Soviet side. I saw from the inside how images of an "enemy" are made but also how patience and attention to facts can produce deeper insights.

It was a fascinating process. We met days, and often nights as well. I observed in Olof Palme a true leader; he created friendship and trust among us. He took his time and contributed to the atmosphere that made it possible to reach peaceful conclusions.

I walked on two legs, one Nordic and one NATO. Together with Olof Palme and others, I searched for a way to build a bridge between the United States and Great Britain, the leading members of NATO, and the representatives of the Soviet Union. It was a daunting task that often looked impossible. But Palme never gave up. He often worked into the small hours of the night. Personal bonds and comradeship developed. We wanted to understand each other. Facts and common insights brought us gradually closer. A common platform of facts is decisive. It reduces the room for tactical maneuvers.

For some time it looked as if Arbatov was unwilling to accept that there existed a rough balance between the arsenals of East and West. He insisted that the Americans always had been in the lead and that the Soviets had had to follow and keep pace in self-defense. The rest of us understood that Arbatov always had centrally placed people in Moscow following him carefully and preventing him from going too far.

He had brought along, as his number two, General Mikhail Milstein. They were both very charming. But we were in no doubt: They were assigned to check one another. We could rarely talk to one of them alone even in social settings. These were the years of Brezhnev and Andropov. The KGB was active. It came as a great surprise that we managed—although not before the very last meeting—to eliminate a number of important Soviet statements of reservation.

In the end we enjoyed a broad agreement. The arsenals were much the same in East and West. This was very different from what the Soviet Union, the Reagan administration, and the NATO governments had been saying about the situation. The analytic report of the Palme Commission, *Common Security,* met with much skepticism from the right wing in numerous countries, not least Reagan's United States. But Cyrus Vance persisted. He knew the facts and he had guts.

The struggle over NATO's "dual-track decision" had continued since December 1979. NATO had agreed to deploy more than five hundred new medium-range missiles on the soil of Western European members and at the same time invited the Soviet Union to negotiate over reducing the numbers of such weapons on both sides of the Iron Curtain. The background for the decision was the deployment of the Soviet SS-20 missiles that could reach targets in Western Europe. Today these weapons have been removed.

I had brought along Johan Jørgen Holst into the secretariat of the Palme Commission. He was a participant and observer during my absence while I was Prime Minister in 1981. He possessed a solid background in arms control and had much expertise to lend. I think he also learned a lot. He drew on this experience when, as Foreign Minister ten years later, he took part in the negotiations between the Israelis and the Palestinians in Oslo.

Sharp Divisions

The arms race could not be allowed to continue. In the nuclear age no one can obtain security at the expense of another. It took years before Reagan and Gorbachev came to the same conclusion: A nuclear war cannot be won and must never be fought. But it was far from easy to make a breakthrough for these new ideas. The Cold War was on. Two years previously the Soviet Army had invaded Afghanistan.

At home a great struggle was breaking out between left and right. The Conservatives were concerned that new thinking on nuclear weapons could undermine NATO cohesion. Prime Minister Willoch was the main combatant. But not everybody in the political spectrum to the right of Labor agreed with him. Many young Conservatives were confidently engaged in the struggle against nuclear weapons. At the same time, our own party was divided, some taking more radical stances on nuclear disarmament than others.

After the general election of 1981, when I stepped down from the premiership to become the Parliamentary Leader of my party, I had to take leadership on the nuclear arms question. My experience on the Palme Commission gave me a good background. And so did my experiences with international cooperation among labor parties of the so-called Scandilux group, including Egon Bahr, whom I knew from the Palme Commission and party friends from the Nordic countries, Benelux, Switzerland, the United Kingdom, and Germany. Our development of common principles and guidelines for policy lent support and inspiration to my work on the domestic political scene.

In 1983 I was elected rapporteur for the Parliamentary Standing Committee on Foreign Relations on a very important security matter. The government had presented a controversial white paper on nuclear strategy and arms control. My ambition was to create a report to Parliament that could reestablish the broad parliamentary consensus on security policy, which had been the trademark of Norway since our entry into NATO in 1949.

The Labor Party was already fully engaged with the issue; we stood clearly in defense of our NATO membership. But our ideas about arms control differed from what the Conservatives thought both in Norway and in other NATO-member states. We believed strongly in the path of dialogue and balanced arms reductions.

Visits with Helmut Schmidt

In the spring of 1981 West German Police came to our summer holiday home at Helleskilen. The upcoming visit by West German Chancellor Helmut Schmidt was to take place in a peaceful and beautiful setting, an informal place that offered the possibility of getting to know each other better. Why not my summer house? Well, the weather is fine in August, and we have a panoramic view of the Oslo fjord. But the accommodations are primitive. That's fine with Schmidt, my staff told me. But the plan was vetoed by German security: The mountain north of the house could too easily serve the purposes of possible terrorists.

I was relieved. A state experimental farm outside Hamar with a lovely view of Lake Mjøsa was chosen for the meeting instead. We had two fine days of exhilarating conversations from dawn to dusk in an atmosphere of privacy.

During the years I have sent many friendly thoughts to German Security. It is okay to rough it, and I was brought up that way. But without a road to our summer house, with bunks, homemade food, no shower, and no indoor toilets, I would have suffered hostess-nerves and been distracted from the political discussions.

The West German Chancellor had made it a tradition to have an annual bilateral get-together with the Prime Ministers of each of Germany's neighbors. We were pleased that Schmidt had included Norway in spite of the fact that we have no common land border.

In this way I met both Helmut Schmidt and his wife, Locki. We touched upon a number of Norwegian–German questions of economic cooperation, particularly with respect to oil and gas. Most important for me was the opportunity to discuss the history of NATO's dual-track decision and the American idea of a neutron weapon. Schmidt had been a longtime insider in the direct contact between West Germany and the United States regarding central security issues. What I best remember was his reaction to the idea of a Nordic nuclear-free zone. Spontaneously he advised us to make comprehensive demands of the Soviet Union and the Warsaw Pact countries.

We were on the same wavelength. We had to make sure that the pressure was balanced on both sides in order to achieve real disarmament and increased security.

Negotiations Are the Only Way

It was necessary to stand united against the Soviet ambitions and their oppression of our neighboring countries in Central and

Eastern Europe. That was why NATO was created. That is why we needed NATO during the 1980s.

But we could only stop the arms race by developing trust and co-operation with our adversary. This had become clear to me and to a number of other people in Norway, Western Europe, and the United States. Negotiations were the only possible way. We considered it our responsibility, even after having left governmental offices, to continue our work on these most vital questions.

Reagan and Willoch

Ronald Reagan was elected President of the United States and the message from Washington became tougher. Most dramatic was Reagan's characterization of the Soviet Union as the evil empire. He went on the offensive against the peace movement both in the United States and in Europe. New language came into use. It was now more important to be the strongest, not to find solutions based on common interests.

There was uneasiness throughout Norway, too, reflected in most of the political parties in Parliament. The fear of new escalation in the armament spiral and a more offensive emphasis on the role of nuclear weapons produced in us a willingness to fight with conviction for another and better result. A number of issues split Parliament during the years when the Conservatives conducted public policy. We had a very aggressive Conservative Party in the 1980s with Willoch in the lead. There was less interest in searching for common ground.

It is not useful to ignore a substantial part of the electorate, or a majority of women and the young by telling them that what they held at heart was of no interest. One could not dismiss them by simply saying that they were leftists. Some tried to do precisely this, however. And this is part of the reason why the debate was filled with hatred.

How did I experience the challenge? I did believe in taking people seriously. I believed in dialogue. I felt it was my responsibility to contribute to a forward-looking and inclusive political platform for

Labor. This would also be the best starting point for a comprehensive Norwegian line. But I had no guarantee of success either within Labor or in Parliament.

The Freeze Movement

In June 1982 I was invited to a congress for the U.S. Democratic Party in Philadelphia. I met centrally placed politicians including Edward Kennedy and Gary Hart, who was then expected to be a contender for the presidency. I also met Madeleine Albright in seminars on international relations, NATO, and nuclear weapons.

There was a lot of discussion about the so-called freeze movement. A group of well-established political scientists and experts—McGeorge Bundy, George F. Kennan, Robert S. McNamara, and Gerard Smith—had recently published an article in *Foreign Affairs* in which they argued against first use of nuclear weapons and urged a closer study of the role of conventional weapons. The article served as an inspiration for all who wished for new approaches to get out of the nuclear arms race.

In New York I was asked to open a discussion on common security for the Norwegian U.N. delegation. I discussed the basic idea of mutual dependence. The forces of the arms race could not be brought to a halt if we did not accept the impossibility of ever winning in the race for superiority. States could no longer attain security at the expense of one another. Security can only be achieved through acts of cooperation. A bilateral, mutual freeze on nuclear weapons and their delivery systems constituted an effort for mutual advantage, not for one-sided victory. This is different from the "arming in order to disarm" sort of security policy.

The ideas in the U.N. document from the first special session are closely related to the notions of common security, including the concept of a nuclear freeze and the political program that the Democrats had agreed upon in Philadelphia.

Did the Democratic Party support the aim of the freeze campaign? At the seminar were centrally placed advisors for both Edward Kennedy and Walter Mondale. When I asked them to comment on a freeze with regard to the NATO dual-track decision, I got not one, but four different answers.

Nevertheless, my main impression was this: Successfully achieving a freeze presupposes consultations and treaties. Both intermediate range nuclear forces (INF) and the strategic arms limitation talks (START) had to be included in any agreement based on mutuality and balance, all things considered. The balance needed to be global and I was reminded that Senator Kennedy had turned down the idea of an isolated European freeze.

The Democrats did not support the Reagan administration's view regarding a limited nuclear war and the idea of superiority in the arms race. They understood that would lead to less security and even more dangerous levels of destructive power. They disagreed with the Reagan presumption that the Soviets had nuclear superiority. No responsible U.S. military commander would trade the U.S. nuclear arsenal with that of the Soviet Union. The Democrats also thought it was both dangerous and irresponsible to raise any doubt about the ability of the United States to defend itself. My knowledge of the Democratic Party's position on nuclear arms became a great inspiration for my work within the Norwegian political setting.

The philosophy behind the freeze also ran parallel to the analyses of the Palme Commission in that it stressed the necessity of avoiding any form of circumvention of an agreement. Finding ways to evade treaties had driven the arms race. Many agreements had been entered into but later circumvented. Loopholes in the treaty texts had been exploited to accelerate new forms of arms buildups. This is what happened with the Soviet SS-20 missiles and with the U.S. MX and Trident, which in my opinion constitutes a breach of the SALT agreement.

I had acquired a conviction. Disarmament was possible. But I also was convinced that any unilateral declaration from Norway, or from NATO—such as our Socialist Left Party demanded—was no road to the goal. It was through joint East–West action that the answers would be found. Disarmament could only be achieved through negotiations, through pressure on both parties, through the acceptance of the idea that the competition had to spiral down and not up.

Deep Divisions Within the Labor Party

In spring 1982 a drama had unfolded in Parliament during the examination in the Parliamentary Standing Committee on Defense of a seemingly very routine issue, NATO's commonly financed so-called infrastructure program. The question arose as to whether Norway at this point should go along with and finance the construction of new nuclear rockets. The dilemma traveled the corridors and picked up many a Labor representative's involvement.

On May 28 I received a letter from Bjørn Tore Godal, chairman of the Oslo Labor Party. Their board had decided to ask the Parliamentary Group to vote against financing any construction connected to the deployment of the new medium-range missiles in Europe. Godal's letter referred to a recent decision by the Labor Party Central Executive Board asking for a new examination of the question of deployment if and when there were any results from the East-West superpower arms-control negotiations that were supposed to follow the dual-track decision.

We had a deep division down the middle of the party. As in so many other political tugs-of-war, I understood both sides all too well.

Knut Frydenlund was our faction leader in the Committee on Defense. Our faction thought it was our party's duty to contribute to the preparation for deployment in case the Soviets did not pull down their SS-20s. At the same time, Frydenlund underlined that this would not be an automatic road to deployment on our side. The letter from the Oslo Labor Party pushed the issue, arguing that we should not cooperate with NATO's preparations until negotiations had advanced further. It was up to the Parliamentary Group to decide.

In his charming and reflective way, Frydenlund suggested that the government should at a later stage come back to Parliament and ask for the money. He made it a condition that the government would then have to evaluate whether the preparatory work for deployment would weaken our negotiating position in the dual-track decision.

Norway Must Not Be a Spearhead

My speech to the National Executive Board in early October 1982 was well prepared. In the days leading up to it I had long conversations with Knut Frydenlund and other influential members of the party. Knut was, like me, concerned with the cohesion and logic of our policy to help finance new nuclear arms while we were searching for the time necessary to create a joint position in our security policy.

Knut and I did not know what proposals the government was preparing, but he was uneasy. There had been little contact with the biggest party of the country and no will to ask counsel from us.

I became convinced that any new round of requests for money only a few months after the first would not at all serve either us or NATO. The most responsible thing would be to make this clear now. The National Executive Board supported the suggestion I put forth:

"It would have been a break with our security policy traditions if we exercised any form of pressure on other NATO countries, which in contrast to us would be directly involved if deployment were to take place. A number of the most directly involved countries have until now made no decision either on deployment of missiles on their own soil or on direct appropriations of earmarked sums for NATO's common financing of preparations for any deployment. Therefore it would be neither right nor natural that Norway should spearhead and now make direct appropriations of earmarked sums.

Norway should take a wait-and-see position in conformity with the thoughts on which the Norwegian government based its support of the decision of 1979."

Hullabaloo. "Labor Breaks with the Dual-Track Decision," read the headlines in the non-socialist press. *Dagbladet*, however, saw it differently: "The Government placed a trap for Labor. It is the Government which has asked for this fight. Prime Minister Willoch and his defense leadership were thinking in the short term and in a tactical mode. Mr. Willoch behaves like a politician in opposition. It is impossible that national interests can have motivated the conservatives."

The "disciplined" majority behind Willoch shrank steadily. That spring, three MPs from the parties of the Middle had voted with our minority. The nuclear protests and the terror of the arms race had had an impact across party lines. This Willoch understood too late.

Steen Once Again

In late October 1982 *Arbeiderbladet* ran the headline: "Labor Will Under All Circumstances Say No." It had been declared by Reiulf Steen, speaking from his new position as Member of Parliament, that Labor would never support the appropriation of funds to build nuclear arms.

This was Reiulf's way of undermining the agreement we had arrived at after the meeting in the National Executive Board. He did not like it that I had been working systematically to have the party support a forward-looking strategy.

For Knut Frydenlund, Odvar Nordli, and Guttorm Hansen, just to mention a few of the heavyweights on the committee, this was quite untenable. They were in charge of formulating the party's position with regard to other NATO members and the dual-track decision. These three had been very flexible in accommodation for agreement. Reiulf Steen chose self-promotion over party loyalty.

The Oslo Christian daily *Vårt Land* was close to the truth when it wrote, "We hesitate to believe it, but Reiulf Steen's latest solo gambit looks like part of an offensive against the Party Leader." My sentiments, exactly. But I chose to remain silent. My responsibility was to keep the party together. I had to make sure that in the spring the National Party Congress had a political platform that would combine the two positions on missiles.

Fortunately our Parliamentary Group unanimously supported the proposition from our people on the Defense Committee: The question of a Norwegian contribution should be postponed till regular budget examination the following fall. At that time we would also have a clearer view of the parliamentary treatment of this matter in the countries in which these weapons would be deployed.

"Let's wait until the fight is necessary," Knut Frydenlund had said to the press when our proposition had been made public. But Willoch wanted to have his voting on the appropriations for missiles, and, by pressuring parliamentarians on the Right, he won with a majority of one vote!

Former Prime Minister Nordli accused Willoch of concealing the fact that in other NATO countries there had been criticism of the way the government handled these matters. A minority government cannot treat these issues of security and defense with a nonchalant attitude toward Parliament. The strength of a government is not measured in terms of its stubbornness vis-à-vis its Parliament. It is the support that a government gets in its own country that is decisive.

Unanimity Alone Will Do

After the Christmas party at party headquarters in 1982 I invited to my office Thorbjørn Jagland, former Leader of Young Labor and now serving as Foreign Policy Secretary at party headquarters. I gave him some of my thoughts about the work of the Labor Party Missile Committee, which we had had to establish. We had worked well together since I had become Party Leader.

Several times we had discussed the common ground we had to find in order to advance disarmament and create unity. The principle of the arms freeze had to be the groundwork if we were to look forward and not be stuck discussing who was right about the consequences of the dual-track decision.

It was necessary to have unanimity on the Missile Committee if the party was to establish a joint platform and create consensus within.

Be It Agreed

Finally, the Missile Committee came up with the following recommendations:

- The United States and the Soviet Union had to agree on a mutual freeze of all types of nuclear weapons.
- They had to issue parallel declarations about this, to be followed by a decommissioning of the Soviet medium-range missiles.
- There could be no deployment of the American Pershing II and cruise missiles.
- In assessing the balance between U.S. and Soviet arms, British and French nuclear weapons had to be taken into account as part of the U.S. arsenal.

The committee also recommended an agreement for a comprehensive test ban and stressed that no arms race should take place in space. Negotiations over strategic weapons (START) had to include production and deployment of cruise missiles on aircraft and ships operating in the northern waters.

After discussing the recommendations from the Missile Committee both in the International Committee and in the Central Executive Board, the freeze was accepted as Labor's strategic alignment. This was later that winter supported by the individual annual meetings of the party at the county level.

The wings of the party followed one another with Argus eyes. The stronger adherents of a straight no to missiles got bloodthirsty.

It stimulated a rebellion in the Parliamentary Group the week after. Many reacted against radical MP Grete Knudsen and debate was fierce. The day after, *Dagbladet* ran the headline, "Labor Rebellion Against Gro's Formalism."

It's easy to write headlines with a short name like mine. But "Gro's formalism" was in fact the decision of the Group, accepted by a great majority. It was Grete herself who had used the word that entered the headline: formalism.

Real Support

On Christmas Eve *Dagbladet* carried an "at-home-with" report with a picture of Olav, Ivar, and me. No breakfast without nuclear debate, the article suggested. It was plain truth. "Before the devil has got shoes on and when night frost still covers Bygdøy, four newspapers are dumped at the door step of the family Brundtland. Shortly afterward the discussion is in full swing over Pershing II, MX, and about the daily editorial over the coffee cups and bread knives."

Sixteen-year-old Ivar answers thus when asked if he too participates in the discussions: "Someone has to listen as well." I cannot say it was ever simple for our teenagers during the time when Olav and I were super-occupied by daily political challenges, but they always seemed to rise to the occasion.

Olav is a fine supporter in difficult matters. He is himself heavily involved and knowledgeable—international politics is his field of expertise. I can discuss my attitudes and reflections with him having complete confidence in his integrity.

Olav told the *Dagbladet* reporter that he had nothing against the Willoch government's having followed a straight line and remained firm, "But the critique of the opposition has at times been out of proportion. There are two models for such a debate. One, free, in which one draws the majority against oneself. Another, not free, in which one barely keeps the majority. This cannot go on for very long. It does not help to be right if one does not command a real majority. I am furthermore uneasy with viewpoints that are not exposed to examination and debate, that might turn brittle and break when put under pressure."

Olav was right. It was a preview of what was to come for the non-socialists.

The Old Boys

When I had been Party Leader a few years, Knut Frydenlund asked me to meet with some of the old boys. He had noticed considerable concern among people like Haakon Lie, the old party secretary; Jens Christian Hauge, the Secret Military chief during World War II; and Tor Aspengren, former TUC boss. They had grown uneasy about the security policy debate. Knut Frydenlund thought it would be better if I met them alone.

I invited them for cake and a cup of coffee at home. Finn Lied, former Industry Minister and longtime Director General of the Defense Research Establishment, joined us as well.

Our conversation was not comfortable. Jens Christian and Haakon took the lead. They were critical. It was dangerous for the party to put such a great emphasis on the views and wishes of the anti-NATO group. Did I not understand how important it was to show firmness? Now things were out of control.

My temperature rose. They underestimated me. Did they really believe that I was so lacking in reasonable knowledge of these important matters? Silence. I searched for the appropriate tone. I did not want to answer as a little girl—neither as the idealist Progress girl nor as Gubbe's daughter to whom they could give fatherly advice.

I answered calmly and factually. I described the different issues we had labored with and the need to establish a comprehensive and unifying platform. I told them about the work of the Palme Commission and the possibility of getting to a negotiating result on the idea of the freeze. I believed that it was possible to unify for NATO and a durable disarmament strategy at the same time.

My talk must have had some impact on Tor Aspengren at least, for in a telephone conversation with the notorious furniture dealer

Arvid Engen at Jessheim, he offered this opinion: "She does not listen to anyone, Arvid, to no one at all."

The criticism from the old boys continued even in public. Haakon Lie called it treachery to hold new views on nuclear weapons and on the conflict in the Middle East.

Salmon Fishing

The intense and nervous disagreement on nuclear weapons would dominate the political landscape for five years, from the preparation for the dual-track decision of NATO in late 1979 until May 1984.

A prominent and strongly conservative newspaper from central Norway noted in May 1984: "Parliamentary circles are really impressed by Gro Harlem Brundtland's tactical gifts in the nerve-racking play around the recommendation from the Foreign Relations Committee on disarmament. She enjoys herself like a salmon swimming upstream. At the same time she keeps her own left-wingers under strict control. This is no small achievement. Former Foreign Minister Knut Frydenlund, now being rapporteur for the Defense Committee, is holding back his recommendation on the future of defense in order to let Gro put down some more NATO-friendly formulations in her report. It looks like the moderates once again have taken command inside Labor."

On May 24, 1984, I introduced my report from the Foreign Relations Committee. Our recommendations on arms control were unanimous, with only one exception. The report evaluated all the questions central to the debate on security and disarmament during the last five years and built on my analysis and that of my party.

Willoch had lost much of his sway not only over the parties of the Middle, but over his own party's MPs as well. The Conservative Parliamentary Group in the end avoided both isolation and the risk of splitting down the middle by going along with the consensus.

At Home, in Opposition 9

Time with the kids was always in short supply. I missed them. So I did what I could to be free on the weekends. At the vacation homes I could relax and be a mother. The newspapers were not brought along. I liked cooking and the preparation of meals, good time for lengthy conversations and laughter. There was something special about Christmas and the days before. Olav normally shouldered the main caretaking responsibility at home, but I was in charge of the holidays.

Mamma had taught me to boil caramel. We took the recipe from her *Big Swedish Cookbook*. It had to boil for hours and needed attendance. It was always surprising when it came out right, with the proper degree of sweetness and cohesiveness. You could check it by removing one teaspoonful and plunging it in cold water to see if it stiffened.

Once when Jørgen was twelve and Ivar thirteen, they took the bus to the Parliament building to go shopping for Christmas presents with me. We went to the big department store. It was overcrowded. I had to concentrate on keeping hold of the two boys.

Then I sensed it. Everything I did was observed. If I looked for them, to be certain, someone else was following my gaze. If I raised my voice, it became worse. Christmas shopping that evening became a nightmare. The boys must have sensed my discomfort. It increased their desire to tease and test me. They could hold their mother prisoner, in the palms of their hands. I didn't want to object in front of an audience.

Returning to the Parliament building with my two menaces, I felt totally exhausted and unable to cope. Later that evening I told Olav what had happened. The boys were given a lecture. I had learned another lesson about how difficult it was to combine my public status with my role as mother.

I had experienced such things before. During summer vacations we often do our shopping at a big supermarket. Other shoppers are intensely interested in our conversations. They examine our purchases. Most are curious but discreet, saying nothing. But occasionally they make comments: "Is that environmentally friendly?" or "Surely that's not healthy." Like other children, Ivar and Jørgen would want candy. My dilemma was whether to fight over every whim or give in and escape unwanted attention.

One Easter we were at a restaurant at a tourist cabin in the High Mountains. I ask Ivar to pick up a chocolate candy wrapper from the floor. He had not dropped it, but I thought the kids should learn to pick up after others as well. Some years later, during a very intense debate on where to run electric power lines over the mountains, I received the rudest letter from someone strongly opposed to the decisions made by the Ministry of the Environment. His furious letter also contained a reference to the wrapper incident. He described me as an intolerant chatterbox, interfering in everything, even demanding that other people's children pick up garbage from the floor!

Married to Arne Olav

Olav and I had belonged to different political parties and different student organizations from the very start. Even after I became Minister, our differences were manageable. I defended our relationship tooth and nail on the principle of equality. Independent men and women did not have to hold the same points of view or vote for the same party.

After I became Deputy Leader in 1975, this stance became more difficult. Political opponents could exploit our relationship. I began to be concerned. It took much longer for Olav to realize that this was a problem, and I didn't immediately express my uneasiness.

While I stuck to my principles, I only complained when points were made in the press or by others. By and large we distanced ourselves emotionally from all the criticism. But there had to be a limit.

When Olav was in the running for Parliament as a Conservative in 1981, the stress became too difficult. I also was surprised at how long it took for him to realize that this was too big a burden for me. In his book, *Married to Gro,* he wrote that I gave him the impression that if he was elected I might divorce him. Well, it's true, I felt forced to make that abundantly clear. In fact, I meant that divorce was the only natural consequence of such a victory. But I said it to illustrate how inconsiderate he was in not realizing that he had to refrain from placing such a great burden on me. My remark was necessary to get him to draw the conclusions that he should have drawn long ago. After all, I was Deputy Leader of the Labor Party and had been a cabinet Minister for five years.

Olav has always been an optimistic soul, sometimes even a naïve one. I have always had more reservations about difficult situations, and I am quicker to see problems. We differ, so I do not criticize him too harshly.

Children Under Pressure

What did the kids feel? During the 1970s and the first half of the 1980s, the political debate in Norway was much sharper than to-day. The children were sandwiched between parents holding different opinions.

I think we managed an open and pleasant atmosphere in the political debates within our own home. They saw that Olav and I communicated in a civilized fashion, examining issues such as taxation, security policy, welfare, and education. But perhaps even such civilized disagreements made the kids feel insecure.

Moreover, when the children were away from home—in the schoolyard, in the homes of their friends, and in clubs—they were often attacked and got into lots of arguments. Though they did not report the difficulties they encountered, they often came under fire, particularly when their mother and her party were under strong attack. I know that they fought back.

Kaja told us about a close friend who insisted that the Brundtland family surely were tax evaders. Kaja was shocked, knowing how strict we were about following the rules. How could the friend say something like that? You own an ocean-cruising sailboat, the boy said. People living on two incomes from public service could not afford that. He had been told this at home. And he seemed convinced.

Knut was also confronted about the boat, told that a real socialist would not own one. "Why not?" I said. "That's our business. We have paid for it with our own money after taxes and we own the boat on a fifty-fifty basis with your grandparents. The discussion about the level of taxation and how to use public funds for equality and justice has nothing to do with how we spend our private money. Whether you buy clothes, go on vacation in the South of Europe, or keep a sailboat is your choice, as long as you don't harm anybody else."

"We knew what you stood for, Mamma"

Kaja knew the intense contempt some had for the word "socialist." She knew very well from discussions at home and from her own reading of history that Mamma was no socialist in the senses hurled at her. They made it sound like Communist, Stalinist, believer in centralized government. She knew I was a social democrat with traditional Labor values, just as my father was.

Kaja was the only one of the kids who said that she was a social democrat and would vote Labor when she turned eighteen. The three boys kept their own counsel. Olav and I did not push them one way or the other. Quite natural. Voting is secret, the boys argued. So it is. It was important to us that the kids learned our attitude toward democracy and the individual. We respected the children's choices made on the basis of their own consciences.

After she turned twenty, Kaja occasionally said that she would have been happier had we given her more distinct advice and that our neutrality was not always easy to take. It reminds me about the decision I had to make about my own education when I was eighteen. It had not been possible to make the choice without knowing both Mamma's and Pappa's points of view—even if I did not follow either.

Today Kaja laughs: "Mamma, naturally we knew what you stood for, what you thought. We could read the papers and watch you on TV. So could everyone else. During the seventies, the big political confrontations happened on one TV channel and on one radio station. Everyone tuned in, and the agenda was set for discussion in all workplaces the following day. Times have changed!"

Olav on the Move

Everyone read *Aftenposten*. The paper's political editor served as the media leader for non-socialist policies. He fought for the Conservatives and for Kåre Willoch. He exploited the inner tug-of-war in the Labor Party in the most effective way. But *Aftenposten* was at the same time a newspaper with a broader outlook.

A reporter married to the editor in chief told me about the very strong reactions her husband had experienced in 1977 after the paper had printed a front-page picture of Olav and me in our sailboat on Norway's charming south coast. Letters to the editor criticized the paper for presenting the Deputy Labor Leader in such a favorable light: "The picture was too sympathetic and positive. Signed, Conservative Voter."

I don't know how Olav voted in 1981; I'm pretty sure it was Conservative. But it became clearer over time that our political views had grown similar. In particular, in security policies Olav had a great deal of sympathy for the fight my closest allies in the party and I waged to make defense strategy more solid and popular.

Olav gradually became convinced that education and health are so central to society that their administration has to be under public responsibility, guidance, and financing. He was skeptical of the attempts to privatize the health sector in such a small and sparsely populated country as ours.

Nor did I know how Olav voted in 1985. But by then I had grown suspicious. At that time I enjoyed so much support from him, not only for my work generally, but also for my viewpoints, that I couldn't believe that he continued to vote Conservative. But I never asked, and he never let on. We both continued to respect each other's independence.

In 1989, during the campaign, Olav decided to go public in one of his monthly columns in a regional paper and explain why he was about to vote Labor. Security, welfare, and the economy were most important in his analysis. He later stressed the importance of voting Labor in order to secure a platform for having a choice about joining the European Union. A Center–Right government would not allow the possibility of Norwegian membership in the European Union, because of the negative attitudes of the Center Party.

At Sea

We used the sailboat on summer vacation. During the 1970s we sometimes sailed through the Swedish skerries. One day, we sailed along the south coast of Norway. By chance we met my younger brother Lars. We sailed in tandem for a few days all the way past Lindesnes before we decided to return east. Local sailors had informed us that winds were only 6 knots, and although the waters were treacherous and strong currents can create mighty waves, we decided to have a go.

The wind rose. And so did the waves. My heart beating fast, I shouted to Olav, "We have to lower the sail!" We took the mainsail down with relative ease. Then the jib. Olav was wearing his life jacket, but I asked him to fasten a line as well. A little irritated, he knotted a rope around his chest, the hook on the other end clasped onto the railing. On the front deck he ran into trouble. The jib sail hit him over the head, and he was suddenly thrown over the railing and into the water.

I was struck by fear, trying to remember the right things to do. His line was long enough to let him fall into the water but so short that he was beaten against the boat as he was dragged alongside it. There was no way to lift him right away. I decided to try the winch, used for tightening ropes for the sail. I remembered reading about that once in an article.

Olav managed to put another rope around his chest and his right leg. It seemed to work, and with the winch I had the strength to haul him up. But halfway up, Olav screamed for me to stop. The rope was nearly strangling him. We had to abandon the attempt.

He was remarkably clear and collected. He shouted for a new rope. And just as he'd tied himself in, the railing at the other end broke. A terrible moment. Olav suffered another blow, and had he not been so alert, it could have ended disastrously.

He managed to get himself to the rear of the boat, in an effort to reach the ladder as I lowered it into the water. He struggled but the boat danced in the waves. We learned later that the wind was nearly 12 knots.

Olav could not climb high enough, and I couldn't help him. If he'd been able to find a foothold on the lowest step, another lifeline would have done the trick. He was worn out, but still thinking clearly. With a loose rope he fastened his hands to the ladder to prevent drowning should he lose consciousness in the cold water, only 57 degrees Fahrenheit. I was trying to get the boat into calmer waters.

By this point, Olav had suffered that cold water for more than an hour. He was beaten. We talked to one another to keep him awake. But I knew we didn't have much time. His body temperature was dropping every minute.

Then I saw a motorboat with a couple and an adolescent boy. However, to my great dismay, the man could not leave his steering position, and neither his wife nor his son could operate the boat! I was shocked. Luckily, another boat came along. The newcomer took command of the first boat, and the skipper of the first boat now came to our rescue. He put on his life jacket, dove into the water, and finally gave Olav the help he needed to get his feet on the ladder. I pulled him up from my position, helping a tired, battered, but happy Olav on board.

I took his wet clothes off, found dry wool clothes and blankets, and set about restoring his body temperature right away.

We were both scared but managed to sail the boat back home to Oslo. I was fully aware that it had been a narrow escape, that I had very nearly lost my husband and the father of my four children.

A Child Leaves the Nest

During the summer of 1979 Olav, Kaja, Ivar, Jørgen, and I had sailed to the south of Norway. While taking an evening walk along the lovely beach, the longest sand beach in Norway, Olav told me that Knut was moving out in the fall. Olav had known before we went on vacation. He took it easily. For me it was a shock. Knut leaving home? He hadn't yet graduated. That was much too soon!

Knut wanted to live with friends that last year. He wanted to be president of the graduates of Oslo Business College, and he thought that all the commotion and telephone calls that would come with his activity would interfere with his mother's work. I had to accept. But I will never forget that evening and the devastating loss I felt.

Later that year Knut met Cecilie Malm. They were both eighteen. Their encounter became all-important for both their lives. In the summer of 1985, when they were twenty-four, we celebrated the first wedding of the next generation. A grand wedding. They were married in a stone church seven hundred years old, situated close to Cecilie's family's summer holiday home. It was a happy day. The entire family was there. We all liked Cecilie and felt very lucky.

The press was there. Privacy in a public place does not come easily when you have been Prime Minister and may very well be again. Cecilie had ancestors of great standing in business and shipping, and *VG* suggested that Gro, the Labor Leader, was now personally crossing the divide and entering as mother-in-law into a family dynasty of private wealth and conservative persuasions. Knut's in-laws, the menu, and all the rest of the wedding were displayed for all to see. The press did not respect our privacy.

Kaja, too, graduated from Oslo Business College and left home at nineteen for a little college in Evanston, Illinois. It was somewhat less of a shock to see my second child leave home. The next year she moved with a childhood classmate to an apartment in Oslo and studied public law and social economy at the university.

Kaja later transferred to the National Business University in Bergen. I was on my way to Brazil when Kaja asked what I thought she should do next. Olav had advised her to take a master's degree in international business administration. Olav's strong interest in international affairs was persuasive. At the same time, diplomacy was tempting.

I thought Olav had been somewhat forceful in his advice. Why did Kaja necessarily have to go to graduate school? The training in the Foreign Ministry was also of value. Did we have to put pressure on her? I hoped she'd feel free to make her choice, and told her so. She applied for the diplomatic service and was accepted.

We felt the loss of Knut and Kaja. But we saw them often on weekends. The family collective still functioned. Not infrequently three generations would meet at our holiday homes at Lake Mylla in the winter and at Helleskilen in the summer.

Ivar and Jørgen

Kaja was all the more relieved to leave home when she did. Her younger brothers behaved like typical noisy, untidy, dependent adolescents when they were fifteen and sixteen.

Ivar mostly kept his thoughts to himself. When he turned sixteen, he suddenly started to concentrate on schoolwork. Why? He wanted to be admitted to the Norwegian Technical University in

Trondheim, and he needed top grades in mathematics and physics to do so.

One day in the fall of 1985 I came home and at the door Olav said: "Ivar has a girlfriend you should meet. Her name is Suzuki." I was surprised, but prepared to take it well. But there was no girl in the living room, or anywhere in the house, and Ivar shrugged coyly when I asked him.

Behind the house stood a black motorcycle. Some girlfriend! Ivar was on his way to Trondheim and wanted to leave on the motorcycle. I despaired. I knew all the statistics.

I told Olav: "Give Ivar your car. We'll sell his motorcycle." The next morning Ivar got an offer he could not refuse. I was tremendously relieved to see Ivar drive off in his new car.

My father had kept his apartment in Trondheim since his professorial days. Ivar, who took after him, both in facial complexion and temperament, moved into the apartment with some of his new student friends.

Jørgen started his studies at the University of Oslo in the fall of 1985. He had just turned eighteen. Later that fall he asked for early admittance for his compulsory military service, before starting his law studies. I thought it was too early. But his two elder brothers and Olav, who had all completed their own compulsory military service, thought it was okay.

In the winter of 1986 Jørgen came home with new friends, all in the midst of officer's training. Jørgen was physically and mentally in superb form. It was not until later that year that his difficulties began.

Life in Opposition

In October 1981 Labor became the opposition party, and so we undertook a thorough evaluation of our party's policies and strategies.

The Labor Party and the trade unions had solid roots in all areas of Norway. I stressed the value of decentralization, of strengthening the party in the municipal branches and at the county level. We wanted inspiration from voters and local officials. On the Central

Executive Board we sought representatives from outside Oslo, and during the 1980s the Board was also broadened. This has made the party stronger.

In Parliament there is a risk that members will become specialists and lose their breadth of knowledge and depth of experience. In our Parliament every member sits on one of the committees, which roughly equal governmental ministries in number. Labor frequently has several MPs on each committee, forming what we used to call our faction. Every committee faction had its own leader, elected by the Parliamentary Group.

Though a fraction is a microcosm of the Parliamentary Group, it should not be permitted to perform as a "state within the state." No one should "own" policies in a democratic party. When a piece of legislation is taken up in plenary sessions in Parliament, it is often brought up on a recommendation by a rapporteur from the concerned committee. In preparing the party's views for such a recommendation one can be misled if the work is done by the fraction all by itself in isolation from the Parliamentary Group. It is important that many members be active in the discussions in order to involve the whole Group. Then people will not vote along party lines out of loyalty but because they feel ownership of the Labor Party's line on the issue.

Life in opposition often involves courting voters by demanding larger budgets than the government is willing to set aside. But the budget ultimately has to be balanced. We had to make sure that nobody lost sight of the economic picture, and we strove to strengthen our team of Party Secretaries to be able to develop our own budgetary alternatives on a much more solid and reasoned foundation than parties in opposition generally had done.

Throw Out the Old Receipts

Our party's main goals remained the same, but I wanted renewal. We who had been the architects of the welfare society should be the first to criticize it. How could we get rid of rules and regulations which no longer were necessary? How could we check the unintended side effects of social programs?

We had to examine the monopoly of the Norwegian Broadcasting Corporation. It had been with us since the years between the world wars. The media situation was different in the 1980s, and people were asking for more variety, particularly in light of international competition.

The Conservatives had popular success with their slogan "Forbidden Norway," which pointed to a lot of things that were prohibited. Labor had to admit that some regulations were difficult to comprehend or to defend. There were complaints about working hours, the shortage of nursery schools, and housing policy. Perhaps the most important problem had to do with the fact that we had created a system of cooperative housing that made it virtually impossible economically for a resident to move into another municipality. We had struggled with this for some time. There were two housing markets: One was low cost, cooperative, and municipality-based in which would-be homeowners put their names on a waiting list for area housing; the other was free and private, and consequently had higher prices. Since you could not sell your house in the cooperative scheme for market prices, you could not get enough to buy yourself a new house on the private market in the next municipality. We did not tackle this dilemma soon enough.

Labor could not continue to look like the party of regulation. A new round of work toward a more "open party" became necessary, and we started to draft a program in 1983, which we called "New Growth for Norway." The notion of growth, however, was not universally popular. In fact, we really needed new economic growth, although not just any kind of economic growth. Norway needed new technology, new markets, and a new way of using research and development in both the public and the private sectors. The new workplaces had to be established in areas that needed an improved quality of life. There were lots of demands, including better care for the elderly, more nursery schools, and more homes for the sick.

We had heated debates about privatization of health services. The Conservatives used the United States as an example. But I knew the costs of the U.S. way, and I didn't want a system in which the less privileged were less able to afford good care and treatment.

My Closest Collaborator

Mamma was the office worker with the most experience in the Labor Parliamentary Group. From 1981 until 1986, I really benefited from the skills she had acquired while serving former Prime Minister Trygve Bratteli when he had been Parliamentary Leader. When I took over his position in October 1981, we thought it natural that she continue. Yet it must have been strange for Mamma. She had worked in the Parliament building since the 1950s, when I was just a small girl. Now I was entering her workplace.

Mamma knew her job. She knew Parliament, and she knew the Group. She was used to speedily and efficiently finding and preparing all material politically relevant to the work at hand. She helped me a great deal and never spared herself, working overtime whenever necessary.

I had always enjoyed Mamma's support. I don't know how Olav and I could have managed when the children were small had she and Pappa not been there to help out at almost any time. Now she also took care of the practical sides of my daily work both as Parliamentary Leader and as Party Leader. Svein Roald Hansen, a journalist from Fredrikstad, became my political counselor in June 1983 and established a close relationship with us both. He was clever, loyal, and hardworking just like her. Our little team could manage an incredible workload, one that would only increase when I was asked to chair the World Commission on Environment and Development in the fall of 1983.

I appreciated that Mamma never stopped being an educator, though it was sometimes burdensome to be her daughter and her boss at the same time.

One day at the office I knew that I would hear from the maternal side of my assistant. I had been across the street to a hairdresser and had my ears pierced. I knew Mamma's attitudes about such silliness. I had postponed this frivolous step for a long time. I was now forty-three years old. My attitudes were after all not so different from hers. "Mamma, do you notice anything different?" I asked. No? I turned my head. "Do you see something now?" I asked. She saw, but she did not say a word. Her facial expression said it all. Everyone in the room laughed, as Mamma turned on her heel and went to her office.

The Murder in Stockholm

It was the middle of the night when the telephone rang. I awoke in an instant. Prime Minister Olof Palme of Sweden had been shot. It seemed completely unbelievable. The caller was from the Swedish Labor Party office and knew only that Palme had been on his way home from the cinema with his wife, Lisbeth, when it happened: He had been murdered. I tried to pull myself together. The media was bound to call for my reaction to this tragedy, which would shake not only Northern Europe but the whole world.

That weekend I was due to examine the political situation at the annual meeting of the Oslo Labor Party. Instead my first assignment was to commemorate Olof Palme. My thoughts were with Lisbeth and their sons. The meeting room was packed with delegates and press. Stern faces. Many in tears and in shock. I dug my fingernails into my skin. My voice could not be allowed to crack completely.

He was one of us. The Labor movement in Sweden and Norway had no dividing boundaries. This meaningless and brutal murder was terrifying and the loss of Olof Palme was devastating. As Leader of our sister party, he had been an exceptional source of inspiration not only to the Nordic peoples but to people everywhere.

I had vivid memories from the most recent meeting of the Palme Commission in New Delhi that past January. It had been a very special week, with optimistic signals from both the Soviet Union and the United States. Our Soviet member, academician Georgi Arbatov, had helped to get an important declaration from Secretary-General Gorbachev two days before the meeting started. He had presented a three-step program for the elimination of nuclear weapons before the year 2000.

In my capacity as former Norwegian Prime Minister and as a close friend and colleague of Olof Palme, I had been invited to stay on and join his official two-day visit in India after the conclusion of the meeting. He had such natural and spontaneous warmth and closeness toward the people we met along the road that I remarked on it. He told me that he knew the Indian villagers from his visits when he was a young student and had remained impressed with them for life.

What was it that made him so extraordinary? It was his personal qualities. But it was also his ability to inspire trust in the ideals of Northern Europe and the United Nations, trust that fueled his restless drive toward bettering the lot of the underprivileged. He was genuinely the world's symbol of hope for a better and more just future. Olof Palme's legacy is great, and I have considered it my duty to carry on his work.

We flew together from Frankfurt to Delhi. We talked about the challenge of being a Party Leader. It is with you night and day, on weekends and during vacations. We talked about the children, the family. What did our position mean for them? We talked about the relentless responsibility and also about slander and threats, about factions of the right wing—particularly in Sweden—which fomented a pure hatred of social democracy and Olof Palme. There was also an international movement that abhorred the Nordic social democracies.

Palme remembered picketers holding posters linking him with international Communism. Over time he had seen many of the same faces while speaking to large crowds both in Sweden and abroad. Sometimes his staff could identify these faces, but sometimes not. Palme told me this disturbed him even when he tried not to dwell on it. I could feel his worry. I saw his eyes, and I cannot forget his expression.

The Brundtland Commission

10

One day in March 1982, I found this note in my office:

> GHB, See the attached telegrams.
>
> Ulf Svensson called on behalf of Tolba, the UNEP director, to try to get you to say yes. In particular, because you are being considered to chair a new committee on environmental matters similar to the Brandt Commission and the Palme Commission. Tolba is traveling to Stockholm around March 15–16 and would stop in Oslo on the way to talk to you. Perhaps you should call him first.
>
> 8.3.82.
>
> IH

IH is Inga Harlem, Mamma. That was the way she wrote when in the office.

In Stockholm in 1972, the U.N. had set up a separate environmental organization—United Nations

Environment Programme (UNEP)—based in Nairobi, Kenya. The intention was to provide a stronger environmental profile.

Ulf Svensson was one of those young and enthusiastic Swedes who wanted a commission whereby one would really be able to review the range of problems that environmental difficulties imposed upon the world.

A number of key countries had long since worked toward giving the international effort for environmentally friendly development a new political platform, but few believed that reforms could come about from within the U.N. system itself. The director of UNEP, Mustafa Tolba, a strong-willed and dynamic Egyptian, was skeptical about the idea of a commission, although the attached telegram was an invitation to the tenth anniversary celebration of the Stockholm Conference, and to the open hearing that Tolba was arranging in Nairobi.

Assignment from the U.N.

I had heard some weeks earlier that I had been short-listed for the commission, along with former U.S. President Jimmy Carter and former British Prime Minister Edward Heath. I had some doubts about taking on an international commitment. It was enough of a job being both Party and Parliamentary Leader.

In the middle of December 1983, however, the U.N. Secretary-General, Perez de Cuellar, approached me and asked me to head the new international commission. It was to be called the World Commission on Environment and Development.

I consulted my closest colleagues in the party; they all thought this was too important to turn down. I remember what Tolba had said when he was trying to persuade me: "You are the only Environment Minister in the world to have become a Prime Minister." Many others had also placed considerable emphasis upon precisely that fact.

My U.N. assignment was to establish and head the commission. Sweden had promised to provide help with the actual start-up, in the form of both expertise and financing.

Advice from Willy Brandt

On December 18, 1983, I was in Bonn for Willy Brandt's seventieth birthday. He was appropriately feted at Bahnhof Rolandseck, a small converted train station, now an artists' restaurant, immediately south of Bonn. It posed a good opportunity for me to draw on his experience of having headed a similar agency.

Brandt stressed the role that the World Bank had played for his own North-South commission. He said that it was critical for me to build further upon the bank's role. We spoke about various people, including Sonny Ramphal, Secretary-General of the Commonwealth of Nations. Ramphal was committed and possessed an extraordinary knack for interpersonal relations, which meant a lot when people needed to exchange ideas and arrive at conclusions.

Sonny promised to help me get the commission up and running, but said that he had too much to do to come in as a member. Later on, I made a strong appeal to him: "You consider it important that I take on this job. We both believe that development must be central to the commission report. If I am now to take on this huge and demanding task, then I must have the reinforcement that comes from being able to work with you, someone I know and have experience with. This is going to be tough. If you do not want to do it, then neither do I." I convinced him. He proved to be of enormous importance.

Nominations for members came from many quarters and from every continent. Among the more startling names to be proposed were those of Jane Fonda and Prince Claus of the Netherlands. There were difficult choices to be made: I wanted to have a good North/South balance. I also felt it was important to find good women for the commission, but almost exclusively men were suggested. However, I managed to recruit two fine women: the Italian senator Susanna Agnelli and the Colombian scientist Margarita de Botero.

Tolba and Khalid

The commission had a turbulent beginning. The Secretary-General of the U.N. initially wanted to appoint President Senghor of Senegal as vice-chairman, but Tolba refused to cooperate further unless his good friend and confidant Mansour Khalid was appointed instead. Khalid had previously been Foreign Minister in the Sudan and had good contacts in the African and Arab world. He knew George Bush well from long ago. He was certainly the commission member who would spend the most time on the telephone in the next few years. He always kept several balls in the air.

The fact that the commission was not a U.N. agency but an independent entity was to be of major significance right from the start. Khalid and Tolba had argued that it should be a U.N. agency, a designation that would have allowed Tolba to exercise direct influence.

The Swiss government offered us the old Palais Wilson in Geneva for our headquarters. There I met representatives from Sweden, Canada, Japan, India, and the Netherlands, our sponsor countries. They helped to get the commission on its feet during the first weeks of 1984. The Indian ambassador brought greetings from Prime Minister Indira Gandhi, whom I had met during her official visit to Norway in 1983, along with a recommendation that Nagendra Singh, president of the International Court, be a member of the commission.

There were many who wished to offer advice, but I did not want to be coerced. Mansour Khalid considered me a relatively young and inexperienced woman and clearly believed that it would be easy to wrest control from me. He would be disappointed.

Conflicts arose when Khalid came under the impression that we would lead the commission jointly and that he should approve all decisions. However, he had been appointed vice-chairman, not co-chairman. The U.N.'s legal experts also made it clear that Khalid had been mistaken. He was upset and difficult and would telex commission members as they were appointed, in order to promote his own views.

The Bear in Geneva

I arranged to recruit experts in different disciplines, and I wanted them to have a leader who was able in terms of expertise and administration. Jim MacNeill had headed the environmental department of the Organization for Economic Cooperation and Development (OECD) in Paris for several years, and had been Deputy Environmental Minister in Ontario, where the greater part of Canada's industry is located.

Jim thought our commission had an impossible task; the U.N. mandate was too indeterminate. "So we will write our own mandate," I said. Jim later claimed that it was largely this attitude that had persuaded him to join.

Environmental thinking had long been characterized as a "clean-up-once-the-damage-is-done" policy. However, we wanted to integrate environmental considerations at all political levels. And we were intent on looking at all types of policy that could influence the environment, from the belief that economic policy is the real and substantive environmental policy.

We agreed to hold public hearings wherever we had meetings. This proposal was met with considerable skepticism, including from several of the commission's own members. Khalid believed that this practice would violate national sovereignty. Jim argued that the fact that hearings were allowed to be held was itself a manifestation of national sovereignty.

We also agreed to place as much emphasis upon disseminating the commission report as upon drawing it up. We had learned from the mistakes of the Brandt Commission, which had not had any clear information strategy, even though Willy Brandt had given hundreds of lectures.

Jim would not be controlled from Oslo. He was the one who was surrounded by the international staff morning to night, working full-time, while I sat in Oslo with all my responsibility in party and Parliament. I had deliberately chosen a strong person. Jim MacNeill could be obstinate, and there were occasional conflicts with other colleagues, but he had an extremely tidy mind and an enormous capacity for work and for reading. We decided early on that the commission should obtain scientific and political reports relating to the matters we were dealing with. I believe Jim read everything.

I also believe that Jim purposely chose to act tough. He had been through some difficult trials in his life, something that I would only become aware of when tragedy struck my own family.

Feverish Start

We held the first commission meeting in Geneva in May 1984. For the previous few weeks I had had a bad cold, sinusitis, and a temperature. Two days before the scheduled meeting I became very ill.

Good advice was at a premium. I had to get back onto my feet. The X rays revealed pronounced pneumonia, no minor ailment by any means. Massive doses of penicillin were administered in consultation with my doctor, who felt it was my choice, considering how important this meeting was.

I was listless, but my senses were sharpened and I was able to concentrate. I recall the atmosphere that first day, while I was still feverish. Was this going to work or not? Had I overextended myself?

There were twelve commission members present. We still lacked members from the United States and the Soviet Union. It soon became clear that both the United States and the Soviet governments wanted to be involved.

We agreed on our principal strategy. I told my colleagues that we had to complete the report in 1986 so that it could be discussed by the U.N. general assembly in 1987. It turned out to be difficult to finance this major undertaking. We started with practically no funds and had to ask governments and organizations for voluntary contributions. We began with Swedish money, set up our own account in a Swiss bank, and operated as Brandt and Palme had.

Maurice Strong, the Canadian member of the commission, suggested Warren "Chip" Lindner as head of administration. Lindner, who worked for the World Wildlife Fund, came to Oslo to meet me. It was a two-way interview; he asked me about my background and my views on leadership in order to decide whether he could work under me. The American heard a great deal that day in Oslo, about Scandinavian concepts of democracy and leadership, and about the style I call my own.

Chip was to be the practical problem-solver who organized our work throughout the world and in Geneva. He and I would often have to intervene and restore a positive atmosphere when the somewhat more direct McNeill had trodden on too many toes.

Visions

What, then, was this commission's goal? We were to examine and evaluate with independent eyes the structures of our societies as they had been developing in the era of industrialism. Ultimately, we were to sketch out new ways of protecting the environment and of combating both poverty and uncontrolled population growth. Our mission was more a matter of politics in general than of traditional environmental protection. It concerned finance, resources, energy, and industry, as well as education, health, and family planning. The list was long!

No previous international commission had reflected the international spectrum as we did. A clear majority of our members were from developing countries. This was an important point for me, and it proved to be a real strength in the years that followed. As a result, we managed to get our message across in Africa, Asia, and Latin America.

Jim, Sonny, and I advocated an open working system to enable us to gather accounts from many quarters, from the scientific elite as well as from average families living with environmental problems in developing countries. We encouraged everyone who wanted to submit written reports, ideas, and opinions. We gradually amassed an enormous volume of material.

We were quick to make our basic view known: It is possible to construct an economically sounder and fairer future based upon policies and behavior that can secure our ecological foundation. But fundamental changes were necessary—in attitudes, lifestyles, and politics. And it would require an entirely different kind of cooperation between countries, and among trade, industry, and research.

The Ministry of the Environment cannot be the only place where environmental policies are pursued. The Ministries of Finance and Energy, and local government—these are the real Ministries of the Environment, with authority and budgets that can be applied so that they really make a difference.

In Indonesia

The first meeting outside Geneva was held in Jakarta in March 1985. It would not be possible to celebrate Easter in the Norwegian manner that year. Olav was disappointed, since we always had Easter in the mountains. There was only one solution: Olav—and Jørgen—would have to come along.

Jørgen was seventeen and about to graduate from college that year. He did not consider a trip to the Far East a poor substitute for our usual sojourn in the mountains. He enjoyed himself on the flight to Jakarta, and he was able to make use of his English. He charmed everyone, including his mother.

The commission had decided that public hearings were to form part of all our meetings. That was simple enough in countries such as Norway and Canada, but not in Indonesia, Brazil, the Soviet Union, or Zimbabwe, where such events had never before happened.

Emil Salim, Indonesian Minister of State for Population and the Environment, was our liaison to the Indonesian government, which was decidely opposed to the public forum.

We made it clear from the beginning that if there were no public hearings, we would not come to Indonesia. The government acceded. The hearing was covered on television, without censorship. People were brought in by boat from across the huge country of islands. We ignored the fact that some of those who spoke had been selected by the authorities and security police to appear "on behalf of the people." Many, many other speakers were nevertheless able to see and hear things that they would not otherwise have experienced.

Borneo, or Kalimantan as it is known in Indonesia, had just had the worst forest fire in history, a fact of which the rest of the world was oblivious. Forest tracts were being burned to open up new agricultural areas. Then the fire got out of control. The commission flew to Borneo and viewed from the air the devastation caused by the fire.

To fly from one end of Indonesia to the other is like flying from Oslo to New York. The country is the fourth most populous in the world, after China, India, and the United States. Environmental and development problems are ascribable to particularly large industrial projects, the use of agricultural chemicals, deforestation, and demographic shifts from densely populated Java to the outlying islands.

Emil Salim was quite simply a warm person. On one occasion when the commission was discussing urban problems, his eyes almost popped out of his head. We were talking about effecting economic transfers through the country, from population centers into the rural regions, with an infrastructure—roads and bridges—to connect the various parts of the country. Salim had an entirely different view. He thought it was the villages that had to be taxed so that the money could be used to develop the big cities.

Least Possible Damage—Greatest Possible Benefit

"We cannot give up. Passivity and pessimism have never helped the earth to advance." This was the message I brought to a Norwegian television interview in January 1985.

Environmental problems will not disappear without an active desire for change. Public pressure is crucial in many countries whose politicians will not take a matter seriously until the pressure from ordinary people is strong enough to be effective.

Environmental protection forces us to think in global terms. We cannot avoid the major contexts that extend beyond the frameworks that the individual nation-state has laid down. International cooperation has already become a necessity, not a choice.

Environmental protection can no longer be an afterthought, but rather it must be the leading edge of development. We chose a new perspective: Economic plans are to be assessed on the basis of their effect on the environment and on development. And our goal must be the least possible damage and greatest possible benefit measured in human values. Everyone has the right to food, health, education, and work.

I reported on the greatest problems.

Agriculture: Current farming practices undermine the opportunities for lasting yield. The soil is not renewable. We are using it up.

Tropical forests: Developing countries' debt increases their need for export income and gives rise to excessive felling of trees for new cultivable areas, fuel, and timber. When the roots which had retained moisture die, the earth dries up and we have soil erosion.

Fresh water: Providing clean water is the greatest problem in many places. Seventy percent of freshwater is used for food production.

Fishing: We are overfishing most species. We need to lessen the world's total catch.

Nature must be made use of in such a way that it is not diminished but rather continues to provide enduring yields in the longer term as well as in the short run. The advantages of environmental protection efforts, even when the costs are factored in, far outweigh the outlay.

Extensive poverty and unequal distribution of resources cause most of today's most serious and most threatening environmental problems. We must build environmental considerations into economic development.

Our next meeting was held near Oslo in June 1985. The Conservative Prime Minister, Kåre Willoch, spoke during the opening ceremony, in keeping with the way that we organized things in every country we visited. It was perhaps not with great enthusiasm that the government supported this meeting so close to the parliamentary elections in 1985, a time when environmental awareness was rapidly increasing in Norway.

During the Oslo meeting the famine in Africa and the worldwide population question commanded particular attention. Two hundred and fifty delegates from European voluntary organizations took part in the public hearings, together with our own Norwegian organizations, including both the trade unions and the representatives of business and industry.

We studied research projects for wave power on Norway's west coast, and the measurement areas for acid rain in the south. Being at Oslo fjord on Midsummer Eve was an experience none of the members has forgotten. To this day, they continue to talk to me about the light Norwegian summer night.

The Land of the Rain Forest

At the end of October the commission convened in São Paulo, the largest city in Brazil—the largest in South America, in fact. Brazil had just replaced a military regime with a democratic government. The most sensitive question politically was the rain forest.

The Brazilian authorities made it clear that they did not want us to discuss only the Amazon. They did not want any interference in domestic affairs. We would simply have to discuss rain forests in general. We had no problem with that.

In Brazil there were allegations that Indians were being forcibly uprooted in order to clear space for modern economic operation and investments. Brazil also had some of the world's most polluted industrial areas, such as the city of Cubatao, which we visited. It was frightening. The great attention that has since been focused upon the city's unusually high mortality rate had its effect. Today the city has been totally altered, and people can live there.

We also visited Manaus, the city that lies right in the heart of Amazonas, where the river is so wide that you can hardly see the other bank. The governor of Manaus had a reputation for being extremely well disposed toward industry. Rain forests and Indians had no place at all in the many plans that required his approval. We were invited to dinner with the governor with representatives from the media present. I prepared to give an after-dinner speech that dealt with these politically difficult questions. We worked hard to come up with the best formulations.

Perhaps the governor had an inkling that we might make our attitudes known in this speech as, early on in the dessert course he rose, thanked us for our presence, disappeared, and never heard my critical remarks.

We held public hearings in both São Paulo and Brasilia, dealing specifically with tropical rain forests, the international debt crisis, and the impact of the crisis upon the environment and development. The hearings in São Paulo turned into the most enthusiastic affair. The newly acquired freedom of expression and the Latin temperament brought things to a boil. When the hearings were officially over, some of the participants climbed up on stage and proclaimed that the proceedings must go on. They were too important to stop.

There were thousands of people there. It was hard to know whether to end the meeting as planned. We didn't want to disillusion the delighted participants. Things quieted down gradually, but it was a profound experience.

To Win Africa

We were very anxious to win support for the commission's recommendations from African quarters. We could live with the fact that the conservative Western governments were critical, because when our work was brought before the U.N., approval or disapproval would ultimately be expressed by a majority of countries' votes. But we could not survive if fifty African countries were unreceptive.

And in Africa environmental considerations had long been regarded as something that would slow development and increase the cost of industrialization and general progress.

In the summer of 1986 Mansour Khalid had attended the summit meeting of the Organization for African Unity (OAU) in order to ensure that we were able to present the commission's report at the summit meeting in the summer of 1987, before the U.N. was to consider the matter. We wanted to show Africa respect in this way. Khalid was one of Africa's own and was conversant in the special social code that applied in the OAU.

Zimbabwe's Finance Minister, Bernard Chidzero, was a member of our commission. He was an enormous man with a deep, resonant voice. A man of few words, whose words weighed heavily. He was an old revolutionary colleague of the Prime Minister and future President Robert Mugabe. Together they had overthrown the colonial power of Great Britain, but in a manner so careful that the upheavals were perceived as a model for the future peaceful transition to majority rule in South Africa.

Chidzero was now chairman of the development committee of the World Bank, one place where we were determined to bring about changes. The World Bank and the International Monetary Fund (IMF) are not like the U.N., in which each country has one vote. In the World Bank and the IMF, votes are apportioned according to economic strength. This was something the developing countries were greatly dissatisfied with, as it afforded the United States a very strong position and the opportunity to influence conditions governing loans and aid.

We were particularly anxious to introduce environmental considerations into World Bank affairs. Should, for example, the World Bank provide loans for the development of meat production in Botswana? What would the consequences be for the soil there if a rapidly expanding cattle population were to graze there? And, more problematically, who was to determine which environmental factors were to be considered? If Botswana's government had no objections, should the World Bank have any?

This raised the question of the limits of the countries' sovereignty, an emotionally charged question in Africa, especially in light of its most recent history.

The Air Zimbabwe plane from Frankfurt to Harare was full that September night. At the airport stood Prime Minister Mugabe, along with his whole government and the diplomatic corps. It was six o'clock in the morning and the diplomats could not have been enthusiastic about being called out to the airport, as was required by Zimbabwe's protocol.

I was quite unprepared for such a large-scale reception, but I had a dress that did not crease and managed to fix my hair after a night on the plane. We pulled ourselves together and stood stiffly at attention while the Norwegian national anthem, *"Ja vi elsker,"* was played. Then I inspected the honor guard. I worried that such press photos could be used to criticize my travel activity back home in Norway; fortunately the press showed other pictures of Mugabe and myself, with flowers in garlands around our necks.

The jacaranda trees have blue flowers. The whole city was full of blue trees. It was September, spring south of the equator and "fruit blossom time in Harare."

Julius Nyerere, the erstwhile President of Tanzania, had come to meet us. He was accompanied by Tanzania's Minister of Natural Resources, Gertrude Mongella, who later became the Secretary-General of the U.N. Women's Conference in Beijing. Our discussions won Nyerere over in favor of the environment and development. He said our broad approach had persuaded him.

Sanctions Against South Africa

During the official opening meeting, the convention hall next door to the Sheraton Hotel was completely full of schoolchildren who cheered and waved flags. Mugabe's national ZANU party had made a popular festival out of the meeting, busing in droves of supporters and onlookers.

Back home in Norway, in the U.N. and the world press, the situation in South Africa was the main issue. In my frigid, air-conditioned hotel room, I wore a lovely woolen shawl given to me by Margaret Thatcher during her recent visit to Norway, an ironic item of clothing given that South African apartheid had been a real point of contention between us. I was putting the finishing touches to my evening's speech, which would powerfully address the apartheid regime and the policy that Great Britain supported.

The main thrust of the speech concerned the world economy and the effect this had upon Africa's resources: More money was leaving Africa to pay loan interest and debt installments than was flowing in as investments and development aid. African countries were forced to gear their agricultural production to exports, rather than to food for their own populations. As more and more countries fell into the same straits, prices fell, and they had to produce even more to service their debts and to pay for essential imports. Thus, relaxation of debts was absolutely crucial. Strong agricultural subsidies and high tariffs in the north took the bottom out of the markets for those countries in the south that wanted to export agricultural products.

I concluded by making a comment in my role as Norwegian Prime Minister, since not everybody on the commission was in agreement with Norwegian policy. I announced the news that Norway would impose unilateral sanctions against South Africa. That was when all hell broke loose.

The African National Congress and the so-called "front-line states" had been calling for such sanctions by the West. But the West had resisted; many major companies had made good money out of trading with the apartheid regime. In Norway, the argument against unilateral action was that it would hit our trade and industry unreasonably hard and give our competitors an edge, without having any appreciable effect upon South Africa's economy.

But we had reached the point where we believed that Norway had to take the lead. The apartheid system was so extreme that unilateral measures were justified.

The press conference following my speech dealt with Norway

and South Africa, and the news circled the globe. For a whole week we were to have commission meetings and public hearings. Now everybody knew that we were there!

The public hearings in Harare showed that Africa was prepared to discuss the limitation of population growth. Hitherto there had been strong cultural barriers to this discussion. During the hearings Professor Dedeji, who headed the U.N.'s Economic Commission for Africa, proposed some drastic notions of imposing punitive taxes on families that had too many children. In some African countries the annual population growth was nearly four percent. With an economic growth close to zero, there would be even less money per inhabitant for schools and public health care. A rapid population growth is a sure road toward poorer living conditions for all. And where there were already food shortages, it was even clearer that poverty and population growth create a vicious circle. The same message would stand at the center of international politics in the nineties—in Rio in 1992, and even in Cairo in 1994.

Nairobi–Frankfurt–London–New York

The meetings in Africa took place just before the opening of the U.N. General Assembly. I was the only member of the commission who had access to the U.N. speaker's rostrum. Norway has kept its traditional position on the list of speakers all these years—second in the afternoon session on the actual opening day—a position that ensures good attendance among representatives.

I was told that it was in fact possible to reach New York in time if we were to follow this breathless itinerary: fly out from Nairobi at midnight on Sunday; land at about six in the morning in Frankfurt; then on to London and, from there, take the morning Concorde to New York, arriving at about nine on Monday morning, New York time. I agreed.

In Africa I had worked on the U.N. statement in the evenings, usually on my hotel bed. I consulted Maurice Strong on how I might best talk about the need for reforms in the U.N. organization itself. Maurice was highly critical of what he perceived as excessive bureaucracy. His proposals amounted to a powerful broadside. The diplomats in the Norwegian Foreign Ministry would be stunned.

The Sunday before our departure we were going to fax the proposals to New York so that copies could be made. At the telecom center that housed Nairobi's only fax machine, the man behind the counter replied in a mild, explanatory manner: "We don't send faxes on Sunday, sir." Our staff dictated the whole statement by telephone to New York.

In London we saw the morning papers. The previous night there had been a breakthrough at the European disarmament conference in Stockholm. Oslo hadn't advised us about this. And now my statement for the U.N., a few hours away, needed adjustment.

The Concorde takes three hours from London to New York. This meant we could get there in time for President Reagan's lunch for the NATO members. But on the runway the captain reported an oil leak that would need repair.

I managed to get to New York just in time for my speech to the General Assembly.

I said that even the U.N.'s strongest supporters, such as Norway, found ourselves allowing grounds for doubt as to whether the U.N. was able to discharge its tasks. I spoke of deficient personnel management and discipline, and the increasing lack of confidence in the U.N. budget, which provided for many redundant measures and duplicated efforts.

I criticized countries that had withheld their contributions, a criticism that I was to repeat for many years to come.

I spoke firsthand about the commission and of course about the unilateral Norwegian sanctions against South Africa, and I urged all countries to follow Norway's example.

The next day we flew back to Norway so that I could give a lunch in honor of West Germany's President, Richard von Weizsäcker, who was on a state visit. I gave a speech for him in German at Akershus Castle. I had accomplished a great deal over the previous fourteen days.

The Report's Conclusions

In Moscow in December 1986, the commission was ready to discuss in greater detail our conclusions and recommendations. We agreed about how to describe the principal content of the concept, "sustainable development."

The report had to contain a fundamental appreciation of the international economic conditions that composed the framework for social development. We were agreed upon "sector chapters" on population policy and the development of human resources; food security, regarding both the production and distribution of food; the protection of living species and ecosystems; the selection and composition of energy sources and technology; how industry could produce more while consuming fewer resources; and, finally, major urban problems, the challenges of the mega-cities growing at an explosive rate.

We also wanted to deal with peace and security, and address how war and rearmament could influence the resource base, and how a failing resource base could lead to catastrophes and war. A separate chapter was to deal with the earth's common resources, such as outer space and the oceans.

We would have to be measured and careful while proposing changes to the U.N. What we said here would be studied closely, that much we knew.

Those who had visited Moscow in advance to prepare the meetings were asked, "Is she going to meet Raisa?" There were many who thought it natural for the Norwegian Prime Minister to meet the Soviet leader's wife.

My colleagues gave an emphatic "no." This was as silly as asking if Gorbachev was going to meet Dennis Thatcher in London. After all, both of them were men. This was 1986, and still the Soviets as well as the Americans working on the commission considered it natural for me to meet Raisa.

"Sight-seeing in the Kremlin"

"Friday, December 5. Reserved time. Sight-seeing in the Kremlin," my Soviet program read. The commission was to be in Moscow for a whole week, and Norwegian planners had arranged a meeting for me with Gorbachev. It had been twelve years since a Norwegian Prime Minister had met the Soviet leader. The Soviets had continued to be noncommittal on whether the Prime Minister from a small country like Norway would even be allowed in to meet the Soviet leaders. It should not be seen to be an automatic right. That is why the program read "sight-seeing," when it actually meant a meeting with the top man.

The previous evening we had gathered to make preparations at the home of the Norwegian ambassador. The list of concerns we wanted to take up with the Soviet leaders was long. We discussed the ways in which we might bring up individual humanitarian matters. A number of dissidents under persecution needed outside help, and a visiting Western Prime Minister might ameliorate the situation by raising the matter directly with the Soviet leader.

The Kremlin really is worth "sight-seeing." A British Labor Party politician once wrote that there are no clocks in the Kremlin. The Russians and the Soviets have always had time on their side, in negotiations and in war. In the Kremlin, that is clear. Its walls tell about the eternal Russia.

During the Cold War years, the Kremlin and Red Square were used as a military parade ground for the Soviet Union to display its military strength. Many foreign guests have come to the Soviet Union and been cut down to size. In Stalin's day they were kept waiting in ignorance in their hotels until they were summoned to a meeting in the middle of the night—as then-Norwegian Foreign Minister and later U.N. Secretary-General Trygve Lie experienced in 1944.

Official talks between the Norwegian government and the Soviet leadership since World War II had often taken the form of Soviets' perpetual criticism of Norwegian security policy and our membership in NATO. I had myself experienced such criticism on many occasions, both in Oslo and in Moscow. At the same time, as neighbors, we had a number of other recurring issues, such as the question of Spitzbergen, the Arctic archipelago where the Soviet Union constantly kept an eye on Norway, despite the clauses in the Spitzbergen Treaty (which in 1920 neutralized the territory) that prohibit activity "for purposes of war." We, for our part, were strongly concerned that the Soviet Union should recognize and respect Norwegian sovereignty on Spitzbergen. On several occasions they put our will to the test.

At the beginning of the 1970s the question of demarcation between the Norwegian and Soviet continental shelf was tabled. The fact that this matter still remains unresolved shows the Russian reliance on time for help, and we have realized that we must show the same patience as they do. In this way, a small country can manage to be treated with the necessary respect by powerful Russia.

Human rights were also important to discuss with the government in Moscow. I chose on this occasion to take up the case of the Jewish dissident imprisoned by the Kremlin in Siberia, Ida Nudel, whom I had also discussed in previous contacts with the Soviet Union. Sometime after she was liberated, she visited me at my office in Oslo.

Since Andrei Sakharov was awarded the Nobel Peace Prize in 1975 and was exiled to Gorki in 1980, it was also completely justifiable for me to raise his case.

Mikhail Gorbachev and the Soviet Press

Gorbachev was a new kind of Soviet leader. He was well traveled in the West. Margaret Thatcher had said that he was a man she could do business with. Coming from her, this was clearly an expression of the greatest respect.

What was quite clear to me on the way in through the red walls of the Kremlin, past guards and gilded onion cupolas, was that Gorbachev represented a new generation. He wished to exercise strong influence upon the global development. It was essential for me to use my time with him well, because it was by no means certain that we would have many such opportunities to put forward Norwegian views and Norwegian foreign policy to the new Soviet leader.

I was anxious, and concentrated on figuring out how to leave the most important impression behind. What would I need to say before the meeting ended?

It was a special time. Eight months had elapsed since the Chernobyl accident, and it was barely two months since Reagan and Gorbachev's summit meeting in Reykjavík, where the two leaders had sat down together and nearly agreed upon a comprehensive nuclear disarmament, to the great joy of many people and to the dismay of others.

Gorbachev was open, with a clear gaze, sympathetic and sure. He received us with outstretched hand, clearly far more at ease among the press and the storm of their flashbulbs than other Soviet leaders were.

We established an immediate rapport. He explained, without prompting, that his daughter was also a doctor, and that she had recently advised him about the effects of industrialized society upon health and environment. Precisely what the commission was to discuss over the next few days.

He appeared to be inadequately briefed regarding our borders in the Barents Sea, though he would become better acquainted with the issue in the years to come. His genuine and immediate reaction was that our two nations could not continue to have unresolved border issues. Here his bureaucracy had clearly held back information from him about a matter that had already been under negotiation for sixteen years. After our talks in Moscow, we would shortly experience some movement in these matters from the Soviets.

———

On the Saturday evening of our stay, our hosts invited us to see *Sleeping Beauty* at the Bolshoi Theater. It was a fabulous production and we had the best possible view from what was still referred to as the Czar's box. In the intermission amid amazingly extravagant pastries, sugar-icing sculptures, and fruit centerpieces, Soviet deputy ministers conversed shyly with us about environmental protection.

The meeting of our commission was to be an important test of the new openness in the Soviet Union. The press swarmed around us. Nature programs were popular on Soviet television, and the Norwegian explorer Thor Heyerdahl is a well-known and respected figure. Nature programs were permitted even during the most repressive periods, and consequently environmental issues did not seem threatening to the "Establishment."

We noted a greater candor among the Soviet press than we had been used to. We had engaged Juri Senkevich to lead our own press conferences. He had been with Thor Heyerdahl on the *Kon-Tiki, Ra,* and *Tigris* voyages, and enjoyed high status in the Soviet Union.

The list of Soviet media who wanted interviews was long, and we wished to be accommodating and to support the new openness.

Hectic Final Stretch

After the Moscow meeting, we put together a writing team led by Nitin Desai, an economist from India who had worked in Geneva from the very beginning and who became Deputy Secretary-General of the U.N. following the Rio conference. He was joined by Lloyd Timberlake, a well-known writer on environmental matters, and Linda Starke, an American who edited the annual report from the World Watch Institute, *The State of the World.*

Almost every member of the commission was given responsibility for a specific theme or chapter of our report. There were many drafts. Some wished for a report with drastic proposals, and some for just the opposite.

It proved to be easier to agree upon the actual analysis than on our expression of it. And the U.N. Environmental Programme and the diplomatic quarter in Nairobi were now extremely impatient to see the report. We believed it was still too soon, but we requested a meeting with a UNEP representative. The chairman, A. Moumen Choudhury of Bangladesh, came to Oslo for a briefing from me.

He arrived in a state of shock. He had been picked up at the Grand Hotel by a staff member who brightly suggested that they might walk, since it was no more than five minutes to the government building. It was freezing cold, and Choudhury was a man of the tropics. After the meeting he was driven in a warm car back to the hotel.

An international office such as I held enabled Norway to have a range of contacts in these years that we had never had before. Of course, we had previously seen Olof Palme's commission give Sweden a high profile, and we saw no reason not to do the same for Norway. The Foreign Ministry even asked me to investigate ways in which the commission's international circuit of meetings could best be used to promote Norway's interests at the same time.

Akasaka Prince Hotel in Tokyo. The decisive meeting. We were almost at the door. We had to review every sentence in the report and create the feeling of joint responsibility necessary to position the report squarely on the international agenda.

There would have to be compromises, but our report must not be diluted.

The meeting room had no windows. We could not see whether it was night or day. Nor could we feel it, so heavily jet-lagged were we by the time difference.

In the middle of it all, there was Project Japan, an initiative for Norwegian fish exports to Japan. It was an example of Norwegian events run in tandem with the commission's meetings. Norwegian fish exports to Japan have been a success for ten years now, and tonight, two hundred Japanese fish buyers had been invited to sample the wares. That evening there were prime culinary opportunities involving sushi made from Norwegian salmon and mackerel, and—most exotic—whole, deep-fried capelin, a small fish that, along with herring, is a key species in the Barents.

The secretariat worked night and day. They sat in on our meetings in order to help us find workable formulations. In the evenings and at night they sat in front of their computers and wrote and amended, amended and wrote.

Near the end we still had a handful of unresolved issues. Nuclear power was one. The U.S., Soviet, Japanese, and German members and the Colombian, Margarita de Botero, made a drama of the final phase. She would only agree to a complete rejection of all nuclear power. She was Green, she said. How could she disappoint the many people who believed in her?

The American and the Soviet did not know what to do. It was totally alien to their concept of normalcy to reject all use of nuclear power. I spent a lot of time with Margarita in the breaks, tried out different wordings that might untangle the problem.

We managed in the end. "Nuclear power can only be acceptable if final solutions are found for all the unresolved problems that it causes." Some called this a round egg that satisfied everyone. No, the truth is that we have not solved the problems of safety, and the results of nuclear accidents are such that society cannot accept the risk.

Margarita was moved when we found a solution. She gave a spontaneous speech in which, with strongly emotional turns of phrase, she said that love for the commission and the people who believed in it had enabled her to put her future and her career at stake by agreeing to a compromise.

My own relief soon turned into sorrow when I was informed that my Foreign Minister, Knut Frydenlund, had been taken unconscious to the National Hospital and that doctors held no hope for his recovery. Knut was older than I, but we both belonged to that generation that was fundamentally positive toward NATO. With his good judgment and wise words, he had been a very close and good colleague for many years. He had his own way of recognizing a small country's possibilities. I took the first plane possible back to Oslo.

Not the End, but the Beginning

The whole winter we had carried on work to prepare the launch of the report. Bill Ruckleshaus, our U.S. member, was a Republican who had been head of the Environmental Protection Agency (EPA) under Nixon. Bill wanted us to come to Washington and present the report there. He would take up the matter with George Shultz, the Secretary of State. In civilian life, Bill was a lawyer and had a lucrative practice. Bill had a great sense of humor, and his capricious human aspects made it difficult to believe in the stereotype of Americans as the poor countries' opponents, as it is often portrayed in the U.N. We nurtured no illusions about U.S. policy, but Bill made it possible to find consensus in the commission. After Tokyo he was reasonably satisfied. He had learned a lot.

Contact would be made with Howard Baker, Reagan's chief of staff, whom we knew, and with Gus Speth, head of the World Resources Institute. Jim and I agreed: If we did not get to meet Reagan, but only a Deputy Secretary of State, we would not go.

From then on, there was a complete lid on all information. The launch was to take place in London on April 27. It would not be a real event if everything in the report was already known.

Still, it was in keeping with protocol for the U.N. to receive the report before it was published. U.N. Secretary-General Perez de Cuellar was going to attend a meeting of the U.N.'s special organizations in Rome on April 22. So we would present the document there and then.

As letters, invitations, and requests for interviews started to stream in from all over the world, it became clear that our good report was not the end, but the beginning. But the U.N. mandate held that the commission would cease to exist within a reasonable time limit.

Jim sent me a long note asking me to take on the principal responsibility for ensuring that the report was followed up on in the best possible way. This required access to diplomatic resources, which in turn required a government willing to take on such a task.

Norway was willing. And Norwegian diplomats and emissaries had first-class status in many international organizations and capitals.

We set up a schedule for my activity that year that was quite demanding.

After the Rome meeting with the U.N. Secretary-General, it was off to London, to launch the report and meet with Margaret Thatcher. The spring and summer would include follow-up dates in Brussels to meet with European Union ministers; Stockholm, for the Nordic launch; Nairobi, for the committee meeting of the UNEP; New Delhi, for official presentation to India and Asia; Addis Ababa, for an Organization of African Unity summit meeting; and Denver, Colorado, for the North American launch of our report at the World Wilderness Congress. Finally, there was the report's formal presentation at the U.N. in the autumn.

In Rome, the U.N. Secretary-General received a decidedly short version of our study. The main points were: We could not continue with the current energy-consumption pattern without destroying the atmosphere; we had to come to grips with poverty and bring about a new era of international economic growth; the 1960s had made a significant contribution to the world's development, and in many respects had had a positive effect upon the world's population, but the 1970s landed the environmental bill on the table.

The commission had been careful to show that it *is* possible to simultaneously achieve a better environment, more health care and education, and less poverty.

In our meeting I placed particular stress upon the responsibility of the U.N. Secretary-General for coordinating the work of U.N. agencies toward our goals.

The report delivered, Perez de Cuellar sent Tolba and Khalid away and we talked about Norway and the U.N. He expressed his thanks for Norwegian General Martin Vadseth's service, at the disposal of the U.N., toward termination of the war between Iran and Iraq. We also talked about various people. Perez de Cuellar was positive with regard to Shimon Peres, and skeptical about Yitzhak Shamir. On the American side he considered Deputy Secretary of State John Whitehead to be an important supporting player. He was surprisingly open with me.

This was one of many conversations I had with de Cuellar, a sensitive, intelligent man who was quite clear that his mandate was to be not too strong a leader. He spoke quietly and diplomatically, apparently wishing to avoid confrontations.

The Environmental Movement Goes to London

The British Ministry of the Environment was the enthusiastic host of a successful launch of our report in the Queen Elizabeth II Centre in London on April 27, 1987. The report was a convincing contribution toward international cooperation for a more just distribution between countries and within countries. And it was a thorough analysis of the need for growth, for a new kind of growth that strengthens the resource base.

Least satisfied were those in the environmental movement in favor of zero growth, a solution that the commission considered to be totally wrong.

Even if not everyone was in accord, the Norwegian environmental movement was to change from a relatively strong pro-commission attitude in 1987 to an out-and-out campaign directed against the government and the Labor Party. I often spoke with colleagues abroad about this. In the United States and Canada it was normal for people in environmental organizations to be given positions in national environmental administrations, because they were known to be the best professionally. It is my impression that there are not enough economists and engineers in the environmental movement in Norway.

I used this British trip as a chance for a brief visit with Margaret Thatcher about environmental questions and Norwegian-British matters as well as the burning issues of security policy and nuclear disarmament.

Number 10 Downing Street

For Norwegians, indeed for children who grew up in wartime and 1950s Europe, Number 10 Downing Street is part of our own history. In the radio reports from London that our parents listened to illegally during the German occupation, this address was the symbol of free Europe. Britain was our foremost ally, as well as host to the lawful Norwegian government during the war.

A solid, well-maintained door with a brass knob opened into an ostensibly normal house set in a little cul-de-sac. In the hall inside, selected photographers and press representatives were waiting on the left, along the stairs that led up to the building's office section and the Cabinet Office. Shortly after I was announced, my host came out smiling to bid me welcome. A few pleasant words for the reporters and then we went upstairs to the British government's permanent meeting room.

Thatcher pointed out with a smile that she had just evicted a couple of cabinet ministers from the room because she was to meet the Norwegian Prime Minister, indicating that we colleagues had to find ourselves some space, away from the more routine affairs. It was doubtless her way of making clear that she had gone out of her way to find time in her busy schedule to enable us to continue our dialogue from Oslo last fall. I had a couple of members of my staff with me. Margaret Thatcher had only her press secretary and close confidant of many years, Bernard Ingham.

The environment report was not what concerned her most, but she did relay the highly complimentary appraisal from her Environment Minister, who, I noted, had given a good speech that day.

A Conversation About Gorbachev

Thatcher might not have been very interested in the environment, but her commitment was stronger and her analysis was more thoroughly prepared with respect to Gorbachev and the disarmament issues. Since our own last meeting, we had both met Gorbachev. She was concerned about his last major speech, which she considered to have been uncommonly well prepared, and she was keen to hear my impression of it. I said that I had perceived Gorbachev to be a committed, hardworking politician who communicated very well. He clearly wanted results. He expressed a fundamental belief in Communism but wanted to ensure that it worked in practice. Thatcher observed that Gorbachev had conducted talks without supporting notes and that he was a very dominating sort of person.

I gave her my own impression of a person who maintained command of a range of areas brought up in our talks but who still possessed some of the old Stalinist analyses and constructions. This had been evident when he quite simply rejected the idea that there existed any kind of narcotics problem in the Soviet Union!

I also recounted that I had shared with Gorbachev my own medical experience, along with my evaluation of Norway's problems despite our restrictive policy toward drugs. He paused for a while and said, "Why, I have a daughter who is also a doctor." Three weeks later, we heard reports of a comprehensive presentation by Gorbachev about drugs, which he now treated as the new major national problem to be combated. I had no doubt that he had asked for a real briefing and updated information as a direct result of our conversation.

Thatcher pointed out that information continued to be heavily filtered before it reached the new leadership. Gorbachev was himself well aware that his Communist system did not work, she said, and that it was not possible to increase production without wage differentiation, accountability for results, and new incentives. Gorbachev knew what he wanted to achieve but not how to achieve it: That was how she put it. It was a quite precise analysis.

I shall never forget how, a year or two earlier, the British Establishment—and no doubt many others within the alliance—had been disturbed, shocked even, at the apparent naïveté shown by the British Prime Minister, a woman who had declared that Gorbachev was "a man we can do business with." I had then not yet personally met Margaret Thatcher, but my intuition told me that here was a courageous lady who was not easily fooled.

"We must maintain a nuclear force"

I was very keen to hear what Margaret Thatcher had to say about the next step in the long struggle surrounding the medium-range missiles (intermediate range nuclear forces, or INF) in Europe. I said that I was soon bound for Washington, where I was to meet both President Reagan and Secretary of State Shultz. To them I would stress the importance of the West's reactions to Gorbachev's latest proposal of a zero option for such weapons. Now was the time to take him at his word. The dual-track NATO decision of 1979 was, after all, a conditional deployment resolution that was to be followed up by a parallel effort to achieve full disarmament in nuclear weapons categories. Politically it would be immensely difficult to win understanding if we were now to reject a solution that politicians and public opinion had worked for since 1979.

Thatcher actually agreed that this was a weighty argument. Then she went through the basic tenets of her disarmament philosophy, which did not argue for elimination of nuclear weapons. She had expressed as much to Gorbachev, and as a result, the possibility existed of a conventional war escalating into a nuclear war. The reality of the NATO dual-track decision had to determine how one was to respond to Gorbachev's proposal, but Thatcher did not believe that the West would be able to withstand a conventional assault by the Soviet Union.

She stressed that we must therefore possess a nuclear capability since we could not trust the Soviets. Total nuclear disarmament, in a "zero solution" agreement, must be capable of verification. She then went into arguments concerning the importance of short- and medium-range missiles—INF missiles were most threatening and destabilizing because of their extremely short flight time. INF missiles were to be a feature of later phases in the disarmament dialogue between East and West. Thatcher stressed that we must at all times maintain a nuclear force as a response to Soviet chemical weapons, since it was our only means of responding. Thus she was able to see the political efficacy of the dual-track decision of NATO of 1979, but she had extremely strong reservations given the possible long-term consequences of the Soviets' superiority in conventional and chemical weapons.

I appreciated that both the political dialogue that Margaret Thatcher had maintained with Gorbachev, and Reagan's "near agreement" with the Soviet leader in Reykjavík the previous autumn would lead to an important step forward in disarmament and arms control. It would be a real breakthrough for the concept of common security, as the Palme Commission called it.

I looked forward to my meeting with Reagan. We had received the go-ahead at the last minute, which tends to be the way with Washington.

Secretary of State Shultz

In Washington it was high summer. I received Secretary of State Shultz in my room at the Hotel Willard, just a stone's throw from the White House, the afternoon before I was to see the President. We had met before. He was a friendly, open, and efficient representative of his country, easy to establish contact with.

I thanked him for his willingness to consult with us and other members of NATO and reiterated our view that we were in favor of the most comprehensive of the three options that the Americans had put forward as a response to Gorbachev's proposal. I actually found it hard to believe that there was opposition to this solution.

Shultz asked me for my position regarding the short-range missiles. He was rather dejected at the widespread lack of knowledge of the facts. Many people believed that the term "short-range missile" included all nuclear weapons other than the long-range ones, and that no short-range missiles would mean a de-nuclearization of Europe. That was simply not the case!

It sounded as though Shultz was slighting the British Prime Minister's cautious position. He stressed that even following a zero solution for short-range missiles, a nuclear arsenal would be maintained in Europe that would keep the doctrine of flexible response intact. Such an agreement would be the first example of a significant reduction in nuclear weapons. The President was very keen to bring this about, said Shultz. Thatcher and Reagan felt that they had virtually come under suspicion for having set objectives and believing in the possibility of achieving results in Reykjavík. Clearly Shultz was ready to follow up on the President's intentions.

The Secretary of State could only shake his head over the Soviet negotiating technique. What was on the table one day had disappeared by the next. Yes, I thought, that was just how the Soviets had perceived things as well, when Reykjavík ended with an empty table. The proposals for a nuclear-free world had been withdrawn because of the disagreement over whether the U.S. Strategic Defense Initiative Program (SDI, popularly known as "Star Wars") should be included in the deal.

Shultz explained that he had discussed the zero solution for short-range missiles with Gorbachev, and had insisted strongly that it would have to be global. Since Gorbachev had said he was in agreement with this, he believed the issue had been resolved.

But in Geneva, the Soviet Union had recently proposed a solution limited to Europe. Furthermore, they had for the first time included the warheads of the West German Pershing I missiles in the negotiations. Shultz quoted Reagan, who had said that it was not that weapons created distrust, but rather that distrust led to arming.

Shultz had had meetings and an open discussion with Soviet authors who were now able to publish what had long since been banned. Like Thatcher, he had appeared in a long interview on Soviet television, on condition that it was not to be cut or edited. The only thing to mar his appearance was the Soviet failure to translate a few words: "You should leave Afghanistan; they don't want you there." The omission only attracted greater attention—and Shultz was able to say how many troops the United States believed they had there.

My comment on this interesting account was that this, of course, showed that progress was happening in the Soviet Union. Then Shultz rapped his knuckles against the table and smiled: "It remains to be seen what this will lead to and how long it will last."

"In my opinion the trend is irreversible," I said. "People will remember what happens." Shultz had received a similar reaction from

Soviet intellectuals. Moreover, Gorbachev knew that the society would stagnate unless it was opened up.

Nevertheless, Shultz said, the Russians had an inbred capacity for cruelty that could be traced right back to the old Czar and that was embedded far deeper than Communism. So, "We must keep our fingers crossed."

I took up the question of what we in the West should do in order to stimulate the right kind of development in the U.S.S.R. He repeated his characterization of Soviet maliciousness but then agreed that the Soviets' positive steps were to be encouraged.

I proposed that we should do more to strengthen economic exchanges with the Soviet Union, which could contribute toward greater openness. Shultz agreed, providing there was a commercial basis for trade, excluding state subsidization. Care must also be shown with regard to trade involving goods of military significance. Even though there was not much ground to be gained, I again emphasized the importance of active U.S. involvement with regard to influencing international economy and world trade. Shultz concluded by pointing out that it was the solidarity of the alliance that had created the opportunities that now existed.

Shultz visited Norway later on. It was just before Christmas, and in the evening, after the political talks, we gathered around the grand piano at the government's guest house after dinner. Arm in arm, we sang "White Christmas" and other American Christmas songs. I had learned the lyrics in school in Brooklyn.

The Man in the White House

My first meeting in the White House thus came about as a direct consequence of the commission's report on environment and development. The environmental issue was not the most popular one during the Reagan administration, but still, many Americans took it seriously—and Norway was an important ally.

When I arrived at the White House, the Norwegian press was in position in the summer sunshine, in the allocated area left of the lawn by the drive up to the main entrance. I was greeted by a friendly woman from the White House protocol department.

We had to wait a few minutes in the Cabinet Office. Vice President George Bush stuck his head round the door to say hello. I had talked to him about the commission when he visited Norway in 1984, when I was leader of the opposition.

Reagan was friendliness personified, charming in the way we had all seen him on television. "You had a fine talk with Secretary of State Shultz yesterday, I hear." He asked me to brief him about Norwegian views on arms control.

I thought it right to point out that we were in the middle of a gratifying development, and that we could now bring about an agreement we had wished for ever since 1979, especially in light of what he himself had initiated and achieved.

Reagan believed that an agreement appeared to be within reach, but that it would nevertheless not bring about a change of heart for our Soviet friends. The skepticism was deep-rooted, in him as it was in Shultz.

I said that Europe should appreciate the good results being negotiated, and expressed consternation at a strongly critical article by Nixon and Kissinger, which had appeared earlier in the *New York Times*. We must not now put obstacles in the way of every sensible agreement, I argued.

The President then touched upon the problem Margaret Thatcher had discussed in London: the danger of Soviet superiority in conventional weapons. I pointed out that President Reagan himself had gone for the zero option in his speech in 1981. Now that the Russians were meeting him halfway, it seemed a shame to withdraw.

The President wanted to know if I thought that the Chernobyl accident had made Gorbachev more receptive to new ideas. I confirmed that it had made a deep impression in the Soviet Union, which I had visited the same year that the accident occurred. Reagan's comment was that one warhead alone equaled two Chernobyl accidents.

Shultz had asked me to summarize my conversation with Margaret Thatcher when I finally met with Reagan. Doing so gave me the opportunity to put forward some important arguments about the historical context of the current negotiations—and the chance to say that I now felt that the British Prime Minister would ultimately support President Reagan. I also declared that European countries would now have to support the U.S. President, who had requested clear advice in a letter to the allies.

Reagan added that the issue also had a moral aspect. Humanity had developed weapons that were "horrible." We based our peace and security upon the threat of using such weapons. There must be another route toward security.

We were agreed on this point when National Security Adviser Frank Carlucci entered to remind the President of an imminent cabinet meeting on trade policy. I was aware that our meeting had already far exceeded our allocated time, because we had established such a good dialogue.

Reagan had not finished. He shared with me a little anecdote before moving on. At an economic summit, Thatcher, who had chaired the meeting, had taken a delegate to task for being "out of line." The person concerned had remonstrated with Thatcher, who had remained silent. When, after the meeting, Reagan told her that she had been right and should not have accepted such a scolding, she answered: "Women have the wisdom to know when men are being childish." *He* was quite a different sort of man, and he admired Margaret Thatcher. We established a fine contact—and I was able to go out to the Norwegian press in excellent spirits.

Capitol Hill Launch

The letter inviting fifty selected guests to our presentation of the commission's report before the U.S. Congress made it appear as though our work were the most important that had ever occurred politically in this area. The letter made wonderful reading. It was signed Albert Gore, Jr., Democratic Senator from Tennessee. But, as usual with Congress, those who had been invited did not necessarily turn up. The key people concerned, senators and congressmen, might drop in or send a staff member.

Nonetheless, it was a full house, with some hundred people assembled, when we presented the commission's report. We found
that we had many supporters in the United States from then on.
Environmental interest was increasing. Knowledge was increasing.
The ozone layer and climate changes were demonstrating that environmental action was now more than a matter of protecting plants
and animals or fighting industrial pollution. We underlined the relationship between the environment and the economy, as well as
the technological level we had reached. We had to stop our hereto-
fore uninhibited competitive behavior and move toward forward-
looking and environment-friendly patterns of development, with
less pollution, more recycling, and less consumption of energy.

Jacques Delors, president of the European Commission, had
shown interest in our report right from the start. And soon, in early
May, I was in Brussels to discuss the report with the European
Union and Belgium's Prime Minister, Wilfred Martens. Then, on
May 9, the first anniversary of the Labor government, we were in
Saltsjöbaden, near Stockholm, where the Swedish government had
arranged a conference on development policy. I felt it was right to
carry out the Nordic launch of our report in Sweden, which had
played such a central role in the setting up and financing of the
commission.

India and Addis Ababa

When the report was considered by the U.N.'s Economic and Social
Council, as was the normal procedure for any UNEP proposal to
the U.N. General Assembly, the developing countries were reported
to be skeptical. They perceived "sustainable development" as a new
set of conditions to be imposed on loans and aid from North to
South. This was a very sensitive issue for many developing countries.

I often explained that in my estimation, the countries in the
North were also dependent upon broad political support from their
own people, and that it would not always be easy to make funds

available to developing countries unless it was sufficiently demonstrated that the objectives were sensible from the perspective of both the environment and development.

The series of regional presentations took us next to New Delhi at the beginning of July. Rajiv Gandhi met me at the airport; it was 113 degrees Farenheit. In the course of my stay I was invited to the home of Gandhi and his wife, Sonia. We talked about heading governments. Rajiv Gandhi seemed to approach his job with mixed feelings. In the garden right outside the window where we sat, his mother had been gunned down by one of her own bodyguards.

His thoughts while we sat together must also have touched upon Olof Palme. There was, after all, a geographical and thematic relationship between Palme's work and mine. The three of us had been together in February 1986 when the Palme Commission had held meetings in India, just weeks before his assasination. Tragically, it would happen also to Rajiv, when a Tamil woman blew herself up in front of him, only a few years later.

Travels then took us to the headquarters of the Organization for African Unity (OAU), in Ethiopia's capital, Addis Ababa. There was a certain symbolism to this. Ethiopia has never been a colony. The Ethiopians are a proud people. Even the poor and the hungry, of which there are many.

Africa's support was important in the U.N. With me in Addis Ababa was the Foreign Ministry's newly appointed special ambassador for environment and development, Bjarne Lindstrøm. He had extensive U.N. experience and knew Africa from having been consul general in Cape Town and a principal connection with the ANC and opposition groups in South Africa.

Once a year the African nations' government heads meet at the OAU summit. This was the meeting that we had wanted to be invited to. Never before had any Western head of government addressed this assembly.

The headquarters consist of, among other things, fifty identical bungalows. This is where the heads of state stay. Over the course of the days-long meeting, we saw small and large delegations wandering to and fro between the bungalows. This was the time for bilateral talks between Africa's leaders.

The Secretary-General, Ide Oumarou of Niger, invited me to lunch in his home, where we were received by his three wives. They were lined up according to seniority by the entrance when we arrived.

The Ethiopian head of state, Menghistu Haile Mariam, also wished to meet me. Menghistu had come to power by means of a violent coup. There were stories of violence within the imperial palace itself, which Menghistu had converted into a presidential mansion—a fairy-tale building. It now appeared to be completely empty apart from the guards, who kept watch inside a somewhat overgrown garden, in which Emperor Haile Selassie had kept lions.

This was a regime that was nearing its end. Menghistu was sitting on some kind of throne when I was shown into the room. At his feet sat the Foreign Minister—the only Ethiopian present apart from the guards. The Foreign Minister took notes and prompted in a way that made me think of *A Thousand and One Nights*.

Menghistu was dissatisfied with the fact that there was no longer any cooperation between the Norwegian and Ethiopian navies. This was something of an unusual element in the talks program, and no one had expected such a twist. He also had some critical comments to make about the freedom that exiled Ethiopians and Eritreans enjoyed in Norway. Menghistu was evidently not used to being contradicted or participating in arguments among equals.

Only Muammar Gadhafi stayed away from the summit meeting; all the other African leaders were present. There were short talks with several people, including Egypt's President Hosni Mubarak, who clearly liked what he had heard about the commission. With him was Boutros Boutros-Ghali, the Egyptian Deputy Foreign Minister who later became Secretary General of the U.N. I also met the South African ANC leader Oliver Tambo and the Palestinian leader Yasser Arafat, whom I had encountered several times before.

I had put a lot of work into the speech I gave. The African

members of the commission who were present, Mansour Khalid, Mohamed Sahnoun of Algeria, and Bukar Shaib of Nigeria, were pleased that it showed respect and understanding for Africa. The conference room in Africa Hall is round, and people sit close together. The atmosphere was one of deep concentration. The reception was good. Many heard for probably the first time the analysis that links the principal inequalities of the world economy to environmental and resource problems.

I went through a list of the international plans and resolutions that had been adopted. Africa had recently subjected itself to considerable self-criticism for unwise development and poverty. Now the countries of the North would have to display greater consideration. The report "Our Common Future" offered a concept around which all countries should be able to unite.

The United Nations—and the Future

Shortly before "Our Common Future" was to be formally presented to the General Assembly, I was asked to speak at the Kennedy School of Government at Harvard on Norwegian oil and energy policy.

On the plane from London I met Henry Kissinger, whom I asked to read through my energy speech. I had taken the previous year's drop in oil prices as a point of departure to argue in favor of a long-term oil price that would reflect the real value of oil. In this way investments could be made more secure and research planned over a longer timetable. Kissinger was quite clearly taken by the fact that I had placed so much emphasis upon policy and upon the reining in of market forces. But there was every reason for the change. The history of oil is a political history. Oil has started wars and has contributed toward ending them. Why else did Hitler want to be in Baku?

Americans have never been keen to hear the international perspective, but they realize that it is necessary. I said that the developing countries would need more energy, while we in the West and North must stabilize our own energy consumption. A 50 percent

reduction is possible, if these countries concentrate on greater energy efficiency and on a far stronger research effort into conservation and alternative energy sources.

The busy summer had given way to autumn when I returned to
the United States to present our report to the U.N. In New York, I
talked with both Prime Minister Robert Mugabe in his capacity as
leader of the OAU and Prime Minister Rajiv Gandhi, who held the
leadership of the Non-Aligned Nations. They had both come on the
same errand. Danish Prime Minister, Poul Schlüter, too, who was
chairman of the Common Market, also came to the U.N. I appreciated this greatly. Together the three represented an overwhelming
number of the countries in the world.

The meeting started off with a speech from the President of the
Maldives. He spoke on behalf of the rest of us, because he was a
head of state, and Mugabe and Gandhi were "only" heads of government. He was not big; shorter than I, he had to have an extra
step in order to see over the lectern. He spoke quietly about his
country and the climatic threats that it faced. The highest point on
the Maldives is only about eight feet above the normal high-water
mark. The country could, quite simply, disappear into the sea as
a result of the greenhouse effect, at some time in the twenty-first
century.

I had dinner with several commission members in the evening.
We had to adopt a position regarding the commission's future. We
remarked that the Palme Commission still existed, held meetings,
and adopted resolutions. Yet two factors argued against our continuing. First, our mandate from the U.N. was fulfilled. That mandate
had afforded us decisive influence, and we would not have its automatic legitimacy if we continued independent of it. Second, the
commission's distinctive openness—the public hearings we had
held in many countries before and after the report—was relatively
expensive. The Palme Commission was less ambitious and so had
been able to manage with a lower budget.

We also noted that the small secretariat we had established in
Oslo would be overtaxed by the inquiries that continued to flow

into the commission from around the world. We simply had no mandate to act on behalf of the commission once it was dissolved.

The head of administration, Chip Lindner, who had barely slept for three years, volunteered to set up and operate, on his own initiative, a separate foundation in Geneva, which could be approached by all those who sought more information about the commission and its work. Indeed, the Centre for Our Common Future began operation by the end of that year. It was a relief, and a wonderful point of contact for which we would be glad on several occasions.

But the assignment itself was over. Now it was up to all who had read and heard "Our Common Future" to put the report into responsible practice.

Government of Women, 1986–89

11

It is May 1986. The days and nights are bright, the air full of anticipation. Norway is about to get a new government, one that is younger, and one in which eight of the eighteen members are women. This was something quite unprecedented, and not only in Norwegian history; the news of the Norwegian government of women spreads worldwide. We are actually setting a record!

But this is not the thought uppermost in my mind as I make my way to the Royal Palace on that Friday, May 9. I know that we are facing difficult times. Willoch's government has resigned, Norway is in an economic crisis, and as a minority government, we now need to summon all our energies and set about creating a viable economic course for the country.

The government of women comes in on a wave of enthusiasm, and indeed, expectations of a new direction are high. But not everyone has realized the gravity of our position. Spending continues, and so does borrowing. This is still the time of the yuppie.

It was a big day, too, for the six-year-old who came up to me after the May First procession and said, "I thought you were just someone in a movie!" Yet there was little glamor those early mornings, when I was up at the crack of dawn, Olav ironing my dress, I washing my hair.

The events and impressions of the last fourteen days are etched in my mind: Willoch's attempt to force the Labor Party to its knees, met with the biggest upsurge in Labor Party support in decades.

The Fall of the Conservative Prime Minister

Kåre Willoch had been no easy adversary. He was sharp-tongued and long on experience. He was fully capable of exploiting his superiority—twelve years older than I, and male—with irony and sophistication. I had been too long obsessed with trying to win by arguing better. As a woman and the head of a so-called "soft" Ministry for five years, I had also felt that I had to demonstrate sufficient knowledge about economic matters.

A younger woman often feels an obligation to demonstrate that she is as competent as an older man. Indeed, this sense of obligation frequently drives many women both inside and outside politics. You not only have to be better than a man; you also must be able to prove it.

From time to time I became truly furious because I saw that Willoch was smart enough to escape from problems by dishonest means. It was foolish to show my indignation. But TV is a most difficult medium because it exaggerates emotions. You have to remember to be calm.

Norwegian TV became the main arena for campaigns as recently as 1981, but media training was not yet common. Nevertheless, I learned from my own experiences by looking at videos taken from debates at the party office and discussing them with close coworkers in the Parliamentary Group and in the Group Secretariat.

It wasn't easy. I could not pretend to be someone else. I also sensed from regular people around the country that they became engaged because I was so personally involved, because they saw that I had a message. No doubt training is necessary, but most important is to be oneself!

In 1985 Labor got 41 percent of the votes. It was my best election as Party Leader, not least because we increased our lead over the single biggest non-socialist party. Prime Minister Willoch and company went on the defensive and would have to give up eight months later.

The New Gro?

During the campaign of 1985 there was much talk in the media about "the new Gro." I had left my statistics at home. I was more relaxed. I was best when I threw my script away and still remembered my message, particularly when I spoke about the future.

Was I new? No, but I had acquired more experience and I was inspired by the feeling of strong support during the campaign. We had come to a crossroads; there was no longer anything to gain by attacking me for being a woman. That approach no longer worked.

The Election of 1985

With the parliamentary election of 1985 the political landscape changed. The Conservative/Center coalition no longer had the majority of the parliamentary vote. To carry a majority vote, they had become dependent on Carl I. Hagen and his Progressive Party's two votes. In the Norwegian parliamentary tradition, however, a government has the option to stay in power until a vote of no confidence opposes it or until the government itself draws the conclusion that it cannot continue due to a lack of support on key policies. A government might draw this conclusion as a consequence of a key vote on an important policy question.

Hagen was a clearheaded and tough player. To make matters worse for the existing government and for the Conservatives, Labor had become attractive to the Center Party and the Christian People's Party because of their strong dislike for Hagen. These two parties considered the Progressives to be worse than the plague.

There was, of course, no non-socialist alternative without Hagen. But instead of resigning, Willoch chose simply to declare that the government ought to have sufficient support both from the Progressives—and from Labor—to continue governing!

I think Willoch was overconfident in his analysis. He first declared that there was still a non-socialist majority and that this was the basis for continuing a non-socialist government. He then argued that Labor had to accept and support his government, in order to avoid being branded as irresponsible. If he did not have his way, he knew he would have to step down. So he chose to try to bully me and Labor into subservience.

Willoch Steps Down

Willoch counted on his minority coalition without first checking the parliamentary basis for it by making an agreement with Hagen. Despite his dependence on Hagen, Willoch treated him as an outsider, and Hagen grew less willing to support governmental policies. And Labor, of course, never gave Willoch any pledge of support.

During the winter of 1986 the economy deteriorated, not least because of dramatically falling oil prices. More than a year earlier, the Willoch government had introduced a budget, typically tailored for the upcoming general election, catering to the special wishes of the parties of the Middle, in particular, offering more money for the municipalities. The result was a more relaxed finance policy with increased public spending yet less public income because of tax reductions, a priority for the Conservatives. The bureaucrats in the Ministry of Finance must have been in great despair. The impact on the Norwegian economy was serious, even before the dramatic fall in oil prices.

Now there was no way around cuts in government spending. The Labor Party did not agree with Willoch's proposals, and Hagen was not willing to lend support either. The government fell. The Conservatives had not been willing to compromise so that we could support the austerity package.

The Conservatives were responsible for the fall. But Labor could not automatically form a new government. There was after all still a non-socialist "majority" for the rest of the four-year term, and under our constitution there is no way to call a new election before that term is over. I made clear that it must be the responsibility of the non-socialist majority to clean up the situation. That majority had existed since 1981, even if the parties of the Middle were closer to our views in many areas. Yet quite a few in the parties of the Middle were tired of the Conservative domination of the coalition. They felt more like hostages than colleagues.

Last-Ditch Tactical Ploys

Kåre Willoch called me on May 2. He wanted me to come to his office at ten o'clock. I told him I would instead return his call from my office a little later. What he wanted to talk about was his upcoming conversation with His Majesty. He wanted to be able to indicate that I was in agreement with the council he planned to give to the King. I decided not to be part of this tactic and said he could not refer to any agreement with me.

In the office I asked Svein Roald Hansen to come in and make a short note of the conversation for the files. I felt that the government was trying to dictate the attitudes of the three parliamentary groups even after its practical demise. In my opinion it should be the parliamentary groups of the three parties that had formed the majority coalition—not only the Conservatives but also the Center and the Christians—that should make such decisions now that the government had stepped down. Svein and I concluded my internal note: "Many representatives from the parties of the Middle have said that, although the three parties formed a coalition government, they in no way make any sort of a coalition opposition to Labor."

When I was called to the Royal Palace at noon that day, both His Majesty the King and His Royal Highness the Crown Prince were waiting. King Olav got straight to the point: "I would like you to form the new Government." I was prepared for his words. However, I had thought about the issues I needed to discuss with the King. I asked to first give my evaluation of the situation.

The parliamentary situation had been and would continue to be difficult. The three-party minority had now been governing since the fall of 1985 without having made any substantial, concrete clarification of its parliamentary basis. That was the reason for the current crisis. We now had to clarify the parliamentary relationships before we could form a new government.

With regard to the political content of this crisis, the disagreement was over how to distribute cuts in government spending. This would be a crucial dimension of Norwegian politics for the years to come, as further and deeper cuts would be necessary.

I expressed to His Majesty that I felt it was important first to know whether a government could be built on a possible majority. I knew how important it would be to loosen the bonds that the Conservatives had had with the parties of the Middle. Set free from the coalition, the parties of the Middle could act in accordance with their own political profiles and in important cases give their support to Labor.

The King listened. Then he asked, "What will be your answer if I ask you to form the government?" I said that such a question would be difficult to answer in view of what I just had said. I wanted to avoid saying a direct no to the King. His Majesty then concurred that he would turn to the President and the Vice President of Parliament and ask them to explore the parliamentary situation. This was what I had wanted to happen, so that I could indeed start forming a new government, but on a more solid basis, with actual majority support.

The President and Vice President conducted talks with all the parliamentary leaders and reported back to His Majesty at five o'clock. This process made it absolutely clear that the Middle parties were not ready to cooperate with the Progressives to contribute to a true Conservative-anchored majority. They both conceded that Labor should take over, and threw their support behind me. Thereupon I was called to the Palace once again, and the King asked me to form the new government. This time we spoke only briefly. My answer was yes.

The change of government took place the next day. I had come to a clear conclusion. A Prime Minister, be she Labor or Conservative, does not govern a democratic Norway, and indeed not in such a situation as we had in Parliament during the 1980s and 1990s, by threatening the survival of a government's majority in order to forge a change in parliamentary priorities. I had become convinced that the lines had to be drawn and the important political priorities secured with the backing of the real majority of Parliament.

Women on the Move

In my new administration, women would really be full partners in the political process. This time I would personally pick the whole team. A very positive effect of the party reform of the 1980s forced us to nominate in every constituency not less than 40 percent of either sex for Members of Parliament. I didn't want my cabinet to be any different.

The seven Ministries headed by women were Family and Consumer Affairs, Justice, Church and Education, Agriculture, Environment, Social Affairs and Health, and Foreign Aid. I was happy to be able to pick four of them from our Parliamentary Group now that so many women had been able to gather political experience. Of the three other women cabinet ministers, one had international experience from her work with the TUC. Another had been State Secretary in the Ministry of Finance. The third, who was made Minister of Agriculture, was chosen from a Labor chapter in mid-Norway and had no national political experience. She nonetheless turned out to be one of the toughest and most enduring Ministers of the 1990s.

What About the Men?

I had wanted Gunnar Berge as our leader in Parliament, and Einar Førde as my Finance Minister. But they put their heads together and came up to my office to explain that each wanted the job I had intended for the other, urging that I would not regret it if I listened to their advice. Although I had had my reasons, I decided to make the switch. They would be my two most important colleagues, in either case.

On the first page of my little green notebook, dated May 6, 1986, there are four names beside the word "Defense," but the post fell to Johan Jørgen Holst. Knut Frydenlund once again became our Foreign Minister. I knew from experience that his warm smile and good humor would contribute greatly to the spirit of the new team.

Dark Rose with a Slingback

There was a sea of people on the hill outside the Royal Palace. Roses and happy smiles. I had managed a quick trip around the corner from the Parliament Building to buy new shoes for the occasion. Dark rose with a slingback. Roses, women, and young, happy smiles: photographers and journalists at home and abroad got the point. A little more color, a little more speed, and a little more determination to press ahead.

This was my second time as Prime Minister. At forty-six, I was five years older and five years richer in experience, experience I would no doubt need. What lay ahead would be no Sunday school outing.

On Friday May 9, at 4:30 p.m. I held my first cabinet meeting. The new Ministers had been to their various Ministries. My notes for that day read, "Trust your civil servants. Treat them openly, show confidence in them, as though they were political colleagues." Advice from former Prime Minister Trygve Bratteli. Then there is a "G.H."—my father Gudmund Harlem: "Be decisive. Stay silent in Parliament if in doubt."

I knew the importance of the advice I had received as a new government Minister twelve years earlier, and I shared it now with my colleagues. I described how it had worked for me. Then I offered concrete advice about how to proceed in our work.

In the first place, it is vital to keep in close touch with our party representatives in the standing committees of Parliament. Secondly, be willing to raise matters with one of the State Secretaries at the Prime Minister's office, or directly with me or another cabinet colleague. It is important that we work as a team and share our experiences. Third, the best solution technically is usually also the best solution politically. Fourth, as members of the cabinet we have a collective responsibility. Fifth, we are each the trusted representative both of the party and of the people. Sixth, beware that any spontaneous act of individual initiative might consequently involve others' unnecessary and wasteful efforts to extinguish the flames of a controversy.

We then discussed the draft of the government declaration to Parliament, the traditional policy platform. Everyone contributes in a debate like this, especially on the elements relevant to one's own field of activity. Yes, indeed, we felt that this could be a fine team and that we had the necessary support in Parliament and in the country. There were smiles all around, exuding optimism and determination.

We Must Do the Dishes

Sunday was a busy day. First I listened to the Sunday morning radio program where Olav had been invited as a studio guest. I enjoyed that he has chosen my favorite song from the days when I was Minister of the Environment. I hummed along as I read my final notes on the economy and drank my morning coffee until it was time to dress: a new green two-piece that would also do for Princess Märtha Louise's confirmation later in the day. My official duties were already lined up and awaiting me. It was lovely to see the young people in their white coats that May morning in Asker church outside Oslo even though my thoughts were somewhere else entirely.

Sunday afternoon the press release made its way into the news agencies: The Brundtland government intended to take immediate action to rectify the crisis in the country's economy. Scheduled for six o'clock was a press conference that both the Prime Minister and the Finance Minister will give. The new government was just fifty-one hours old. For the past few weeks, the economy had preoccupied us all. Unfortunately I was right when I had said, "Willoch's is a government that leaves the dirty dishes for others once the meal is over."

There was no doubt that wide-ranging measures would be required. And it couldn't be done without cutbacks in public spending. Statistics showed that private consumption had increased by 8 percent in 1985, three times the amount planned for in the Willoch government's budget. This had in turn led to a sharp rise in imports and pressure on the Norwegian economy, a pressure that had increased through 1986.

These trends were further weakening the power of Norwegian business to compete in the marketplace. The foreign trade balance was heading for a loss of 50–60 billion Kroner in only a couple of years. In previous months there had been widespread speculation against the Norwegian Krone. The National Bank had been selling foreign currency and the value of our currency reserves had fallen by several billion Kroner.

We were faced with two options. We could either introduce far more stringent cuts, with the attendant dangers of unemployment and social disruption; or we could devalue the Norwegian Krone to ease the long-term pressure on it. The civil service as well as the Bank of Norway were of the opinion that devaluation was the best option, naturally in combination with restructuring and cutbacks in the national economy.

Finance Minister Gunnar Berge and I conferred with TUC leader Tor Halvorsen and his economic advisers before we made our final decision. Halvorsen was fully aware that union interests would be seriously affected no matter what choice we made. He too was concerned about industry's power to compete and the effects on employment, and he advised a more modest package of cuts and a decisive devaluation.

Drastic Measures and Hard Work

Photographers and journalists swarmed around us as we—Hermod Skånland, Governor-General of the Bank of Norway; Finance Minister Gunnar Berge; and I—headed for the pressroom on the ground floor of the government building. In the foyer and corridors leading to the pressroom the activity was frantic as Norwegian and foreign journalists moved in.

Our decision: a 12 percent devaluation, the largest since 1949. Norway's economy had been without direction for too long. Eighteen months of irresponsible expansionist economics had left us with no choice but to devalue.

I stressed that devaluation would enhance Norwegian industry's power to compete, and that our long-term goal was to stabilize our balance of trade and our employment figures. Because this was not a one-time measure, we would have to follow this up with major cutbacks. Demand would have to be reduced, and we would also try to limit the opportunities for gains through market speculation. The revised national budget due later in the month would also introduce cuts in loans and borrowing, to prevent too much stimulus of the economy.

I stressed from the start that those who earned most had to bear the greatest burden. These measures were necessary to avoid even more extreme measures later. Hermod Skånland concurred, "Any country in a similar situation would have done the same."

The newspapers referred to a "dramatic devaluation" and to the "bankrupt shop" that the Willoch government had left behind. The economic realities were harsh. Growth in the private sector would now have to be controlled by higher taxes and reduced public spending. Not exactly a popular program for a new government! Three days into the new government the forecast was crystal clear: drastic measures and hard work, and no time for a honeymoon.

A Concerned Queen

Queen Beatrix and Prince Klaus of the Netherlands were on a state visit to Norway during these turbulent days. For the new government this meant a rapid introduction to the world of protocol, a banquet at the Royal Palace, and the renting of evening clothes. My Minister of Social Affairs and Health asked, presumably in a spirit of republicanism, whether she had to accept the King's invitation. My answer was unequivocal: If one is well enough to go, then one accepts!

As I climbed the great staircase of the Royal Palace in my blue taffeta dress with flared skirt and bolero, I caught sight of the Minister of Consumer Affairs and thought for a moment that I was looking at my own reflection! "Olav, look!" I gasped.

There's a quite simple explanation why two government leaders should turn up at the Royal Palace wearing identical new dresses: little time, and limited selection in the same few shops between Lions Hill at the Parliament building and the Royal Palace. All our shopping had to be done in the few minutes between meetings. Actually, I'm surprised it doesn't happen more often. In a situation like this I was relieved to have been to the Royal Palace before; I'm sure it was worse for the new Minister! One just has to smile and be glad the whole thing is of no real importance.

Queen Beatrix was extremely interested in the new government of women. One after another we were summoned to meet her as she stood with the King and the royal family. The Queen was aware of recent changes in Norwegian political life and was especially interested in the combined roles of politician, woman, and mother. In addition, she was very concerned about environmental issues.

I had told Olav that the Queen's after-dinner speech would be completely nonpolitical. However, the Queen was soon discussing matters of international security, emphasizing the military role of the Netherlands in NATO's defense of Norway, and even recommending that we join the European Union!

Later I saw Queen Beatrix warmly praise the work of the World Commission on Environment and Development in a speech she gave as host at a royal banquet in her own country. On that occasion, too, she was clear, concise, and focused in her message. My impression is that the Dutch Royal House has for many years been an important contributor to the debate on environmental protection.

Please, Not "Mister President"

The atmosphere in Parliament is tense; the press benches are full this Thursday morning May 10. The upcoming debate is awaited with great curiosity and anticipation. All the members of the new government are present.

The President announces Item 1: election of a new Vice President, since our previous Vice President has now joined the cabinet. We elect another woman!

The awareness of gender equality is ever present. The new Vice President acquires a new dignity. Before she opens the debate she makes it clear that the occupant of the President's seat is now a woman. Later in the day she says, "The President would like to inform Foreign Minister Frydenlund that the President would prefer not to be addressed as 'Mr. President.' " Smiles all around.

Old customs die hard, and in the written notes the Foreign Minister had been given by his Ministry, the words "Mr. President" introduced each new topic. That little episode stuck in my mind, and from that day on I made it a point never to say "Mr." "President" alone is quite adequate and always safe. As for "Madam President," there's something about it I don't like, just as I never like it when someone addresses me as Madam Brundtland. My name is Gro!

Dramatic Weeks

During this time we were coping with the enormous effects of the big nuclear power accident at Chernobyl and its subsequent cover-up. It shocked us all and swiftly occupied many of the cabinet members.

Moscow initially sent confusing and conflicting messages about the scope and character of the accident. When Sweden sounded the alarm Monday, April 28, the central authorities in Moscow denied that there had been an accident. Finally, late in the evening, an official admitted the fact and that two people had lost their lives. Two days later the Soviet authorities acknowledged that 197 people had been hurt. But, according to the Soviet news agency TASS, the radiation situation in the area was improved! Air pollution in the Kiev district gave no reason for worry. And both drinking water reservoirs and rivers were unaffected. At the same time, Greek students in Kiev reported that they had been instructed not to drink milk or water and not to wash their clothes in the student dormitory. The cover-up was unacceptable.

A report from the Norwegian Institute of Energy Technology made me all the more concerned. It stated, "We are not at all surprised that such an accident happened. We know that only a few of the approximately fifty nuclear power stations in the Soviet Union are secured. Almost every Soviet nuclear power station lies in the open without any special covers to protect [the environment] from radioactive emissions."

During the following weeks our government had to heed a number of aspects of the catastrophe and to rectify our deficient state of preparedness. We needed to come up with comprehensive actions to protect sheep and reindeer. Nuclear fallout carried by wind from Kiev created dangerous grazing conditions for these animals. It would be many, many years before the effects of this catastrophe would be overcome. The Soviet authorities seemed to lack both the ability and the will to handle the situation. The mishap became a nail in the coffin of the Soviet regime.

Tax Shock

The media was right when it called the economy Labor's greatest headache. Not only would the Labor government have to go back on former promises, but the strength of its government would also be diminished by its need to get support from the opposition in Parliament. Some predicted that the second Brundtland administration would be forced to step down on an economic question. I thought that this very well might be true. But I also felt that we should be thinking long-term. I was sticking to the Labor Party slogan of the 1950s: It's the results that matter.

The weekend after the change of government offered no time for leisure. For 1986 we had proposed to increase taxes by 2 percent for incomes that were well above average. This was the only method by which we could distribute the economic burden in a more just way, in the middle of the budget year. We knew that the Conservatives would use this against us. They called it inconsistent to raise taxes at the same time that our proposals for long-term reform of the system would lead us in another direction.

Tug-of-War and Footnote

Our most important political challenge, both internally and diplomatically, was how to handle the NATO Defense Ministers' meeting which U.S. Secretary of Defense Caspar Weinberger was to attend. The meeting would result in a communiqué from the Allied Defense Ministers on two important issues. One was the U.S. plan to restart production of chemical weapons after a moratorium of seventeen years. The other was the U.S. space weapons program, the Strategic Defense Initiative (SDI), or "Star Wars."

We were against both. We had the parliamentary majority when these questions were presented to what we call the Extended Foreign Relations Committee in Parliament. The parties of the Middle supported us. But the Conservatives and some of the non-socialist press were on the warpath. Norway could issue a clear protest, as did Denmark, the Netherlands, Luxembourg, and Greece. After debate, it was agreed that the communiqué would condone no chemical weapons whatsoever. Thereby Norway and the others issued a strong signal to Reagan. Our Defense Minister, Johan Jørgen Holst, had successfully requested that his speech should be added to the report from the meeting. This would later be presented to the U.S. Congress, which had demanded NATO's support before giving the Reagan administration funds for producing chemical weapons.

The proposed controversial sentence on SDI would offer strong support for the U.S. position regarding medium-range and strategic missiles and space-based defense systems. This last part we could not support. Our opinion had been that Norway's former Conservative Defense Minister should not have accepted the U.S. position in earlier NATO meetings. In the short time that had passed since

Oslo Labor Party Progress Group festivities, May 1, 1946. Truls, son of Prime Minister Gerhardsen, carries our banner. My brother Erik is in the second row and I am in the third, both of us in trenchcoats.

Smiling young medical students, 1962; of the very nearly full-fledged doctors, I stand farthest left. This professor once proclaimed, "Remember that menstruation is only tears from a disappointed uterus." I remain close to the women I graduated with.

Arne Olav Brundtland proposed to me in the spring of 1960.

The Brundtland Family on July 31, 1974, the day I was appointed Minister of the Environment. Our youngest, Jørgen, on my lap, and, clockwise, Ivar, Kaja, Olav, and Knut

The "King in Council": I, as the most recently appointed
cabinet minister, have the most junior position.

The ill-fated train tour, which started
the campaign of 1979. I talk with the
Minister of Finance. Reiulf Steen
(with pipe) and Bjørn Tore Godal ride
in the row behind us.

My first term as Prime Minister lasted but ten
months. On October 13, 1981, I was on my
way to submit my resignation to the King.

Cartoon in *Arbeiderbladet*. The text: "The whole of NATO rejects Labor's views on missiles—I maintain that it is all the others who are out of step."

Hele NATO tar avstand fra Aps rakettsyn
— *Jeg fastholder, det er alle de andre som går i utakt . . .!!*

With Pappa and Robert S. McNamara in Oslo in March, 1984

Dinner in Stockholm with Yasser Arafat, Danish Prime Minister Anker Jørgensen and Olof Palme of Sweden. This picture caused a real stir.

In Halden, just west of our border with Sweden, with Olof Palme during our campaign of 1985

On the rooftop terrace of the Government House with Margaret Thatcher, September 1986

With President Reagan in the White House

Open heart transplant in the university hospital in Xian, People's Republic of China, February, 1988

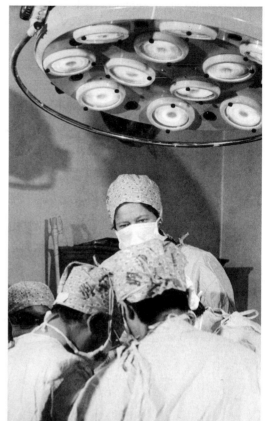

A light moment with Deng Xiaoping discovering that the interpreter had translated his age to be 48 years instead of 84

Heads of state and government meeting in The Hague, March 1989. Helmut Kohl, Michel Rocard, François Mitterrand, Queen Beatrix, Ruud Lubbers, and myself

With Hillary Clinton in 1995 on our National Day, May 17

With Nelson Mandela on Robben Island, revisiting the site of his sixteen-year imprisonment

above: Boris Yeltsin enjoys his "raspberries and cream." Queen Sonia in a red dress
and I in an ivory coat humor the Russian President.

Propaganda posters in Indonesia, 1995. My spouse and I
are depicted alongside Mohamed Suharto and his wife.

the change of government, Norwegian authorities had been in contact with U.S. counterparts and had not seen eye to eye.

In fall 1985, the former Conservative Defense Minister had negotiated a new text with Caspar Weinberger in the NATO nuclear planning group. He pointed to the fact that the majority in the Norwegian Parliament on security policy had been lost through the election of 1985; consequently, he had to ask that the formulations on SDI be removed if the agreement was to be acceptable for Norway. But hours later his U.S. colleague publicly betrayed our Defense Minister. In his press conference Caspar Weinberger declared that the SDI was absolutely nonnegotiable and that the communiqué from the former Defense Ministers' meeting was the valid one!

It was difficult abroad. But at home we faced a storm. Kåre Willoch, who had now become chairman of Parliament's Foreign Relations Committee, was highly critical of our disagreement with the United States. But we had the will to present Norwegian points of view clearly and with determination within our own alliance. My cabinet was backing up the efforts to make the changes in the Defense Ministers' communiqué. We were only partly successful; as it turned out, we had to make our points via a footnote this time.

A splendid article in *Arbeiderbladet* noted that SDI, which had been launched by President Reagan as a vision and without prior consultation with European allies in a five-minute radio speech in March three years earlier, would turn upside down the military strategy of the alliance if put into place. Caspar Weinberger had been fully informed from the very beginning that the real majority of opposition to SDI in the Norwegian Parliament did not initially surface only because Prime Minister Willoch then had control of all central functions in foreign and security policy.

Our new government had gone to Brussels with the intention of now representing the real majority view of the Norwegian Parliament. By refusing the Norwegian proposals for the Defense Ministers' communiqué, Weinberger was rejecting the advice of U.S. Secretary of State George Shultz and relegating Shultz to the role of a dissident. That was conspicuous. Also conspicuous was Willoch's expressed opinion that Norwegian security had been weakened by a Norwegian proposal to use the words Shultz had formulated in the communiqué from the Foreign Ministers of NATO!

Attacks from Our Own Ranks

My second week in office concluded with a fierce attack on the government from Liv Nilsson, the newly elected leader of the Union of Municipal Workers, which had gone on strike. It came as a complete surprise to me. Nilsson had not discussed the bargaining situation with me. Nor had the Trade Union Council leader. Neither the Minister of Consumer Affairs nor the Minister of Municipal Affairs had been informed of any problems.

The government had discussed labor issues and strikes repeatedly in its conferences. We could intervene if conflicts between employers and employees were threatening to important interests like life and health. But no one had suggested governmental intervention in the actual bargaining process. The strike split the labor movement. Nilsson claimed that the Labor government was running the same policy the Willoch government did. Gro is a disappointment, she went on; Gro should have taken the initiative, intervened and secured an acceptable outcome. She also warned the Minister of Municipal Affairs against settling the dispute through compulsory arbitration. The strike was growing. She warned that in a few days TV would be black and radio silent, air traffic limited, the streetcars of Oslo idle. Compulsory arbitration was obviously in the air.

I felt that these strong gambits were both a stab in the back and deeply unjustified. At the same time I was struck by the fact that here was a newly elected female leader. It was her first bargaining. She had operated with an unusually high profile, raising strong expectations among her members. I also remembered a conversation during a dinner a few years ago. A member of her union had told me with enthusiasm that with Liv Nilsson I would soon sense a new and much tougher style. True enough!

We were both interviewed on TV. She spoke in a very strong fashion, as if I had the direct and personal responsibility for all sides in a comprehensive and complicated bargaining process. Neither the Prime Minister's office nor the cabinet controls the negotiators. The Association of Norwegian Municipalities carried the main responsibility for the employers' side in the municipal sector. But outbursts like Liv Nilsson's make their impression. An accusation was hurtled, and it hung there. It hurt, it did damage.

The climate created by Liv Nilsson should have told me not to appear on TV the evening before I went to Canada to chair another meeting of the World Commission on Environment and Development.

Ten commissioners had been traveling the Canadian continent in the previous week. I limited my participation to two days including a public hearing in Ottawa. *Aftenposten* carried a straightforward report about the meeting itself, but in the picture chosen for publication, I am holding a telephone and the text runs: "During her weeklong visit to Canada, our Prime Minister would have to govern Norway by means of the telephone." Soon thereafter the new leader of the Conservatives commented: "She is running Norway from a telephone booth." This incident symbolized, rather ominously, the difficulties of getting across to the media and the public the importance of Norway's involvement in the international community.

The lack of understanding at home for our international work would be a burden in the years to come. Praise and punishment went hand in hand. In this case, Foreign Minister Knut Frydenlund made a most effective counter-blow, which carried the day for some time. Referring to the telephone-booth remark, he simply said about the new Conservative leader: "Presthus is a clown." Sluggers and populists had to be handled that way. Knut was respected and popular. Therefore his words carried weight when he decided to speak out.

In these very first weeks I had another surprising experience. The Minister of Finance conveyed the strong wish that I should be away as little as possible. But I thought I could rely upon my experienced coworkers and my close and trusted colleagues, whose political understanding was considerable. We were always in close contact even across great distances. We knew one another quite well and had full confidence in one another. Nevertheless, insecurity in the "family" was felt when "Mother" was away, as one of my State Secretaries put it.

Looking back on the harsh criticisms of my short visits to foreign countries, I am struck by how strong and persistent they were. Today such a complaint would be completely unfashionable. Perhaps the introduction of the Internet has changed people's ways of thinking. In a time when every second Norwegian has a mobile phone and carrying along a laptop is common, the idea of having to be home to communicate loses its validity. But my international image connected with the World Commission on Environment and Development was something new in Norway. No Norwegian Prime Minister had ever traveled the world as I did. No Norwegian Prime Minister had been received by so many other world leaders. The biggest Norwegian newspaper, VG, decided to follow me abroad all over the world. The paper stressed the speed and efficiency of the lifestyle and often the glamour, as they saw it, of my whereabouts. People were also led to question if this young and photogenic woman really should be moving around in the top political echelon worldwide; and this was used by the opposition.

Hunting in the Fall

During the fall we prepare the two most important government documents of the year: the state budget and the national budget. The Conservative Parliamentary Leader indicated that this fall would be his party's harvest, and their new PM candidate, Rolf Presthus, indicated that bullets and gunpower would be distributed for the fall hunt. But the question was whether the parties of the Middle would once again choose to go along with the Conservatives. My impression was that the Conservative leaders knew that they could not at the same time unite the three parties of the former coalition and summon the support of the Progressives as well. The distance between the Center Party and the Progressives was too great, and both parties were needed together with the Conservatives and the Christians to have a majority in Parliament. We stood a reasonable chance of receiving the support of the parties of the Middle once again. But the Conservative leadership gained new confidence from all our political struggles.

During the spring there had been lots of commentary in the papers about whether Labor should have taken over governmental responsibility. It was perhaps too big a burden for the party and the trade unions. The polls gave no happy return. From 43.9 percent of the public's having confidence in us in April, we fell to 39.9 percent in June and further to 35.9 percent in August. This reduced confidence has an impact. It wears down the spirits of our Members of Parliament, and makes the task of leadership more difficult. But I believed that we shouldn't lose faith—even if criticism of the high interest rates came from our own ranks. Internal criticism is always the greatest challenge.

I had to ask the members of our Parliamentary Group whether we really believed that the measurement of our political work should be the monthly polls rather than the results we could achieve for the daily life of ordinary people. Did we believe that the Norwegian people would be better served by a Conservative government? On the Party National Executive Board I asked what the situation was after four and a half years with a non-socialist government. Where were the 157 billion Kroner from oil? How had the money been managed? I had to go on the offensive to bring the people together in support of our minority government.

I stressed that under Conservative rule, those with highest incomes had received tax reductions, while retirees were paying higher taxes. There had been a pronounced increase in income in parts of the private sector and in groups not organized in labor unions. Not since the end of the 1960s had emigration from the rural areas been greater. The boom let loose by the Conservative government had mostly been an urban phenomenon.

Our party program carried the heading "New Growth for Norway." We prescribed a different medicine, another sort of growth, different from that permitted by the Conservative government. In certain areas the growth was too big and this had created a vulnerable situation for our country. I stated: "When Labor pilots this new course for Norway, we will create the foundation for a new sort of growth. Reforms are urgently needed and four tasks are center stage: (1) We have to guard the welfare society; (2) We must reform the system of taxation; (3) We must slow or reverse the cost increases of Norwegian business and reestablish a sound income policy based on solidarity; (4) We must strengthen Norwegian industry and thereby secure the foundation for future welfare and employment."

Bullets and Gunpowder

The three former coalition parties tried to cooperate on a common budget proposal. The Conservatives demanded that the parties of the Middle oppose tax increases. The demand was rejected. Our proposal on a progressive tax on gross income was not fully successful, but we won support for some increases and for fewer rights of deduction. Our job now was to find a reasonable comprehensive budget solution together with the two parties of the Middle.

Now Labor's program and priorities formed the center of gravity of Norwegian politics. That fall the Center Party and the Christian People's Party supported Labor's budget. At the same time the media commented maliciously on the unfortunate fall hunt, particularly on the leader of the hunting party. His bullets and gunpowder had turned out to be ineffective.

Maggie Visits

Prime Minister Margaret Thatcher of Great Britain was one of my first official guests in the fall of 1986. The program for the visit had been fixed by the previous government, but I too had every reason to welcome a visit to my country by such an important leader of one of our closest allies.

So when Thatcher came, she was not greeted by her Conservative colleague as originally planned. Meeting instead were the only two female Prime Ministers of Europe—from different parties, from different generations, and with different points of view on a number of issues, including the boycott of the apartheid regime in South Africa. The support for boycott was very strong in Norway, as in the other Scandinavian countries. Britain was seen as the most apartheid-tolerant country in Europe.

As North Sea neighbors and allies in NATO, Norway and Britain are close. These dimensions of our relationship were central to the program of the visit. We would stress the military and the maritime community. The program in northern Norway gave Thatcher occasion to show her strong interest in naval matters and the importance of our two navies in the common defense of the Norwegian coast and the oceans west and north of Norway.

Thatcher automatically felt at home. It almost looked as if she had done nothing but relate to military chiefs. She obviously enjoyed inspecting the troops and asked a number of well-informed questions during the briefings and the visits to military installations including a submarine base in one of our fjords. Of course the role of the military was more real for Britain than for most countries in Europe at the time. As Prime Minister, Thatcher had led a war to recapture the Falkland Islands. I had had no such direct experience. But I was very much in charge of our security policy.

The media's interests and expectations were focused, however, on the fact that we were two female Prime Ministers of Europe; they almost turned the meeting into a test of our "manhood." *The Observer* called our encounter "The Iron Lady Versus the Super Woman." I was the " 'Iron Lady of the North,' tougher than any man." Foreign Minister Knut Frydenlund was quoted: "I would not miss this meeting of these strong-willed women for anything in the world."

I was not at all happy about this advance brouhaha. We had problems to discuss, including acid rain and policy toward South Africa.

Margaret Thatcher saw no connection between female influence and soft values. But just before she came, a colleague had suggested that the British Prime Minister was about to change her position on acid rain. She could no longer maintain the British point of view that acid rain from Britain was not as damaging as had been reported by other countries, and she could not reject what British researchers had told her. Acid rain from Britain had serious effects far away from the British Isles, not least in Scandinavia. The fight against acid rain that others and I had fought in international forums since 1974 had finally produced results.

My approach was not confrontational. I had every reason to believe that I was meeting a knowledgeable, dedicated, and conscientious political leader.

VG reported, "It started so nicely. A silky-soft encounter between two iron-willed ladies in Tromsø." Everywhere I observed the tendency of the press to write about women differently. What two men in a similar situation would have been characterized as iron-willed, or the encounter as silky-soft?

The demonstrations started in Tromsø. Posters proclaimed, "Maggie Go Home" and criticized the British policy in South Africa. Thatcher took it with good humor both in Tromsø and the following day in Oslo when the Oslo police had difficulty controlling a crowd. "So cozy of you to make me feel at home," she joked in Tromsø.

She was well prepared to discuss Britain's responsibility for acid rain and had announced a plan for cleaning three coal-driven power stations. Both in our conversations and in my speeches I praised this step and expressed the hope that the country would go further and also join the protocol on 30 percent reduction of acid rain. She did not agree with me, citing the need for reductions in Eastern Europe first.

We spent hours together in the plane going from Tromsø to Oslo. Dennis, Margaret, Olav, and I sat around the same table. Dennis had strong opinions about the policy toward South Africa: It should not change. Margaret left much to him. We returned to the issue in our conversations the next day but were unable to arrive at a joint conclusion on what role the world ought to play in order to end the brutal and undemocratic regime.

I raised the theme of women in politics. I asked what she was doing to increase the number of women in the British government. I assumed that this was an area that she was as interested in as I was.

But instead she demurred. It was difficult to find qualified women for cabinet posts. There were only a few female Members of Parliament from which to choose. Very few women were qualified for Ministership.

I got the message. She was Prime Minister because she was the best. If other women were best, they would certainly manage what she had managed. We were fifteen years apart in age. She was British. She was conservative. We had important differences in background, culture, political platform, and personality.

Thatcher dazzled everyone who met her. She was sure of herself and domineering, but also charming. In the meeting at my office with several of my cabinet Ministers she impressed all of us. The Minister of Oil and Energy was affected by a method Thatcher used to stress the importance of her arguments. She wore a heavy bracelet on her left wrist, and I can easily recall the sound of it hitting the table while she spoke. No wonder she rendered some people speechless!

In Oslo, too, we had expected demonstrations about Britain's position on South Africa. I had noted our disagreement about this issue the day before in my speech at lunch. I felt I had to do so because most of Norway's population felt so strongly about the situation. Neither the Prime Minister nor her delegation responded to that with enthusiasm.

On our way to Akershus Castle in downtown Oslo my driver was told to use the back door. People were rioting at the main gate. It was an alarming experience. The police had lost control. The situation might have turned dangerous. Later we learned that the potential for danger was compounded by internal conflicts in the Oslo police which we later rectified by replacing some of the leaders. We never experienced again such lack of professionalism. Margaret Thatcher was relaxed about it all. She comforted the Chief of Police of Oslo, who was one of the guests at our greatly delayed dinner. "It is no easy job to be a policeman."

Memorial in Japan

One day the Japanese Embassy inquired whether I had reservations about a monument in honor of my government being raised in Japan. They wanted to acknowledge the unusual number of women in my cabinet with a memorial. Memorial? I was only forty-seven. My government was only a few months old. Reservations? No, why? Whoever they were, they should feel free to do as they pleased. If somebody wanted to honor the first "woman government" of the world, that was certainly fine with me.

A few months later *VG* carried a fine picture of young, smiling Japanese women in front of a 3 × 6-foot granite rock, which had been put in a school in Sakai. The stone had been imported from Sweden, polished and cut on Shikoku Island, and then transported to Kyoto. The names of all our female cabinet members are chiseled into the stone, along with a poem by Yosano Akiko in Japanese and in Norwegian.

Our ambassador to Japan read a greeting from me at the inauguration, then joined a thirty-member female choir in song. Yosano Akiko, who died in 1942, is known as the first feminist author in Japan. She wrote the poem "The Day the Mountain Moved," inspired by women's liberation. The philosopher Shunzo Toumimura conceived of the monument. After having read in Japan's largest newspaper about the new Norwegian government, he thought: At last, after more than seventy years, Akiko's dreams have come true, not in Japan, but in Norway.

A miniature copy of the monument was given to the Prime Minister's office later in the fall. It is now on display in the Ministry of Family and Consumer Affairs.

This small episode illustrates the intense attention directed toward Norway and its new cabinet. The news about a government of women traveled all over the world. Foreign Minister Frydenlund reiterated his comments from the blowout in the North Sea of 1977: Norway has not enjoyed more attention since the invasion of 1940. Women and the environment were exciting news. It created lots of work for my coworkers and for me personally. I regretted that I had to disappoint so many enthusiastic people all over the world by not having had time and opportunity to respond properly to their warm letters and cards.

Hunting in the Spring

In the spring of 1987 the Conservatives, the Christians, and the Center Party continued their efforts to reestablish a non-socialist platform for an alternative government. But the three parties disagreed about the political basis on which to force a change of government. Many in the Center Party were closer to Labor in practical politics and wanted no new alliance with either the Conservatives or a conservatively oriented policy. Nevertheless the three parties developed a common platform in reaction to the revised national budget to be examined that May. They hoped to use it as a launch-pad for a vote of no confidence.

During that spring there had been great struggles over agricultural subsidies. The government usually negotiates with the Farmers Union and the Smallholders Union on the amount of subsidies to be paid by the state. Organized agriculture was strongly disappointed with the offer from the state regarding the amount of subsidies, some hundred million Kroner less than in previous years. They organized strong demonstrations by busing members to Oslo from all over southern Norway. The spirits of the three non-socialist party leaders were high. They clearly believed their efforts to oust Labor would be successful this time.

Bound for a Crisis?

By early summer, the opposition's negotiations had slowed. *Aftenposten* revealed on June 6 that the Center Party was not willing to commit itself to a new government of the three parties. The Conservatives and the Christians were tired of negotiating without any guarantee from the Center.

The following day brought reports on a non-socialist summit in the Parliament building. The Central Executive Board of the Conservatives had met with Carl I. Hagen of the Progressives. The paper reported smiles and a positive atmosphere. Problems had been ironed out and the candidate for Prime Minister himself, Rolf Presthus of the Conservative Party, looked happy, although he cautioned against jumping to conclusions.

A change of government would require the agreement of all four parties. The Conservatives found problematic the inclusion of the agricultural subsidies in the political package for a change of government, and Presthus therefore said publicly that basing the vote of no confidence on the issue of agricultural subsidies was simply a technical measure. The Christians had no such reservations, and the Center Party had in any case only been willing to participate on the basis of an agreement to increase the subsidies, not as a general criticism of the Labor government. The Progressives, however, were not at all in favor of increasing state outlays for agriculture.

During those days I was in Nairobi for a meeting of the World Commission on Environment and Development. Labor's Parliamentary Leader, Einar Førde, called to inform me that we were bound for a crisis. I had great difficulty believing that the four parties had come to agreement about their means of attack and told Einar that I had serious doubts about Hagen's willingness to go along. Would new subsidies for farmers be the basis for the formation of a new non-socialist government? I'd believe it when I saw it! Perhaps distance made for a little more clarity.

As recently as April 1986, many journalists and politicians held the view that Hagen would ultimately give in to Willoch if pushed to the limit. Now there were new speculations. Could Hagen sustain a new round of pressure? Could he bear the blame if a non-socialist government were not established?

On my way home from Nairobi I had ample time to analyze the situation. My comment upon my return was this: When they try to provoke a crisis on agricultural subsidies, it is because they have neither the will nor the ability to form an alternative to the policy of the government. It is far easier to provoke a crisis than to form a new government, especially without knowing where to lead it. I

chose to speak out clearly. I felt it necessary to throw some cold water on those who already seemed to have forgotten how my administration had arisen.

A few days later Norway watches on television a Carl I. Hagen who
is calm and determined. Not only does he contend that a three-party
government would point in all directions at once, but he also says
that increased subsidies to farmers would destroy calm among the
trade unions. He further suggests that gradual but substantial reductions in subsidies to business in general and agriculture in particular
make good economic sense and that the Labor government has exercised great political courage by its moderate proposals to agriculture.
After a month of negotiations and proclamations of unity, Hagen says,
the Center Party and the Conservatives are still issuing divergent
statements about the meaning of a new agricultural negotiation. A
coalition government that comes to power by undermining cohesion
and moderation in the nation has the poorest possible foundation for
firm and effective government, particularly since a Labor Party in opposition cannot be relied on to help a new government.

This was very clear talk. The Progressive Party had chosen its
line. They had demonstrated their independence and humiliated
the Conservatives, who had stretched far beyond their limits to establish the basis for another non-socialist government. At the same
time, Hagen chose to challenge the Center Party. He stressed that
Progressives could vote in favor of no confidence on a general basis
if the Center now was prepared to work actively for a comprehensive non-socialist alternative in which the Progressives would be
taken seriously.

But the non-socialist alternative now lay in ruins. The Willoch
government had already fallen. The basis for a non-socialist government was destroyed by the non-socialists themselves.

My government would continue!

Labor at One Hundred Years

In the summer of 1987 we would celebrate the one-hundredth anniversary of the Norwegian Labor Party. Was it something to cele-

brate? Yes, we were proud of the legacy of the Norwegian Labor Party. But we wanted even more to look forward to the next hundred years. We launched a new debate on freedom and personal liberty, and would take more care to place the individual at the center of our considerations. It was not certain that we had organized for work, education, and leisure in a way that would fit into the emerging postindustrial society.

Our party had always been in the vanguard on gender equality. Those who had met in the city of Arendal to start the Labor Party were all men, but they were extremely radical in demanding general voting rights not only for all men but for all women as well.

The upcoming anniversary invited forward-looking questions. A reporter asked me, for example, if our labor ideology was as relevant in the culture of service and information as it was in the age of industrialization? In my view there was no great difference in principle. New occupations were not the issue. Attitudes of egoism and cynicism will function even more poorly in the future. It is still important to combine the driving force to create and be productive with the will to distribute resources fairly. Without the will to share, you will not maximally release the creative gifts of all individuals. Without unleashing individual creativity, you will not achieve the highest quality in society.

The Labor Party still needs to be a party of radical reforms.

More to Celebrate

Our family had more to celebrate. On August 16 our first grandchild, Oda, was born. Kaja had married Njaal during the winter.

I did not sleep well during Kaja's labor. Kaja and Njaal had traveled to the hospital Saturday evening. The birth seemed to be a drawn-out event. Njaal called us at half past two in the morning. Kaja had given birth to a daughter. I talked to her on the telephone. She was happy and at ease. The sounds from the newborn whom she held in her arms were wonderful to hear. This is a new era, Njaal there with Kaja during birth. I had been alone, only with the midwife. No Olav. No telephone. Things improve!

The happy event gave me further inspiration to write my speech to the Jubilee Party Congress about social democracy's major challenge to help improve the conditions for children in society, and to secure a safe environment for all. In infant care, progress had been made and technology had improved. But we still felt Norway and the Labor Party were lagging behind when it came to child care. Our first day-care center was established 150 years ago, but at present there was available day care for only one of every three children of preschool age. We formulated as a political goal that before the year 2000 there should be a place for every child who needed it.

Last Days of "The Father of the Nation"

In August 1987, Einar Gerhardsen was again hospitalized. We had celebrated his ninetieth birthday in May with a large meeting in Labor House. Mamma told me he was getting weaker. I wanted to see him.

Prime Minister Einar Gerhardsen was not only our country's most significant political leader in the twentieth century. He was also a part of my childhood. I was very fond of him. I had good memories of camping and walking with him, and of sharing evenings at our holiday homes. He was warm and serious at the same time.

He sat up in bed and took my hand: "Gro, I have known you since you were a small girl. Your parents have been my close friends. I have always believed in you. But you have far exceeded my expectations." It was a solemn moment. I felt overwhelmed. I was silenced.

He continued, "Make sure that the younger generations get familiar with the idea of working together, of exercising the value of solidarity. It will be quite decisive."

Three weeks later he died. I received the news while speaking about the World Commission on Environment and Development in Washington, D.C. I said on Norwegian television, "Einar Gerhardsen is the most towering personality of Norway in this century." This was no exaggeration: the Labor Party with Gerhardsen as its leader had built the new Norway.

I wonder what encounter in other political cultures might equate to my visit at the sickbed of Einar Gerhardsen. If you can imagine President John F. Kennedy visiting a proud but ailing President Franklin Delano Roosevelt in 1961, you might have an American version of it.

Uphill Struggle

The year 1987 turned out to be one of the most difficult years for me politically. So, too, for the Minister of Finance. We were constantly asked by party members and elected representatives why the government would not advocate lower interest rates. It was difficult to explain how current economic conditions circumscribed our freedom of action. We first had to get on a sounder economic course and we had to reduce the large deficit in our balance of trade. The wishes of the Parliamentary Group far exceeded any realistic framework. Norway had just experienced an explosion of easy credit. A reduction of interest would be like throwing oil on a fire. Criticism and impatience came from all quarters. But no one offered alternative economic solutions.

A heated labor market put pressure on wages and prices, and there was a very strong demand for substantial income hikes. I maintained that there existed only two alternatives: cooperative compromise to bring about economic moderation, or—the method used by most European countries at the time—a trimmed-down economic policy with a resulting steep rise in unemployment. However, there was some light at the end of the tunnel. I was very pleased that the outcome of the first collective bargaining in 1988 was successful. Nominal wage increases were moderate. The solidarity alternative was under way.

Ups and Downs in Popularity

We benefited from the lack of cohesion on the non-socialist side. And for a brief period I enjoyed a rather high standing in the press and at the polls. Much to my dissatisfaction I was then pronounced political "queen" and the press predicted a landslide for Labor in the municipal elections of 1987. The outcome, of course, turned out to be surprising. The Progress Party made the best showing, relatively speaking.

Later I was chosen Woman of the Year by Gloria Steinem, the editor of *Ms.* I did not really like it. I knew that such international praise, however personally rewarding, had a tendency to produce envy and criticism at home.

The test of political leadership is not what support you command outside your country, but how you manage at home! Another version of Tip O'Neill's maxim: "All politics is local."

Adjustments in State-Owned Industry

In the late summer of 1986, Kongsberg Weapon Manufactory (KV), the venerable state-owned company in the city of Kongsberg, was once again in acute financial difficulties. Two years prior Parliament had appropriated 250 million Kroner to ensure that KV would be able to join the British corporation Pratt Whitney as a subcontractor for aircraft engines. An emergency meeting of the board reported that KV was now asking for an additional 500 million Kroner! A new investigation by the Ministry of Industry estimated that the firm actually needed nearly three times as much for refinancing. We discussed the situation all winter long.

Then a new tragedy hit the factory, the Kongsberg community, and Norway. The United States charged that KV, together with the Japanese firm Toshiba, had exported electronic steering systems to the Soviet Union and had thus helped to tip the submarine balance in the Soviets' favor. We took these accusations very seriously and even ordered a police investigation. However, only one person was found guilty. The United States believed that Norway had sought to minimize KV's role. The United States found it hard to imagine that the cooperation with Toshiba had been the work of one person only.

In order to minimize the damage I wrote to President Reagan

about the wide-ranging measures we had taken. We also sent Minister of Defense Johan Jørgen Holst on our behalf to meet with the U.S. administration and Congress. Holst had a prominent name in Washington, especially in U.S. academic circles. This was the only time the Norwegian government ever sent one of its cabinet members to lobby a foreign Parliament or Congress.

In the spring of 1987 the possibility of this state-owned enterprise going into bankruptcy was raised. A storm of protest ensued in which almost every conceivable argument was used, including ones about national security. No one had ever imagined that state-owned companies could be terminated, and such a decision would affect creditors as well as management. But I felt sure that we could not any longer pursue an industry policy that used the state coffers as a bottomless resource.

A number of the most senior Labor Party members came to see me asking for a bailout. They were obviously relying on the old-boy network to fix things. Among them was Jens Christian Hauge. I remember that while he spoke at length and without much focus, I realized I had forgotten my wristwatch and grabbed the hand of the Minister of Industry to check the time. Hauge took the hint and said that he understood that time was running out. So was the time for lavish state subsidies for state-owned industries. On October 7 KV had to accept liquidation. A new company took over defense-related work.

KV was one of many difficult cases of this kind during the 1980s. State-owned industry had been built up mainly during the 1940s and 1950s when Norway was reconstructing after the occupation. These companies could not maintain their old traditions, given the new technology, changing market situations, and new demands on productivity. Much conflict was provoked when we had to take seriously such problems and dare to change. During those years I was happy to have had a most capable and trustworthy Minister of Industry.

Changes in Europe

Norway is a founding member of the European Free Trade Association (EFTA), which was established in 1960 as an alliance counterbalancing the European Economic Community (EEC). The EEC had been formed in Western Europe to better implement the Marshall Plan of 1947 for postwar recovery, but it split over irreconcilable opinions about the degree of integration a transnational union should demand. Six countries—France, Italy, West Germany, Belgium, the Netherlands, and Luxemburg—established the European Common Market by adopting the Treaty of Rome in 1957. The original EFTA members were the United Kingdom, Denmark, Portugal, Switzerland, Sweden, and Austria. In 1973 both the United Kingdom and Denmark left EFTA and joined the EEC, which later became the European Union (EU). Norway had put the matter up for resolution in 1972, and in a close vote, our people chose against following suit.

Jacques Delors, the president of the European Commission (the governing body of the EU), visited Norway for the first time in 1986. He was a Social Democrat and I found him easy to talk to. As French Minister of Finance, he had found it impossible to increase employment in France alone! One needed wider markets and wider vistas.

I told Delors in confidence that Norway was not in a position to renew an application for membership in the EEC and was now searching for a more secure and comprehensive agreement for cooperation between EFTA and the EU while the EU further developed its internal market. He and I shared this vision for a wider union and in the years to come we kept in close contact through his chief of staff, Pascal Lamy, who is today the EU commissioner for trade.

A first step at home was to present a white paper to Parliament in 1987 in which we argued for the need for establishing a European Economic Area (EEA), consisting of the eighteen Western European countries, "on the basis of our current form of association, that is, the limited partnership of the remaining EFTA countries with the EU." It was essential to be able to avoid a new round of heartbreaking discussion in the country on the contentious issue of Norwegian membership in the EU, which had split parties, communities, and families in the early 1970s.

Letter to the Ministries

Under the terms of the European Economic Area (EEA) Norway would become, in essence, part of the EU internal market, wherein there would exist equal conditions of competition for enterprises in Norway and the EU countries and "the free movement of goods, services, capital, and persons." EU legislation was young, and Norway would have a chance to shape it, in the EEA.

I now wrote a letter to all Ministries. Based on the great importance of the development of the EU's internal market, new Norwegian laws and regulations in the field of the internal market would have to be evaluated also with regard to an eventual harmonization with EU rules. In cases of discrepancies, our deviations must be explained. If they were motivated by overriding concerns, laws and regulations that did not comply with EU regulations would not be precluded.

Some protested that this was highly unconventional. Indeed. The world changed, Europe changed. Norway had to keep awake and be prepared.

As it turned out, Norway was already 90 percent compliant with EU regulations before negotiations even started.

The letters I sent created increased focus, but not everyone cared for my systematic approach. The forces of opposition to a more committed relationship to Europe were everywhere, including in public offices and Ministries.

But this was the easy part. In the coming years, my efforts to keep a broad consensus on European issues would prove to be nearly impossible. It became a defining issue between parties and key to the ability to govern Norway.

In fact, as we approached a new national election in 1989, it became more and more obvious that the Labor Party was under fire. The Conservatives criticized us for choosing the "half-way house"

EEA, and not full membership in the EU. They wanted to use this against us in the election campaign.

The Center Party also wanted to focus this election on the EU. But to oppose our membership! The two former coalition parties were indeed far apart, and on a crucial question for the nation.

I felt we were very much alone in seeking a workable solution for Norway, one that would obviously agree with the Conservatives. After all, their primary goal of membership in the EU still seemed beyond reach, as it had proven to be in 1972 when 53.5 percent rejected membership for Norway in the European Economic Community, which was the name of the EU at that time.

Renewal

At certain intervals it is only natural to consider changes in the cabinet. At the end of the spring session of 1988, my cabinet had been at work for about two years and we had some ideas about how to strengthen it.

Certain confrontations between the Minister of Consumer Affairs and Parliament had also sparked a reshuffling. Other issues, such as the government's struggle to win parliamentary approval of the location of the new national airport, contributed to the need for change. All in all, six portfolios changed hands. As one must always do in such cases, I worked speedily and secretly, but a few people had to be consulted. I managed to prepare the changes in the intervals between my public appearances during the state visit by Queen Margrethe of Denmark. Whenever there was a small opening in the program, I rushed for the nearest telephone!

When I introduced the changes, the press was most interested in why the Minister of Consumer Affairs had to go. I told them that this was a comprehensive reorganization so that we could better prepare to meet future challenges. The outgoing Minister was unhappy to go and complained to the press that she had had no prior warning.

Regarding the latter point, my experience tells me that each Minister has to be mentally prepared that the trust given to him or her is for a limited and unknown period only. One has to be prepared to step down the very day that new political evaluations or events lead to such a conclusion.

Invitations from Abroad

There seemed to be no end to what people both at home and abroad asked me to do during the years that followed the report from the World Commission on Environment and Development (WCED). This was a dilemma. My participation in various events could help further the process the commission had set in motion, so I was unhappy when I had to turn down many of the invitations.

My popularity also created opportunities for Norway. It was unusual for a Norwegian Prime Minister to be asked to open the 1988 Conference on the Atmosphere in Toronto or to deliver the main address to the World Health Assembly that same year. Norwegian political values were well represented by the WCED report, which was celebrated around the world.

I was invited to accept doctoral degrees from universities in Britain, Canada, and the United States. In Norway, honorary degrees are not common. If I accepted, I could be misunderstood as snobbish, especially as a Labor Prime Minister.

I followed a cautious line. I never accepted such degrees, even from my alma mater, apart from the time when Vice President Al Gore asked me to deliver the commencement address at Harvard University. I had twice previously declined. Later it also became difficult to say no to Archbishop Desmond Tutu when he asked me to accept an honorary degree from the University of the Western Cape while on an official visit to South Africa in 1996.

We had to search for the right balance between what was appropriate in Norway and what was appropriate abroad. Often the difference was considerable—and it could be embarrassing to say no. After all there is something called political good manners.

Even more recently, my current staff at the WHO strongly advised me to change my mind when I was about to turn down an honorary degree from the Catholic University of Louvain. This is a most prestigious university in the Catholic world. They would not understand a refusal. There were two other recipients, the President of the Commission of the European Union, Romano Prodi, and the French Prime Minister Lionel Jospin. It would look strange if they could accept an honorary degree while I said no. Moreover, the honor from this university seemed like a gesture of appreciation from the Catholic Church, which had previously rebuked me because of my views on family planning.

Secretly to The Hague

The Prime Minister of France, Michel Rocard, called me in December 1988. I had known him for quite some years. He had a plan for protecting the atmosphere, and had spoken with the Dutch Premier, Ruud Lubbers. They suggested that the three of us should meet secretly in The Hague between Christmas and New Year. It sounded a bit rushed, but if I could help France be a pioneer in this matter, the trip would be worth it.

In Lubbers's house we discussed how supranationality and majority voting could be used in international questions concerning the climate. International cooperation can be difficult and terribly slow when agreement must be unanimous.

No one in Norway noticed my absence, but the meeting stayed on my mind for a long time. Indeed, I would have a physical reminder of the trip for a while: on my return flight, the very small aircraft in which I rode fell so abruptly in airspace that I was thrown to the ceiling and got a concussion.

On March 11 we held a summit about the atmosphere in The Hague. Twenty-four heads of state and government were present. It was a good beginning. We concluded that it was possible to disregard the unanimous-consensus principle in matters relating to ozone-depleting gases.

Neither the United States nor the Soviet Union was invited to The Hague, and the Americans were particularly annoyed. I pushed a little for contacting Washington. But Rocard did not want to. He had tried to call President Bush in December 1988 between Bush's victory and his inauguration, but the staff of the president-elect had not been willing to put through a call from the French Prime Minister. Rocard had not forgotten. In addition the French are traditionally less than enthusiastic about including the "superpowers."

Getting the Winter Olympics to Norway

Not many people really believed it was possible for Norway to host the Winter Olympics, not even my Minister of Culture, who put forward the cabinet brief suggesting that the state give the necessary guarantees. In Parliament there was widespread support for the notion. Politicians from different parties would stop me in the parliamentary corridors: "Can't you find time to make a trip to Seoul, Gro?" "Try, try, it will mean so much." (The International Olympic Committee was meeting in Seoul.) For once there was talk of a trip abroad that would enjoy widespread support!

All the same, the prevailing government mood was one of cautious pessimism. In reality our chances were slim, and that view was the one generally held in the press.

So when the enthusiastic people of Lillehammer asked me to attend the meeting of the International Olympic Committee (IOC) in Seoul during the Summer Olympics in 1988, the advice I received from my office was unusually varied. Lillehammer had after all been a candidate for the 1992 games, which had ultimately gone to Albertville, France. Some felt that Norway would again be deemed too small and would lose. One argument consistently used against Norway by the Swedes was that Norway, after all, had already hosted a Winter Olympics in 1952!

Certain quarters felt that the powerful economic interests involved would prove too much for us, and that we would have no chance, since we would naturally play by the book. Others sensed that the Lillehammer people were right to be encouraged and that the basic preparations were a lot better now than they had been for the previous bid.

Prime Minister Chirac's support for Albertville had been considered decisive; there were also rumors that the Swedish King was willing to promote Sweden's bid. These were strong arguments in favor of my offering public support for Lillehammer's request. There were a number of reasons that I did in the end decide to join the campaign. The most important of all was this: if Norway lost, then in good conscience I would have done all I could.

Thorough Preparations

Hosting the Winter Olympics would be a major undertaking, but thousands of Norwegians would be the beneficiaries. From our work on the economic guarantees put up by the state, we knew that the games would provide widespread employment and investment opportunities.

All four potential hosts had to present their case to the IOC meeting, which was held a few days before the opening of the summer games. Each candidate was supposed to offer a video presentation supported by a speech—in our case, my speech.

We tried to understand the internal culture of the IOC. What were the motives at play behind each vote? All the candidate towns had spent time and money on their campaigns, courting the various IOC members. My staff and I had a hunch that the Lillehammer people, though they had certainly done an outstanding job, were nevertheless a trifle overoptimistic. Long experience with international affairs had taught us that a promise of support didn't necessarily mean much when the critical ballot was a secret affair.

Morten Wetland, later my State Secretary for Foreign Affairs, had been extremely skeptical about the whole trip, saying that it was "like fetching a snowball home from hell." But now he gave everything he had to the preparations.

I discussed the basics of our strategy with him and with my closest associates. What was Norway's strength? What was my strength? Many of the IOC members from Asia and Africa undoubtedly knew of the work we had done on the World Commission on Environment and Development. We realized that these were members who were perhaps more interested in the summer games and not likely to be overly impressed by the shape of a fifty-kilometer ski course or meteorological documentation about the stability of the local snow.

The little secretariat in Geneva that had succeeded the secretariat of the World Commission on Environment and Development sent out an information packet about the World Commission and me to all members of the IOC. They had also exploited the network that had been established over the years by the commission, especially in Africa and Asia. The IOC members were encouraged to ask themselves the following question: Has the role played by Norway in supporting the Third World over the years been a valuable one?

The Lillehammer people had hired an advertising agency to make the presentational video that would be shown to the IOC immediately before I spoke. We wanted to make sure that the film didn't contain sequences that might seem incomprehensible or unfortunate to those looking at Norway from a considerable cultural distance. Two of my state secretaries gave it a preview in Oslo, and the agency ended up making a few cuts.

We studied the Olympic charter. What we were doing, after all, was extending an invitation to visit our country on the basis of the mandate and the values of the Olympic movement.

Walk and Talk Like Winners

Olav came with me on the whirlwind journey from Oslo to Seoul, via Copenhagen and Bangkok. It was dusk when we arrived in Seoul. TV towers, modern bridges spanning the river, the lights of a big city. At the hotel we called together the whole Lillehammer delegation before going to bed. We ran through our plan and tactics again.

I showed the group my draft speech and asked for comments. This was a final double-check. Morten Wetland worked away in the wings. He told the delegation: From now on we have to walk and talk like winners. There's always one who wants to have voted for the winner, so we must convince that person that we are going to win!

The next day we convened in a large hall for presentations. Opposite the presenters were the IOC members, already seated in rows of chairs. At one end of the room was a large screen. Lillehammer's video was good. I spoke immediately afterward, and I felt that I got through to them. I chose to give a third of my speech in French. It had been recorded onto a cassette, and on the plane to Seoul I had practiced it. The IOC President, Juan Antonio Samaranch, Princess Anne of Great Britain, the Archduke of Luxemburg, former King Constantin of Greece, and all the rest of them listened.

In my speech I focused on the importance of the IOC's ideal to unite young people from all over the world, especially in a world characterized by war and conflict. I stressed the environment and the idea of sustainable development. I cited the principles of equality and solidarity between countries. The quality of the snow in Lillehammer and the other technical questions had already been presented. A number of those present in the hall that day were rumored to want a Nobel Peace Prize for the IOC, and the message of brotherhood and peace was clearly appreciated.

We all took note that the application from Anchorage was only supported by a video message from U.S. President George Bush. Its chances of winning were probably not the best.

It had been arranged for me to meet Senegal's powerful M'baye—the most important African on the IOC—after the presentation. He was also vice president of the International Court of Justice in The Hague. The World Commission's Indian member, Nagendra Singh, was president of the court. Later I heard that these two had been in touch with each other about Lillehammer, Norway, and me. Norway has always been a strong supporter of the court at The Hague, and Jens Evensen, my former cabinet colleague, had been a judge there for many years. Some of those present from Lillehammer no doubt thought it strange that I said nothing about Lillehammer but spoke only about international affairs and the importance of the court.

Later we met with some of the Norwegian athletes in the South Korean Olympic Village.

"The decision is 'Lilly Hammer' "

After about twenty-five hours on the ground in Korea we all gathered in Seoul, then headed home again. The mood was good. We had done all we could.

The night flight took us over Anchorage and the North Pole. At breakfast over the North Sea heading toward Oslo I finished off a few notes of what to say if we didn't win. There were three different texts. We didn't think Anchorage would get it, but all the other cities had a fighting chance. I did not prepare anything in the event of Lillehammer's winning. I am not superstitious, but all the same . . . Should we win, my remarks would be spontaneous. We arrived back at my office minutes before the live broadcast of the result from Seoul.

Samaranch emerged on the stage. He was handed a sealed envelope. He opened it, removed a small sheet of paper, and announced, "The decision is Lilly Hammer." It sounded as if he were introducing a female star. My heart did a little flip. I heard the sounds of celebration in the offices all around me, and the wave of joy spread across the whole country. I'll never forget that moment, not least because I found myself wondering for a moment: Was there an expression of slight surprise on Samaranch's face? I don't know how he cast his own vote. Then I said something I've always liked and used in several speeches: "If you doubt your case, then your case is lost before you start."

A few hours later we saw an interview with an angry and disappointed mayor from Sweden. Norway had used dishonorable methods, he maintained. This was arrant nonsense. We had simply used our imaginations!

The lesson is this: A small country can never make headway as a candidate on the international stage if it doesn't exploit the resources at its disposal.

The Winter Olympics in 1994 gave us fourteen wonderful days, and in sporting terms, a formidable success. We had a priceless advertisement for Norway as pictures of the winter landscape and of cheering Norwegians were beamed to TV screens around the world.

Losing and Winning the Government

12

As we entered the third year of our government in 1988, we were still struggling to get the national economy back on track. I knew that to have any chance of success we had to maintain the traditionally close political cooperation between the government, the party, and the Trade Union Council. Given all the criticism from the ranks and from certain trade unions, many believed that this was not possible.

But this year we received the support of the Center Party and had majority support in Parliament for the Law on Regulation of Incomes. This law was an important part of the framework for cooperation on income policy. We had to avoid wage increases and inflation, and were able to contain such a policy through time-limited legislation prohibiting wage increase, unless it was part of a broad, negotiated agreement. In the fall of 1988 we again collaborated with the parties of the Middle to be able to present a state budget that we could successfully defend in Parliament. By contrast, there were hardly any close connections among the three former government parties when we entered

1989, the year of the next election. For Labor, a lot of things were going well.

Many on the non-socialist side and in business circles thought that our government had been doing a good job with the economy. But it was no regular thing to read a senior political reporter's editorial in *Aftenposten* about the Labor leader: "No one can take away from the Prime Minister that she has been a virtuoso on the untuned instrument that Parliament is for any government. Deep into particulars, she has procured a majority for the policies Labor wants to implement." The headline of the editorial captured the overall tenor of the piece: "Strong leader for weak government." I did not care for praise that did not include the Party. But such partial praise was typical of the times. My international position and experience were highlighted but at the same time characterized as a problem. My every absence was said to weaken my control over what happened at home. Meanwhile, unemployment had started to rise sharply during the fall of 1988. Trade union leaders as well as the leader of the Socialist Left Party were up in arms. Unemployment continued to be a central economic and political issue far into the 1990s.

The National Congress in an Uproar

The Party Congress of 1989 focused on the selection of a new deputy leader. Thorbjørn "the Lip" Berntsen had announced his candidature long before. He was a popular politician, famous for his sharp tongue and his infectious humor. Many might have thought that he would have been an exciting deputy. A colorful trade unionist was easy to market. But selecting a deputy leader also means selecting a potential future leader and perhaps even a Prime Minister. The TUC leadership did not think Thorbjørn Berntsen would be the right candidate. The TUC leader is regularly chairperson of the election committee. The Party Congress election committee is always broadly recruited from all over the country.

When I arrived at the Party Congress Sunday, which was the last day of the meeting, Leif Haraldseth, the labor union leader, had presented the idea of two deputies for the election committee. His condition was that Gunnar Berge should be senior deputy and Thorbjørn Berntsen junior deputy. Berntsen protested and would agree only if the two deputies were equal. One paper characterized as masterful the presentation of the two-deputy compromise, calling it a "well-timed adaptation to the perestroika of the party."

In order to elect two deputies, the Party Congress had to agree to change the rules. A congress has the sovereignty to do so, but some party members stirred themselves into fevered oratory against this solution.

So now, as I listened, my heart fell. There was a clear risk that the proposal wouldn't pass. I knew that the election committee had done good work and had tested the proposed models with each of the different factions. Now there was no easy way out. I had written some notes, but I was very tense. Heart beating fast, I stood up. I looked into the faces of three hundred delegates, knowing that the only chance I now had was to present my inner thoughts totally openly.

I myself was convinced that the committee had presented the best possible proposal. We had been through a difficult period carrying the responsibility of government while negotiating in an economically difficult time. Thorbjørn Berntsen represented tradition. For some he had become the symbol of the trade unions and a guarantor against the party's going too far in modernizing. Now we would need both Gunnar and Thorbjørn.

I spoke my mind. I felt that my message came through. And one of my happiest moments as Party Leader came when my speech ended and, after a moment, the applause was thunderous.

Thorbjørn Berntsen served the party well. Eventually, he became Minister of the Environment.

The Sixth Year's Reform

In my political introduction to the Party Congress of 1989 I pointed out that we had just endured the most demanding few years since the reconstruction after World War II. Had the initially high income from North Sea oil simply blinded us and made saving seem old-fashioned? We had borrowed much more than we had saved. We had to be realistic and not use more than we created. When facing great challenges there is only one solution: More work, stronger effort on all fronts. Labor had a slogan: "Make your contribution to the common future." We wanted to reestablish the respect for everyone's duty to make a contribution.

The whole country had the Trade Union Council to thank. For the first time in the 1980s, prices in Norway would be on an equal level with the prices of our competitors. Norwegian commodities and services would stand a better chance of competing for customers at home and abroad.

The congress of 1989 also laid the groundwork for the great reform of the elementary and advanced school systems of Norway. It was a giant step forward. I felt strongly that our children should start compulsory learning before the age of seven. But there were many issues to be sorted out. Should the beginning school age be lowered to six? Should the new school be of nine or ten years' duration? What percentage of the school day should be totally free for recreation? Everybody felt strongly: parents, teachers, kindergarten professionals.

It would take some years before we could start implementing the school reforms. As recently as 1997, opposition to the reform stressed the insufficiency of school building-safety standards and educational material as well as the security of roads to the schools on which most pupils walk or bicycle to school.

Birthday

I turned fifty on April 20. I dreaded it. It had been difficult enough to be celebrating my fortieth birthday in 1979. Then we had had a private and informal party at home for forty or fifty people.

My preference was to drop the celebration for my fiftieth. I argued that I hardly had the time. But many others—family, friends, colleagues—insisted. I had to give in.

"We will have a family party that weekend, and there will be a small birthday party with cabinet colleagues at Foreign Minister Stoltenberg's house on Thursday evening," I explained to the journalists. I also used that interview as an opportunity to comment on my work outside of Norway: "I regularly spend about 10 percent of my time on international work. But I have the feeling that many imagine it otherwise." I had often given accurate information about the time that I spent abroad, and my coworkers had done the same, but it never turned up in the papers!

I was asked whether I was aware of the criticism of my international engagement. Yes, I answered, but we ought to have the nerve to do what is right in spite of criticism. It would have been wrong and irresponsible if we in Norway had simply looked at our own navels. We had to participate internationally. It would have been meaningless to stay within our own borders on principle. There were our children and our grandchildren to think about. It takes time to arrive at results. We have no reason to expect that everyone else will solve the big international challenges on our behalf. We must engage ourselves. We were facing an enormous process of internationalization. In ten years, I predicted, the Norwegian Prime Minister would travel internationally twice as much as I did. The 10 percent I devoted was necessary to care for Norway's interests in the revolutionary globalization then under way.

My birthday itself opened with breakfast in bed and a surprise visit by the whole family, grandchildren included. The nine o'clock music hour on NRK radio (the Norwegian equivalent of the BBC) was full of greetings from friends, opponents, and artists. Yet it was a Thursday, and the governmental schedule was followed routinely. But at three-thirty there was a reception for three hundred guests in Labor House. The whole family was there, little Oda at center stage, one and a half years old, smiling and running around. She was given a tricycle from the Socialist Left Party to symbolize our children, our environment, and our future.

I was overwhelmed. When I thanked everyone, I grew teary. My voice thickened. I had to break out of my emotions. I looked for my daughter. When our eyes met, Kaja laughed a little, shyly. She helped me that way. I talked to her directly from the rostrum: "Kaja, do not laugh!" Then I could go on. Togetherness, solidarity, and collaboration have given my life richness and excitement. This was my message of gratitude on that very special day.

The 1989 Election Campaign

Toward the end of the spring parliamentary session, the political climate was very much affected by the upcoming election. At the eleventh hour and to our great surprise, the Conservative leader, Jan Syse, proudly presented twenty-two points of agreement among the non-socialists. It was a common platform for a future non-socialist government. Most of the points could be supported by all parties, even Labor. There were no precise dividing lines. Nevertheless, these points became the nucleus for Jan Syse's successful post-election project to again establish a non-socialist three-party government.

During the campaign, however, we were optimistic. We had clear results to show for ourselves after three years in government.

But intervening factors helped change the atmosphere. NRK radio aired a report about shady contacts between Labor politicians and the Secret Service. It threw a dark shadow over the start of the campaign.

It went from bad to worse. During the summer, new sensational-istic headlines revealed that furniture dealer Arvid Engen, unknown to most of us, was unmasked as the leader of a mysterious network involving former Party Leader Reiulf Steen. It became publicly known that Mr. Steen had for many years conducted telephone conversations with Arvid Engen in which he gave his version of meetings, events, and persons in the party in full knowledge that Engen taped it all and then played the tapes for selected journalists. In this way, Steen manipulated media interpretation of many issues within the party and effectively attacked his adversary, former Prime Minister Odvar Nordli.

From the end of July until mid-August these shocking findings dominated the media. We in the party leadership could do little to limit the obvious political damage to the party.

The last week of July, while we were vacationing at our summer holiday home at Helleskilen, new Party Secretary Thorbjørn Jagland called to tell me about Steen's open admission of the main facts during a press conference to launch his book, *Power Struggle*. We publicly denounced his actions as disloyal and a violation of democratic principles. "Such actions cannot be tolerated," we maintained.

Steen's admissions were certainly not a good start for the last leg of the election campaign. The party was clearly thrown on the defensive.

We were helped by one of my positive performances on TV. Our spirit was reinvigorated. I received many positive comments. Whereas once I had been too tense and perhaps overly prepared for tough treatment by reporters, I now appreciated the effect of a smile.

A professor who was an expert on body language had previously criticized me: "She eagerly uses lip smiles, but almost never eye smiles, which are the genuine smiles. Her body often leans backward in protest and not forward in anticipation of the questions." Well, he had a point. Under pressure, one sometimes smiles too frequently and too shallowly. It seems necessary, because of the high temperatures in the TV studios, to consciously prevent viewers from experiencing the debate as a gladiator fight. To settle down and take deep breaths is the best way to prevent the temperature from rising. I had learned from my many confrontations with mediagenic Conservative Kåre Willoch during the early 1980s.

We were now faced with two relatively large right-wing parties, the Conservatives and the Progressives. My TV duel with Carl I. Hagen of the Progressives was no success. He is a clever debater. He managed to get on the offensive.

Labor did poorly in the 1989 elections, while the Socialist Left did well. Their new party leader, Erik Solheim, could take much of the credit. He had picked good issues—the environment and unemployment—and had directed his cannons against Labor and the government. It was tough to have the environmental cause used against us. We had made substantial improvement, and I personally had for many years made a contribution on the international level. After all, air and water do not respect national boundaries drawn on a map. Yet Solheim's continuous accusations that we did not do enough at home produced political results, and persuaded voters, especially the young.

I campaigned a great deal in northern Norway. We were using a chartered plane, the rear of which rattled disconcertingly when one of the photographers suddenly took ill. He lay down flat between the seats. I had to call upon my medical skills. Landing at the old Oslo airport, the body of the plane emitted a loud noise such as I had never heard on any of my numerous flights.

A few days later we held the final debate between party leaders on TV. Only minutes before we were scheduled to go on the air, I received a note: A chartered plane had been lost on its way to Denmark. No further information. I conferred with Syse, and we decided to go on with the debate. When it was finished, we concluded that all other campaign activities during that weekend should be postponed. The plane had crashed in the sea, and more than fifty people had lost their lives. I later realized that the lost plane was the one we had used in northern Norway only a few days before. This tragedy impressed me deeply. At the time, only Olav knew of my additional personal uneasiness about the whole tragedy.

Non-socialist Government Once Again

In the weeks after the election, the Conservatives, Christians, and Centrists again sought to establish a non-socialist government, with only a minority, and without including the Progressives. Few believed they'd be successful. But I knew that more unlikely things had happened. We would have to see. After a lot of leaks to the press and publicity pictures from their convention hall, they managed in the end. The next question was what the Progressives would decide to do. An agreement between the three non-socialists did not in itself produce a non-socialist majority or, for that matter, any real basis for a change of government.

Late in September I analyzed the situation in both the Central Executive Board and the Parliamentary Party Group. A declaration of will from the three non-socialist parties was not enough to overturn our government. Only if the Progressives supported the platform would there be the required majority; then we would have a new situation. And how would they ever stand together and handle our EEA negotiations?

I also analyzed our own poor showing. We had lost to both the Socialist Left and the Progressives in the municipalities where the economic problems were the most difficult and the pessimism most conspicuous, specifically in the areas dominated by traditional industry and in the coastal regions where there was a crisis due to the limitation in fishing quotas and where unemployment was high.

Suicide Paragraph

In the first days of October it seemed dauntingly clear that Carl I. Hagen had moved toward supporting a non-socialist government. Pressure mounted on Labor. Some suggested we give up right away.

This would be the easiest way for Syse to establish a new government. But was this really wise? We had experienced this situation in 1985–86 when the Willoch government had the Progressives on the tip of the scales but without any clarity about their support. Should we not instead wait for the non-socialist majority to prevail by itself in a vote—for example, the vote over the content of the "Speech from the Throne," the King's annual speech at the opening of the new session of Parliament, in which the main lines of the government's policy for the coming year are expressed? Should we not let them demonstrate whether they would have a real basis for majority government?

In essence, the outcome of the election had made no difference.

It could not be Labor's task to make the establishment of a non-socialist government as easy as possible. If we had the nerve to hold on and wait for the debate on the "Speech from the Throne," the four non-socialist parties would have to get together to vote down the policy of the Labor government.

My line was difficult to present publicly. It would make it easier for others to attack us. After the Progressives had declared that they were in support of an alternative government based on the twenty-two points, I chose the simplest way out. It was to ask for the floor after the budget was presented by our Minister of Finance. In my short declaration to the Parliament, I said that my basis for resignation was the declaration of the three non-socialist parties and the words from the Progressives. My declaration did not change the fact that the government, Labor, and our Parliamentary Group had clear points of disagreement with the twenty-two points from the non-socialists. We maintained it was unfit as a basis for governance.

A major concern was Norway's continuing negotiations for the agreement on the European Economic Area. We of course all knew that this had been the difficult issue in the discussion among the three non-socialist groups. This was the central problem for the Center Party. In reality they opposed an EEA agreement. So a key political challenge for this new government was just being swept under the carpet.

In public the new government published what was characterized by the media as the "suicide paragraph" on its relationship to the EU. It simply stated that the three parties reserved their rights to keep their respective positions on the relationship to the European Union. We did not refrain from remarking that such deep disagreement was a strange starting point for a new government.

Royal Burial Party

Each time our King bids good-bye to a departing government, he throws what is known as a "royal burial party" at the Palace. King Olav's warm words for me and my cabinet in 1981 had made a great impression on me. He discussed my time as Minister of the

Environment and as Prime Minister. He remembered events we had both attended. He thanked me for an inspiring cooperation. He also noted the importance of Norway's having had its first female Prime Minister.

When he spoke to us eight years later in 1989, King Olav referred to the demanding and difficult tasks that my second government had inherited in 1986. He touched upon what a thankless task it often is to be at the helm. During our personal and informal conversations, the King had expressed his uneasiness over our weak relations with Europe. To him this was an important failing in our national security policy.

In the weeks after the election of 1989, he too was worried about how the governmental situation would develop. He referred with concern to the governments of the interwar period and the situation before the Second World War. His Majesty feared much disagreement about foreign and security policy in our relationship with Europe.

I had conducted many a personal and confidential conversation with His Majesty, King Olav. I greatly valued his wise reflection, his enormous knowledge, and his sharp insights. I felt he appreciated being updated on my minority government, on our relationships with the trade unions and the Confederation of Business and Industry, on our struggle to obtain a defensible and long-term income policy. He often asked questions. He was a keen newspaper reader—and an astute observer of our country's position, at home and abroad.

In Opposition Again

By the middle of October, the Labor Party was again in opposition in Parliament. In my speech to our Parliamentary Group, I observed that the new Foreign Minister's comments on the Middle East had contributed to the impression that our new government had moved in favor of Israel and consequently was outside consensus on national views in foreign and security policy. We had to check this and help make sure that our country had a government that took care of Norway's interests based on the attitudes of the majority of Parliament. If not, we would have to speak up in the confidential exchanges in the Extended Foreign Relations Committee or, if need be, in public.

There had been much discussion as to whether the three government parties would be able to carry through consistent policies regarding an EEA agreement. In my speech I argued how important it was that people both inside and outside our party see that we stick to our policies. In opposition we would not deviate from the line we had followed at the helm. We noted with satisfaction that the government, at least for the time being, was continuing on our own course for the negotiations on an EEA agreement.

We had to think long-term. This new government could, in principle, last for the whole parliamentary period. New elections could not be held before 1993. We might be facing four years in opposition, and we had to plan our strategy in opposition accordingly. We had to establish working groups in which several different committee factions could join together and better hammer out our policies.

It was important to communicate informally and among factions. Nobody should "own" any issue without sharing with others. Communicate more rather than less, was my advice. We created theme groups across factions on the EU, the environment, coastal Norway, and family policies.

Together on Europe

In November we conducted a Parliamentary Group meeting to analyze the negotiations between EFTA and the EU. I was the only participant in that debate who had not previously opposed Norwegian EU membership. We now stood together to fight for the EEA solution.

Our overall strategy was to help the Syse government to stand on the majority view and pull the Center Party along as far as possible toward a "yes" vote on the EEA.

We enjoyed a high degree of agreement in the Parliamentary Group. Almost all of us supported the strategy for an EEA agreement. Everyone understood that if we did not succeed, then in the next issue—the debate over EU membership itself—great disagreement would prevail in Labor as well.

We debated at this point how we could move to protect Labor values by influencing the European internal market in the social dimension, labor rights, and environmental values. Like every other candidate for the EEA we had to start with the four freedoms: free movement of commodities, services, capital, and persons. This had been the situation in our own country as well as in the rest of Northern Europe for a long time. The big question was more exactly what rules and laws should govern the internal market. Would we be able to safeguard our social values, our environment, our commitment to a just and fair society?

Slow Motion

The negotiation process between EFTA and the EU for the EEA agreement began slowly. The EFTA countries, and in particular Norway under its new three-party government, operated with long lists of demands for exceptions from the basic rules. Norwegian Laws on Concession gave Norwegian authorities the right to privilege Norwegian citizens and enterprises in questions of market competition, and there was strong opposition in the Center Party against changes to those laws. The EU was growing impatient. EFTA solidarity held for some time, but the situation soon became untenable. Norway was perceived as the stumbling block to an agreement. The lack of tolerance for Norway became stronger. At the same time Sweden started to reevaluate its position. It looked like our neighbor would opt for membership in the EU.

In October 1990 the Minister of Trade informed Parliament about the situation in the negotiations. The government had great problems. The Minister of Trade believed that Norway had to reconsider the many special reservations we had presented to the EU, but she had no concrete proposals to make.

Norway seemed unable to act, unable to take care of our long-term interests in cooperation with the other Nordic countries and our EFTA partners. We would suffer a great loss if we ourselves should contribute to the breakdown of the important EEA agreement.

One point was clear. The old Free Trade Agreement of 1973 between Norway and the European Common Market, as the EU was then called, was no longer adequate. Without an EEA agreement, the possibility of EU membership would disappear. Either the three-party government had to find a solution, or we'd have to change the government so that it could fulfill its responsibilities as an EEA negotiator.

By now, no one on our side had any desire for Labor to take over and to work from a minority position as we had done between 1986 and 1989. But as leader of the Foreign Relations Committee and as previous Prime Minister, I felt the government had to change course. The EEA negotiations could not be stranded because of Norway. The alternative to EEA would be to force the issue of outright EU membership, and this certainly would mean moving from the embers to the flames. Labor now had to do its job as the biggest party in the land.

Meeting the "Queen of No"

In September 1990 the Foreign Relations Committee was in Africa. On the long way home I sat side by side with Anne Enger Lahnstein, who by now was the leading force in the Center Party and strongly dedicated to preventing Norway's entry into the EU. She was later dubbed the "Queen of No"! We actually discovered much in common. We agreed on the value of solidarity and democratic governance, the necessity of a strong public sector to care for a just distribution of resources between families, groups, and districts. We talked about the positive role of the trade unions. I told her about our internal party and trade union discussions on the EEA issue.

We were obsessed with finding good social solutions to take care of important national interests. Among the Laws on Concessions, we had to replace the ones regulating access to ownership of real estate. Foreigners faced stricter rules for obtaining obligatory concessions from our Ministries of Industry and Agriculture in order to acquire buildings or land, regardless of purpose. We would need to devise new instruments that would not be rejected by the EU and the EFTA countries as unfair privilege.

Lahnstein praised our national tradition of cooperatives, and we were both devoted to trade union rights, environmental and social concerns, and employment, although we differed sharply about the EU and whether to sign the EEA. We both thought that the role of the state would be important in the future, but also that there needed to be more cooperation in Europe.

Some later speculated that Anne and I had laid plans for the events of the subsequent weeks. But we did not talk directly about the Syse government, though everyone knew it had only a short life left.

Syse's Tight Spot

After a meeting on October 23 between the EFTA Ministers of Trade in Geneva, Parliament was to be briefed on EEA matters, with the parliamentary debate to follow a few days later. The Trade Minister of Switzerland, Jean-Pascal Delamuraz, was chairman and had demanded that all EFTA countries relinquish demands and long-term reservations about the rules of the EU if they wished to proceed with the negotiations. The Swedish Trade Minister posed the direct question to her colleagues: Is everyone ready to give up demands and reservations? All except Norway's Minister nodded.

Just before our Minister of Trade was to brief Parliament on the proceedings she asked my advice on how to proceed with the viewpoints she was unable to speak about in an open meeting of Parliament. She had to fulfill her duty to inform Parliament, but she ought not to say something that could undermine the negotiations. I suggested that what she could not say in public she could say to the Extended Parliamentary Foreign Relations Committee, which could be called to meet just after her speech to the full Parliament.

She took my advice and it became clear that the disagreement between the three government parties could not be resolved. The planned debate was postponed. Prime Minister Syse announced instead that the government would step down.

Demanding Days

I had begun to prepare myself for the eventuality that Labor would have to take over. I had many names on my list for Ministers. But the situation was not clear.

On Monday the Christian People's Party and the Center Party conducted their respective Group meetings. The Christian People's Party wanted to support a minority Conservative government. The Center Party recommended that Labor take over the government. I was in my office when Anne Enger Lahnstein informed me of her party's wish. I stayed in my office, preparing myself to appear on TV a little later.

On television, Lahnstein explained that the biggest party ought to take the job. At the same time she made it clear that the priority question for the Center Party now was the fight against membership in the EU.

I was guarded in my public comments. There was no constitutional call to form a government. Labor alone had no majority. We had to further explore the political basis for a future Labor government. Labor would not take office if we did not have a reasonable chance to pursue our policies. We had already hammered out an alternative state budget, which we were willing to pursue either in government or in opposition.

The basis for the three-party government had not been sufficient. Yet the Center Party stressed that if Labor formed a government, the Center would be a free party in opposition. Labor risked being alone with the main responsibility, as the Conservatives and the Progressives would also be in clear-cut opposition. Thus the Christians and Socialist Left Party would be able to pressure us on a number of different issues. We ourselves would have a burden as heavy as the outgoing Syse government had had in Parliament. Only Labor and the Christian People's Party would be fully committed to a comprehensive EEA agreement. And Norway was in the middle of crucial international negotiations.

It was incredibly important in this situation to pressure the other parties to take some co-responsibility. I stressed within the party that we now needed to establish a parliamentary majority's support for the formation of a Labor minority government. We wanted to build more nursery schools and day-care centers for children. We wanted to secure the role of the state banking system, and increase the efforts for environmental protection and collective transportation. We had to secure support for some of our key policies by presenting them to the parties of the Middle and to the Left Socialists. And I had to be certain that in any attempt to form a new government I had the support of our own party and of the labor union movement.

Negotiations

We called a meeting of the Coordination Committee of Labor and TUC and held it in the Parliament building in order to save time. I knew that it was all-important that the trade unions support us, so that we could present a coherent and responsible political line.

I also took up our alternative budget, our tax profile, and our six points for improving Norwegian industry and business policies, which I would present to the leaders of the three other parties.

The TUC boss, Yngve Hågensen, said that the unions were concerned on the basis of their experience from the 1986–89 period. A minority taking governmental responsibility had to adapt its policies in order to obtain the necessary majority. This meant that one later had to explain such compromises to the voters. Hågensen stressed the importance of sticking to the main lines of our alternative budget. The non-socialists had not been able to stick to theirs.

He pointed out that cooperation on income policies represented a clear dilemma. If the TUC should link up we ought to be able to ensure results. And we, of course, did not control a majority. Regarding the EU, Hågensen said we had to move slowly.

My own experience from the 1986–89 period was that the unions had withheld their support. The difference between a Labor government backed by the TUC and one that is not is like day and night. One of my deputy leaders said it straight out: If TUC did not want a Labor government to take over, we had better not make the attempt. I think that Hågensen understood the point and became more forthcoming as a result.

We had a six-point plan, a comprehensive intiative to improve industry and business policy in order to secure employment. Many firms were low in equity and so handicapped in the efforts to exploit the possibilities for growth, making them vulnerable for takeovers. Our six points had been developed in a partnership between the Labor Party and the TUC, based on our traditional ideology. We asked Parliament to approve this plan as the basis for our new minority government—and we found more support than we had expected. A majority asked Labor to form the new government.

Labor by now had the support of 46 percent of the country in nationwide opinion polls. The brief Syse era had actually built support for us. In forming a new Labor government, we would not have any binding agreement with any other party, so our government could lose power at any moment. But it eased our task that the Norwegian people clearly felt that the Conservative coalition was incapable of leading the country.

Chapter 13

Safety Net: The European Economic Area

EEA in Its Own Right

In Parliament our new Minister of Trade put it this way: Our adaptation to the EU's internal market had to be understood as an integrated part of the modernization of the Norwegian economy. Globalization had arrived to stay and would be even more comprehensive than we imagined in 1989.

For me it was clear from the onset of the EEA process that EEA was important in and of itself, apart from the question of EU membership. I was not sure that the Norwegian people would decide to join the EU within a reasonable period of time. And the most enthusiastic supporters of membership—in my own party, in the European Movement and among the Conservatives—created a considerable political problem by not treating the EEA question separately from the issue of EU membership. My main argument was that by adopting the EEA, we would not forgo our freedom of choice at any future crossroads. We would need a three-fourths majority in Parliament to pass any future treaty. Thus, we were absolutely dependent on the votes of the Christian Party, which was uncompromisingly against EU membership. Joining the EEA would not open the door to any eventuality regarding the EU and so was safe for EU opponents to support.

The Battle for the EEA

That winter, as Norway and the other EFTA countries were negoti-ating a final EEA agreement, a comprehensive set of regulations for the internal market had to be finalized. The Center Party felt free to wage an active campaign against anything that smacked of the EU, including of course the EEA.

At the annual general meeting of the Nordland County Labor Party, there was no doubt that opposition toward the EU and the EEA had established considerable grass-roots support. Strong speakers, particularly on behalf of the fishing and agricultural in-dustries, made their opposition very clear. Nevertheless, a clear ma-jority in favor of the EEA had emerged, even in Nordland. I came away with an even stronger impression of how crucial this issue was in the provinces, especially in northern Norway.

In March I visited the Northern Norwegian Labor Party branch of Troms County. Up here the opposition to the EEA was much stronger. The county Party Leader was himself an acknowledged skeptic about many issues, and many times over the years the party leadership had encountered dissent from his branch. To counter his opposition, I spoke with great conviction. "Look at all the good fea-tures of the Troms County Labor Party program," I said. Yet, I added, one of the principal problems of the county was that exports of processed-fish products to the EU were hampered by tariff barri-ers of up to 30 percent! I stressed that our demand was a clear one: free trade for fish throughout the EEA. We would also issue a clear rejection of the EU's counterdemands (in exchange for free trade they wanted new access to Norwegian waters, and to establish higher fish quotas). But we had a strong hand to play, and we could prevail!

The EEA was actually much like the North American Free Trade Agreement (NAFTA). But whereas NAFTA consisted of only three countries—Mexico, the United States, and Canada—the EEA was meant to be made up of all European Union members and all EFTA members alike.

The Troms County meeting adopted a unanimous statement that the EEA should be treated as an independent alternative, unrelated to EU membership. It criticized the continual intermixing of the EU and EEA debates.

We were constantly exposed to pressure from all quarters. Carl Bildt, the leader of the Conservative Party in neighboring Sweden, had several times directed sharp criticism at the Labor Party and at me because we had restricted the debate to the EEA agreement. He said that the Nordic region would be damaged by any delay in Norway's application for EU membership. There had been lots of headlines: "Gro Harlem Brundtland is a coward." "She is dragging her heels over the question of the EU." "The EU train is leaving now."

I actually agreed with Carl Bildt that I should be involved in educating people about the EU and EU membership. It was not my intention to sit and wait for opinion to form. I wanted to carry opinion with me in favor of an EEA agreement in such a way that we could later convince Norway to join the EU. So I kept a cool head, even though I was immeasurably irritated by Bildt and Norwegian Conservatives.

I was quite certain that, despite Bildt's urgency, the EU would not place decisive weight on whether Norway applied for membership early or late in 1992. There were, to be sure, several signs that a clarification of the Norwegian position was wanted, but at the same time there were expressions of respect for our own democratic processes.

Will the EEA Slip Through the Net?

Speculation was rampant both before and during the EEA negotiations meeting in Luxemburg in June 1991. Both the unresolved fishery questions and other problems looked as though they might upset the whole EEA agreement. In spite of it all, I was never in any doubt myself. Solutions would be found.

Between midnight and one o'clock on the morning of June 20, I received a telephone call from my Foreign Minister, Thorvald Stoltenberg: "We have reached agreement." Happy and relieved, he tells me about the principal features of the political agreement that has come about during the Ministers' working dinner. Full market access for Norwegian fish products, and in return Spain would take over all of the EU's present catch quota in the Spitzbergen sector. This was happy news!

VG and *Dagbladet* celebrated the next day—"EEA Agreement Last Night" and "Total Victory Last Night"—and reported that the Norwegians earned considerable praise from Jacques Poos, the Luxemburg Foreign Minister who presided for the EU, and from Austrian Trade Minister Wolfgang Schüssel, presiding for EFTA.

The press pressured me for interviews all day. I usually prefer that those who create the news be the ones to talk to the press, but on this day, in reply to a newspaper question, I confirmed that the agreement was the most important thing to have happened during my premiership. Then problems began to surface.

The next day my Trade Minister gave her report to Parliament. She started by referring to skeptical remarks that were said to have emanated from Brussels that afternoon. The chairman of the EFTA and the chairman of the EU Council of Ministers have both said that a political agreement exists in respect to the fisheries question, but that important work remains to be done at the technical level.

A new EEA meeting is scheduled in Salzburg. The majority had once been hopeful that this meeting would be the great day of victory for the EEA process, resulting in the provisional signing of the EEA agreement. Instead EFTA and the EU continue the tug-of-war about transport, funds, and fishing.

Foreign Minister Stoltenberg reported that Jacques Poos confirmed on the phone everything he had said at the press conference in Luxemburg: that there had been political agreement reached with regard to the main points, but that the details were still to be sorted out and discussed by experts on both sides. Such a thing can be difficult when nineteen countries' fishery experts have to reach an agreement. "That is why I am not surprised at the reluctance from EU member states that we have recently experienced," said Stoltenberg.

I was less optimistic a few weeks later. It gradually became clear that the EU would not be able to deliver what had been expected after the Luxemburg meeting.

Consequently, we considered withdrawing our offer of access to fishing grounds off Spitzbergen. From the meetings in Brussels, it emerged that several countries' representatives had adopted positions that were counter to what their own Ministers had approved in Luxemburg!

The problem was this: Only the Norwegian politicians actually saw the fishing issue as being important enough to involve politicians at a high level. With the exception of Iceland, no other country in Europe fully comprehended the dimensions of Norwegian fishery policy. In no other country did the coast play the central role that it does in our country. The politeness and friendliness with which we were generally met often concealed a lack of insight into the complex fishery issues.

Labor and the whole trade union movement rallied behind our cause. Young Jens Stoltenberg, who would become Prime Minister nine years later, said, "The world is unfair. When other countries demand our fish, we get the blame for saying no!"

A Government Under Attack

But at the Conservative Party's Central Executive Board meeting in August, the new Conservative leader Kaci Kullmann Five attacked me outright, as if we were in an election campaign. "Gro still maintains that EU membership is not on the agenda," she said. "That is totally wrong. Out in the country, membership is on the agenda! Gro did not think that Sweden would seek membership before Norway. That happened. She promised that the EEA agreement would be ready in July, and then in August. That did not happen. She 'celebrated' the agreement on free trade for fish. She relied on talks with the EU Commission's President, Delors, to solve the problem in the final stage. That has not happened. Conclusion: Norway will have learned that things can go seriously wrong by relying blindly upon Brundtland's assessment of the European developments, upon her contacts and initiatives to get Europe to dance to the Labor Party Leader's tune!"

Norway's considerable difficulties, and those of the minority government, were now being exploited to the fullest. I was deeply disappointed with the way the Conservatives were behaving. In Parliament, however, I replied in a moderate tone that I did not find it very constructive for us to use time and energy discussing whether we should have been satisfied with the result that the EU announced after the Luxemburg ministerial meeting now that we knew that the EU was not in agreement with that announcement. Whether we liked it or not, we would not reach a final goal until all nineteen EU countries said yes to the arrangement we had worked out. We could not now conduct a public debate about Norway's position, for we were still in negotiations, fighting for a vital interest. Those who sought to gain short-term political advantage from the fact that we had an unresolved conflict would themselves have to accept the responsibility for the negative consequences for the country.

No one could be in any doubt about for whom my words were intended. The Conservatives had themselves been running the government recently, and they were in favor of an EEA agreement. Yet now they chose to work against the Labor Party on an issue that was vital to the country. It was incredibly disappointing, and it had significant damaging effects. The EU countries opposed to the agreement were now in a stronger position. And even though the Conservative attack was directed against the government, it of course left a negative impression toward the entire EEA agreement. The criticism went so far that the Conservatives' leader found it necessary to point out, after the debate in the Parliament, that the Conservatives were still in favor of the EEA!

I felt real indignation when I encountered the Conservatives' Kaci

Kullmann Five in a radio debate soon after. It was no gala performance, for either me or Kaci. The bitterness between us was clear. I can confirm that mine was genuine.

Electoral Defeat

The local elections in 1991 were far from satisfying for the Labor Party: 30.9 percent, 10 percent less support than in 1985! We tended to drop a couple of percentage points in local elections, but there was no way to explain the 1991 outcome as anything other than weak. There was no doubt that the combination of the EEA debate, the nascent "No to the EU" campaign, and the effects of the economic crisis had made an impact.

My September 19 diary entry records my impression of the tough postelection debate: "The thought of leading once again toward an election and of being the subject of assessment every minute, for weeks and months, is daunting. If you hammer, or are hammered, then—either way—there will be wailing." I further noted that the Young Labor leader had stated that our plans for increasing the number of nursery schools were not visionary enough—because they would not provide an adequate number of schools.

This little note illustrated how much I had been hurt, for I took this very personally. The Young Labor leader was putting emphasis on popular reactions to our policies, our programs, and our overall political results. Yet now she was critical of me. Throughout all these years I had felt that Young Labor was among my strongest supporters. Young people looked for renewal. Young people wanted to talk concretely. They were impatient. They were less constrained by old traditions. Was I now losing their support?

In my address to the National Executive Board I emphasized that we had no doubt lost support because we were not perceived from the outside to be standing together. Disunity could not fail to erode our reputation among the voters. Internal strife is always costly. Very costly.

Alone

In my postelection comments, I had placed increasing weight upon the self-evident connection between the solution to the country's problems—employment, trade, and industry—and the arrangements we would be able to make through cooperation with other European countries.

It was frustrating now to observe that both the Socialist Left and the Center Party had completely withdrawn from the whole EEA process, ranging themselves in a clear "no" position against both the EEA and the EU. At the same time we were dependent upon these two parties in domestic policies. The Conservatives had also allowed themselves to think most of all about their own party and the battle for votes, rather than about Norway's best interests.

I was more than ever convinced that we would have to write a very different "Speech from the Throne" this year. The speech would be read as usual by the King to Parliament at its opening in October. Queen Sonja and Crown Prince Haakon Magnus would be at the King's side. It would be the first time that King Harald, who had taken over the throne, had read such a speech. As clearly as possible, we would need to speak out on the direct connection between our key national challenges and the international frameworks surrounding us, particularly the vital EEA agreement. It was not enough that we had finally won support from the Christian People's Party. We still lacked the three-fourths majority for adopting any EEA agreement. I did not feel I could take responsibility for the country's government if the Labor Party did not gain sufficient support from the other parties, both for the implementation of a domestic economic rescue operation and for bringing about the EEA agreement that the country so badly needed.

The beginning of the "Speech from the Throne" reflected precisely that understanding: It stressed the close connection between our high unemployment and the rapid changes in the international environment. It called for comprehensive cooperation between political authorities and labor, trade, and industry in order to regain full employment and to preserve and renew the welfare state. Then came the one sentence that everybody took note of: "It is absolutely necessary that there be support for a policy that is able to secure these goals."

The speech went deeper into the seriousness of the situation: "The government sees it as a major task to ensure working conditions in Norwegian businesses that are as good as those of businesses in other European countries upon the introduction of the internal market on January 1, 1993. The government will therefore work toward the successful completion of the negotiations between the EU and EFTA leading to a comprehensive agreement on a European Economic Area and presupposes that the agreement shall gain the requisite majority in Parliament."

If we did not gain support for these principal lines of policy, then there was no basis for our government's mandate. I had gotten my point across. The words, though spoken by the King, were mine. It was a strong declaration of intent. It was my duty to remind the Parliament that a minority administration must be able to mobilize sufficient support around key national policies. In our situation, we were dependent upon support on international issues from parties other than those that were, on principle, behind us on the domestic policies. This was the defining comment that it had now become absolutely essential for me to make. The words that King Harald had spoken caused a stir and were debated over the ensuing days. Most people realized that there was an implied warning about a possible stepdown of the government in these words, though I never openly confirmed this.

There is a long tradition for the "Speech from the Throne" to have a specific and real content, and neither King Olav nor King Harald had ever indicated that they had any objections to this tradition. This occasion was no exception: His Majesty had had no problem laying out the political message inherent in these important sentences. On the contrary, I knew that both King Olav and King Harald had been very concerned about the difficulties inherent in a minority administration's governing the nation, and also about that very important aspect of Norwegian politics—our relationships with other countries.

The New Swedish Prime Minister

When Sweden's new Prime Minister, Carl Bildt, planned to visit Oslo, I anticipated that his once aggressive and excessive criticism of me would assume a different character. He was now himself in a position of responsibility. He represented Sweden. He had to cooperate with Norway.

I assumed correctly. With a self-critical humor he put his previous comments aside, and I refrained from rubbing salt into the wounds. We were in the same boat; we had to stand together to bring about an EEA agreement. We were also going to conduct a debate regarding the future relationship of Norway and Sweden with Europe, in which we needed to support each other. In this context, party politics were of secondary importance.

And so it was that Carl Bildt and I, with the help of our two offices, came to be a driving force behind the work of revitalizing Nordic cooperation. It represented an important milestone when we managed to see our way through to a platform for all-inclusive Nordic cooperation. Moreover, it was of immense importance for me to affirm that if one of the Nordic countries did not wish to become an EU member, it would not cause a split between us.

This was hard for Carl Bildt to swallow at first. For him it was self-evident that all of the Nordic countries should become members of the EU. But we could not establish the foundation of Nordic cooperation in such a way that any country would be excluded.

Three days after Bildt's visit, in a joint ministerial meeting in Luxemburg, the EU and EFTA countries came to an agreement regarding our cooperation in a European Economic Area. Finally, we had the result we had wished to achieve two months earlier.

We had struggled with the question of fishing right up to the last moment. The long tradition in the EU (which in many ways is based on reciprocity) had been to link access to markets with access to resources on the fishing grounds. We on the Norwegian side had exactly the opposite point of departure. But we had come to compromise. Norway was asked to allocate catches in Norwegian waters to EU countries, and we accepted an agreement with partial free-market access and granted cod quotas to Spain and Portugal.

There were to be new setbacks in a few weeks, when the EU Court rejected the EEA agreement on the grounds that its planned institutional solutions were of questionable legality within the Treaty of Rome, which is the EU's constitution. The whole affair seemed like an endless war!

A Union Discussion at Lake Mylla

In December 1991, trade union boss Yngve Hågensen and his wife, Astrid, drove up to visit Olav and me at our vacation home at Lake Mylla. With time and quiet, we could have a pleasant meal together and go through the issues about which there might be disagreement. It had been a self-evident assumption that the trade union movement was an integral part of our political work. Yngve and I had spent a lot of time together; our party had placed considerable weight upon the labor movement's views; and no major issue was decided without our having talked about it beforehand.

All the same, from Yngve's point of view, his movement's access to power was clearly not good enough. He felt that the trade union movement did not possess sufficient influence over the issues that concerned it.

What the TUC concludes about an issue before submitting a demand must be its own responsibility. What the party's leadership and the government decide with regard to the overall management of the economy is our responsibility. But in both cases there must be a dialogue. We must help one another and learn from one another.

Labor had been suffering a stream of criticism of a more ideological nature. The party and government were being accused of not building upon the right values. We did not place sufficient emphasis upon employment, upon evenhanded distribution among people and industry. We did not endeavor well enough to help the weakest among us.

During the hours we were together, Yngve was quite open about the things that most dissatisfied him. He felt that we had given too much ground while balancing the state budget in Parliament. Here, of course, was the problem of ruling without a majority and of having to make compromises with other parties in order to pass the most important parts of our policy. Under such conditions, problems that most interest the union movement do not necessarily find optimal solutions.

Yngve pointed out that there had been some disagreements between his economic adviser and mine, and he stressed how important it was for us to be able to have agreement between the Prime Minister's office, the Finance Ministry, and the TUC. He was critical of the State Secretaries in the Ministry of Work and Administration and in the Finance Ministry.

He also brought up what he referred to as "the wear-and-tear" issues for laborers: unemployment benefits, leave of absence schemes, retirement age, sick pay, the social security net, and apprentice wages, among others. These were all practical matters—and difficult matters. We had always discussed changes of this type very carefully with the trade union movement, but we did not always end up agreeing.

Nonetheless, we soon agreed that we had to make even more time for discussion, not merely between Yngve and myself, but also between the various unions and the political leadership in the Ministries. This was the kind of line I had intended to follow right from the start. If one takes time, and considers all the questions about which there can be disagreement, then solutions can often be found.

Economic Upturn—At Last

At the start of the election year 1993, Labor was in agreement about its strategy. We would stand together on our values and our policies for the coming years. Differences over EU membership should not derail us. But as the Center Party and the Socialist Left Party had started campaigning against EU membership long ago, and as the Conservative Party could hardly hold back its determined push for membership, it was a fearsome task for Labor to win support for our agreed solution, the European Economic Area. Meanwhile, most EFTA countries wanted not just an EEA, but actual EU membership. The negotiation for the shrinking remainder of the EFTA with the growing force of the EU would not be easy.

The media was to a considerable extent dominated by the question of EU membership for Norway. Finland and Sweden were by now already negotiating for their own EU memberships. We planned to start negotiations in order to assess the prospect for Norwegian membership sometime later in the spring.

This year's May First celebrations became controversial. Some anti-EU activists chose that day to demonstrate against membership. As a result, our Party Leader, Thorbjørn Jagland, declined to speak at an event in Oslo.

I was to speak in Kristiansand this First of May. It is always exciting to see who comes and what the mood is like on a day like this. Spirits were high, and the weather was beautiful. At least two thousand people thronged the main square in "the Capital of South Norway." In my speech I stressed international solidarity and our duty to help the victims of wars, as well as the refugees on our own continent.

My remarks reflected the dramatic developments in Europe. Civil war was raging in the former Yugoslavia. In other countries, fear of foreigners and isolationism had led to attacks on asylum-seekers and refugees; Jewish memorials had also been desecrated. It was of central importance that our long-term assistance to the developing countries continued. We had to help create a new and more just world. The developing countries must be allowed better access to our markets for their products. We must assist by forgiving the past debts of the new democracies. Let us not forget, I implored, that we once upon a time were a developing country, too. It was only when we managed to combine political democracy with the building of a strong state that we made economic progress, when we managed to invest in both welfare and employment.

Norway could not turn its back on the international community, I declared. That was the reason everything went bust in Eastern Europe: Those countries had isolated themselves economically and politically, and worse, they had blocked free contact among peoples.

This First of May I was pleased because the interest rate finally was going down. In just a short while the Bank of Norway had lowered interest rates from 11 percent to 7.5 percent, a reward for the economic discipline that had been the government's policy, a policy that had enjoyed the support of the trade unions.

I felt that something relaxed that sunny day. Our message was heard. I became so inspired by the warm applause that I could not resist stepping up to the podium to join the local women's choir singing our best labor songs. So the TV viewers saw their Prime Minister singing out! I was happy!

Great Skepticism

Two weeks later we debated the government's long-term national plan in Parliament. It was now possible for me to describe a number of the most important results of our policy: moderate increases in nominal incomes and very little inflation, with cooperation from the trade unions. At the same time we had put through measures for business that had made a great improvement in Norway's ability to compete. This job had been more difficult while the world economy was in a serious decline in the early 1990s. Internationally, unemployment had risen dramatically and the trend had hit many sectors of the Norwegian economy.

Our economic policy, however, had finally brought about a reduction of interest rates. We had performed far better than our neighbors during the European currency crisis of the previous fall. In contrast to Sweden and Finland, we did not have to make cuts but could continue to develop our welfare programs.

Nevertheless May 22 brought an alarming opinion poll: Conservatives were ahead of Labor! Many now took for granted that we had already lost the next election.

The Nordic Prime Ministers Meet

Meanwhile, the EU issue was constantly in the media. The Nordic Prime Ministers' summer meeting was in Reine, a village in the Lofoten Islands off northeastern Norway. Our focus was coastal Norway, Norwegian traditions and culture, the fisheries, and the principle of sustainable development and management of resources. I have never been any good at fishing, but Swedish Prime Minister Carl Bildt put his heart and soul into winning the competition we held on a boat one evening. His catch weighed twenty-two pounds and he was instantly as happy as a boy. Then suddenly my eye caught some grampus and I proudly shouted, pointing: "Look here, we have the whales!" This was quite something for the visiting delegations from our neighboring countries, which, with the exception of Iceland, were rather skeptical about the Norwegian whaling policy. They themselves had only limited experience with whaling and did not support our whaling even for scientific purposes. But at least here they could see real whales, and for most of them it was a first.

Three Nordic countries were now busily negotiating with the EU. For us the control over resources and fishing rights was the most important issue. We wanted to educate our Nordic neighbors on this particular point. But our own voters were skeptical. "No to the EU" was now far ahead in the polls.

Cabinet Cabaret

The first opinion polls after the summer recess showed support for Labor mounting. The results came in the same day we held our campaign launch in Labor House. It was covered live by television, not a testament to our solid political message, but rather because three of our cabinet members had prepared a "Cabaret Surprise." They had mobilized the whole cabinet, myself included, to perform songs and poems.

Per Kristian Foss of the Conservatives was asked to comment. He made a mistake we politicians should stay away from: He made critical remarks about the quality of the Prime Minister's singing voice! People thought the cabaret was great fun. They liked our audaciousness.

Our Minister of Fishing and I sang "We Are Whaling," written to the hit song "We Are Sailing." At my annual summer press conference in June I had announced that the government would reinstate traditional whaling. After years of a moratorium and subsequently only small quotas for research purposes, this was great news for coastal Norway. This was Norway's attitude to the resources in the oceans—long-term management built on a scientific basis.

We opened the campaign with two questions for the average voter: Who should govern the country? and, Are you willing to take the risk of new non-socialist experiments? In my first campaign speech I could declare that Norway was on the right track economically after a number of difficult years. We should stay the course. Unemployment was still too high, and we could do more about it.

Labor Carried Aloft

The Conservative approach was to make a massive critique of Labor's economic policies. It did not work. People could see the results of our policies in their daily lives. Rents and interest rates were lower; price increases no longer ate up wage increases.

There was dissent in the Conservative ranks. The message of the Conservative leadership for tax reductions and reduced public spending was not accepted out in the country. Toward the end of the campaign, the Conservative Party changed its message, trying to minimize their differences with Labor's policies. To change horses midstream, however, does not convince the voters.

We were confident. A first report about the mood of the voters regularly emerges from the voting arranged in public schools. Although this takes place while there are still several days left of the campaign and in spite of the young age of these "trial voters," this mock election normally serves as a good index of the actual outcome. That year we did very well in the school voting.

In 1989 we had chosen to fight two right-wing parties, the Conservatives and the Progressives, which actually played into the hands of the Progressives. In 1993 we decided to concentrate on the Conservatives, the largest of the non-socialist parties. The Progressive vote sank from 13 to 6 percent and the Conservatives won only 17 percent.

Aside from Labor, the Center Party was the biggest winner. Their Leader had stuck to her strong opposition to Norwegian EU membership. She was rewarded. Postelection surveys showed that the Center Party took voters from every other party and that the loyalty of their own voters stayed high. For the first time in the history of that party, they won MPs from all constituencies and became the biggest of the non-socialists.

We had secured a substantial basis for continuing Labor government. But the Center Party had strengthened its basis for winning the Great War—the war over Norwegian membership in the European Union.

The Long Struggle Toward EU Membership

14

When was Norway going to make up its mind? For several months there had been impatient attention from many different quarters. Would the country seek membership in the European Union? The effort to decide began in 1992 when the Labor Party completed a wide-ranging debate throughout the country. We needed to have as many people as possible involved in this debate. There had been six hundred study circles with twelve thousand participants. A total of twenty thousand consultations had been conducted. The results of the extensive survey on the European question were presented on April 1, 1992.

A full 50 percent of all Norwegians were in favor of applying for membership, 25 percent were against, and 25 percent were undecided.

Did I not have an opinion myself? Certainly, and so did many others. But this was a historic decision, and the matter was one that would finally be determined by means of a referendum. So other key leaders of Labor and I had to carefully choose our timing.

Together with Our Neighbors?

Things had changed dramatically since the question of EU member-ship had first arisen in 1972, and the changes were becoming more and more rapid. The Berlin Wall came down in November 1989. The Cold War was over. The Eastern European countries were knocking at the door of the EU. And so were our two neutral neigh-bors, Sweden and Finland. In the course of the last two years, the pace of political development had been so rapid that deep-rooted attitudes had to give ground. The EU had now become the most important coalescing political force, not merely in Western Europe, but throughout the whole of Europe.

In November 1990, when the National Labor Party Congress es-tablished the lines of our debate about "Norway in a new Europe," we knew that Sweden was going to apply for membership and that its neutrality was no longer an obstacle. We agreed that we should place great emphasis upon our relationship with the other Nordic countries and achieve close cooperation with them. Two years later, in 1992, when we had still not brought the big EEA agreement safely into harbor, the National Labor Party Congress still had to adopt a position about whether we, too, should seek membership in the EU.

Our French Socialist colleague Jean-Pierre Cot had recently put it this way when talking to the press: "The EU is a supranational co-operation that means that social-democratic values and policies are, for the first time, promoted within an arena that had hitherto been restricted to the multinational companies." Margaret Thatcher's fears of socialism sneaking in via Brussels had not been entirely un-founded!

Democracy Across National Borders

On Sunday, April 2, I participated in the Hordaland County Labor Party's annual meeting in Ullensvang. Others in the party leadership

and several members of the government were going to attend other
annual county meetings around the country. This was "Super Sunday," Norwegian style. Our Agriculture Minister had already given
the grounds for her "yes" in a newspaper feature article. The Foreign Minister, the Minister of the Environment, and the Party Secretary were all going out into the field. How would they argue? What
would they emphasize? Would they all strongly promote a "yes" decision? Nobody knew.

There was no doubt that our nerves were on edge. It was an important day. What kind of mood would our representatives encounter? How would they react? I had scribbled before actually
writing my own speech, drawing concentric circles around a black
spot at the center. The dot was the single individual. The first circle
was the people locally; the next circle was regional, within the
larger national circle of Norway. An order of democratic decision-
making processes. But what was beyond that? How could we develop democracy beyond our national borders? My work with the
environment had strengthened my conviction: We had to have
greater democracy, not merely within each individual country, but
across all national borders.

In my final remarks, I took up these central themes. To say "no"
to participation in a binding international cooperation was to impose limits upon government by the people. We would then re-
nounce our opportunities for achieving our democratic goals!

I formulated my own conclusion: "As on so many occasions before in the history of our nation, a crucial choice rests, first and
foremost, with the Norwegian Labor Party. Cooperation within the
EU does not provide an answer to all our challenges, but it makes
us better able to confront them. I believe that we serve Norway's interests best by joining the EU. Then we shall be able to fight for the
solutions we believe in, both in Norway and within the European
arena. We must not wait to see what the future will bring. We must
create our own future, now!"

"A waterfall of arguments"

The meeting hall was full. There were almost a hundred representatives of the press. The TV cameras had been on throughout most of my hour-long speech. My own personal conclusion would not end the debate. The party would not decide whether Norway ought to send an application for membership in the European Union until the National Congress in November.

The reception was generally good, but varied. One newspaper's commentator felt that the text did not appeal to people's hearts but was more along the lines of cool rational argument. That was true enough. It was much easier for those who were opposed to membership to make emotional appeals by creating suspicion and distance, calling Labor's motives into question, purporting to defend everything that was ours—our culture, our history, our traditions. Defending what is familiar, defending what is close at hand, is easy. We had to argue for change.

In the days leading up to the Ullensvang meeting, the Prime Minister's office had received several inquiries from groups who wished to have their own meetings with me. Normally this would not be a natural thing to do when I was going to a party meeting that required full involvement on my part. This time was different; the pressure was strong. "Surely she can let us have five minutes?" "We must be able to hand over a petition to her!" I decided to let people present their concerns.

The petition that we had agreed that I should accept was from a grandmother my own age, who appealed to me on behalf of the shared future of her grandchild and my own little Oda, Kaja's daughter. The Norwegian press and TV cameras were in position, of course. Standing around her was the Marxist-Leninist committee from the Odda smelting plant. Also in our company was my Secretary of State, who had lived in Hordaland County himself twenty years before. He actually had had many doubts along the way to his eventual "yes" conclusion. But our interlocutors had entertained no doubts whatsover about their opinion. The television coverage that

evening contained a large element of the "no" side's activity in Ullensvang and gave extensive coverage to the petition. My daughter
Kaja was not pleased, feeling that she and her daughter had been
exploited in a political battle in which she herself had no part!

The Danish "No"

One afternoon in early June 1992, in Rio de Janeiro, where I was
taking part in the big U.N. conference on the environment and sustainable development, I received the news from Copenhagen: The
Danish people had said "no" to the Maastricht Treaty negotiated by
the EU member states to further intensify European integration. My
heart sank. Yet another blow. The atmosphere among the press was
electric. "What would Gro say about this? Surely now she will lose
heart about Norway's membership bid." I prepared to comment at a
hastily convened press conference.

Could we allow ourselves to be influenced by this? I asked. Denmark is an EU member, and now the Danes are opposing major
new steps toward greater integration. As a member, Denmark's re-
sistence may lead to a compromise within the union. We are *not* yet
a member. That is the big difference! For that reason we are without
influence!

Certain journalists believed that Denmark would secede from the
EU, but I considered this a hasty and uninformed conclusion.
There were bound to be new attempts, new negotiations and
adjustments. The Danish people had not been asked whether they
wished to leave the EU, but whether they were in agreement with
the changes that the EU countries had proposed jointly.

I did not wish to give the impression that the political events
in Denmark would be decisive with respect to Norway's future. This
was the same basic attitude I had had about Sweden's surprising
early application for EU membership. People are quick to react negatively if they gain the impression that we are coerced by choices
made by other countries.

Still, in the wake of the Danish referendum, the disagreement
within the Labor Party became more prominent. At my biannual

press conference, the problems of both the Labor Party and the country were examined. I focused on the combination of unemployment, unrest, and pessimism in provincial Norway and the struggle surrounding Norway's attitude toward the EU.

The papers wrote that Gro Harlem Brundtland had admitted that she had entered her toughest phase as a political leader. But, they said, she does not depart for one moment from her message that Norway's interests are best served by EU membership.

In talks with Chancellor Helmut Kohl of Germany, who had visited Norway in mid-July, I had stressed the need for our membership. I expressed my views in the same way to the Oslo daily *Today's Business*: "There is now much to indicate that the tempo of extending cooperation within the EU will be reduced. The Danes are an alert people. The Danish 'no' may be an expression of the belief that the development in the EU had run ahead of the European populations themselves. In such an event, it is wise to slow the tempo of increased integration. The need to place renewed emphasis upon the the right balance between integration and individual nations' own freedom of action is a question that I have taken up with both British Prime Minister John Major and with the German Chancellor."

The journalist asked whether I saw any need to slacken the tempo of movement toward Norwegian membership in the EU, whether delay would not be more democratic. I replied that I could not see how it was disadvantageous to seek membership now when the EU was opening up to the EFTA countries, and when our neighbors had already applied. Now we could negotiate membership in tandem with Sweden and Finland and other EFTA countries. In this debate, I said, it sometimes seems as though it is only the opponents of the EU who possess democratic rights. What about EU supporters? Indeed, it is the Norwegian people themselves who will be responsible for our country's relationship with the EU, in a referendum that will settle the issue.

The Norwegian Parliament Passes the EEA Agreement

Right in the middle of the preparations for the Labor Party's National Congress, the great debate about the EEA agreement came before Parliament. We now were to make our final considerations on the most extensive and significant economic cooperation agreement that Norway had ever contemplated. This agreement represented the best means of securing Norwegian interests when the internal market came into full force in 1993.

On top of that, it would be a breakthrough for the Nordic society model when nineteen European countries in an economic charter agreed upon working toward sustainable development. It was also an acknowledgment of our values that the internal market would be working with new rules that safeguarded a high level of protection for health and the environment.

There had been, of course, a great deal of tension surrounding the EEA agreement for a long time. We could never allow ourselves to feel quite sure that we had a sufficient majority. It had been my argument that one could support the EEA and still oppose EU membership. Indeed, that summer we in the party's leadership had agreed that it was important to appoint a new Fisheries Minister, given the sensitivity along the coast in the wake of the resource crisis and the EEA negotiations, and I myself backed a jaunty fellow from Troms County, Jan Henry T. Olsen, an active party loyalist, but a "no" man. Others balked: But Gro, will that work? He may be a "no" man, but he is wholeheartedly pro-EEA, was my reaction.

I believed quite simply that we would not be able to bring about a "yes" in a national referendum if the points of the agreement were not good enough for a man of Jan Henry's attitudes and background to be able to support it. For Jan Henry, it was the question of natural resources and fisheries that constituted the decisive argument against membership. He took up the challenge. The daring appointment was well received.

The EEA agreement was finally approved by a three-fourths majority in Parliament.

Only one month later, the Labor Party National Congress decided, by a two-thirds majority, to recommend that Norway should apply for membership in the EU. A few days later, I was in the Parliament recounting the entire history of this question, beginning with the government's accession declaration of November 6, 1990, when negotiations toward an EEA began. I suggested that the proper conclusion to the path we had followed was that Norway now should seek membership. I received support from a substantial majority in Parliament. But the big challenge lay ahead: Negotiations with Brussels and getting the support from the Norwegian people.

Number 10 Downing Street

On November 24 I traveled to London in order to hand over our application for membership to my colleague, British Prime Minister John Major, as Great Britain had the EU presidency for that half-year. I got a warm and friendly reception. Major had himself been encountering heavy political weather over the last few weeks. This particular afternoon he was in a good mood and immediately said that mine was the only pleasant letter he had received for a long time! He asked that champagne be brought in to mark the occasion.

In the Prime Minister's meeting room, there were only myself and my two staff members, across from John Major and a colleague seated at the other side of the table. No press, no photographers. I could toast in champagne without any reservations. I was not terribly preoccupied with the symbolic value of the occasion. This was hard political work designed to secure important values that touched upon people's everyday lives.

Negotiating

Our application was delivered in London and Brussels; Bonn and Paris would be next. The commission in Brussels was responsible for negotiating on behalf of the member countries. But I was convinced that the capitals of the member countries were at least as important. That's where the national governments and parliaments are. That's where the Prime Ministers and the Foreign Ministers are to be found, as well as the other cabinet Ministers who can have a decisive influence on the position of an individual member country at important junctures.

It was important to make Norway and our special problems known in the different countries and to build a position of personal trust with the key personalities in Europe. The recipient of a message must be willing to listen. Genuine attention, will, and engagement are necessary. A small country needs this much more than a large one does.

I was concerned not to let Europe overshadow my domestic agenda, but all the same, I systematically followed up my contacts with European colleagues. And we also had to consider a wider circle. In the United States, President Bill Clinton took office. I went to Washington the last week of January and met with my friend, incoming Vice President Al Gore. He received me warmly, but was rather cool regarding whaling. I delivered an engaged defense of Norwegian policy and stressed the scientific basis for management of natural resources. This matter was also important for the EU negotiations.

European Round-Trip

In Paris, Prime Minister Pierre Bérégovoy was interested in Norway's problems. He wanted all the Nordic countries to become members of the EU. We discussed the foreign and security issues, along with the general political aspects of Norwegian membership. Cooperation for economic growth and employment was important to us as well, and that issue was also close to hearts in France.

Central to our conversation were Norwegian geography; our recent history since 1972 when the people had first refused membership; and questions of fishing, agriculture, and energy. I told Bérégovoy that the population density in Norway is 13 persons per square kilometer as opposed to 145 for the EU. In northern Norway there are only 4 persons per square kilometer, and in Finnmark, the number is less than 2. I told my colleague about the centrality of the fishing industry. It was perhaps true enough that the EU concept of reciprocality held too few benefits for Norway to grant further access to its waters; but beyond that, the tenuous stability of our established fishing management was vital for habitation and economy along the very long coast of Norway. This was my way of saying Norway had no fish to give. Concerning agriculture, our total production was less than 1 percent of the EU's, and our growing season was only half as long as the the EU average because two-thirds of our production takes place north of 60 degrees latitude, where growing seasons are short and relatively cold.

We brought the same themes to Bonn two months later, in my official visit with Helmut Kohl. The Chancellor gave us a grand dinner, and our conversations were useful. As in his official visit to Norway the summer before, he was once again inviting, open, and direct, and he asked me not to hesitate in contacting him if we needed his help. The Chancellor of Germany surely wanted Norway and the other Nordic countries as fellow members of the EU.

Between European visits, I rushed home to Norway. Then on to The Hague for a luncheon meeting with Prime Minister Ruud Lubbers, whom I knew from many years before, when as a new Minister of the Environment I had accompanied Prime Minister Odvar Nordli to the Benelux countries. Early the next morning, I flew to Rome to see Prime Minister Amato. The next day I met Foreign Minister Colombo and President Scalfaro. It was a very effective European round-trip.

Going to Brussels

The contrast often becomes stark when you visit different places abroad at high speed. But the challenges do not become smaller when you travel in your own country. On the local ferryboat in Oslo harbor, a fellow passenger stared at me and then came over: "You look just like the Prime Minister, though you look much kinder."

Well, a live human being probably looks much less severe than one trading short and sharp remarks in a heated television debate with a political opponent!

Two weeks later my Minister of Trade, Bjørn Tore Godal, went to Brussels to inaugurate the formal EU negotiations. We had worked together on his speech. At the last minute Johan Jørgen Holst delivered a number of suggestions for corrections. Holst had become Foreign Minister only three days before, having replaced Thorvald Stoltenberg, who had officially responded to a call from the U.N. Secretary-General to work for peace in Yugoslavia. Holst was an intense colleague, knowledgeable and strongly engaged. I knew his work from the Palme Commission and the World Commission on Environment and Development, so I was not surprised. Bjørn Tore, who himself had long experience in writing political texts, was not so pleased; he asked over the phone from Brussels to cut out some of Johan Jørgen's suggestions. I opted for a compromise, feeling that it was fine for the new Foreign Minister to have his say on some points.

Other Ministers had to go to Brussels as well. I followed the situation closely when the Minister of Fisheries, Jan Henry T. Olsen, went for his first visit. I knew that his field would be the most controversial. Jonas Gahr Støre from my office, the adviser on European affairs, went along to support Jan Henry and to keep us informed.

Jan Henry emphasized the importance of the fishing industry for coastal Norway and our critical need for sufficient control of resources. The EU Fisheries Commissioner, who was from Greece, had been well prepared and responded to each of Jan Henry's points. He confirmed that Norway was ahead of the EU in fishing management but pointed to the need for an organizational change regarding the Norwegian fish sales associations. He added that the EU policy was under development.

On whaling, the EU Fisheries Commissioner had quite a different attitude from his Spanish predecessor. He agreed that the International Whaling Commission had to set the framework. He also knew that the scientific arguments were more in Norway's favor, "but we have to deal with public opinion."

The Fisheries Commissioner accepted our invitation to visit Norway for three days in July. This was to our advantage because he also was responsible for the environment, a combination that made him sensitive to arguments for sustainable management of fishery resources.

Occasionally we have used songs as a diplomatic vehicle. At a dinner given by Norway's Ambassador to the EU, my Minister of Fisheries chose to end his after-dinner speech by singing two verses from one of the songs he really liked. Full jubilation followed his performance in a clear voice of "Another World" (*"Ei anna jord"*). Once given a translation of this fine text, the Fisheries Commissioner in return sang a song from his home island in Greece.

Peace in the Middle East

In the middle of August an excited Foreign Minister, Johan Jørgen Holst, asked for a confidential meeting. He brought the message we had longed for but hardly thought possible. It looked as though, after many months of secret meetings, the parties to the Middle Eastern conflict might be prepared to sign the main elements of a peace agreement.

The Norwegian labor movement's long-standing relationship with both the Israeli Labor Party and the trade unions was important. And so was the will of the Labor government to acknowledge the rights of the Palestinians. This combination functioned as decisive precondition for Norway's positive role in the peace process. For years the Labor Party had cooperated in the peace-building efforts within the Socialist International, the international body of socialist and social-democratic parties. Within this group, envoys from the Israeli Labor Party and the PLO had a meeting ground for an important ongoing dialogue.

The Oslo accords attracted enormous attention when they were made public in September 1993, and they fomented a formidable excitement, not least in our country. Johan Jørgen Holst, who formerly had been perceived only as an icy intellectual and thorough expert, now became a popular hero as well.

In the preceding weeks, Johan Jørgen had traveled constantly to keep the puzzle pieces together. He was available to the parties on the telephone twenty-four hours a day. When I saw him at our cabinet meetings, I often observed that his eyes were red from lack of sleep.

A few weeks before Christmas Johan Jørgen was admitted to the National Hospital after an episode of dizziness and a severe headache. He told me his blood pressure was a little high and that he had been treated for it over the last few years. But he waved away all worries.

December 16 a new alarming message came. My colleague had once again been admitted to the National Hospital after a serious episode on his flight home from Madrid. This was much worse. He had suffered a stroke.

Bjørn Tore Godal took over the daily responsibility in the Ministry of Foreign Affairs. But Johan Jørgen was kept up to date through his civil servants and his State Secretary when his condition permitted.

I saw him a number of times and called during Christmas. The symptoms receded somewhat and his ability to speak improved a little, but the doctors at the National Hospital believed that he needed several weeks of rehabilitation in a hospital south of Oslo before they would be able to make judgments about his long-term condition.

His intense work, long trips on airplanes, and important contributions made the situation all the more tragic. He had not spared himself, and now he was paying a severe price.

I saw Johan Jørgen January 12, the day before he was scheduled to be transferred to the rehabilitation hospital. Early the next morning, the press representative for the Foreign Ministry, who had been in close contact with Holst, caught me on the phone as I was at the airport, due to go to Helsinki: "I have a sad message. The Foreign Minister died early this morning." I could hardly believe it. I had seen him the day before. He was recovering. We returned immediately to my office.

We had lost an unusual force, a human being with great knowledge and deep insight. Norway had lost a Foreign Minister who was not only respected at home but also enjoyed a strong international esteem. His gift for foreign policy was fully employed in the negotiations for peace in the Middle East, where he had played a key role. His name will forever be associated with the promise of this historic accord.

Tangle in Brussels

We were facing decisive moments in the EU negotiations in Brussels. We had started two months later than the other applicants and our problems with agriculture and fishing were much more difficult.

We did not know whether an outcome would be ready in the spring, under Greek leadership, or in the fall, when Germany would have the chairmanship of the EU. It was easy to imagine that the change in leadership would be advantageous for Norway. At the same time impatience on both sides was great, and many had decided for themselves that everything must be in place by January 1, 1995.

The following weeks brought an intense negotiation on agriculture. Hans van den Broeck, the EU Foreign Policy Commissioner, wanted to deny adjustment periods to the applicants, expecting full implementation of EU regulations for all new members from Day One. For both Norway and Finland, this created enormous difficulties.

My Minister of Agriculture kept in close contact with her Finnish colleague. Our problem was compounded by the fact that the Swedes in fact were in agreement with the commission. They wanted free market access from Day One. The Swedes would not help us. But in Finland we hoped to have a partner.

I went to Helsinki to try to convince Prime Minister Esko Aho that if Norway and Finland stood together we would have a good chance of instituting adjustment periods. I got the impression that, as chairman of the Center Party—the former Agrarian Party—Aho appreciated my appeal, but that he was being very careful. The body language of some of his civil servants gave me the impression that there must be differing attitudes within his government. Perhaps some thought that I frankly did not know how the Finns aligned themselves. Perhaps they did not know themselves.

I also invited Paavo Lipponen, the Finnish Labor Party Leader, to the Norwegian embassy to brief him on the most important points in the final phase of the EU negotiations. There was no support to be found on agriculture. Finnish trade unions and the Labor Party had aligned with the Swedish. Enough was enough, they reasoned, for agricultural subsidies and special market conditions; the better solution would be adaptation to the EU rules and prices from Day One. My best hope was that other forces in the Finnish political setup would be more forthcoming. But I left Helsinki uneasy.

Norway Once Again Alone

The Winter Olympics were in full swing at Lillehammer. The whole nation participated. Never before had the Winter Olympics drawn so many TV viewers the world over. Hillary Clinton visited during the games, and we had breakfast together in a stylish house from the seventeenth century at the Maihaugen Folk Museum. We talked about American politics; the challenges to the new U.S. President, health questions, and, of course, the sporting event. The kitchen had gone out of its way and served both elk and bear meat. I had to tell Hillary that this was no normal breakfast menu. Inside, the flames in the fireplace made the room feel quite cozy, even though outside it was far below freezing. It seemed a good omen that a gold medal went to an American skier while the First Lady was in Lillehammer.

On February 27, during the concluding ceremony of the Lillehammer Olympics, a new message arrived from Brussels. The other Nordic countries have nearly reached a solution. We were late—naturally, because of our later start.

Brussels negotiated with four countries at the same time. Sweden was most interested in the size of its contribution to the EU budget. Austria had difficulties accepting EU demands for use of the Austrian transport system and transit through the Alps. Finland had concerns over agriculture. As did we, in addition to the major matter of fish.

But much was already in place for Norway's membership. Coastal waters to twelve miles out are reserved for Norwegian fishermen under the U.N. Law of the Seas. The EU was also prepared to abide by the established rules for technical regulation of catches. Important issues still remained, however. Our negotiators sensed that their continental counterparts felt it natural that Norway should give some additional resources to the EU.

The EU had not brought forward any exact figures, but suggested that the demands of Spain and Portugal should be taken into consideration. The Spanish demand we knew: They wanted seven thousand tons of cod in compensation for what they called historic rights, and eleven thousand tons as a contribution to economic and social development. We rejected both demands out of hand. Spain had no historic rights, in our view, and our contribution to development would be taken care of through our eventual contribution to the EU "cohesion" fund, whereby member states provide money for trans-European projects to the least prosperous members.

Others thought both Spain and Norway were being difficult. In spite of the years I and other people had spent on thorough explanations in the EU capitals, most politicians in the EU countries still saw fishing as a difficult technical question—and they were impatient for a quick solution. We were asked to make a compromise. I said to Jan Henry over the telephone, Remember that London, Paris, Bonn, and Copenhagen refused to give Spain and Portugal not a single fish in 1986 when they joined, and now they want us to give way in 1994. It was unacceptable!

Cool Heads

We had to show that we were keeping our heads cool and not giving in to pressure. But the pressure against us was formidable. Of the other EU members, Germany was notable for trying to act as a counterweight and a broker of compromise.

In the end a deal was put together which combined the petitions of the four countries seeking accession, Norway included. The essence of the Norwegian input was to make available earlier the access to the fishing grounds that had been allocated to EU countries as an element in the EEA deal. Fish resource projections had grown faster than anticipated. In popular terms, "we were stretching the EEA fish": we allowed our partners to consider their rights as a kind of bank account from which they were permitted to draw at an earlier point in time.

Toward the end, all seemed fine with the member states and the candidates. It was late evening, after the final day of negotiating. Surprise, surprise, at literally the last minute the Irish made a demand regarding mackerel. They wanted the right to fish their quota of mackerel in the Norwegian zone at certain times. We considered this a stab in the back. But it was not enough to destroy the whole agreement. The Irish won, in part due to their surprise tactic. The irritation that our concession created among the fishermen in southern Norway was instrumental to the "no" movement at home, and we often thought in hindsight that we ought to have refused the eleventh-hour demand.

"The people shall decide"

On March 17, 1994, I gave a report to Parliament. We had obtained good solutions for Norway on all central issues. The most important idea of the European Union was the committed cooperation among independent states. We had applied for membership because we needed democratic governance and cooperation across national borders.

I stressed that we had demanded special tools for maintaining living conditions in our country, with its unique climate and geography. One of our conditions was that we continue to control our natural resources. And the negotiations had been a success! Our vital needs had been acknowledged. The text of the treaty stipulated our sovereign right to our energy sources. There were new paragraphs for northern agriculture as an integrated part of the Common Agricultural Policy of the the EU. Our own policy for sustainable management would be the basis of the EU's management of fisheries policy in our northern waters.

Fishing was central in 1972. I knew it would be equally important in 1994. That's why we had been so insistent about this issue and had fought so hard. We had secured ownership of our fish resources. Norwegian fishermen would not face competition on their fishing banks. As before, we would own 95 percent of the Norwegian codfish. No one would be allowed to come in and threaten the resources belonging to Norwegian fishermen.

This central point of the treaty would be a bone of contention until the day of the referendum. The "no" side argued that a simple majority in the EU could alter the text. But that was nonsense. Unanimity was required for changing the texts of the treaty, and naturally Norway would never agree. We had arrived at a really good solution.

I went to two different annual meetings of county party branches and was encouraged that party activists received our membership treaty so positively. The EU was now the centerpiece of political debate in our party, and in the country.

In northwest Norway, even the large number of people in favor of membership consistently refrained from saying so because of the pressure from the "no" side. Even in fish-processing industries, where new jobs had been created because of the EEA treaty, the mostly female workers were opposed. Many were from fishing families or were engaged or married to fishermen. The fishermen's main concern was other countries' potential access to resources in our fishing grounds. They were less worried about their own access to the market, since they delivered their catch at prices determined by fishermen's organizations. That most of the fish—a precious national resource—had to be sold abroad did not concern them. The surprise Irish mackerel victory was driving scores of fishermen from southern Norway into the "no" camp as well.

Another reservation was over Germany's strong position in the EU. The fact that Germany had developed into a new democracy could not overshadow the memory of its five-year occupation of our country during the Second World War. The EU was also seen as prioritizing economic growth over the environment, which concerned many people.

In September, I attended the U.N. Conference on Population in Cairo, where I spoke out against the criminalization of abortion. There was great pride in Norway, but also a smart new criticism that claimed that with Norway in the EU, Gro would not be able to make such independent policy statements. The critics were wrong. But their comments had an effect.

In Hattfjelldal in Nordland County I visited a farmer and his family. He proudly showed me his new barn. He had fifty cattle, of which eighteen were milk cows. He said he stood to lose hundreds of thousands of Kroner a year if EU prices were introduced. A regional agricultural officer was with him. But I was equally prepared and told the farmer that the agreement with the EU had given Norway the right to keep the subsidies to northern agriculture at today's level and for as long as we wished. It was up to the Norwegian Parliament to decide.

Again I saw that some people simply did not believe the facts. The farmer stuck to what his organization, the Norwegian Farmers Union, had told him. And it had not taken its data from the treaty. So it turned out to be impossible to agree on what data to use. The Farmers Union clearly had a solid grip on its members!

That farmer made a strong impression on me, and in a subsequent party meeting I analyzed his thoughts. I was careless enough to say that it looked like he had been brainwashed by his organization, as no fact could enter his mind. Two days later, the local workers' paper printed my words. The farmer was interviewed as well. He had contacted his union. They threatened to take me to court. I was reprimanded for my lack of decorum. The farmer had the upper hand. It was a foolish mistake. I was sorry, and mad at myself. I had been in politics for twenty years; I knew that nobody was watched more closely than I was. But it is difficult to stay engaged, fresh, and optimistic and thus be a good communicator without running the small risk that a word or a sentence might backfire.

The TUC Congress Says No

TUC boss Yngve Hågensen had been careful before the TUC congress. He remembered the "no" of 1972. The "no" side was active, but Hågensen knew the delegates and estimated that the end result would still be "yes."

Both Party Leader Thorbjørn Jagland and I were in the hall. I was uneasy. I listened to the very demagogic "no" speeches and the ensuing applause. The majority turned out to be slim indeed: 156 to 149. But the majority said no. Yngve and I were very displeased, but we tried to conceal it. Now we had to tone down the difference between the "no" and the "yes" figures at the TUC congress. Labor had of course a majority for "yes," but we had to let the "no" side enjoy its full rights within the party. It was mandatory that the minority of trade unionists still enjoy their full rights to work for a "yes," at least in principle. But the help we could get from the TUC was now effectively diminished.

I had a heavy feeling in my body when I left Labor House. A "yes" from the TUC congress would have given us a much better chance. It would have made a big difference in a close referendum. Again I have to underline that the difference between having TUC pushing from behind and TUC as an opponent is like day and night. The whole "no" movement now had an extra legitimacy.

The Fisherman's Union

Should I go straight into the lion's den? We had discussed it carefully. The Minister of Fisheries, Jan Henry T. Olsen, had to go to the national convention of the Fisherman's Union, but that union had always invited the Prime Minister as well. I felt it right to go. I was heavily engaged in the fishing questions. Twenty years had passed

since I was first at this national convention as a young Minister of
the Environment. These people preferred straight talk. I had liked
the tone. If I attended, that would be my style.

What drew the most attention was the part of my speech decry-
ing a pamphlet on EU membership distributed by the Fisherman's
Union. Like the Farmers' Union, the Fisherman's Union had disregarded the facts. From the rostrum I said, You are trying to create
quite a dramatically different picture from reality. The pamphlet
does not at all mention that Norwegian quotas are secured in the
treaty and that we are guaranteed Norwegian fishing management
in the North. You will have the same quotas whether or not we become members of the EU. Recommendations from the biologists
and researchers determine quotas, not our status as an EU member.

I had no hope of convincing the Fisherman's Union to change its
viewpoint. But I could create a certain doubt over the factual basis
for their arguments. And more important, I could defend my position even in hostile territory.

The press agreed. Even if it looks like she is running her head
into a concrete wall, they wrote, at least the Prime Minister gives a
convincing impression that she holds a solid conviction for the issues she fights for. Some papers picked up the humorous little
point that the three yes votes in the Fisherman's Union convention
was triple the total yielded the last time the question was debated,
twenty-two years before.

In the final week of the campaign, something quite different took
place in Kristiansand in southern Norway. The Workers Association
hall was crowded. My message: We could not vote away the existence of the EU, but we could vote away our influence in it. My
sentences were shorter than usual. The issue demanded directness.

We felt that the country's attitudes had finally turned our way.
On November 21 our polls had indicated 49 percent yes versus
51 percent no among the decided. The undecided tended to emphasize peace and security over the economy.

However, Socialist Left sympathizers were wary of conceding our rights of self-governance. The fact that we had less support from our own voters than from the Right made me insecure.

The final TV debate on the Friday before voting day on Monday was naturally viewed nationwide with the utmost attention. At the end of the debate, Center Party Leader Anne Enger Lahnstein, "the Queen of No," proclaimed that EU membership would weaken trade union rights. I was fed up with false statements. I said: "This is the limit. This is a lie." Strong words but nevertheless the truth.

I knew that my exact words could be more easily exploited by the "no" side than appreciated by proponents, although telephone polling interviews pronounced me the clear winner in the debate. But my uneasiness continued. Anne was not ashamed to say that my statement about her lying was an undignified form of debate. I told the journalists that I did not regret my words. Trade union rights were fixed in the Treaty of Rome and were further strengthened through the Maastricht Treaty.

I believe certain standards must be met. If you argue that membership means weaker trade union rights, you should be able to substantiate it. I was willing to be sorry for my earlier use of "brainwash." But this was something different. I was demanding facts and fairness from a responsible party leader. But privately I thought, yes, I should have used a less emotionally charged word.

We ended the campaign in the city of Drammen just south of Oslo. The momentum was superb; the polls now showed a fifty-fifty split. I hoped we were finally out front at the finish line. There was no time left to say "maybe." I told a reporter that we could have our "yes" if everyone turned out. "You can use that as your headline!"

The Referendum

They took exit polls at different places around the country. Throughout the evening, figures tilted a little in favor of "no." We were together in Labor House, as was election night custom. A lot of "no" results came in from the smaller constituencies in provincial Norway, and we waited for results from cities and more populated areas. We had to stay composed. But spirits were not high.

I was prepared for this situation as well. From the very day when it had become clear that the question on EU membership should be debated anew, I knew one thing for sure: We would have to conduct a referendum if the Labor Party said "yes." I was prepared for another "no." That was first and foremost the reason I had staked our fortunes on cooperation between the EU and EFTA in the EEA. I feared a new divisive debate in Norway. From the very beginning my opinion was that in a referendum the people decide, and we then respect the outcome.

A big majority of Parliament had asked for a Norwegian application for membership. This majority had also stated its obligation to respect the outcome of the referendum. This was in contrast to the view of the minority in Parliament, some of whom declared that they would not necessarily respect a "yes." There was a basic principle here. When I was younger, I had reacted skeptically to Prime Minister Bratteli's 1972 decision to make of that year's referendum an ultimatum of his own. His threat to resign in the face of a "no" decision had actually helped to produce the "no" decision. People do not like to be pushed around. For me it would have been unthinkable to do the same in 1994.

Together with Party Leader Thorbjørn Jagland I went to the last television debate. It was the final hour. I was filled with conflicting thoughts about how Norway could now best handle the situation. In my dossier there were two different draft press releases, one for yes and one for no. I cleared the "no" version to be sent from the Prime Minister's office around midnight.

"It is today decided that Norway will not be a member of the European Union," my statement said. "The government therefore will not make any proposals to Parliament for formal voting. The Labor Party and the government have made it clear that we will without reservation respect the decision of the people.

"I will not conceal that the outcome is a disappointment. We gave our advice. In a small majority, the country has decided not to follow this advice. The government will do whatever is in its power to take care of Norwegian interests. The state budget must be adopted. We must do whatever we can to secure as much as possible of the EEA treaty. It will now be a more demanding task to reach our aims and be heard in international cooperation. No one can escape the responsibility. Therefore I make this appeal to all: We will be forced to work even harder in caring for our country and our welfare. The government sees no alternative to conducting an active European policy. Our dependence on our closest friends and allies, our relations with the Nordic countries and with the European ones, are of the greatest importance and will be given high priority by the government in the future. Our responsibility is to do our best for our country. Democracy has played its role. It is that simple, and we all have to accept it."

These thoughts filled my mind as I struggled to get through to the national TV studio for the final comments of the night. The place was full of journalists and TV cameras. I was somber, but focused as I conveyed this message. The debate was over.

Early that morning, after two or three hours of sleep, we all met at my office. I told my staff that the Norwegian people had not said "no" to the EEA, or to Nordic cooperation, or to an active role for Norway in the international community. Later in the day I got a note from one of the State Secretaries: "When this morning at the office you had already put behind you the great loss and only were concerned about the future, you gave us all new courage. I for my part had decided to leave politics in the event of a 'no.' I thought it mattered that much. Your behavior last night and this morning made me change my mind. In view of your performance, it became totally unthinkable to jump ship."

The Future After the People's "No"

There was no point dissecting what had just happened. There was no longer a no-side and a yes-side. We were together. That was my view. It had to be that way. Now we needed a new course. The idea that the "no" alliance could build on these results to advance its political views had no basis in reality. There was no basis in the "no" to ask for a different Norwegian national policy or foreign policy. The "no" alliance was composed of people with very different outlooks and perspectives. There were both radicals and reactionaries, from many different political parties. They had been fighting together for one goal and that was what had united them. Moreover, the EEA treaty had obtained a three-fourths majority in Parliament. Our first priority was to take care of that agreement. But nothing was automatic. Many within the European Union perceived our internal vote as a distancing of Norway from Europe given that the three other Nordic countries, Denmark, Sweden, and Finland, had joined. If Norway had decided for itself, why should the rest of Europe take care of the special needs of Norway?

It was important to make sure that Norway was not forgotten. We had to swiftly contact both the established and the new members of the EU to dispel resentment. Together with the Foreign Ministry, I devised a strategy for immediate action.

Most important was to secure the EEA treaty. The complicated decision-making structures would now include only Norway, Iceland, and Lichtenstein on the one side, and the European Union on the other side—altogether fifteen member states.

We were treated with kindness and politeness. Everyone perceived that the government had done everything possible to obtain another result and that we were now doing our best to take care of our national interests. We wanted to secure the political dimensions of the EEA treaty. Regular political consultations were a part of the basis for the treaty. It became clear that this was now seen differently by our EU partners, who prioritized on the basis of EU membership.

I was thankful that we had substantially re-formed the basis for Nordic cooperation. I had in fact had a tough fight at the time with both Swedish Prime Minister Bildt and Danish Prime Minister Schlüter, both Conservatives, in establishing the EEA as a European framework for the Nordic reforms. I had known that it was an open question how Norway would vote in the end and had therefore worked hard to secure the EEA agreement to protect Norwegian interests in case of a "no."

During the "trial period," between the end of our negotiation for membership and the final decision by the people, the Nordic Ministers of Environment had begun meeting ahead of scheduled meetings of the Environment Ministers in the EU when important issues were on the EU agenda. This was one of the ways in which we were able to examine what was on the European agenda. But now we had lost access to the European microphone. We could no longer speak for ourselves in that forum.

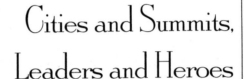

Chapter

Cities and Summits, Leaders and Heroes

15

Action for Sustainable Development

From 1987 to 1992, the report of the World Commission on Environment and Development retained its authority, and was increasingly regarded as the central document of development and a reference point for further international cooperation. We on the commission had proposed that our conclusions must be accepted as a program to enact sustainable development. We had proposed a major conference five years after the launch of the report to chart the progress made so far and to determine future direction.

Maurice Strong, one of our commission members, was named Secretary-General of the conference, a post he had also held at the first environmental conference in Stockholm in 1972. The chosen venue was Rio de Janeiro. The Brazilian president, Fernando Collor, came to Norway in the summer of 1991 to discuss Brazil's role as the host country. He was clearly eager to be prepared for this important event.

Mitterrand and Delors

The 1992 Rio summit was interesting because it so clearly demonstrated the extent to which the various heads of state had involved
themselves personally in the issues of the environment and the des-
tiny of developing countries. A summit meeting forces the participants to start the preparation procedures in their home countries.
Here the heads of state or government are more or less summoned
to attend meetings. And it's important for them to be on the ball,
because new initiatives can be launched. In the Ministries the civil
servants need to study the existing legislation and policies, and
there will typically be several briefing meetings before a summit
meeting.

In Norway we discussed the topics on the conference agenda at
government level several times, and all of those most intimately involved—the Ministries of Foreign Affairs, the Environment, Foreign
Aid, and Finance—cooperated closely with one another and with
the Prime Minister's office.

In Rio I was scheduled to speak late in the conference, which
meant that people would have heard ideas repeated a great many
times before it was my turn. That was unavoidable. Sitting behind
my place-marker at a big conference, it's interesting to study my
colleagues. Often it's just as interesting to note what is not said. Not
everyone can be bothered to listen. Personally, I try to keep my seat
as much as possible out of respect for my colleagues. A number of
people wander about and say hello to each other. Conversations
both formal and informal take place at all times.

I remember one incident in particular: Mitterrand had arrived.
The French President always makes an entrance. He generally had
an aide-de-camp behind him carrying a little black case to indicate
that France was a nuclear power. Jacques Delors arrived with Mitterrand in the French Concorde. No doubt there were practical
reasons for this, but it did illustrate the relationship between the
sovereign nation France and the international organization the EU.
It isn't possible to officially register a plane as an "EU" plane.

Mitterrand gave an impassioned speech in which he confirmed
an increase in French foreign aid. The speech was well received,

but it was distinctly different from the collective EU speech on foreign aid that was also presented at the conference. The individual EU countries obviously enjoyed considerable freedom within the union. Not long after Mitterrand had finished his speech he left. Visibly annoyed, Delors followed Mitterrand. He didn't get to give his speech. Instead, it was distributed in printed form.

Most government leaders and heads of state were full of praise for Rio and what had been achieved there. I chose to take another line. "We have an obligation to the world to be honest about what we have really achieved here: moderate progress in some areas, slight progress in other areas, and in many areas no progress at all," I said.

That was the truth. The wide-ranging Agenda 21 had been agreed upon, an agreement on climate and on biological diversity, but much of what was contained in the resolutions was insufficiently forward-looking. Agenda 21 was binding, but its deadlines and enabling procedures were inadequate to really protect the environment. Still, significant processes had been set in motion. To be talking about the climate at all meant we were on the right track, even if the content of the agreement on climate was vague. The agreement to preserve the biological diversity of life on earth had been signed, but it was more a framework for future meetings than a strong, legally binding document. The most disappointing aspect of the follow-up conference has been the lack of money for environmental and development aims.

Something else that dampened our spirits in Rio was the activity of the Norwegian environmental movement. They had made the trip there to throw stones at their own country. They were extraordinarily parochial. The thousands congregated in Rio were not interested in erroneous claims that the environment in Norway was bad, that Gro Harlem Brundtland was a two-faced hypocrite, and all the rest of the claims they had dreamed up. They were obviously disappointed to find that others did not at all agree that Norway was setting a poor example, and it must have been extra galling for them that Norway was voted "most constructive country" by the

nongovernmental organizations (NGOs) at their alternative conference, which was being held in Flamingo Park, another neighborhood in Rio.

"This is Senator Al Gore"

It was in Rio that we heard that Bill Clinton had nominated Al Gore
as his vice presidential candidate. Here was a young and dynamic
team to challenge the establishment government of George Bush.
From the perspective of Rio, this was good news. Al Gore was
passionate about the environment, so much so that Bush would
perjoratively dub him "the ozone man" in the autumn election campaign. The Clinton-Gore partnership had an aura of victory about
it. My conference route was Oslo–Rio–Boston–Washington–Oslo.
For some years I had been receiving invitations from Harvard University to give their annual Commencement Speech. I had had to
refuse so far because their commencement had an unfortunate tendency to collide with the last hectic days at Parliament before the
summer recess.

The term "sustainable development" was beginning to enter the
general vocabulary, and the concept became the subject of a number of academic studies. Al Gore was known as a knowledgeable
and visionary politician with a special interest in the field of sustainable development. I had met him for the first time in 1989 in
New York, when we both participated in a worldwide television
broadcast entitled "Our Common Future." On that occasion he
came to Lincoln Center on foot, with his wife, Tipper, and two of
their children. What I recall best is the sympathetic impression he
gave. I also met him when our Parliamentary Standing Committee
on Foreign Relations visited Washington in 1990. That was the first
time we discussed the issue of whales. Now it was the spring of
1992 and he was on the telephone: "This is Senator Al Gore calling
from Washington." He was a member of the commencement committee. Would I please come to Harvard this year? If so, it would be
the day after the opening of the Rio conference. Gore asked if I
would travel back to Rio with a delegation from the American Con-

gress. No, thanks, wrong direction, I answered. After that I'm off to Norway. But I did say yes to Harvard.

There is a certain responsibility attached to giving the commencement lecture at Harvard. Morten Wetland is a marvelous speechwriter, and he knows me and my beliefs inside out. He and I put the finishing touches on my speech as we set off northward to Boston.

There are many things to consider in planning a speech. What type of audience is it? What is the occasion? How much does the audience already know? And there is a difference between a speech for an audience of fifty or one hundred and one of over twenty thousand, as at Harvard. Here I could count on a knowledgeable audience, but it was by no means certain that they were especially knowledgeable on the topic that interested us most that week. It would be a shame to misjudge the audience.

I chose to draw upon twenty years of political experience. Technology, global business, and the new communication media had steadily assumed much of the power that had previously been exercised by democratic institutions. Nation-states were now too small to solve problems that were essentially of a regional or international nature. If we continued to foster the illusion that countries could operate independently of one another, then we risked postponing vital decisions that could only be made effective by countries reaching decisions and acting together. We also ran the risk of adding to the mounting skepticism with which politicians were viewed, and the accompanying lack of respect for democracy as a seemingly impotent political system.

We were accustomed to holding our politicians accountable and to judging their results on the basis of how they affected our daily lives. If they disappointed us, we were quick to turn from them and from the political system. This type of alienation from the democratic process could lead to an insidious weakening of democracy's institutions. Recent and dangerous antidemocratic demonstrations in a number of countries and renewed calls for the Strong Man were symptoms we had to take seriously. Democracy isn't a process that starts at the top and extends downward. Rather, democracy must be based at the local level, in the hearts and minds of ordinary voters, in political parties, voluntary organizations, and pressure groups.

Poor countries—the majority of countries in the world—used only a small proportion of the world's resources. The more greedy industrial nations were in the process of using up within the space of a few decades what it had taken the earth millions of years to produce. The widening gap between the fortunate minority and the poor majority was a potentially destabilizing tendency. It was both dangerous and morally unacceptable.

In order to achieve sustainable growth, deep-seated changes were necessary in all societies. Would it be possible to feed a world population two times its current size in an environmentally defensible way? How could poor countries become our partners in cooperative ventures when on average only 8 percent (in some countries as little as 2 percent) of citizens in developing countries had the option of higher education? How could we provide the energy for a world economy potentially five times greater than the one we currently had without destroying the environment and the earth's atmosphere?

If we didn't manage to help the underdeveloped countries bypass the most polluting stages of development and develop their human resources, we ourselves might well end up the losers.

The failure of the Rio conference to make proper resolutions aimed at limiting population growth had been almost shocking to note. States with no population problem—and in one case a state with no births at all, the Vatican—did all they could to prevent the acceptance of resolutions involving family planning. Contraception should be available everywhere. The status of women must be raised. Their education must be improved: "For too long women have been treated with condescension!"

These were the central points of my Harvard speech, a strong argument in favor of supranationality in the name of international cooperation. And I urged the students not only to dream of a lucrative career in business, but to consider public service as well.

"Journalists of the worst sort"

After a speech like mine it often happens that both acquaintances and strangers approach you to continue the discussion. John Kenneth Galbraith held a reception in his nearby garden. He had been an adviser to President Kennedy. Jerome Wiesner was there, an adviser to the Palme Commission and for many years president of MIT.

The next day I went to Washington and met with President Bush. He greeted me with these words: "Gro, we don't make a habit of spying on visiting Prime Ministers, but we hear you gave a good speech at Harvard yesterday." Afterward, as we were relaxing in the comfortable armchairs by the fire in the Oval Office, Bush told me that "a wave of journalists" would be admitted in groups. U.S. journalists shout out questions and hope that theirs is the one the President answers. "Just ignore them," said Bush. "Our American journalists are some of the most ill-mannered in the world. I hope they're better in Norway!" I said maybe so, yes, generally speaking they were all right. The result was that Bush paid more attention to the Norwegian than to the U.S. journalists!

John Sununu, the White House Chief of Staff, was present during our conversation. He was known as an active opponent of the environmental lobby and probably wanted to make sure that I—an environmental troublemaker in his eyes—didn't trick his boss into saying something silly. Among other issues, the environmental lobby in the United States held Sununu responsible for advising Bush against signing the treaty on biodiversity because it would undermine United States sovereignty.

Bush was genuinely interested in hearing about the Rio conference. We also discussed the biodiversity agreement, and I think I managed to sow some seeds of doubt in his mind about America's refusal to sign, which henceforth made the United States a legitimate target of criticism of all the Rio participants.

In 1988 Bush had run for office as, among other things, the environmental presidential candidate. But the choice of advisers is crucial. William Reilly, his Environmental Protection Agency (EPA) administrator, functioned more as leader of the state commission on pollution than a member of the government, more as a civil servant than a political leader. Reilly came from the NGOs and in those circles his appointment was popular. It was therefore Sununu, and not Reilly, who became the big bad wolf for those who perceived the United States as a slacker in the field of international cooperation.

Bush seemed glad that the allotted time for everyone in Rio was only five minutes. "God, I hate it when people go over time," he sighed, obviously straight from the heart. I later learned that while giving his speech at the closing ceremony in Rio, Bush had had no problem keeping himself well within the allotted five minutes.

To Capitol Hill

Clinton won the 1992 election. He inherited the Cold War on its last legs and a number of unfulfilled expectations both at home and abroad. It was clear that his real passion was for domestic affairs.

Al Gore's position as Vice President meant that we in Norway already had an important contact. Things ought to change for the better. I knew the international network of those passionately committed to the environment and noticed that the expectations of Clinton and Gore were high. One of the first definite statements Clinton made was that the United States would now resume its support for the U.N.'s population program, which had been stopped under President Reagan. This program looked forward to, among other things, the U.N.'s next big conference on population in Cairo in 1994.

I was invited by the U.S. Congress to be one of the main speakers at the Forum on Technology and Governance that was to be held on Capitol Hill at the end of January 1993, just one week after the changeover of power. The theme was so close to the one I had addressed six months earlier at Harvard that I chose to accept. Maybe now, with a new team, we might have more influence.

John Gibbons headed the congressional office for the evaluation of technology. The U.S. Congress has a large apparatus for undertaking its own studies. My father's former colleague Robert S. McNamara was there, again impressive in his vitality. Clinton's economic adviser Laura D'Andrea Tyson took part too, and the room was full of familiar faces like Lester Brown of the World Watch Institute and Gus Speth, Director General of the United Nations Development Program (UNDP).

In my speech I particularly recommended the use of carbon dioxide taxes and other economic sanctions to reduce the amount of fossil fuel used as energy. I also made a strong appeal to the United States to play a leading role in environment and development. The chance had come.

Hillary

On this same trip, I was asked if I would like to meet Hillary. Yes, it might be interesting. She was probably a very talented and goal-directed person. Some of my staff were very negative. You can't! Remember all the bother when you were to meet Raisa Gorbachev? And how will it look? The Norwegian Prime Minister meets not the President but the President's wife? On this occasion I ignored the objections and our ambassador to Washington was told to request the meeting. President Clinton had gone to the electorate with a program in which health-care reform had a high priority. He had chosen his wife to lead the reform. This was something new.

We met at Hillary's office in the West Wing. I told her about my own experiences with the Norwegian health service, both with and without a white coat. We got on well. My own time in America had made it clear to me that something had to be done about health care there. It was too expensive and too inefficient, reaching too few people in spite of the fact that the country boasted the world's most advanced medical and technical facilities.

The document containing Hillary Clinton's planned reforms ran to fifteen hundred pages. It was reviewed as a book in the *New York Review of Books*, and Morten Wetland made sure I read the review. That made a good impression, and Hillary said when I met her in Lillehammer in 1994 that she was prepared to leverage my effort against those members of Congress who had not read even the book review: "If the Norwegian Prime Minister can read it, then so can you Americans!" The most pressing reforms were in the areas of insurance coverage and the administrative cost of the system. In the United States, 14 percent of the GNP goes to health. In Norway, where everyone is covered by state insurance, the figure is only 9 percent.

Hillary took a lively interest in the operation of the Norwegian health service, and her attitudes in many respects echoed my own social-democratic approach.

Serious Questions of Population Control

Preparations for the U.N. Conference on Population and Development in Cairo were spread over several years. I said yes to the invitation from United Nations Population Fund (UNFPA), the U.N.'s population program, to deliver a lecture in New York on the topic a few months before the conference. I had known UNFPA Director Nafis Sadik, a female Pakistani doctor, for a number of years. She was from a Muslim background herself, but had an almost Scandinavian perspective on the issues. Yet she had to be careful not to offend the countries that were major financial contributors to UNFPA. I think she felt it would be better if someone else advanced the series of broad health initiatives for mothers and children, as well as for future mothers, which were absolutely necessary and would also include advice on family planning and the provision of contraceptives. Equal rights for women and men to make the key choices in life, about how many children to have and when to have them, had always been a key concern of mine.

Since the time of my studies at Harvard and my work as a young doctor, I had been aware that the number of births per woman drops as the general standard of living in a society rises. A rise in the standard of living goes hand in hand with improved access to education and greater mobility within a society. In those countries where access to leading positions was dependent on something other than personal qualities and abilities—for example, inheritance rights or genealogical background—the result was an underuse of human resources.

At the same time, my study of ecology had taught me that the extent to which a society burdens its environment is a function of the number of individuals involved, the technology used, and the scope of the economy. To have a chance of overcoming poverty, new generations needed education. If the population expanded more rapidly than the economy—if the population grew by 3 percent as in certain African nations, yet the growth in the economy was 2 percent—we can see what a job it would be to build enough schools and train enough teachers. In order to succeed, a redistribution of resources in the society in question would be needed, for example, away from defense expenditures and over to education. These were the kinds of issues we considered in Norway as we prepared for Cairo.

Support for progressive population policies has to be regarded as a global responsibility. There are a number of global issues from which we cannot run away without serious consequences: peace-keeping, environmental initiatives, the war on poverty. But if we can't address the growth in population, we run the risk of all the other international problems getting completely out of control.

The developing countries were skeptical of Western attitudes toward population control. They claimed that a European or an American uses a much higher proportion of the earth's resources than an Indian or a Chinese, and this made them question the West's motives in advocating population control. Was the West's hegemony as a user of resources something it wanted to preserve, and was it the West's real intention to keep the developing countries down? There was also the question of oil and the related question of air pollution. For the developing countries, the strongest argument against enforceable limitations on atmospheric emissions was the demand for justice. By comparison with the West, the individual Chinese or Indian had a very modest consumption of oil, so it was immoral of the developed countries to maintain that we wanted to continue with such an unequal distribution. Clearly, we had to cut down oil consumption in the West and reduce the population growth in places where it was highest. Otherwise there would always be too little for us all.

Many of the most economically promising developing countries today have also succeeded with their population policies, even if their methods have been controversial. Indonesia and China are examples of this.

Population isn't just a question of numbers but of the relation between the size of the population and the available resources. Presently the poor countries are minimal consumers of resources compared to the Western countries, which in the course of a few generations have used up resources that the earth has taken millions of years to produce.

Sometimes the obstacle to population control is religion. This happens when family planning is turned into an ethical question. But morality isn't just a question of controling sexuality and protecting unborn life. Morality becomes hypocritical if it means that mothers suffer and die during unwanted pregnancies or illegal abortions, or that unwanted children grow up into a life of wretchedness!

Fortunately, pragmatic attitudes to the demands of religion were possible. In my address, I mentioned particularly Buddhist Thailand, Muslim Indonesia, and Catholic Italy as examples of countries with drastic reductions in the number of births over a strikingly short period of time. Countries that had successfully curbed their population growth tended to have a relatively good economy and a fair way of distributing resources. Those countries did best which also laid greatest stress on health, education, and an improvement in the position of women; which stressed the availability of information on family planning and made these services readily available to women at a local level.

The single most rewarding investment a country can make as a whole is in educating its women, which actually means fewer infant deaths and a reduction of growth in the population. Economically, it might be as profitable to invest in men as in women, but this is far outweighed by the social profit to be had by investing in women.

The world has listened to thousands of speeches on the subject of population policy. In other countries a politician's options are often severely restricted by weighty political and religious considerations. I was fortunate to have the support of people in my own country for making such points so explicitly.

The lecture was well received. There was a spontaneous suggestion from the floor that I should travel to Cairo to try to make my influence felt there. I answered yes on the spot, and Nafis Sadik followed this up by saying that UNFPA would give me a place at the conference.

Clash with the Pope and the Mullahs

During preparations for Cairo it became clear that the Vatican and a number of Catholic and Muslim countries were preparing to obstruct progress. This wasn't the first conference on population arranged by the U.N., but the motions tabled from the countries most opposed to change represented a serious reversal, especially for the women of the world.

A number of the conflicts that arose at such U.N. conferences must seem quite incomprehensible to the average man and woman. For example, the Vatican was strongly opposed to the use of an expression like "reproductive health" in the conference's final document, since one could not exclude the possibility that such a formulation implied methods of population control, which they could not accept.

During the Pope's visit to Norway in the summer of 1989 I had met him for a talk in which population and family planning were central features. He had evidently been well briefed beforehand on the Norwegian Prime Minister's background as a crusader for abortion on demand. When I raised problems of a general nature which the Catholic Church by reason of its teachings might find difficult, he chose to reply by saying that he would think about it, thus avoiding the need to give a direct answer.

I was particularly keen to voice this problem: "How can the Catholic Church be against the sale and distribution of condoms? Think of those parts of Africa most hard hit by AIDS: Should not women there be allowed to protect themselves? They can't even be sure they're not being infected by their own husbands. The main point here is not the prevention of conception but of the spread of a deadly disease."

The Pope said it was a difficult problem. He would think about it. On issues such as this, the Pope's attitudes remain problematic over a decade later.

I think the Vatican seriously miscalculated its approach to the Cairo conference. The entire international press pointed the finger at the Vatican as perhaps the most obstructive participant.

There was great tension in the preparation for the Cairo conference. The general feeling was that we had reached a crossroads: Would reactionary forces succeed in turning back the clock?

Large U.N. conferences are usually opened by the head of state of the host country, in this case Egyptian President Hosni Mubarak. After this, the U.N. Secretary-General or his representative speaks. Boutros Boutros-Ghali had made the journey to his homeland in person. Being Secretary-General of the U.N. is not an enviable role. He has his mandate from the member countries and is scarcely at liberty to express an opinion that is at odds with that, least of all in an environment like that of the Cairo conference, with its powerful emotional and religious overtones.

After we arrived, the Norwegian delegates, my own staff, and I talked over the most obvious remaining areas of conflict and discussed how best to stress our point of view.

There were about three thousand people gathered in the conference hall. In my first sentence, what I said could not have been more direct: "Let us put to one side these symbolically loaded issues that the press have written about so much recently, and let us instead concentrate on the main questions."

There was spontaneous applause. I thought: What have I started now? This is going to get out of control, because what comes later on in the speech is real dynamite!

I stressed the value of giving equal education to girls and asked the conference to consider the misery and deaths that came in the wake of unsafe abortions. We should not add to these burdens, and women in such desperate life conditions should not be persecuted as criminals. For that remark, there was a standing ovation.

Back at the hotel after all the enthusiasm we met several members of Al Gore's staff. They were in high spirits. Gore aide Kathy McGinty gave me a hug and a huge smile: "Poor Al, having to talk after you. He really didn't have a chance!"

That wasn't true. Gore gave a good speech. I never doubted that Clinton and Gore's attitudes toward such matters lay close to what we in Norway and the Nordic countries believed. But the Americans had to take into account large groups whose skepticism they could not afford to arouse. The most important thing Al Gore did in Cairo was to announce clearly the shift in U.S. policy. No one who saw or heard him in Cairo could doubt that the man's heart was in the right place!

We made time for a private conversation. He was preoccupied with the problem of climatic change and the importance of getting the Germans to play a leading role in defending the environment.

The day following my speech a Norwegian paper wrote: "It is doubtful whether any Norwegian politician before her has aroused such international interest as Gro Harlem Brundtland did with her speech in Cairo on Monday. What she actually did was challenge the Christians and Muslims on the Right with a strong appeal to common sense and humanitarian considerations on the issues of abortion and birth control. News media across the world have registered her clash with the Pope and the mullahs. Her courageous speech has set the agenda for the rest of the conference."

"Hate-filled response to Norwegian speech," wrote another Norwegian paper and reported the attacks on me in Arab world newspapers. One wrote that the theme of the conference was adulterous sex. In Norway one of the most fundamentalist MPs of the Christian People's Party said that I was as hypocritical as the groups I criticized.

Can a Man Be Prime Minister?

It wasn't easy for me to attend the U.N.'s Women's Conference in Beijing in September 1995, but once preparations in New York got under way it was soon made clear that people were keen for me to be there.

Karin Stoltenberg, wife of Thorvald Stoltenberg, had a political career in her own right and was now the senior civil servant in charge of the preparations on the Norwegian side; she communicated to me the degree of interest in my attending. But with ongoing local elections in Norway, I could at best travel to Beijing only in time to give the closing speech to the conference. Still, I decided that it was worth it.

It was evident that the work of the U.N. was no longer hampered by the political polarities of the Cold War. There was a general understanding of the fact that an improvement in the position of women was not only a simple matter of justice, it was the key to the attainment of goals vital to the success of any society.

The Chinese were probably not fully aware of what they were letting themselves in for when they offered to host the conference. Control of the press is not what it once was in China. Chinese leaders may have come to the conclusion that China's image abroad was not improved by television footage of police officers placing their hands over journalists' camera lenses for no apparent reason. Was it Deng Xiaoping who once said that if you open a window, a fly might get in?

In private conversation the Chinese are open about the way their country is developing. I met people from the upper echelons of the hierarchy who were of the opinion that free elections and a multi-party system such as we have in the West would be introduced within fifteen years. In all my bridge-building with Asia, which I stepped up considerably after our EU vote in 1994 in order to forge

contacts for our trade and industry, I stressed that we understood
their difficulties in embracing certain aspects of Western life, but
that we all—not least politicians—must learn to accept criticism.
Constructive criticism is absolutely vital. But even criticism that is
less than constructive is only irritating, not dangerous.

I broached this subject in the opening of my speech: "What is it
we will remember from this conference? An unnecessarily high level
of security? Police officers with their hands in front of the cameras?
All those who were not given visas? Yes, but such memories cannot
survive for long. So let us instead count our strategic triumphs, not
our tactical reversals. What we have succeeded in doing is to create
a new and safer framework in which girls can grow up and women
can live out their lives."

After Jan Syse took over the Norwegian premiership in 1989 I
got a nice telephone call from a woman in Fredrikstad. Her son,
aged four or five, had been watching TV and been told that the man
there was the new Prime Minister.

"Yes," said the boy, "but can a man be Prime Minister?" I used
that in my Beijing speech, and the accompanying laughter from an
audience of the world's women could perhaps show how far most
countries still have to go before women have the opportunities that
we in Norway take for granted.

The Beijing conference focused attention on the fate of women
and girls in many lands. Women's rights are human rights too. Cultural diversity is a strength, but we should always challenge any
culture's dismissive attitudes toward equality and the self-evident
right of girls and women to lives of dignity and integrity.

The Loneliness of Leadership

President Mitterrand had extended invitations to a summit meeting
in Paris in November 1990 as part of the Conference on European
Security. This was a new era for our part of the world. More than
forty heads of state and government were assembled. Mitterrand
reminded us of the meeting in Helsinki fifteen years earlier. He

praised both the United States and the Soviet Union for their efforts to slow down the arms race, so that we would not even need to make changes to the Helsinki Treaty.

How was Europe faring? Democracy was still vulnerable, still weak. The old habits and thoughts lived on. Mitterrand supported Prime Minister Michel Rocard when Rocard contacted the Dutch Prime Minister and me in an effort to acquaint heads of state and government with a major new issue: the ecological challenge. Major and mostly positive changes had taken place on the European continent over the last year; democracy was on the march.

I had previously met most of the Presidents and Prime Ministers who attended the summit, but some were new to me. There were two representatives from each country, so I had my Foreign Minister beside me at one arc of the enormous elliptical conference table. Diagonally opposite me sat Soviet President Gorbachev, and the Norwegian delegation could not help but notice his frank gaze, as well as his interest in us and in the remarks I made about Norway.

I had visited Gorbachev twice before. Once of course was in 1986, not long after he became Soviet Secretary-General of the Communist Party; the second time was in January 1990, in the Kremlin, when I addressed a large international conference in Moscow with future U.S. Vice President Al Gore. Now, this autumn, Gorbachev had been awarded the Nobel Peace Prize, although we had still not received official notification that he would be in Oslo to receive his prize on December 10. So we were keen to see whether, during the course of the two-day conference, he would commit to coming.

Later that day, just before the official luncheon, the Soviets requested a meeting between us on behalf of their President. We had been following the dramatic developments in Moscow over the last few months. All the indications were that Gorbachev's situation was now more difficult than ever before.

The Soviet President and I sat down alone. He looked directly at me and expressed his regret that he had to decline the invitation.

He was naturally very appreciative of the Nobel Prize, but with the prevailing situation in Moscow it would be impossible for him to leave the country.

He was unusually frank: "They were not happy about my coming here to Paris and made it quite clear that there could be no question of my going to Oslo. They won't let me leave the country a second time."

It made a strong impression. Here was the mighty President of the Soviet Union, the much respected and admired reform politician to whom a whole world felt grateful, and what he was actually telling me was that he was a prisoner in his own country. So a good question might be, Who were *they*? They had to include strong forces in the Duma, the Russian Parliament, which was not elected by the people! And no doubt there were other forces at work within the Moscow power structure, the conservatives and even reactionaries of the Communist Party, and not least the hardliners in the Soviet secret police, the KGB. These were the ones who were responsible for Gorbachev's eventual fall from power.

Gorbachev held my hand. It was obvious he deeply regretted this situation and really would have liked to come. I knew there would be disappointment back home in Norway, and this was not a pleasant message for me to deliver, but what really struck me was the political reality behind what I had just heard, as well as the human aspect of the man's situation at that time.

It's a lonely life being a leader. No doubt Gorbachev was often lonely in facing the difficult decisions he had to make, with his wife, Raisa, by his side, but without really knowing, in the atmosphere prevailing in Soviet political life, who were his friends and who his enemies. I sympathized greatly with him in his difficult situation, and I didn't really need to express my sympathy—he knew how I felt.

"What's needed is patience!"

Seven months later Mikhail and Raisa Gorbachev visited Norway and were welcomed warmly at Fornebu airport. The press was out in force and the Soviet leader radiated calm, warmth, and self-confidence. There was no external sign at all of all the pressure he was under at home.

After he had exchanged friendly greetings with my team we had a twenty-minute talk in my office. Our conversation was first and foremost about the Socialist International. Gorbachev was concerned about the future of the Soviet Union and its progress with democracy, which, he said, would also involve the Communist Party. He was concerned that the world perceived the troubles in socialist countries as the failure of the very idea of socialism and was interested to hear what we had to say about the Socialist International in light of the November 1989 fall of the Berlin Wall. His own Politburo had admitted that the Soviet Union had much to learn from Europe's social-democratic parties. Was a broad alliance possible involving parties of the Left, Social Democrats, and Socialists? Gorbachev liked to think that the future of the Soviet Communist Party lay in some such alliance.

I didn't want to give Gorbachev the impression that such a development would be easy. The Socialist International had always been willing to allow observers at meetings and to cooperate with others, even nonmember parties. I said I thought such a solution might be possible, and that this was something to aim for. But the Socialist International has always stressed certain basic criteria for all member parties. A self-evident criterion is freedom of choice. Free elections, free trade unions, and freedom to negotiate in the workplace were essential in any social-democratic party's view of democracy.

Our conversation was optimistic, but I think Gorbachev realized that there was no simple way of avoiding the difficult choices that now faced him.

In the official bilateral talks we spent a lot of time on our shared regional problems: the environmental problems, nuclear pollution, development on Kola Peninsula, and the need to deal with the large-scale sulfur emissions from nickel production. We also spoke in depth about the principles involved in offshore oil production where the delimitation of a line between Norwegian and Russian continental shelves had been contested since 1974. Gorbachev was certainly well informed. All the same, I soon sensed that he had nothing new to add at that point. He was cautious, though keen for progress.

I think Gorbachev would have liked to have done more but felt that he had no mandate and no real power given the situation in the Soviet Union. So it was all the more gratifying when at his large press conference later that day he gave a crystal-clear answer to the press on the question of the maritime borders: "Yes, I'm sure we'll manage to work this out. We've come a long way already, nearly three-quarters of the way there!"

Indeed, in the months that followed, it became evident that he hadn't had the political basis to back up such an optimistic prognosis. It might also be that this public statement had awakened certain sleeping dogs in the Duma and elsewhere in the Soviet system. Unfortunately, the progress we had achieved and the constructive atmosphere of the dialogue so far were less evident in subsequent discussions with the Soviet Union, and then Russia.

A President Under House Arrest

Three months later the Socialist International met in Berlin in the magnificent old Parliament building virtually sitting on the remnants of the Berlin Wall. It was to be the last time we'd see Willy Brandt at a large public gathering; he fell ill and died about a year later.

We were meeting just after the August 19 coup in the Soviet Union, when an eight-man junta had announced that they had taken over the running of the country and deposed Mikhail Gorbachev. The world was shocked, and many governments, including the Norwegian, denounced the coup. The takeover collapsed after two days, and Gorbachev returned to Moscow from his summer home in the Crimea, where he had been put under house arrest. It was in these days that Boris Yeltsin appeared on the scene as the new leader, condemning the coup and giving a fiery speech from the top of a military tank outside the Soviet Parliament building.

Former French Prime Minister Pierre Mauroy, who was the new

President of the Socialist International (SI), gave a report from an extensive visit to the Soviet Union he had made with a delegation from the SI. They had spoken to the former Foreign Minister Eduard Schevardnadze, as well as to Yeltsin and Gorbachev. Now work was under way on the new constitution establishing a federation of sovereign republics, a development that would weaken Gorbachev's role as leader of a united country. The platform for the new federation was that of the broad democratic movement led by Egor Jakovlev, to which Schevardnadze belonged.

Yeltsin had been open and friendly and had made a good impression on the delegation. A democratic Russia, that was Yeltsin's platform. He had expressed the desire to see a new form of economic union between the independent republics. And according to Mauroy, Gorbachev had seemed relaxed and full of energy. He had been open with them about the situation and readily admitted the mistakes that had been made. The timetable had been organized in such a way that the individual leaders of the republics acquired their legitimacy before the federation did. This left the federation's leaders in a weaker position than those who had just been elected. Felipe Gonzales of Spain believed that Gorbachev as a person seemed more democratic.

Finnish Party Leader Pertti Paasio spoke of how difficult it was to understand the power structure in the Soviet Union and to know who was who. Even though Gorbachev had been in good spirits, the truth was that he was out of touch with the realities in his own country. I remember being struck by Paasio's pessimism, knowing that he had contacts upon which to base his feelings. Paasio also said that we must expect a very difficult three-month period in the winter, with tendencies to social disintegration. Indeed, much of Paasio's prediction was borne out.

As early as 1988, Yeltsin had proclaimed himself a social democrat, for which he had been ousted from the Communist Politburo. Gorbachev had expressed the view that the Soviet people had strong roots in socialism and that he regretted that the Soviet Communist Party could not be saved and reformed.

Felipe Gonzales praised Gorbachev as a leader and a man. He believed that Gorbachev had his feet firmly planted on the ground. It had been Gorbachev who had started the whole reform process, but he could not control everything. Serious mistakes had been made, too.

Karel van Miert, EU commissioner, said that the EU's problem was this: To whom in the Soviet Union should we relate? Was the federation or the republics responsible for the banks and the finances? In reality, the Soviet Union no longer existed! We were in a situation where there was widespread disquiet over what was happening in the U.S.S.R. There were enormous environmental problems—for example, the life expectancy on Kola was down to fifty-one, the same as in Bangladesh. In Moscow, life expectancy had fallen by ten years over the past two decades. It was becoming increasingly clear that we would have to talk directly to the regions, the republics, and the big cities in order to be of assistance, promote stability, and develop democracy.

Yeltsin

I met Boris Yeltsin for the first time in Helsinki in 1992 at the Conference on Security and Cooperation in Europe. There was no time for a deep discussion, but I managed to impress upon him the need to clear up the problem of nuclear waste on the Kola Peninsula, and that delimitation of the offshore lines was necessary. He was charming, obviously enjoying himself. In his speech he held up his neighbor Norway as a positive example, giving us the clear impression that he had added a few spontaneous touches to his speech after our exchange.

In 1995 there were celebrations of the anniversary of the end of the Second World War. We had our own large committee at work, and the Norwegian celebrations began in 1994, with a major event in the small city of Kirkenes to mark the liberation of East Finnmark. The Red Army had performed well up there, and had afterward withdrawn to the Soviet side of the border. This was not the case in the other European countries where Soviet forces had driven out the Nazis.

Yeltsin invited us to attend a commemorative ceremony in

Moscow on May 9. There were discussions in NATO about how to react to the Russian plans. Some felt we should stay away in protest against the fighting in Chechnya.

I was the first Western head of government to accept the Russians' invitation. At the same time I wrote to Prime Minister Chernomyrdin telling him that I wanted to discuss the modernization of Petsjenganikkel, a huge factory producing nickel and a tremendous amount of air pollution close to the Norwegian border, as well as other matters of common interest to Norway and Russia during my visit. My thinking was that my quick answer might earn us some goodwill at a time when there was a lot of muttering among Western diplomats about boycotting the Russian celebrations. According to a Russian source, Yeltsin wrote on a corner of the letter he received from me, "When the lady says jump, we jump."

I believed it was right to distinguish between the 1995 conflict in Chechnya and the huge effort that cost millions of Russian and other Soviet lives during the Second World War. I had powerful memories of my 1978 visit to Leningrad and the Russian war memorial to all the dead soldiers.

Later I heard that my gesture had been much appreciated in Moscow. And in the end they all came: Clinton, Mitterrand, Kohl, Jiang Zemin, and Boutros Boutros-Ghali. My encounter with President Clinton would be brief. I offered my sympathy for the lives lost in the Oklahoma bombing only a short time before. He thanked me and replied that now no one could be safe.

Olav and I arrived at the Kremlin an hour before the veterans' parade. Outside a modest little entrance to one of the Kremlin buildings, on a narrow cobbled road leading to Red Square, four middle-aged people stood waiting. There were no bodyguards, no staff members. Just these four: Yeltsin and his wife, and Prime Minister Chernomyrdin and his wife. They seemed calm and peaceful, these representatives of the mighty Russia, as they waited together.

It was a very stirring experience to watch the veterans, thousands of men and women in their old uniforms, marching across Red Square. Some had trouble walking, but their pride was radiant. When the military orchestra with its thousand members knelt in the square during the final movements of Tchaikovsky's *1812 Over-*

ture, and the bells rang out from the Spasski tower, I was not the only one deeply moved.

Prime Minister Chernomyrdin had made time in the middle of these solemn festivities for a Norwegian–Russian meeting in the White House, which had been so badly damaged during the disturbances in 1992. Chernomyrdin had been in Norway in 1985 as Minister of Gas and Oil and knew the Norwegian oil industry. He had himself been head of the Soviet Gas Company, Gazprom.

I said it was paradoxical that progress on the question of delimitation offshore in the Barents Sea had been halted once Russia had taken over negotiations from the former Soviet Union. We also discussed the modernization of the Petsjenganikkel factory on Kola, which polluted so heavily on both sides of the border. And we discussed the nuclear question and arms reduction, as well as the war in Chechnya. Many had advised against mentioning Chechnya, and other foreign visitors who had done so had been given an earful. My experience is that it is possible to discuss difficult subjects if one adapts the form of the question in order to analyze the situation. And Chernomyrdin was quite open. He made no secret of the fact that in his view the rebels were just bandits, but he respected my interest and knew that we regarded that conflict as a war that raised serious questions about human rights.

A Russian Bear

The preparations for Yeltsin's visit to Oslo in March 1996 were hectic, and my State Secretary for International Affairs, Morten Wetland, had been working around the clock. The Russian ambassador made a great many demands and suggestions, among them that on no account were we to raise with Yeltsin the key issue of the offshore delimitation in the Barents Sea. The Russians pointed out that the matter was now being discussed by experts, and there was nothing that Yeltsin and I would be able to contribute.

I knew this scenario well. In my experience, leaders do not usually share their associates' anxiety at the prospect of such matters being raised at a meeting. So a message was sent from my office saying that we did indeed intend to raise the question, to see how far we could get.

Yeltsin asked to meet me alone before we joined the delegations. "Alone" meant the two us with our interpreters and a stenographer. On the sixteenth floor my staff members were lined up outside the entrance to my office for a look at the visitor. Yeltsin came to a halt and accommodated them with a broad smile for the girls. It was obvious that he was enjoying himself.

After a while one gets used to speaking to the Russians. We learn how to express ourselves in such a way that the translation will be good, we learn what kind of humor works, and when to use it—often. Humor is an excellent tool, and the Russians, too, have a lot of it, in their fashion.

Boris Yeltsin seemed too big for the table he was sitting at. It made him look like a friendly teddy bear. The contrast with his chief of staff, Ilyushin, who was also the stenographer, was memorable indeed. Ilyushin was a small, thin man, completely expressionless, and he chewed gum constantly and rhythmically.

We began by reminding each other of our last meeting in Moscow during the war commemoration. Soon Yeltsin was saying that as leader, there were also certain unpleasant and unavoidable things he had to deal with, that just the day before he'd had to intervene in the way the Russian authorities were dealing with four cargo boats that were being built in Russia for a Norwegian ship owner. With a crooked, pleased smile, Yeltsin stuck his big paw across the table, and I took it, to confirm that a problem had been solved. "Now and then leaders have to intervene in order to solve problems," Yeltsin said, hugely pleased with himself.

He's a real joker when the mood takes him. During a lunch at the U.N. building in New York for the fifty-year celebrations, the press was lined up in the dining room to take pictures of the guests. Yeltsin got hold of a wooden chair, sat down in front of the press photographers, and began to strike poses. When Clinton came in during his carrying-on, no one even noticed.

"In just the same way we have to deal with other problems," Yeltsin rumbled at our private meeting. "This business of the Barents Sea, for example." Now he was going straight for the one thing the diplomats had been doing everything they could to prevent us from discussing. "What we need is a political solution. I suggest as follows. Three-quarters of the line is already drawn. What's left might be rich in resources. Let us form a joint body to search for oil and gas. We share the investment, and we share the profits."

I said it was very difficult to understand why we could not clearly draw the offshore lines. I said too that we had heard this suggestion before, from Prime Minister Ryshkov during his visit in 1988.

"Is it the same suggestion?" Yeltsin seemed genuinely surprised. I produced a map to demonstrate the situation and show how we could, for example, split the territory equally.

"You mean fifty-fifty?"

"That's a good idea. Then we can cooperate on exploiting resources on both sides of the divide."

"There are lots of uncles and aunts against that."

"But it's the best idea."

Yeltsin continued to press ahead with his original suggestion. "Let's form a consortium."

"But which will be the operative law? Norway's or Russia's?"

"We have laws in Russia."

"But they are for Russian soil."

"They are also for foreigners."

"Yes, for foreigners on Russian soil. And Norwegian law covers Norwegian soil."

"You've got a law like that; we've got a law like that. That means we can work together."

"I don't think that's advisable. If we don't have a border, it will only cause confusion and trouble."

"That means carrying on for another twenty-six years," said Yeltsin, rolling his eyes. I produced a pencil.

"If we've managed it here then we can do it here too. It isn't difficult."

"How long will this take?"

"A few months. It isn't difficult."

"Do you think so?"

"Yes."

We agreed on how the experts should proceed and moved on to the question of fishing.

"You trick us over the fish," said Yeltsin. "You get the cod and haddock and all we get is the herring. But we're simple people."

We went over the case of Nikitin, the former naval officer who had been arrested in Russia on charges of spying while working for the Environment Foundation, "Bellona," on the nuclear pollution issue. Yeltsin promised that Nikitin would be allowed to choose his lawyer.

"There's a third thing I want to talk about," said Yeltsin.

"Petsjenganikkel?"

"No, that is the thirty-third, but we can tackle it now," said Yeltsin, smiling radiantly at his own good humor.

"We're keen to see investment get started," I said.

"Yes, tomorrow I will be signing a decree. Forty-two million dollars are to be invested by Norway, and the same from Russia. We've earmarked ten million dollars for 1996. Next year it will be twenty million."

"Yes, that's direct state investment. What remains unresolved is whether the factory should be allowed to keep enough of its own money to finance the investments above and beyond what the state is prepared to cover. There's some talk of lifting the Russian export duty."

"Yes."

"Has that been arranged?"

"They must be given certain tax exemptions."

"This is urgent. The Norwegian firms say that if the problem isn't solved during the Soviet President's visit then the project will fall through."

"I'd better be certain about this. Let's get Blatov in here."

Blatov was the director of Petsjenganikkel and one of many in Yeltsin's delegation who were waiting on the floor above. Yeltsin sent Ilyushin out to look for him.

Blatov seemed to have vanished into thin air. But Yeltsin had located the Russian customs director, Kruglov, and he pointed to him. "Do you know about Petsjenganikkel and the export duties?"

"In principle, yes. Material imported from Norway will be tax-free." Yeltsin turned back contentedly to me.

"Right. Everything coming from Norway to Petsjenganikkel will be exempt from import duty. I can arrange that."

"What about export duty?"

Kruglov pointed out that this duty would in any case be lifted after July 1. I said if it was that easy, then maybe the whole problem was solved. "But it's even more urgent than that. The companies have to get started by April 1." Yeltsin said he would find a solution before then.

"I think that's necessary," I said.

"We can do it tomorrow," Yeltsin agreed. "But we need to sign a protocol so that I can sign a decree. We'll sign it today, before I leave. There are forty-five minutes left of the scheduled time for the talks. Deputy Prime Minister Soskovets will sign for us. Who will sign for you?"

This time it was Morten Wetland who went on a mission to the next floor up and organized the drafting of a protocol with the right content that could be signed in the course of the next forty-five minutes. While we waited, we discussed Chechnya, and I stressed how important we felt it was for the hostilities to cease. But Yeltsin was merciless in his view of the rebels.

"We must rid one area after another of bandits and terrorists. Mr. Dudaev is dug in somewhere in the northwestern area."

Just then the elusive director of Petsjenganikkel appeared. Yeltsin fixed him with his eyes: "What is it that you need?"

Blatov ran through the financial help the company needed. Yeltsin was not completely satisfied.

"How much money do you need, and for how long?"

"Four years duty-free should be enough at the price of nickel today. I've lived in the area all my life and conditions are terrible."

"If we drop the duty by decree in the next few days, will you be able to solve the problems?"

"Yes, with complete exemptions and no new taxes."

"Then that's what we'll do."

"Thank you, Boris Nikolaevich."

Yeltsin was clearly happy: "Rulers have to solve problems!"

He felt we'd done an honest day's work. The big bear paw extended over the table again; then we left and went to the meeting room on the floor above to continue our discussions with foreign ministers and advisers.

Raspberries and Cream

Yeltsin had been ill-mannered in dealing with NATO's Secretary-General Solana when Solana was in Moscow shortly before this Oslo visit. I was therefore interested to see how he would react when I brought up the subject of NATO again. Yeltsin was firm, yes, but by no means unpleasant. I summarized Norwegian policy as a NATO member since its inception and stressed the right of every country to define its own policy within the framework of the alliance's mutual obligations. Yeltsin asked if Norway had any particular opinions on the question of the enlargement of NATO. I emphasized that Norway had supported all NATO's resolutions on principles for the process of enlargement, but that no firm conclusions would be made in 1996.

Yeltsin's view was that NATO expansion would be a great mistake for Europe. He wished that other lands besides Russia understood that together we could fight for European security. In his view, Europe—without the United States—could unite in a common defense policy. I stressed that, on the contrary, all-European security included the United States and Canada. Moreover, the United States and Russia were also natural partners. Yeltsin pointed out what might happen if NATO military forces advanced to the Russian border and Russia made an alliance with China: We would once again be back with two great power blocs. I said that this scenario was completely unrealistic; that U.S. weapons would not be deployed close to the Russian border; and that, moreover, democracies do not go to war. I stressed our commitment to ensuring that Russia always had channels open to NATO. NATO wanted to be in dialogue with Russia, and this conversation was a prime example of that.

My staff and I were impressed by the degree to which Boris Yeltsin was familiar with the questions that most interested Norwegians and with our views on international questions. His staff had already made it quite clear that they wanted Yeltsin to look good for the people back home whenever he was abroad.

Yeltsin clearly enjoyed himself greatly in the company of our royal family. He characterized the spirit of the whole visit when he took hold of the Queen and me, one on each arm, at the farewell banquet. The Queen was in red and I in white. "Raspberries and cream," Yeltsin said to the big crew of photographers.

Nelson Mandela

There is something very special about Nelson Mandela's personality. You feel as if you've known him all your life. He is intimate, direct, open. He radiates warmth and dignity. People across the world have felt a closeness to him. We in Norway have followed him and the struggle against apartheid throughout his time in jail, and then in hope and faith when the dialogue in South Africa started toward the end of the 1980s.

I was to participate in a conference on conflict prevention at the Norwegian Nobel Institute in Oslo in August 1990. Its organizers included Elie Wiesel. A member of Fredrik Willem de Klerk's government and Nelson Mandela were also due to attend. As a former Prime Minister and Leader of the Labor Party, I had a private meeting with Mandela. I had listened with pleasure and admiration to him and his "opponent" in the hall. Both sides seemed willing to find solutions, and I think all of us who were present felt new hope for South Africa's future.

At the hotel we ate a simple meal together, just the two of us. He expressed his thanks for the long years of support offered by the Norwegian Labor Party and the Norwegian trade unions. He thanked us for our political contribution to the struggle against the apartheid regime and expressed the hope that we would continue to offer support in the years to come for all the major reforms that would be taking place in South Africa. He was secure in his belief in the future and certain of where he wanted his country to go. He carried the responsibilities of leadership within him, and I did not doubt for a moment that I was speaking to the future leader of South Africa.

How certain was Mandela of a successful conclusion to the protracted negotiations on the dismantling of the apartheid regime? There had been so many disappointments and setbacks, acts of violence in which the regime's own police force seemed to be implicated. Yet Mandela had put his suspicions aside and made up his mind that he could and should proceed along the way of peace. He wanted political support to put pressure on the de Klerk government in the struggle against violence, but he did not want to overdramatize the situation.

Did Mandela feel confident that President de Klerk sincerely desired a solution? Did he feel that he could trust de Klerk as a person? I left our meeting with the impression that the answer was yes. "You must remember that de Klerk has problems of his own to deal with," Mandela told me. "Opponents in his own ranks."

Less than two years later I was able to welcome Nelson Mandela to Oslo on our National Day, May 17, and to speak to him as host to guest: " 'Struggle is my life,' you once wrote. 'I will go on fighting for freedom until the end of my days.' Sentenced to a lifetime in prison under apartheid, which used the law to abuse justice, you never lost your fundamental faith. Your struggle for freedom, human rights and democracy is the story of life itself, and will remain an example to us all."

Mandela visited Oslo a third time in December 1993, when he and President de Klerk jointly received the Nobel Peace Prize. In the years that followed I had the pleasure of again meeting Mandela on several occasions both at the U.N. and in free South Africa when the Socialist International met there.

A Living Legend

My strongest impressions of Mandela were those from my visit as Prime Minister to South Africa and Robben Island. On Sunday February 13, 1996, exactly six years to the day after Mandela was released from the prison on Robben Island, we sat in a military helicopter on our way out to the island from Cape Town. It was a great honor, and perhaps a special thank-you to Norway because of the way we had stood in the front lines in the struggle against apartheid. Nothing like this trip had ever been arranged before.

I had arrived at the President's house in Cape Town early in the morning of that warm summer day. Mandela shook my hand and we went out through the French windows onto the upper lawn, from which some steps led down to the lower lawn, where the helicopter stood waiting. Considerately, Mandela demonstrated the hearing protectors and made me promise to wear them as we flew over the sea.

The most striking thing of all was to see the warmth and respect with which the South African military helicopter crew and the bodyguards treated President Mandela. He had clearly won a special place in the hearts of South Africans; no other politician of our era even comes close to inspiring such affection. No one felt any doubt at all about his unique position symbolically, morally, and politically among most South Africans.

Throughout the world, Mandela was a living legend. I saw white South Africans—members of a social class one might expect to feel very unhappy about a black president—treat him with the sort of love grandparents sometimes receive, offering him a supporting arm to navigate the icy pavement or securing his scarf on a cold winter's day.

The security service in South Africa had a very special responsibility, for if something happened to Mandela the effect would be as terrible as when Martin Luther King was murdered, and so many young and optimistic Americans lost faith in their own country. Nelson Mandela was the glue that held the peaceful revolution together. His society was on the brink of winning its battle.

Our official visit had opened with a journey directly from the airport in Cape Town to the suburban slum at Kayelitsha, where half a million people live in tin shacks. These people were born on the shadow side of the earth. It was concern for their lives and their rights that had dominated Norway's attitude toward the apartheid system in South Africa. Now the Norwegian Athletics Association and Norwegian Olympic Committee had made it possible to build an athletics field—a pyramid of soccer balls marking the start of a campaign that would make sport available for everybody—and South Africa had just won the African Nations Cup! The team's nickname was "bawana bawana," which means "dribblers," in essence the same nickname carried by Norway's national team.

South Africans are every bit as sports crazy as Norwegians, and after all the years of the athletics boycott, they are also sports-starved. Mandela himself had once been a boxer, and I'm sure during all the years of apartheid, he would have liked to have been standing cheering at the game when the national team played. Now he was standing in the VIP box wearing a South African team shirt.

If you've been in a room when Nelson Mandela enters, you would almost swear afterward that there had been music there. Nelson Mandela has a special stride, and Africans accompany him with a rhythmic clapping that involves the entire body. He greets everybody, and he takes his time. A ten- or twelve-year-old boy got what must have been the thrill of a lifetime when Nelson Mandela asked when his birthday was and got someone to write the date down so that he could call the boy on the day.

With Nelson Mandela on Robben Island

Mandela himself is my guide for the tour of the prison. The prison governor, a woman with the rank of colonel, follows in the background. Mandela asks politely, "Can we see the exercise yard?" "Can we go in here now?" Cell number 16. Six feet square, a window with iron bars, a bed, a wooden chair, a little table. He takes me in with him and says: "This was my home for sixteen years."

He describes how the prisoners communicated with one another, how they tried to keep each other's spirits up. Slips of paper were smuggled from cell to cell. And you had to be concise, he says with a wry smile, because paper was in short supply. I stand and look through the bars and try to imagine spending sixteen years here. I can't.

We continue along the narrow prison corridors, enter a spartan washroom with four toilets. Swinging doors in the middle of each cubicle give just a couple of feet of coverage. He pushes open a swinging door, points with his arm—"This is where we sat."

He turns to the prison governor and asks, "Can I meet the prisoners? I would like to meet the prisoners." This causes some unease among the security men; they have to arrange something quickly so that we can meet some of the three hundred prisoners still being held here, in an island prison whose name the whole world knows. In Mandela's time it was the leaders who were held here, those who presented a threat to the regime. Many of those men are now government members and active politicians. There are no political prisoners here now.

The current prisoners are assembled in a large hall seated on benches. Excitement spreads, and clenched fists are held high through a chanted swirl of Zulu and Xhosa words. The leader is being praised. Mandela raises his fist and addresses the prisoners. "Today I have brought with me the Prime Minister of Norway. She is my honored guest. I want to thank her for all her country has done for us. When I was being held here, it was Norway, along with a few other countries, who supported us in our fight against oppression."

Pause. "Do you study?" he asks the group. Discomfort appears in the eyes of many prisoners, along with surprise and defiance. "You must study," Mandela continues. "You must prepare yourselves for your lives on the outside; you must become useful members of society. While I was here one fellow prisoner received a Ph.D. Another fellow prisoner received two Ph.D's. And yet another earned three. Today they are highly respected members of society and are well able to take care of themselves and their families."

He knows quite well that not everyone will take his advice. All the same, this is the best appeal he can make. The men regard him with respect and trust. Mandela finishes his talk, and the cheering breaks out again. Fists punch the air, voices chant. Mandela responds with a broad smile and a raised fist.

There is a farewell ceremony out by the limestone quarry where Mandela and the other prisoners once did their day's work. The dust gets in your eyes and forms an acid with your own tears. The prisoners' eyes are always red. We ourselves feel it at once. Mandela again thanks Norway and the other countries that had supported the ANC in the struggle. We will always be the friends of Mandela and of South Africa.

I brought a present for South Africa. After thorough investigation we had decided to donate 14 million Kroner toward promoting reconciliation among the races in South Africa. Robben Island was to be converted from a prison island to a museum of South African heritage with a center for freedom and reconciliation.

The following day the Norwegian Progressive Party strongly attacked the gift, saying it was a waste to spend Norwegian foreign aid on a statue of Nelson Mandela. No doubt many others shared this view. How the myth of a statue arose I have no idea, but the press statement criticizing the project certainly garnered a lot of attention in the media. Those of us who had spent such a special day on Robben Island with Nelson Mandela looked at each other and shrugged. As for the statue, we had already seen it. Nelson Mandela, the historic figure, on the historic island.

Traveling back to Cape Town one member of our party put it this way: "Mandela is the closest we'll get to a real-life Jesus!"

The People's King of Norway

The phone rings on Thursday, January 17, 1991. It is only half past nine in the evening but I am already in bed and can hardly rise to answer the call. The night before I had been in Helsinki for a meeting of the Nordic Social-Democratic Committee of Cooperation and was awakened after midnight by my colleagues who had been following events on CNN. The Gulf War had broken out. At about one o'clock in the morning I had a talk with Prime Minister Ingvar Carlsson of Sweden. The attacks on Baghdad had commenced. I decided to leave for Oslo in order to be at home to deal with this latest development. I didn't get much sleep.

Amidst all of this, one of my staff was now telling me that the King was very ill. I later heard that the events in the Gulf had affected him deeply. He was watching television in his Holmenkollen home when he suddenly felt unwell.

Even as I considered whether to warn the government, we were informed that the King had died at the age of eighty-seven. He had been King of Norway for thirty-four years. In a flash I remembered when King Haakon, his father, had died. Pappa, who was Minister of Social Affairs and Health at the time, was summoned to the Palace at night. The cabinet always meets in the event of the King's death. Then there was the long march, past Parliament, where Mamma and I stood, down to Oslo Cathedral. Pappa and his cabinet colleagues were in top hats.

Now it was my responsibility to manage the formal side of the government's role. A cabinet meeting was convened at midnight in the main government building, and then we traveled together to the Royal Palace. King Harald, our new King, received us. With the somberness of the occasion, we took our accustomed places in the cabinet room with King Harald at the head of the table. He formally gave us the news that his father, King Olav, was dead, and that he had taken over the throne. He had taken the name King Harald V and chosen the same motto as his father: "All for Norway." This was a historic moment. We had a new king.

The next morning candles, flowers, and cards from children appeared in the snow outside the Palace. Such a gesture was previously unknown in our country, the result of a desire to express how great a loss Norway felt. The sea of candles and flowers, photographs and drawings, continued to grow, along with the greetings from the thousands who wanted to express their gratitude and their love. The horror of the war now raging in the Gulf must have strengthened the feeling that a vital anchorage had been lost to us.

Preparing the speech I was to give in the cathedral, I wrote on a piece of paper, "We all feel as though we have lost a member of our own family." But I crossed it out. I can't say that. My feelings would overpower me and it would be my own grief I was expressing—not what I must say on behalf of so many.

The country grieved, but we also felt a deep gratitude for all that King Olav had been for us. King Olav incarnated our whole history as an independent nation and our struggle to hold on to our freedom when we were most in need. From the November day in 1905 when he was carried ashore in his father's arms into the harbor as the snow fell, to the day he fell asleep among the snow-laden trees of Kongsseter, King Olav V's hold on our hearts grew steadily stronger, first as Crown Prince, then as King.

King Olav was everyone's king. The explanation is as true as it is simple: He represented the best in what it means to be Norwegian, the best in us all.

Along with his father, King Olav faced his most difficult days when war came, and he faced those days with courage, vision, and decision. We remember both father and son: during the bombing, beneath the birch trees, dignified under pressure, the symbols of a living nation in an occupied land.

But King Olav's life's work was first and foremost in the service of peace. His commitment far beyond the call of duty was the reason for his subjects' love.

We all recall him smiling on the Royal Palace balcony on May 17, National Day, greeting the children's parade. Hour after hour, year after year. The image of our freedom and independence was at the same time a person we all felt close to. He brought us all closer together.

King Olav met more Norwegians than anyone else, and everyone had a personal memory of him. The people he served saw how he carried out his obligations with infectious humor and charm. He was an example to us all. Through his inexhaustible efforts, his firm leadership and real warmth, our young royal house—fewer than one hundred years old—had become one with our nation. Tens of thousands expressed their affection for the late King. The candles and the flowers outside the Palace helped us to convey what we could hardly express in words: grief over our King's death, quiet joy and gratitude for everything he had been to us all. As the children put it, "He was the nicest King in the world."

The dramatic events and the dark days around the King's death made clear to all of us the stability we sought from the one taking over the mantle. To King Harald V, and his family, we sent hope and courage.

A nation is united in gratitude, I thought at the time.

Blessings be upon the memory of good King Olav V.

Pappa

"Pappa died yesterday, March 22, 1987," read my diary. "Admitted [to the hospital on] Thursday with a heart attack, front septum. Recovered well and was in good spirits. Looking to the future, talked to his nearest and dearest about future adventures, times to come, the walks we would take. Was to be moved to the ordinary ward yesterday morning. It happened before they could move him, in the shower, at 10:35. His heart stopped, three-quarters of an hour resuscitation in intensive care was attempted but with no success. I was informed over the telephone while I was having a meeting with two of my Ministers.

"My sister Hanne screamed 'No, no, it is impossible. I don't want Pappa to die!' That's how we all felt. We had all been afraid these last few days. We comforted ourselves with the thought that he died feeling optimistic."

I wrote these sentences in my little book the next day. That was my way of trying to ease the pain. The thought of Pappa's courage, his love of life, and his strong faith that he still had a future with his loved ones was our only consolation.

I had seen him for the last time on Sunday evening, a day and a half before he died. When I arrived, a longtime colleague was at his bedside. Before he left I heard their half-jocular farewell—"If not before, then I'll see you for a day's skiing in the forest!" Pappa at only seventy was certain he would be back on his skis again soon. That his heart would give up on the tenth day after his first attack was a possibility that he, a doctor and an active sportsman, never considered.

I couldn't help thinking about our common professional identity. Doctors are not always best suited to take care of themselves.

An "Incident or Episode"

One weekend in early February Pappa and I were sitting in front of the open fire in his home at Lake Mylla. I had been uneasy about the state of his health since the Christmas holiday. At about ten o'clock on Christmas Eve I noticed that he staggered a bit when he got up. We'd drunk beer and a little aquavit with our pork and a cognac with our coffee as we always did, but he certainly couldn't be drunk, could he? I asked him when he came back, "What was that, Pappa?" He just brushed it aside. The next day he didn't go out on his skis, saying that he felt a little dizzy. He promised that as soon as the holiday was over he would go for a checkup. Of the two of us he was the one who was primarily a doctor; I had been away from the clinic for years. Pappa still saw patients and moved in medical circles and discussed medical matters.

Later I asked him whether he had had his heart checked. Yes, there was nothing the matter with his EKG reading. Had they checked his head too? I asked. Somewhat reluctantly he said, "Yes, there were signs that a small incident had taken place, but it is nothing to worry about."

So there had been an "event" of some sort. Was it a slight stroke? I did not even dare to use the word, just said, "You must have your heart checked more thoroughly, Pappa. Promise me that."

"No," he replied, "there's a waiting list for heart examinations. I don't want anyone to accuse me of jumping the line." His mind was made up, and I had the impression, although he did not say so, that his status as father of the Prime Minister made him even more determined on this issue. I felt uneasy, but said no more. Now after his much too premature death, I regret that I allowed myself to be silenced.

Then it was the second weekend of March. The ski runs are in excellent condition, the sun shining. Olav and I ski north toward Mylla. We are there by five and hear that Pappa has been there ahead of us. He'd arrived an hour before but has gone to nap. That's what we do, too. At about six-thirty, we are awakened by Pappa, who brings me a piña colada. He knows how much I like that. What I did not know was that this was the last time I would experience Pappa's warmth and the hospitable way he treats family members who spend time with him and Mamma at their winter cottage.

It was a pleasant evening. I didn't notice anything unusual about Pappa, and a week later I asked him, as he lay in the hospital bed, how this could have happened. He must have had his first heart attack during the ski trip about two and a half miles from the cottage. He said later that he suddenly felt terribly tired, as though all the strength had drained out of him, but there was no pain. It was sheer willpower that took him the rest of the way to Mylla.

The next day the weather was again beautiful. I was a bit surprised when Pappa said that he didn't want to come skiing with us, that he would stay back and help Inga. That wasn't the usual refrain on a fine Sunday out in the woods. He said nothing about feeling unwell, as he later admitted he was.

Feverish and ill, he turned up at the office he still kept at the Norwegian Research Council for Technology and Natural Science on Monday. But by Wednesday night, Mamma told us, he couldn't sleep and lay awake in pain, considerable pain; yet he refused to call a doctor or allow Mamma to do so. The next day he got into his car, ashen and in great pain, and drove down to the hospital, where he sat down in the corridor to await his turn to see the head doctor, who incidentally was an old boyfriend of mine and a friend of the family. There was something the matter with his chest. He thought it must be something to do with his esophagus. After a while they gave up looking for that. After an EKG test he was admitted at once with the diagnosis: a major heart attack.

Gathering Round the Sickbed

Days had been lost, days when he should have been receiving treatment. Days when he did not go to a doctor. Months had been lost, months when he should have let himself be properly examined so that these developments could have been prevented. I knew his behavior had been careless. As had my own. But now it was too late.

Poor Hanne was the same age as our own children! How would I have fared if I had lost Pappa when I was only twenty-two? She sat there, my little sister, huddled up in the corner of the hall. I couldn't give her any real hope.

Over the next few hours we tried to get in touch with all the children, grandchildren, and cousins. This was the last thing any of us had imagined. He was the pulse of the family, its center, and the one we all turned to in times of trouble.

Jørgen, where was he? He was the last one we got in touch with, the last to arrive. I was pleased and relieved when I saw him come walking along the glass corridor and into intensive care. So Jørgen, too, would manage to say good-bye to his grandpa!

A Big and Tightly Knit Family

Pappa was the center of our large family. He kept in touch with all of us and cared about his grandchildren and nieces and nephews, impressing upon them the values he had imbued in his own children: joy in nature, joy in physical activity, the joy of overcoming problems, of setting goals and attaining them. He also made sure every Harlem knew how to use a map and compass!

But Pappa could also be both serious and determined. He compelled respect, sometimes even fear. His demands were high, but we always found them reasonable. And in times of crisis he could surprise us with his tenderness and compassion. For example, one evening I, aged eleven, came home and found a four-gallon glass container of juice in the kitchen. As I was trying to pour myself a glass, the container fell and broke, flooding the whole kitchen floor with thick red juice. This was in 1950, hard times with rationing. I was inconsolable and dreaded when Pappa would come home and see what I had done. I remember my relief and gratitude and love when all he said was, "Gro, just forget about it. It was only juice." He had the ability to put things behind him and go on.

Olav, who was for many years my parents' only son-in-law, set store by our family traditions of togetherness at the holiday homes. He soon became a part of it all and brought with him his sense of humor. Pappa too had a ready smile and enjoyed an exchange of wits. The young political scientist looked up to the older politician. Olav knew he had much to learn here, despite the difference between his politics and Pappa's. Olav could never get enough of Pappa's analyses of political situations in historical contexts, and there is no doubt that Pappa was one of the inspirations behind Olav's 1968 book on national security. For me, too, these conversations on international affairs, foreign policy, and national security would later prove useful.

In the early years, Pappa had less influence on our everyday lives than Mamma. Work took up most of his time. But at breakfast and often at suppertime, too, at about nine or ten at night, we spoke about everything, discussed the social issues of the day, international affairs and crises, the rights and wrongs of society. And on the weekends he was there all the time: on the ski runs, by the fireside, in the forests and fields, in our old open fishing boat *Sugga* ("The Fat Pig") with its six-horsepower outboard motor and its fishing net.

Pappa was a good sailor, and a patient man. He taught us the practical side of things and was good at explaining the theoretical side too. Wind, current, waves—how did these affect the boat, the sail, the rudder? He showed no gender favoritism and spent equal amounts of time with me and with my brothers, Erik and Lars, and later with Hanne.

Everyone in our family learned to play bridge, and everyone was welcome to join any conversation. Several generations and people from all sorts of different environments all had much to learn from the community that Pappa and Mamma created around themselves and their extended family.

The summer before Pappa died we were all gathered at our holiday home at Helleskilen to celebrate his seventieth birthday—the extended family, Gegga and Ola, and his closest friends from the doctors' club. In his speech, Pappa said that he had been lucky enough to live an interesting and eventful life, and that he looked forward to more of the same. He shared with us his reflections on the things that really mattered in life, on what was most important of all: the family, the adults and children, and then the friends, those who had meant most to him through a long life.

A Life of Learning

Pappa's political and medical activities went hand in hand from the start. He started at the Institute of Hygiene, where he carried out social policy studies. In addition he worked for the Central Register for Rehabilitation, involved in getting the war-wounded back to work and training them in how to face a new everyday home and work life. After this he was in America on a Rockefeller scholarship, specializing in the treatment of the handicapped. Upon his return to Norway, he began his doctoral research into types of occupational disability, work that was interrupted when he was appointed Minister of Social Affairs and Health in 1955. But these studies he could apply to his work in the field of the law on sickness and disability benefits, which he introduced at this time.

As a member of the government from 1955 to 1965, Pappa was also part of the policy discussions on international questions and national security. He was a natural successor to the Defense Minister in 1961.

By 1965, he had been away from the medical profession for more than ten years. He made up his mind to bring his knowledge of medical matters up-to-date and acquire more experience before he returned to head the Rehabilitation Institute. So for the first year after the fall of his government he was an assistant doctor at the National Hospital, dividing his time between the medical and surgical departments. He kept patient logbooks, pulled night duty, and did everything else that would normally be expected of a junior doctor.

I remember how impressed people were by Pappa's ability to see his own professional limitations and his willingness to return to school in this way. But it came as no surprise to me. I knew Pappa's careful and realistic nature and his complete lack of a sense of self-aggrandizement.

Back at the Rehabilitation Institute, Pappa resumed work on his thesis in the evenings and at night. There was nothing the matter with his energy level! When he gave his speech at his doctoral dinner, I recall how he thanked Mamma for the way she let him work such long days in order to finish the work he had begun so many years before. He knew how important her support and patience had been. After all, they had had a child, Hanne, who during these demanding years was nursery school age. And Mamma had her full-time job in Parliament. She had six weeks' vacation a year, but then she looked after not only Hanne but Olav's and my children, too.

But that was not the end of it. At normal retirement age, Pappa set about repeating his efforts to bring himself up-to-date in his profession. He offered to work at the Cancer Hospital for a year without pay, freeing the doctor in charge to do laboratory research while keeping his full pay. Then he started up a private practice! I know he meant a lot to a great many patients. That was evident from all the letters I received in the weeks after his death. The most powerful impression was made by a letter I received from a woman who was suffering from cancer and who gave a moving account of what had happened during a visit Pappa made to her house. This woman was alone and had no one to help her. Pappa washed the floor, tidied the kitchen, and got food on the table and something to drink for her. He didn't just carry out his medical checks and prescribe medication. Showing compassion, taking responsibility to supply the needs of the moment—that was always his way.

I have learned much from Pappa about how to take responsibility. I have learned the meaning of honesty and integrity. I have learned how to motivate others and how to delegate responsibility. I have learned to think systematically and how to take the long view. I have learned the value of precision. I have learned by watching. There were never any shortcuts or easy answers with him! As my younger brother Lars put it in his speech at Pappa's funeral on be-

half of the four of us: "You packed so many good things in our
rucksacks."

In June 2000 while at the U.N. in New York on the fifth anniversary of the U.N. Beijing Conference on Women, I participated in a
panel with four other women leaders in the U.N. system: High
Commissioner for Human Rights Mary Robinson, Director General
of UNICEF Carol Bellamy, Executive Director for the U.N. food
program Catherine Bertini, and the leader of the World Population
Fund, Dr. Nafis Sadik. We were all asked how as women we had arrived at such prominent positions. Catherine Bertini was the one
who found our key point of convergence: All of our fathers had
supported us and allowed us to compete!

Perhaps what a girl has to have beyond the inspiration of her
mother in order to assert herself is her father's support and encouragement. I can hardly imagine my professional and political career
without it.

Jørgen | 16

September 24, 1992. The world stopped turning. A message at my hotel room in Brussels asked me to call home as soon as possible. Anxiety cut me like a knife: Was it Mamma? Had something happened? Had she been taken to the hospital? Or had there been an accident involving my children, as I had always feared?

And yet I had no notion of the terrible message that awaited me once I got through to Olav at home on the telephone that evening: Jørgen had taken his own life.

"No! It cannot be true," I cried out. My youngest son, mamma's little boy. I asked again, couldn't understand what Olav had just told me.

I can see the hotel room in my mind's eye, the desk I rang from, the door to the corridor, the bathroom, the windows, and the bed, all the details are etched in my memory. It was the worst moment in my life. The worst night. The worst morning, with that terrible plane journey home. And there was more to come. The days, nights, weeks, and months that followed were scarcely bearable. My sorrow consumed me. How could I help the others, the children, Jørgen's brothers and sisters, Olav? And Berit, Jørgen's partner, who was pregnant with his child?

To lose a child. I don't think a mother can have a worse experience. You never get over it. The loss is like a bleeding, open wound. The heart is ripped out of you. You can't believe it. It can't be true! You imagine that you can run the film backward, past that dreadful moment, and change the course of events. You do it in dreams and you do it in waking life. But you always end up facing the brutal reality; you know deep down that nothing helps, nothing can save you from the fate that has struck you and your loved ones.

I have lost Jørgen. Forever. Sleepless nights. I'm like someone turned into stone. There's a lead weight in my stomach. I can speak, but I don't understand how. Because a single thought consumes me: Jørgen, Jørgen, Jørgen. Why, why, why? Pictures from the long photo album of his life float before my eyes. The special moments, facial expressions, words, his words, my words, the words of others.

For the most part I say nothing, but I share a few thoughts with Jonas Gahr Støre of my office who sits by me on the plane back from Brussels. A parliamentary colleague was on his way home from a meeting in Strasbourg and saw us as he boarded the plane. A bright smile: "So, you've been in Brussels, Gro?" I hold on tight to the armrests and force my face and voice to be as normal as possible. "Yes, I had a meeting with Delors." That's all I manage to say. Fortunately, other passengers come on board and my colleague has to move on. He knows nothing, and I realize this. I know too that it is unthinkable to tell him here. Now it's home. Home to the others.

I am ill, wounded, lamed. I shield myself together with the rest of the family, with Jørgen's father, brothers and sister, partner. We spend the days together. It forces us to talk, even if only about practical details. The tragedy completely overtakes me, physically and mentally. All the same I have to force myself to think other thoughts and do everyday things. Each ordinary action is an enormous strain.

Knut thinks about the future, about the time after the funeral. We must be together. Let's go to Lake Mylla. I'm grateful for his concern. When we spend six days at Mylla we pass the time talking around the table or walking by the lake. The autumn days are bright, and the memories come flooding in. We find reminders of Jørgen everywhere, in the rooms, on the ski trails. We talk about him. We talk about ourselves. We ask each other questions. We do not understand. Will the loss ever be bearable?

Powerlessness

Just one and a half weeks earlier we had all been at Mylla. Jørgen had seemed so quiet, his spirit and self-confidence so low that last weekend, I remember I was uneasy and tried to get some idea of how he was feeling. How were things going with the apartment? Had he gotten rid of the new lodger who had moved in during the summer when his girlfriend, Berit, moved out?

Jørgen said that his roommate wasn't easy to deal with. He took over the kitchen and the living room, made a mess, drank all the time. But, said Jørgen, how could he get him out? He was strong, aggressive, and difficult to talk to. Jørgen felt trapped in the situation. He would have to wait until the lodger's three months' notice was up, that is, in November. In the meantime he was mostly living at Berit's, in her little apartment, so it was no problem. The two of them were together again after a difficult time in the early summer, and he was looking forward to becoming a father in December.

That weekend at Mylla we were going to cut a drainage channel, and Ivar was in charge of the little digger hired for the occasion. He and his brother joked and laughed, but I saw in Jørgen's eyes that he was really somewhere else. His self-confidence was dismally low. We recognized this—all of us—when he turned down the chance to drive the digger: "Ivar, you do it." Jørgen never hesitated about something like that when he wasn't depressed. When I tried to broach the subject I got the typical reaction, "No, Mamma, everything's all right."

Berit had taken over the role of the most important person in Jørgen's daily life that year. In the late winter of 1992 the psychiatrist had told Olav that now was the time for him to take a backseat and let Jørgen and Berit take over. I remember Olav was uneasy. I was too. But what could we do?

This was one of the hundreds of times throughout these difficult years when we did not know how best to face the challenge of helping our young son with his manic depression. We could see that there were ups and downs in his relationship with Berit, just as there were in his illness, and we both had our doubts. Weren't we after all the best and most stable support for Jørgen's unstable mind?

Yet a sort of compromise was inevitable. We kept in regular touch, called him often. He came with us to the holiday home. Berit and Jørgen came together to family gatherings. But we found ourselves excluded from regular involvement in his treatment.

He was only twenty-five. From the age of seventeen and a half we had known that Jørgen had special mental problems, and that only his parents and the rest of the family would take the responsibility for supporting him and helping him, for trying to get him the best professional treatment available. It was painful to discover that Norwegian society—the running of which was a central concern of mine—had no real treatment or support system to offer young people faced with such severe psychological problems as a psychosis in the formative years of their lives.

Manic-depressives and others could be admitted to a hospital in acute phases of their illness, then released with no structured form of therapy, no after-care, no visits by a health-care professional. They were left to cope completely on their own. The family was kept at arm's length, so that not even they, the young person's nearest and dearest, could offer the best kind of support. No one ever told us about the many faces of the illness, about where we should go to find out about the high risk of suicide in the depressive phases of a manic-depressive illness. These gaps in our health-care system meant that the family wasn't as much help to a sick child as they might have been.

A few weeks after Jørgen's death I found out that Berit had heard Jørgen say several times that he was considering taking his own life, but that he had always added, "Of course, I won't." She hadn't said anything to us about it but had contacted the clinic and the psychiatrist they were seeing. She had said she was worried because Jørgen was talking about suicide so much. They had even been at the clinic, both of them, the day before the dramatic end.

At that meeting they spoke of other things, about the child they were expecting and what that would mean for their everyday lives. They did not discuss the thoughts Jørgen was struggling with and that he had shared with Berit. Today I know this was a mistake. If a manic-depressive is thinking about suicide, then the danger of suicide is there. In this critical phase, it must be discussed and a decision made as to whether some form of protection should be provided. Depression should always be treated, just as other forms of life-threatening illness are treated. That did not happen. A great many deaths should have been prevented, not only Jørgen's.

I found out later about an earlier time when Jørgen had been sent to the emergency room after attempting suicide. No one in his immediate family had been notified. He was just nineteen or twenty at the time and living with student friends.

Our impression was that the health-care personnel had felt no real responsibility for ensuring that Jørgen was given follow-up treatment after such a dramatic episode. I believe that this was wrong. One cannot hide behind the vow of silence and leave sick people to their own devices. Nor is it sufficient here to point to paragraphs in law or principles. Through talking to those involved, one will usually find it possible to establish contact and involve the immediate family.

It is tragic to reflect on how many young people might have been helped at difficult times of their lives. Not all psychiatric illnesses can be dealt with by talk alone. We humans are biological creatures too, with brains that are affected by a number of biological processes. We can find out more about these influences.

After Jørgen's death I got a letter from the psychiatrist who saw him after he showed his first psychotic symptoms just before Christmas 1984. He wrote us that he felt he had not managed to follow up as he should have done because he went away on a study trip and on his return did not renew his contact with Jørgen. He wrote something else that I think is true: For young people who experience a crisis like this, how they are treated by the first person they consult about their illness is of the greatest importance.

I asked Jørgen during the spring of 1985 about the conversations he had had with this psychiatrist. He told me they were okay. But he was not very communicative, and I got the impression that parents were not supposed to get involved in the treatment. For that reason I didn't dare to call. It did not help in such situations to be Gro Harlem Brundtland, former Prime Minister and a physician.

Jørgen had no more contact with this psychiatrist after the spring of 1985. He had a few difficult weeks in the middle of the summer but was in good shape by the autumn. He took his preliminary exams at his university and had a part-time job in the cleaning business.

In the Guardhouse

At eighteen years old Jørgen applied to do his military service. He wanted to get it out of the way before he began his law studies, like his oldest brother. At the draft board examination I don't think he mentioned the problems he had had. Both he and Olav thought it quite natural that he should do his military service as the two other boys had done. And I too hoped that he had recovered by now. None of us fully understood that he was struggling with a chronic illness with good and bad periods.

His first psychiatrist told me after Jørgen's death that he understood early on that Jørgen would continue to suffer considerably with his psychological problems and that he should have warned him not to expose himself to the special pressures involved in regular military service. Again we see it very clearly in hindsight. He, the expert, knew what was right if one were to avoid aggravating the illness. Jørgen didn't know. We didn't know. So how could we do the right thing? It was a tragedy for Jørgen.

At difficult times throughout that year, special aspects of the illness manifested themselves. Jørgen's military superiors knew nothing of the reality of his situation, so on one occasion he was put in the guardhouse in solitary confinement—and he felt he had been unfairly treated. He became oversensitive to sound, slept poorly, lay awake the whole night listening to the card playing and the conversations of those on watch outside his cell. Not a good situation, given his serious illness.

We didn't know about it until we got a phone call from a major at the camp in northern Norway at the end of December 1986. Jørgen was due for home leave during Christmas or New Year's, after one year's service, but he had been sent to the guardhouse and he wasn't to be allowed home for either Christmas or New Year's like the others. Now the major told us he had gone AWOL on his last night on watch after leaving the guardhouse. Unfortunately, Jørgen did not know that his superior had been planning to let him go home before New Year's Eve. The major told us that Jørgen had always been a good soldier. He had experienced a healthy Jørgen, not the Jørgen whose behavior under certain circumstances had so irritated the junior officers.

The military police found Jørgen in the city of Tromsø on his way to the airport. Immediately after the New Year a Swedish paper carried the headline: "Prime Minister's Son Goes AWOL." Fortunately, the Norwegian papers were discreet. But one of the tabloids carried large pictures of Jørgen on the front page. He felt deeply anxious and was afraid of being ridiculed when he turned up to begin studying in the law library the following week. Kaja saw him there one day. He was quietly crying and tried to hide it by turning his head away.

At Knut's suggestion, Jørgen had moved in with Knut and his wife. The idea was for him to have company in his studies—for example, they could walk to the university together in the morning. But before long Jørgen was staying in bed in the mornings. He didn't get up, didn't go out, and was difficult to communicate with. We didn't use the word then, but today we know what it was: depression. One afternoon a few weeks later Knut found Jørgen sitting on the top step outside the apartment in Jacob Aalls Street, sobbing, despairing, helpless. He had gone out and forgotten his key. He was freezing and had been sitting there for hours.

Now it was obvious. He had to have help. Olav rang the psychiatrist who had treated Jørgen originally. He referred us to the health service in Oslo, and in the end Knut and Jørgen wound up seeing the psychiatrists at Vindern Psychiatric Clinic. Not even here did I feel that the main priority was to make a clear diagnosis of the most likely cause of Jørgen's illness. We were all present at a family consultation, and there we tried to talk about the changes we had noticed and what we had experienced over the last couple of years.

This is what I remember best: The psychiatrist turned to Jørgen and said, "Can't you pull yourself together?" No doubt he had his professional reasons and was trying to find out if this was just some passing phase that Jørgen could work his way through. It confirmed a false impression in the rest of the family that I think damaged Jørgen in the years to come. We could be irritated, exasperated, and a little too frequently disposed to wonder "Why can't he just pull himself together?" Imagine how differently things might have turned out if we had had a proper diagnosis back then. A suitable course of treatment could have been arranged. We might all have learned about the illness and been in a better position to help Jørgen. We could have supported one another more through the sorrows and despair that were to come.

I know that it is vitally important to get patients motivated to want treatment. This is one reason that the first psychiatrist could have done a very different job for Jørgen had he, the first in whom Jørgen trusted, given my son signals and advice he most needed. Instead, Jørgen's later experiences with psychiatry were negative. His illness developed without treatment, without the medication that could have stabilized him. Then his psychosis became acute. That summer he became manic and had to be forcibly committed to the hospital. In this phase, a person has no insight into his or her illness, so there is no other choice. But the result is an extremely negative experience with hospitals and with the whole world of psychiatry.

Mother and Doctor

The family is faced with a terrible dilemma in such a situation. We didn't all have the same experiences with Jørgen and therefore didn't always experience his illness in the same fashion. As the years went by and there were new incidents and new phases in his troubles, our discussions intensified. I read books and articles, tried to get up-to-date on the latest methods and theories of treatment. We spoke of how we observed Jørgen in different situations and of how we could best help him. My main aim was to get him to see that treatment was what he needed. I wanted all of us who were close to him to give that same message: You must take the medication to stabilize your wild mood swings.

Our beliefs and doubts were different. Some felt that Jørgen could be just the way he always used to be—happy, bright, quick-witted, knowledgeable, and an intellectually stimulating companion. Then it was easy to relax and think, everything's fine now, he's better now. He's gotten over the worst. But that was wishful thinking. Things could change quickly, sometimes in the course of a few days, even a few hours.

As long as I was there and could react I was sensitive to his moods. Olav learned to identify certain signals too. We did not always react at the same time, though, and we did not always have the same interpretation.

The most dramatic and distressing situations were those in which we didn't recognize our own son. He became confused, spoke incoherently, so that it was impossible to know what he was trying to say. He could be aggressive, or be a danger to himself, like the time he jumped up on the roof at home. He simply didn't sense the danger. It was at times like this that we had to have him hospitalized. What was so sad for us was that we did not learn soon enough how common it is for such manic highs to be followed by deep troughs of depression. Jørgen would think about how ill he had been, he wondered about the strange things he must have said and done, and to whom. It created insecurity, a crippling lack of self-confidence, along with guilt. When the depression sank over him, he became unusually kind, helpful, quiet. He never caused any bother, never protested about anything, was never aggressive. Those phases posed the greatest difficulties for him. They were a matter of life and death. But we didn't know that, didn't realize the dangers—and so we never pushed for him to be admitted to the hospital when he really needed it.

By the spring of 1992 Berit and Jørgen had arranged their wedding. A few weeks before the date Jørgen became very ill, went back on everything he'd said, wanted to drop the whole thing—and within a few days he was in an acute psychotic phase again.

The next time he was hospitalized I had a meeting with the psychiatrist who had had the most contact with Jørgen. The nurse who usually took part in the consultations was present too. I had a copy of *Time* magazine with me, containing an article called "Pills for the Mind." I showed the psychiatrist the article, which I had studied closely. It was not the first time I had asked the question: Why couldn't Jørgen be given medication with fewer side effects and which was demonstrably more effective than what he had been given over the years of his hospital stays? Surely we could try some of the new medicines being used in the United States and in other parts of Europe? Prozac was one. The names of others were given. In the last couple of years there had been several reports of good results and of patients whose lives had been changed, who were again able to work and study. But there was not much response. No discussion. No alternative suggestion. "I'll think about it," said the doctor. But there was resistance: "These medications are not available in Norway."

I felt powerless. Couldn't we apply for these medications to be introduced in our own country? I was willing to pay what it cost myself. But I sensed the opposition and felt that the doctor and nurse were not listening. And again I had the feeling that had struck me so often throughout these years: Mothers were a problem, and even worse were mothers who were also doctors. I found it natural to ask for an opinion and for its basis. On top of that, I was Prime Minister. That certainly did not make matters easier, for me or for others. But as regards Jørgen and his long years of suffering, I was just a mother. I remember thinking, had I been an ordinary doctor and not a top politician as well, I would have found it easier to fight. Gone to another hospital, another specialist, asked for more advice. Why couldn't our son have Prozac? Or Carbamazid? The state was the authority and the power. It was not at all easy to widen our options.

I felt my hands were tied. I hoped that the doctor would do what he said and think about it. And then there was that inner voice that kept saying, "Maybe he's right, maybe it's you who are too critical, who have too many ideas that lead nowhere. After all, he's the psychiatrist, not you." Today I regret that I didn't get more involved. I should have read more, not less. Spoken to more people, not fewer. I think it's true of all suffering and all disabilities: No one is better placed to achieve results than the one afflicted and his or her loved ones.

"Why didn't I call?"

In the days before Jørgen's death, from Sunday to Tuesday, I was in New York at the U.N. general assembly. On Wednesday I returned to Oslo. Thursday I was off to Brussels, where I received the dreadful news. I had thought a lot about Jørgen in New York. I now wanted to see the psychiatrist at the National Hospital about whom I had heard so much and whom I had telephoned just before the holiday. He was on holiday himself at the time, and I did not try again. I wanted to talk about other possible treatments with him, other medications that might persuade Jørgen to have another go. I rang home to ask Olav how Jørgen was, recalling our son's worn expression and aura of helplessness from the weekend before. There were no distinct danger signals at that point, though. Olav had spoken to Jørgen by phone and had even been shopping with him.

That Tuesday, at Newark airport outside New York, I went as usual to the little bookshop where I selected new books to take home. I always looked on the shelves for social studies and medicine, plus general politics and recent fiction. There I saw *A Brilliant Madness: Living with Manic-Depressive Illness*, a fascinating new title. I bought the book and read it almost in one sitting that night, consumed by it, a fantastic book.

This excerpt from the opening page characterizes the book:

Anna, for some time now I have suspected that you might be
suffering from a condition that I would like to discuss with
you. I have not diagnosed it before because it is a difficult diagnosis to make. The diagnosis involves a painful stigma, and
I don't want to stick this label on you and find then that I am
wrong. Don't be afraid, but I think you are manic-depressive. . . .
Even today it feels strange when I tell you how I reacted. I had
heard the words only three or four times before in my life, in
quite other circumstances and obviously without any reference
to me. But the words seemed natural. When my psychiatrist
said them I remember nodding, as though I had known it all
along. They were the best two words I had ever heard. They
described how it felt to be me.

I had read the textbook technical literature on the most common
psychiatric illnesses, including manic depression, but they are often
a few years out of date, and there is a limit to the amount of space
devoted to detail and nuance. This book opened up a new world
for me. It went straight into the patient's own daily life, and the
lives of those around him. Patty Duke, the writer, is the Anna addressed in the preceding quote. She talks openly about her life and
her illness.

When I finished I held the phone in my hand, eager to talk to
Jørgen and tell him as soon as possible about the revelation this
book was. But as it happened Olav came home just then, and
instead I began telling him about the book, and the phone call was
never made.

That was the last time I could have reached him. This is one of
my most painful recurring thoughts, one that has haunted me in
the weeks and months and years since then. Why didn't I obey my
intuition? I later learned how uneasy and afraid Jørgen had been
that night, more so than Berit was used to. A nurse, she had to go to
work at nine o'clock; she told us that Jørgen had almost physically
tried to hold her back as she was leaving: "I wish you didn't have to
work tonight."

Had I called, we might have picked him up and eaten supper together. And naturally he would have stayed the night and we could

have had the morning together. Maybe our conversation could have given him a faint ray of hope; maybe we would have realized just how bad he was feeling. And I was then very clear about the dangers of suicide that are discussed in Duke's book. I was uneasy and anxious, but above all I felt newly determined. This time I would not give up!

The following day, at some point in the afternoon, it was all too late.

I don't know much about what Jørgen did that day. He thought he had the day shift at the nursing home in Madserud Allé, where he had been working occasional shifts that autumn. When he turned up that morning he was sent home. They didn't need him that day. I say it that way because we all knew how Jørgen reacted in such situations when he was seriously depressed. He thought it meant that he was worthless, that no one had any use for him, that he was getting in people's way.

He was alone; Berit was not back from her night shift yet. He had dropped the key to Berit's flat in the mailbox and couldn't get it out again. We think he went down to his own apartment in the center of town and found the lodger there, the mess, the chaos, all the troubles and problems he just couldn't see his way out of. Maybe the two of them argued or had some disagreement? We don't know. It wasn't easy to reconstruct times and details with the lodger, the man who found him that afternoon and called Olav.

Jørgen might also have reread a letter he had received a couple of weeks earlier from the income tax office requesting an extra payment of 55,000 Kroner—the amount he had to live on for the year. Once again, a cruel coincidence. He had said he didn't want help with his income tax form and filled it out alone. He had done so incorrectly. And so when the demand to remit payment came, because of his depression, he viewed it as a hopeless catastrophe about which he could do nothing. When he had been out with Olav on the previous Tuesday he had mentioned the letter, and Olav just dismissed it as an obvious mistake. He told Jørgen to contact the income tax people and get it corrected, but the point is that for him, at that particular moment, the problem appeared to be an impenetrably high wall. And so the letter lay there unresolved, troubling his mind, depriving him in his fragile state of the small amount of courage he had left to go on living.

He was going to be a father but he had failed his university exams. He had years of his life left, and—or so he believed—he owed the tax people a fortune. Deep down he felt worthless. They didn't even need him at the nursing home, and he couldn't solve the problem with his lodger. This last must have been an important factor. It was to the lodger that he wrote the only message he left behind: "You'll find me in the attic."

Reflections Afterward

Now we're all left to reflect and regret. Particularly me. Once again I had quelled my maternal instincts. When I found out about the unwanted person in Jørgen's apartment, my first thought was: We must help Jørgen. Give him the help he needs to solve this problem. But he and others in the family had said that this was something he could handle himself and not to worry. Yet I had every reason to worry, and should have worried even more. I should have done what I thought needed doing and not listened to him or anyone else.

That is still how I think today. We could have helped him survive. We could and should have taken care of problems for him so that he could concentrate on dealing with his own situation when he was feeling so fragile. I wish I had known about the extra worry of the tax demand because money problems can swell out of all proportion to someone who suffers from manic depression.

Nothing can match the pain felt by the person who actually suffers from the illness. I think what must be worst of all is the profound anxiety and doubt about who I am, what I want, and what I will think or be able to do tomorrow. Tomorrow is a terrible burden to bear. Because these thoughts and feelings overwhelm the sufferer, and seem to continue without cease, it is vital to aid the human organism in combating the mood swings and stabilizing the biochemical reactions that contribute to these dreadful and life-threatening disabilities.

"You mustn't give up!"

In the days immediately after Jørgen's death I kept in touch with my
office and with State Secretaries Svein Roald Hansen and Øystein
Singsaas. They took care of the most pressing business. Gunnar
Berge rang the day I got back from Brussels. I felt that his message
was brutal: "Gro, you mustn't think of giving up! The worst thing
you can do is give up your work; it's the central thing in your life."
It didn't quite get through to me. All I could think about was Jørgen. Everything else seemed far away and unreal. And yet the
words must have gotten through at some level of my consciousness,
because the following week I forced myself to begin to think about
the future again, and those words returned to me. Gunnar was
probably right, but on the Friday he said it, it was too early for me
to think about anything except what had just happened.

On the Monday after the first week I went to the office. I had to
do my job. I had to think about something other than myself, my
family, and the terrible blow we had all suffered. There were flowers
everywhere, not just at home and in the holiday home but also in
the office. All the familiar and dear faces of my colleagues reflected
something of how they were feeling. My eyes filled with tears and
my voice grew thick.

We would pick up the usual routines. I would lead the meetings
I normally led. It was possible to put grief aside for a while. Others
helped me to do it. There were papers to be read, discussions to be
completed, conclusions to be drawn. The road forward from lonely
and debilitating grief led from the inner circle of the immediate
family to the next, wider circle, my closest colleagues.

There was the cabinet meeting that Monday. Difficult times too
for those who wanted so much to help. I chose to talk briefly about
what had happened at the cabinet lunch prior to the meeting itself.
It felt easier to share some of my grief with the others. Easier for me
and easier for them. Dr. Werner Christie, the Health Minister, and I
talked a bit about psychiatric illness and the manic-depressive syn-
drome. He too had lost a relative to the same illness.

In the cabinet room I took my place at the head of the table.
Behind me were the great windows looking out over the city. I

thought of the last time I sat there, Thursday, nine days ago. When had it happened? Jørgen's apartment was just half a mile away as the crow flies. On the hill west of the great wall that surrounds the National Hospital. I had sat here that Thursday from twelve-thirty to two-thirty, knowing nothing. The thought of those hours never left me, even as I heard what my government colleagues were saying. I saw the serious faces. I asked some questions. The Minister of Finance was to give the budget speech to Parliament the next day. He mentioned the salient points. Gro, you have to be there, I told myself. The Prime Minister is always present at the budget speech.

I realized that the following day I'd have to meet yet another, even bigger circle of people. On this busy day in "the House" every member was usually in attendance for the budget speech. I arrived shortly before the speech was due to begin at ten o'clock. I nodded weakly to some of those I passed on my way up the stairs and into the chamber. Some stopped and took my hand. I saw the shock and sympathy in their faces. It was very difficult for me. And for others, too. What was the best thing to do under such circumstances? Those I'd known longest came closest. A few words, a hand on the shoulder. I didn't have much to contribute that first day. I've seen the pictures of myself. The black jacket and the dark ribbons. The bleak eyes. A face without life, expressionless.

"Dear Gro"

Letters and flowers poured into the house and the office. I who had previously thought that neither flowers nor words could be of any help in so terrible a situation understood now that such things have a role to play for the bereaved. The warmth expressed arouses feelings inside and makes the tears flow, helping to crack open the armor that you put on. Even the practical details of unwrapping the flowers and reading the cards—all this disrupts the obsessive inward scrutiny that dominates you so completely and jostles the heavy weight of sorrow that seems to have settled forever.

In the three months before the New Year we must have received about a thousand letters from friends, acquaintances, and strangers.

I read them all; I answered them all. I sat late and alone at the office and read the letters from people all over the country, read them again, wept, thought, wept. I wrote very personal replies to many, sharing with them my innermost thoughts. I wanted to show how much I appreciated their willingness to share their feelings and thoughts with me.

Many of them described personal tragedies. Mothers and fathers who had lost a son or a daughter told me what they had been through. Their letters were important. They were my means of contact with a great many others who had known suffering and grief and sorrow. It helps to keep one's own fate in perspective. You can share your sorrow with others, give comfort even when you are suffering grief and loss yourself.

I got letters from many bereaved mothers. I got letters from psychiatric patients. One of them had noticed that we had included a reference to the autumn's TV fund-raising in aid of mental health in our announcement of the death. Money for research, not flowers, was what we had in mind. "It is perhaps inappropriate for me as a private person unknown to you to write this. Yet I feel so strongly for you in your grief. Don't know exactly what happened, but it made a strong impression on me and made me think of those who are left behind, the parents, brothers and sisters, close relatives. As I say, I don't know what happened, but I felt grateful that you chose to support the fund-raising. (Have been hospitalized myself many times after suicide attempts and thirteen years of psychological problems. It is terrible to see how inadequate the health authorities are.) Even though I never met Jørgen I feel suddenly as though in a way I do know him. I respect his decision—but perhaps it wasn't a decision?" The young woman was twenty-eight years old.

To a mother who had written to me about the suicide of her twenty-two-year-old son I wrote this little letter: "It is dreadfully sad when people experience tragedies such as you and I and our two sons experienced. I don't think either of them really wanted to do it. They were overcome by acute feelings of hopelessness and a lack of self-confidence. We must work to improve the health services and psychiatry to try to prevent such suffering." It had been clear from her letter that in her despair she simply could not understand what had happened. Her son had a regular job on the oil rigs, had a girlfriend, and was looking forward to some shore leave. The tragedy is that depressions strike the individual and the family neither knows nor understands what happens.

Several letters were dated October 8 in the evening and October 9, after I had made my first return to public life. One was from an acquaintance from my student days: "I have thought a lot about writing, but not done so, because there really is nothing anyone can say or do to help. But then I received a letter from a friend who had just lost her husband, and I have a cousin and some friends who have experienced what you have been through. The children involved were about the same age, too. So I plucked up my courage this evening after I heard you on the evening news, because I realized how much I—and four million others—have missed that voice these last two silent weeks. It gives us all hope and faith that you will survive what must be the cruelest blow imaginable."

A woman who had met Jørgen when he was a little boy, just four years old, wrote: "It's a long time ago now since we were last at Dalseter Hotel, but little Jørgen became my friend there and helped me through a troubled time. Nowadays I would probably be more 'sensible' and not have spontaneously ignored the family's desire to 'teach him a lesson'; back then I turned his sorrow over the loss of his little penknife to joy by giving him a new one. For me he is not just a name but someone I have thought of now and then. It pains me to see how short his life was." Not until I read this letter did I realize that the young woman who had been so taken by Jørgen at the age of four had suffered from depression herself and that little Jørgen had been a comfort to her at a difficult time. She gave him a little souvenir pocketknife with the name of the hotel on it. For Jørgen it was a revelation that you could get another knife given to you as a present when you have just lost one. Now, through this letter, we had powerful memories of happy days at Dalseter.

The Youngest

When I returned from the clinic with Jørgen, a neighbor friend leaned over the little cot and said, "Gro, he's the most beautiful of all your children."

Now that isn't exactly what one is most preoccupied with or has on one's mind in the first few days after a new baby comes into the world. Is he healthy? Does he seem strong and fit? Does he nurse well? Is he putting on weight? All of that seemed satisfactory. No one could have guessed what would happen twenty-five years later.

He was the baby of the family, the jewel. And it wasn't just mother and father who were so enchanted by the little imp with the lovely smile and the twinkle in his eye—his brothers and sisters were too, and everyone else who met him. He could be full of ideas and determination, fearless, a leader among the other children. But we saw the sensitive side of him, too, sometimes a little withdrawn, two fingers in his mouth and a tear lurking in his eye. I remember particularly something that happened at home. Jørgen was about three or four. I was reading when suddenly I realized he was banging nails into the baseboard at the top of the stairs up to the living room. I called out "Jørgen!" very firmly. He burst into tears, and I felt I had done something wrong, sensed how shocking my reaction must have seemed to him. It was on occasions like this, rare as they were, that I noticed how extremely sensitive he was.

The other family members were probably right when they noticed how often I let Jørgen get away with things and that I demanded less of him than I had of the other children. I believe this is the pattern in most families, that one's rigor and discipline in childraising tends to be more pronounced with the oldest, and that the ones who come later fit into a more relaxed pattern. And more child-rearing happens indirectly, as brothers and sisters "raise" each other.

Jørgen learned quickly, was an early reader, and joined in with what the others were doing from a young age. In certain situations he could be a bit wild, especially when fighting with his older brother Ivar. When they were both very small they stuck together like two grains of rice and were known jointly as "the boys." I'll never forget the experiences of the autumn when Ivar was four and a half and I had just placed him in a proper nursery school, at Mrs. Hjorth's in Bygdøy. Kaja had been there before him and gone on to primary school, and now it was Ivar's turn to move from the nannies in the park and join the bigger children. Jørgen was three and much too young to begin nursery school, where the rule was that children had to be almost five. He had been spending four hours a day in the park with Ivar since he was fourteen months old and had begun to walk. They were always taken to the park together in the stroller. Everything went fine, Jørgen would manage a couple of hours sleep, and he enjoyed being with the other children.

I often heard from the other mothers in the neighborhood what an impression Ivar had made on them. They told me how good he was with his little brother, how he put his mittens on for him, gave him his milk, and made sure he ate his food. I remember one mother saying, "I've never seen anything so touching."

So perhaps what happened late in the autumn of 1970 wasn't so strange, when I came home from work at the Municipal Hospital on Jørgen's first day in the park without Ivar. Our babysitter said that she'd had to bring Jørgen home early because the nannies had told her that he was crying and crying for hour after hour. Jørgen was grieving the loss of Ivar, his big brother. The other children were no substitute, at least not in the beginning. The next day I called home and was told that the same thing had happened again. I said that the babysitter should stay there with him for part of the time and make it a short day, until he got used to the new situation.

Jørgen was again deeply unhappy. I got up my courage and called Ivar's new nursery school. I told them what had happened and asked if it might be possible to take Ivar out again for a while, because it would be good for his little brother—or was there any chance at all that Jørgen might be allowed to start there, too? I presumed that there could be no question of this, but I shared my disquiet with Mrs. Hjorth and she said, "Let's give it a try."

And so Jørgen became their youngest child, the mascot at Mrs. Hjorth's nursery school. He was happy and managed well with the older children. The school psychologists recommended that he begin school a year early, the year after Ivar.

First Symptoms

Over the years we heard now and then that Jørgen was a bit noisy and restless in class, but he had no problems with schoolwork. I remembered someone's remark that I had spent more time under my desk than at it, and that I had "quicksilver in my veins." Similar comments had been made about Knut, our oldest.

It was when Jørgen was fourteen that I wondered for the first time what was the matter with him. He seemed to doze off over his books. None of the children had bothered much about their homework, so in one way it was nothing new. And that schoolwork was boring, that it would be more fun for him to be out, was understandable. But I remember I spent time with him, sat beside him, to listen. "I don't seem able to concentrate," he said. That was odd. None of the others had ever said that. "I can't be bothered. I'll do it tomorrow or later tonight," those were the excuses they used and that I had heard dozens of times.

"What do you mean?" I asked Jørgen. "Can you be more precise, tell me what it feels like?" He said he couldn't seem to see the letters, that they floated into each other so that he didn't grasp what he was reading. My first thought was that it was his eyes. We said we would take him to an optician to see if he needed glasses. But there was more to it.

One day Jørgen was looking out the window. He pointed at the trees and said, "It looks so funny. It looks as though the leaves are so different." I didn't understand. Then he went silent. His eyes were examined and there was nothing wrong with them.

By the time he turned sixteen, things seemed to have improved. He didn't complain about reading and concentration anymore. And that autumn Jørgen and I spoke a great deal. I was uneasy about him and asked about his schoolwork. He said that now and then he experienced those problems we had discussed before, that he couldn't always follow the lesson, that it seemed to him that school wasn't as easy now as it used to be. I remember I said, "Jørgen, I don't know how best to help you." There was nothing the matter with his eyes, so perhaps some other problem was involved, and maybe he ought to see a psychologist? He went to see a female psychologist at the Oslo Clinic and they spent an hour together. He said it had been okay, but otherwise had few words. She had told him that if he felt he needed to or wanted to, he could come and see her again. Fifteen months later I rang the psychologist. Dramatic events had transpired, and now I needed to try to find out what we were up against.

She told me she had gained the impression that here was a mature, knowledgeable boy who had told her he was struggling with a few problems, and she had given him a bit of advice and left the option open for their conversation to continue. She did not seem to have perceived signs that he might be more seriously disturbed.

Jørgen began having strange thoughts and displaying signs that something was seriously wrong. One day just before Christmas, Kaja came running up to Parliament from the flower shop, where all the children had holiday jobs, and said Jørgen was behaving oddly. He had come back to the shop after running an errand to the post office and had forgotten what he was supposed to do there. He'd also pointed to some security men who had come into the shop with the Crown Princess and who were now outside the shop, and said that they were after him. This was a bolt from the blue. Jørgen had never said strange things like this before, and Kaja and the other children were frightened. I was too.

It seemed completely unreal, and I thought of something that had happened a couple of evenings before, when Jørgen came home from a party at ten o'clock on Saturday night. I was surprised to see him three hours before his curfew. He said, "I didn't feel good. I was bored and wanted to get home."

We sat down together by the fireplace. He told me that he was anxious about something that had happened at school. It was his fault, all the problems the headmaster and the teachers at the Cathedral School were complaining about. The pupils had been assembled in the gymnasium and the headmaster described a number of bad things that had happened over the last months. He had appealed to the students to improve their discipline and their behavior. "But the whole thing is my fault," said Jørgen.

"How come?" I asked. "What have you done wrong? Did the headmaster say so?"

"No, but I just know," Jørgen said. I realized I would have to find out more about this. He was unhappy and afraid. And I had no idea what it was all about.

On the day Kaja came running to me I had already called his teacher. No, he couldn't understand it at all. Jørgen hadn't done anything wrong. The headmaster had been speaking to the whole school. Jørgen was having delusional thoughts; his perceptions were unreal. It was frightening. Why was this? What should we do? How should we deal with the problem? I spoke again to his first psychologist. And I spoke to the psychiatrist to whom I had referred several pupils in the days when I was a school doctor. I was given two pieces of advice: Jørgen should take Cisordinol to counter the psychotic tendencies. And we should seek therapy.

It was difficult to get Jørgen to accept that he should take the medicine, but I managed. It emerged that he had for some time now been having trouble sleeping, and the medicine seemed to help there. But he noticed other side effects. He said the pills made him feel sluggish and peculiar, and that he wanted to stop taking them as soon as possible.

Easter Holiday with Mamma and Pappa

If I had known then what I know now, I would never have left Jørgen to his own devices for the next two or three years. He turned eighteen that summer, took his exams, and managed his preliminaries for the autumn. But we saw how volatile his personality was, how he could sometimes be withdrawn and silent and at other times be lighthearted and sure that everything was going all right. The mood swings had begun. The anxiety, the uncertainty, the depressions; and at other times, the overconfidence and excess energy. It is important to deal as early as possible with the serious sort of symptoms he was having. The sooner one works out a proper course of treatment, the better the chance of a successful outcome, and the more likely the person can see for himself or herself the necessity of treatment.

In the Easter leave of the year in which Jørgen did his national service, we had arranged that he would go on a walking trip in the mountains with his grandparents. But when he arrived he was unfocused and didn't have his proper ski equipment and clothing, and in the car on the way up to the mountains it seemed to Mamma and Pappa that his conversation was both very rapid and incoherent. We didn't find this out until later that week, when my parents drove up to the mountain house we had rented that Easter. Jørgen had disappeared, lightly dressed and wearing ordinary shoes in the middle of cold winter. They had realized that something was wrong with him, but Pappa had hoped that a walk in the mountains would do him some good. They returned to Oslo to see if Jørgen had come home. When they didn't find him there, and since we had no telephone in the mountains, they got back in the car and came up to us. What was Jørgen up to? What could have happened? We didn't know what to do. We had no option: Olav and I would have to go back to Oslo. We had to find him. Late that night we arrived back in Bygdøy. No Jørgen. We rang neighbors and friends, but with no luck. We were desperate. What should we do? He had run off from his grandfather in very odd circumstances, but, after all, he was almost nineteen years old.

Between nine and ten the next morning, he came in the door. That we were home was of course a great surprise. Regarding his own plans he would not tell us. He couldn't give any explanation for leaving his grandfather like that. And it was clear that he did not welcome our involvement. We asked him to come back up to the mountains with us. But he wanted to go to Geneva and spend Easter with his boyhood friend, Olav. He was quite determined, could not be dissuaded. Carrying a single piece of hand luggage he left the house and drove off in a taxi. I had tried to stop him. "Olav, we can't just let him go off like that," I said, and ran out to stop the taxi.

The driver looked at us in surprise. "Shall I drive to Fornebu or not?" Jørgen looked furious. Olav was standing beside me when the taxi drove off.

"We have to follow him, Olav," I said. I knew that things were not at all as they should be. Jørgen was not himself. Did he actually know what he was doing? We felt utterly helpless.

Toward the end of Easter we finally managed to get hold of Jørgen at his friend Olav's house in Geneva. "Yes, I'll be home tomorrow. Then we can have a talk, Mamma." It was a completely different Jørgen who came through the door that evening. He was confused and full of regret. He couldn't understand how he had done what he had done. Then he told us what he had done: he had borrowed 20,000 Kroner (about $2,000) from a bank and used between 8,000 and 9,000 Kroner during those five days in Geneva. Now he was in despair and couldn't comprehend how he could have done that. He was going to get a job for the rest of the holiday before returning to northern Norway to complete his military service. He seemed clear, coherent, very determined. He wanted to earn back some of the money. The 12,000 Kroner that were left he gave to me to look after so that he could pay back the loan.

For the next five days Jørgen was thoughtful, considerate, cooperative, and regretful. We talked a lot about what had happened, and he seemed to recognize how odd the whole episode had been. In recollection, Jørgen seemed absolutely helpless. He was going to help Olav screw a plate onto our shed one afternoon but couldn't manage it. Helplessness was a feature of the depression that had now set in. We observed these great changes, but we didn't put a name to them. Quite simply, we didn't understand.

I rang Marit, a colleague of mine from student days and now a psychiatrist in Bergen. I told her what was going on, what had happened at Easter, and asked for her advice. Ought we to let Jørgen go back to his military service all the way back up to the north of the country after what had happened? I was deeply uneasy. Marit knew the name of the army psychiatrist up in Troms County. She suggested I get in touch with him. He assured me that an episode like that might easily be just a passing phase and that it was probably in the boy's best interests to complete his national service. All the same, he would make a point of meeting Jørgen and keeping an eye on him over the next few weeks.

Jørgen went north. He was keen to do his duty, carry out his responsibilities. He wanted to complete his national service.

Jørgen's Letters

The letters I received from Jørgen that year tell their own story. The contents reflect the different phases of the illness he was going through. So does the handwriting.

At the end of April this letter arrived: "Dear Mamma, earlier this week, and last week too, I have tried to answer your letter. My attempts have been hopeless, until now. I promised you I would write on Sunday, but I had to postpone it because I couldn't find your letter. After an intensive search I sat down to write an answer based on what I remembered of your letter, which I last read on Thursday or Friday. It was a letter with no real basis in what you said and full of self-contradictions, and I realized there would be little point in sending it. Now I'll take another shot at it after finding your letter (what luck!). It is a long and important letter and demands a long answer."

When I came across this letter a few weeks after Jørgen's death, I remembered every word. I remember I read that introduction as a confirmation of the lack of self-assurance and the guilt that Jørgen was feeling after that dramatic Easter. Now he was feeling serious and responsible. "It isn't your fault that I have become as untrustworthy and reckless as I sometimes am. Other children have managed fine without half as much support from home as I have had. Let me make that clear from the beginning. You mustn't blame yourself for all the wrong things I have done. I am the only person to blame, but, even more than before, I need help to put right the things I have done wrong and turn me into a decent, upright, responsible, kind and sober person.

"As you must know, I feel rotten to the core. I realize now that I should have taken my 'crazy period' round Christmas 1984–85 much more seriously than I did. To be quite honest, it seemed to me then very embarrassing and shameful to have been mad like that for a period. And so I didn't take it seriously enough, and I didn't take you and the psychologist seriously enough. I ran away from it—and I knew it, which in turn led me to drink too much and enter a vicious circle that was even more dangerous than the one I was already in.

"Just so you know, I haven't touched alcohol since I came back to camp. This obviously doesn't mean I've become a new person, but it does mean that my thought processes are getting back to normal. You and Pappa, and the whole environment in which I grew up, helped me and supported me and tried to build me into a person with a conscience and many other good qualities. Why I should have developed in this negative way is something I can't work out, but I have a strong tendency to want to flee from reality and from my responsibilities. There may be many reasons for this, and I think they are interesting, but they don't give me any sensible explanations for what has happened."

I had written to Jørgen about my worries and my thoughts on the best way to work together with the psychiatrist to try to get to the bottom of the problem and move forward. I wondered whether his problem was chemical and asked whether he thought smoking marijuana might have contributed.

"My most recent and serious 'stressful' period was of course this Easter," his letter continued. "It started when I didn't manage to get on the Officer's Training Course. After that I began to drink a lot. The madness took over again. I didn't care a damn about anything, behaved rudely and egotistically, which only made everything worse. And then I stopped sleeping. I have tensions in the muscles of my back, my face twitches, I sleep badly, I'm sweating and nervous. But I am not heading for a new breakdown, and things generally are going better now. The possibility of my madness being chemical in origin is something I have thought a lot about these last few days. I don't think all the things that happened were when I was high on something, but maybe in the aftereffects. Marijuana can give you flashbacks long after you've taken it. There is no excuse for all the crazy things I have done, and for that reason I am very glad I have you, Mamma, to help me try to solve these problems. I am profoundly grateful not to have been ostracized from the family. It means so much to me, all of you do."

The letter concludes: "And do you think there is any point in my studying to be a lawyer or something similar with a background like mine? Regardless, I would be grateful for an answer. Say hello to everyone for me. Big soldier's hug, from Jørgen."

I read the letter and felt that all we had done wasn't enough. The gratitude was a little too much. And Jørgen expressed his feeling of dependence in a way that made me uneasy. I didn't understand then that this was an expression of depression.

There were a few sentences in the letter that make this even more clear: "Last night I was out on maneuvers. I lay freezing out in the forest and began to think about myself and my future. It didn't look all that good. I wonder if you can help me to decide what I should do in the future."

The greatest difficulty for those closest to the sufferer, those who offer treatment and support, is the uncertainty at the heart of the situation, the difficulty in making the diagnosis and in planning the best course of treatment. We know more today than we did when his letter was written. We know more today than when Jørgen took his own life in 1992. We must work to improve our understanding and treatment of mental illnesses, and take much more seriously the task of actively defusing the risks of suicide in such cases.

Stepping Down

17

We were a month from the National Labor Party Congress in November 1992. Our main task was to agree on the handling of the difficult questions around our links to the European Union. This congress would be a political challenge in many ways, but fortunately there was no controversy about the leadership.

While preparing I had Deputy Leader Gunnar Berge's words after Jørgen's death on my mind: "Remember that you will have to work yourself out of this tragedy." I talked it over with Olav. I realized that I had to have more time at my own disposal than I had had all these years. However, there were critical issues to be decided upon. Could I step down from this big responsibility?

No, it did not feel right. The sorrow was heavy. But would it not be even heavier if I abandoned this responsibility? Olav saw it the same way and he supported me. Gradually I arrived at my conclusion: I had to finish this meaningful job, and it had to be carried out the right way. But at the same time attention had to be paid to the party. Under the current circumstances this time it made sense to split the jobs of

Party Leader and Prime Minister. Personally this was an alleviation of my duties that I would welcome.

How to lay the groundwork for such a solution? Any hint that I was thinking along such lines would immediately create an intense public debate. Not about the EU questions, which were the most important for the party. Not about any other aspects of the program either, but about election of a new Party Leader. That issue would put everything else into the shadows. I knew.

The last three weeks before the congress I examined these questions over and over again, alone or with Olav. I gave no signals to the rest of the party leadership. We had thorough discussions about the political content, the agenda, the handling of the congress. With my staff at the Prime Minister's office I worked on my two speeches, one on Europe, the other on the political situation.

With only one week left, I asked Gunnar Berge, my Deputy Party Leader, to come home with me one evening. I wanted to know whether he was prepared to take up the responsibility as Party Leader if I should decide to step down. Gunnar was skeptical. We agreed that there were other possibilities, too.

Nobody Can Know

The weekend before the congress we were at Lake Mylla. Olav and I went for a walk. I laid out my thoughts about the different ways of handling stepping down as Party Leader. Could I manage resignation so that it did not become an issue until after we had been through the debate on our relation to Europe? That was the question I kept coming back to. What if my resignation contributed to a different outcome on the Europe debate? I was convinced that this "personnel problem" had nothing whatsoever to do with the outcome of the Europe debate. The delegates to the congress should be able to make the decision about EU membership without considering a leadership question.

I read different drafts of my speech to Olav. How could I explain my decision to the congress? My voice thickened, tears began to fall. How to say the right words without suffering a breakdown?

My statement to the congress should not raise new questions. My words had to ensure that the congress would feel fully free to choose a new leader. I also wanted to show my faith that our congress was competent to handle such a process.

The congress examined the EU question on Friday, November 7. The day before I had decided that I had to test out my speech on a close political coworker. I asked my Minister of Industry, Finn Kristensen, to visit my office. Perhaps I felt that Finn would support my personal decision. A lot of times, not only this fall, he had said, "I don't understand how you can bear all this, Gro." But most important for me was the knowledge that our talk would be in confidence. Finn was not a member of the Central Executive Board. He was not a candidate for Party Leader. He would not feel any obligation to inform anyone else. Therefore I could draw on him as partner for counsel and conversation just when I had laid the finishing touches on my speech.

Well, it turned out that Finn had expected my decision. This, in spite of the fact that I had not given any indication in that direction. He expressed his great approval that I was prepared to carry on as Prime Minister. I read to him from my handwritten sheets. Finn had a few helpful suggestions for me.

Friday was a fine day. The congress had opened the day before in the proper manner. It was possible to deliver my introductory speech on Europe fully engaged with the theme. Viewpoints differed, and our debate was thorough.

I had decided that I must ask for the floor when the meeting resumed after the afternoon break. The election committee needed that much time. To wait any longer would be irresponsible. When should I inform the two Deputy Leaders, the Party Secretary, and the TUC boss? It would have to be just before I entered the rostrum, in the intermission between the afternoon session and the evening session.

The hall was empty; everyone was on dinner break. I had asked Gunnar Berge, Thorbjørn Berntsen, and Thorbjørn Jagland for a chat before the evening meeting started. We got together in one of the small back rooms where we would not be disturbed. I also asked TUC boss Yngve Hågensen to come. I told them about the discussions in our family and what Olav and I had been through. I would now step down as Party Leader.

There wasn't much they could say. The way I told them did not invite counterarguments. The decision was already made. I looked at Yngve: "I know that you will have to face a more difficult job than you had prepared for, but I believe that the election committee and the congress will tackle it." Yngve asked for a new meeting of the five of us immediately after I had given my resignation to the congress.

Departure

We convened again at 7:35 p.m. with a song. The meeting's president announced that the Party Leader had asked to speak at the opening of the meeting in order to give a declaration. He had just received this request from me. The hall was full. Our delegates were disciplined about taking their seats on time even after relatively short breaks. Afterward I realized that there were only a few reporters there. The public gallery was almost empty. Nobody expected big news this late in the evening.

I knew that my statement would come as a complete surprise. I had read the text over and over again to prevent a breakdown when I came to the most sensitive words: "President, delegates, I have arrived at the conclusion that now it is necessary for me to ask to be relieved from the position of Party Leader. This is a personal decision. I have not been sure about my decision until the last few days. I was facing a choice. I could have told you in advance before the congress convened. Or I could wait to speak directly to you. I have arrived at the latter alternative. I am sure the congress is familiar with how my family and I have been severely struck. And this happened only a few weeks ago. Such things demand time before one can or ought to make important decisions together with one's closest family.

"Why this decision and why now? Because this congress is one of the most important in the history of the party. We are all responsible for a historic process that demands much in solidarity, loyalty, and dedication in order that a strong social democracy may play the central role that it must and shall play in our country. Like everyone here, I am more than anything preoccupied with doing what is best for this party.

"Being Party Leader requires considerable activity, systematic work, and steady follow-up; that is, total engagement. In addition there is a lot of traveling, which has been a natural part of my life and also the life of my family during the almost twelve years I have been Leader and the six years prior, when I served as Deputy Party Leader.

"I feel that I will have to reserve a little more time together with my closest friends and my family. It will be too much to fill the role of Party Leader as well as the one of Prime Minister in the years to come.

"I know perhaps better than anyone what is demanded in energy, strength, and spirit. The demand is to give one's all in both jobs. The marketing to the public of what we together stand for demands increasing effort and attention in the media age in which we find ourselves.

"I believe that it will serve the party in general if new forces now take over the party leadership. I have notified the central leadership of the party and the election committee leader of this difficult decision only hours ago. The congress and its attendant business has thus been protected in a way that I think is right."

A New Party Leader

Thorbjørn Jagland was elected to succeed me. We had numerous conversations during the following years at which I pointed out that now Thorbjørn was the natural leader of the party and that he had to decide when it would be best that I should step down as Prime Minister so that he could take over the premiership as well.

Thorbjørn said, "Gro, remember that you stepped down as Party

Leader under very special circumstances indeed. Nobody wanted any change. Public concord will be my basis for future analysis." In 1992–93 there was not much more to be said about this. We both thought that such a shift of Prime Minister could come only after a number of years.

Stepping Down as Prime Minister

We are in the cold white ski trails during January 1996. The sun is just looking over the hilltops. A cold haze hangs over Lake Mylla. Olav and I are alone. I am leading. New Year's thoughts turn into thoughts for the future. I stop and turn around. I want to talk. I always like to talk on the trails. Olav usually wants to maintain a higher speed. As the years pass we both feel we have more time at our disposal and can be more relaxed.

Nobody is around in the scenery that we like so much. But serenity is not what I am feeling. I am checking my innermost thoughts. "Olav, what would be the right thing to do? When should I step down as Prime Minister? When should I pass that responsibility to Thorbjørn?" But Olav says nothing. I challenge him: "So, say something!"

"Why this hurry? It is not a popular demand." Well, he had said this earlier when I had brought the theme up for discussion. And he was right.

But this time, I am insisting: "Olav, I have made up my mind. I will not be Prime Minister and go into a new election campaign once again. What I want to discuss is when." He fetches a deep sigh and smiles wryly—but he is not convinced.

This was not the first such conversation I have had with Olav. I have prepared us both for the changes that have to come. It is a great relief to have someone to whom you can tell everything.

It was now more than three years since Thorbjørn was elected the new Party Leader in 1992. Thorbjørn had recently answered the press in a way that caught my attention: "Gro continues as Prime Minister as long as she likes and is willing." These were words I did not like. I thought, This is not right. The responsibility for this evaluation lies with Thorbjørn. He is the elected Party Leader. It is he in his role as Party Leader who has the responsibility to make that overall assessment. I said nothing to Thorbjørn about his statement to the press. But my understanding was nonetheless clear. Thorbjørn showed an increasing desire to be Prime Minister. I was prepared for this and I respected it. Sometime later I reminded him about our earlier discussions and that he needed to make up his mind about the right timing for the shift.

Again he put the whole question aside and repeated that I had to give the signal when I felt the need to be relieved. There was no such wish in the party, so he did not want to end up in a situation in which he could be accused of having pushed me out. But my mind was now quite clear. His utterance to the press had confirmed that Thorbjørn had now begun to look upon a change as a natural thing. From the start I had felt that four years had to be the maximum period for the divided leadership between Prime Minister and Party Leader. I thought that 1996 was the year when it had to happen, but now I had heard from Thorbjørn the clear signal that the gambit for change was mine to bring about.

This was a subject I discussed only with Olav and my chief of staff, Svein Roald Hansen, though occasionally others took up the question and forcefully argued that I stay on. There was an abundance of such opinions at that time—all the time.

Svein Roald stressed that it would serve the party in the general elections of 1997 if I remained at the helm. I reminded him and Olav that in the fall of 1997 Thorbjørn would have been Party Leader for five years. He himself ought to enter the next general election campaign as the candidate for Prime Minister. This he could not do if I stayed on. In political leadership your perspective should be long-term and focused. It does not look good to have leaders who are on their way out. This was important to me. It was better that I took the initiative and relieved my colleague of the difficult demand for change at the expense of a very popular Prime Minister.

The fall was the best time to resign, after the state budget was presented. But should it be before or after the debate over the Speech from the Throne, which is the key political debate of the year? This was a real dilemma. The change would not be a change of political course, but of crew only. So it was logical to have the major debate over with. The same could of course be said about the debate on the budget, the Finance Debate, as we call it.

But another point became overriding. The change should be made before the Labor Party's National Congress, which was scheduled for mid-November. Thorbjørn should be given the opportunity to meet the Congress in his new capacity as Prime Minister.

Thus, in cooperation with the Permanent Undersecretary at the Prime Minister's office, Bjørn Grydeland, I picked the most suitable date: October 23, the day after my return from an official visit to Austria.

No Spontaneity as Expected

I had to keep my decision a well-guarded secret. Otherwise it would dominate the political agenda. Apart from keeping Olav informed, there were only four others who knew it. Grydeland helped me to look up the relevant constitutional references and checked the proceedings from former changes. There are few written rules for such occasions. Grydeland also discreetly made sure that the King would be in town that day. But he waited till late Tuesday evening to ask the King to receive me the following morning. My State Secretaries for Media, Øystein Singsaas, and for Foreign Affairs, Morlen Wetland, had to know my plans in order to prepare correct information for foreign leaders. It was important to get one message across: This would be a change of leader, not a change of policy. There would, for instance, be no reason for adverse market reactions or any kind of political sensation.

The agenda for Parliament that morning was the inauguration of a completely new form for questions to the Ministers, "spontaneous response." Three Ministers would be at the disposal of the MPs for answering any questions within their respective fields of ministerial responsibility, and the questions did not have to be, as before, given in written form days ahead; they could be asked directly from the floor. I had decided to be unavailable for questions that first time since I wanted to stress that the prime responsibility lay with the respective cabinet Ministers. But the introduction of the new format gave me an excuse for asking the President of Parliament to receive me in her office before she opened the proceedings. It also gave me the basis for calling Thorbjørn Jagland the night before to make sure that he would be around in Parliament the next morning. I said nothing about my decision to step down. I had written my short declaration three weeks before and I wanted to present it to Parliament that morning at ten o'clock.

But first I went to the Royal Palace. The King received me at 9:15 a.m., smiling as usual, and asked me to sit down in the easy chair that always is in place adjacent to his desk. This time I took the initiative by asking whether His Majesty had any idea of why I was coming now and not waiting for the next regular monthly meeting with him. Yes, the thought had struck him that perhaps there was something special. The conversation was light as I told His Majesty about my plans and my thoughts about the forthcoming change. In our regular meetings, we always examined the overarching political considerations of every issue. It helped us to find the right words when confronted with the ever more demanding media. Now I told the King that I wanted to make the change official in the regular King in Council the following Friday. He was not surprised that I advised him to turn to Party Leader and Parliamentary Group Leader Thorbjørn Jagland to form the new government as Prime Minister.

My conversation with the King this time was shorter than usual. I knew when leaving that this was the last time that I would have a personal meeting with the King in my capacity as Prime Minister.

He surely thought so too because he was thanking me for my close cooperation and great frankness during many years. I stopped for a second when passing the large window in the Birds Chamber. This was the place where I had so often over the years waited for audiences with the King while looking out at the statue of King Karl Johan and Karl Johan Street, which led down to the Parliament Building. Again I felt the finality of the occasion.

I offered a smile to some of the Royal Palace employees while hastening back to the driver, who took me straight down to the Parliament. A few people who were at Palace Square looked curiously at my black car as we passed. But there was no crowd there. Nobody knew what was about to happen.

The reason I had given for seeing the President of the Parliament, Kirsti Kolle Grøndahl, was the "spontaneous response." Mrs. President was very happy for this renewal in the workings of Parliament. She was eager to know when I as Prime Minister would be available to answer the spontaneous questions. I had thought that this should come later. I looked at Kirsti and said, "But I am coming on a different errand. I will ask for the floor when the plenary meeting starts." Kirsti was taken by total surprise. I started laughing, and we both laughed. "Gro, you have done it once again," Kirsti said, "you have set the agenda."

We could not find Thorbjørn right away. He was not systematic in leaving notices about his whereabouts. This I understood quite well. It can often be complicated, a kind of straitjacket for a Parliamentary Leader to always remember to leave such notices, though I myself had not often left "the Building" when I was Parliamentary Leader without leaving information. Nevertheless, his absence was nerve-racking for those who had been instructed to find him so that he could talk with Kirsti before the 10:00 a.m. plenary meeting.

About three minutes to ten Thorbjørn entered the office of the President slightly out of breath, smiling, somewhat insecurely. This was surely a turning point he had been looking forward to, but he had had no information from me. His wife had no information and neither had his closest political colleagues. They all had been spared from the burden of knowing what they did not need to know.

We decided to follow routine to prevent anyone from knowing anything before the meeting started. So we left the President's office through different doors and entered the chamber from different sides. I chatted with some of the MPs on the way to my chair. While passing the three cabinet ministers who had prepared for the "spontaneity," I checked their nerves, which could have been tense before this new form of meeting. So I lowered my voice and whispered that there would be no "spontaneity" as expected this morning, since I would take the rostrum first. All three kept their faces. But they obviously understood.

My Public Declaration

The last time I stood at the rostrum of the Parliament as Prime Minister, the chamber was packed. Soon surprise overtook many of the faces. This was something they had not anticipated. It was clear also that for many of the others this was a special moment. With my words, a particularly solemn atmosphere descended on the chamber.

"Honorable President, I have today asked to give Parliament the following message: We are approaching a new general election for a new four-year parliamentary period. I am of the opinion that the leadership of the government and the composition of the cabinet should be clear well ahead of the election. Accordingly I have informed the King that I will submit my resignation to the King in Council this forthcoming Friday."

Then the President spoke: "Given the message from the Prime Minister, the President suggests that the meeting be adjourned. Anyone opposed?" No one. The entire meeting was adjourned at 10:05.

I exchanged a few words with the three cabinet members and with a few of the MPs, who pleasantly remarked that this was certainly a surprise, but soon I escaped back to the President's office and left the building by a side door. The two main entrances and the exit from the garage were blocked by journalists. I wanted to be back in my office as soon as possible and to avoid a running press conference on the way. A regular press conference had just been set for eleven o'clock in the government's media center. There everyone would be given the same information. I had prepared my announcement on a sheet of paper. Now it would be typed and made ready for distribution to the press.

In the car I all of a sudden remembered that I had informed no one in the family and wondered whether Olav had done so. Mamma, Knut, Kaja, and Ivar knew nothing. Mamma had the habit of listening to most news on the radio. So by now she would know. Olav later told me that he had asked his boss at NUPI whether he was interested enough in political science to watch coverage of the first "Spontaneous." So Olav was at the TV set. But he had forgotten the kids.

At the Prime Minister's office the atmosphere was somber. We'd maintained a cooperative environment and a positive tone for so long. We had all been happy with the intensity, tempo, and responsibility of our work. My personal secretary, Inger Andersen, whose thrilling laughter and fantastic singing voice often filled the office, was now in a sad mood. We embraced and both of us got teary.

At the media center, Singsaas thanked the journalists and photographers for coming and asked me to start the press conference. I gave the background for my decision by reviewing political developments since I had stepped down as Party Leader. Most of this was second nature to the reporters but they did not hesitate in asking a lot of questions. The atmosphere was solemn and strong emotions surfaced. Laughter, too. The last question: "This press conference is marking the end of an epoch for the whole nation and for you personally. What do you feel?"

I responded by saying that I would not be able to answer for some time. Because when you are busily executing your plan of action, you are concentrating on doing only that.

Thank You and Good-bye

Throughout the press conference, I had a little difficulty keeping my voice clear. The next two days would be hectic and heavy, filled with wistfulness and warmth, thank you and good-bye.

I had had fantastic colleagues—the Secretaries, the advisers, the civil servants, the clerks, the watchmen, the drivers. Many of us had been together for more than ten years.

Bjørn Grydeland asked reticently whether there would be time for at least a short farewell reception for an hour or two. We had always been so efficient. Tempo was concern number one. But this time I felt that I had time for my colleagues and friends. For they had become friends at this office where I had spent ten full and productive years of my adult life. No, I said, we would have to take out a full evening. So I will be able to both laugh and weep. So I will have time for everyone.

We arranged a farewell dinner with everyone at the office invited. We indulged in memories about the stresses and the successes, and the inspiration we took from one another. We remembered the humorous episodes, stories that tend to improve with each retelling. I expressed my thanks to Grydeland, Wetland, Støre, and to my most recent chief of staff, Kolberg. Olav, too, thanked everyone for all the assistance he had received in his many functions as the Prime Minister's "decoration," as he used to say, alluding to the fact that in his view so many wives were escorted to public functions with that as their only role. We were like a big happy family.

Reflections on the Decade of Reform

Ten years had now passed since I took over in 1986. Political work has to be focused; it has to deliver. Had our time become one of reform? In 1986 we had almost five years of Conservative government behind us. As Party Leader and as Leader of the Opposition I had seen so many of our fine visions remain mere statements of intent. Environmental protection, gender equality, family policies—all of these had suffered from lack of progress and vision in the administration we had succeeded.

In those years, we set out first to reform the Labor Party from within. We activated a new policy: to have a minimum of 40 percent of each sex in all elected positions. And with just one exception, we had managed this as of the general election of 1985. Since we took over as a result of that election, we achieved much more than we would then have thought possible.

Investing in education had been an important part of our efforts to increase the number of jobs and in our struggle against unemployment. And just as important was this: Investment in education, with an ever-improving range of options open to all on how to finance it, is in itself an aspect of the democratization of our society. An increasing number of young people had been able to get the education and the job of their choice. The number of university places had doubled between 1987 and 1995. Higher education was now within the grasp of young people everywhere. The result has been a huge influx of human resources into our society.

In the early 1980s, many a sixteen-year-old encountered the adult world for the first time in the form of unemployment. One of our reforms made institutions of higher education a part of the Norwegian public school system.

Young people without opportunities were a major problem in Europe at the time. In Norway the situation was quite different. Everyone had acquired rights. We stood firm through the years of struggle, albeit beneath a hail of criticism. The union movement was a major source of support to the minority government. But in Parliament we had to fight to get from one milestone to the next.

We also introduced schooling for six-year-olds. It was said that this reform in particular was introduced too quickly. Often the opposition parties and the teachers allied themselves against our reforms. The programmatic basis for the policy was worked out as part of our long-term strategy before the election of 1989. Our Education Minister after the autumn of 1990, Gudmund Hernes, led us through the long and hard battles. Often it was a question of keeping one's nerve, of keeping a cool head and a warm heart. The political game in Parliament was complex. Sometimes we had to play the Conservatives and the parties of the Middle off against each other and gamble that if we just stood firm on behalf of the children, we would win. Now it was 1996 and the battle was won. Six-year-olds would spend their first day at school in the fall of 1997! They would get ten years of basic schooling, not nine, a real educational shot in the arm for our country!

With the most important part of the education reform behind us, I had needed my very efficient Minister of Education to change Ministries so he could now work on health issues. We had already carried out a major program of reform and greatly increased our spending on health goals. There had been dramatic advances in the medical world, and it was a continual challenge to make sure that high-quality treatment was available equally to everyone throughout the health service.

Gudmund responded with three major parliamentary proposals to improve primary health service, hospitals, and psychiatry. The Organization for Economic Cooperation and Development (OECD) gives good marks to the Norwegian health service.

In 1986, no one would have believed that within ten years female students would outnumber males. That the number of nursery school seats would have more than doubled. That paid maternity leave would be one year, and that the proportion of employed women of working age would be near that of men. That's where we are today. What we're building is a society of choice and equal opportunities.

In 1993, when maternity leave was extended to one year, four weeks were also reserved for the father. The number of fathers taking advantage of their right increased from 4 to 70 percent over the course of three years. We gave notice of a new, more flexible arrangement, introduced in 1994, which allows that the leave can also be used over a period of years in the form of reduced working hours. Parents can choose six months' full leave and take the rest in the form of six-hour days on full pay until their child is almost three years old.

The goal of a nursery-school place for every child who needs one was another important aim for the Labor Party and our women's movement. We created a special Ministry of the Child when I again took over the government in 1990. I know of no other government having done so before. I have never thought it fair that any parent should be unable to find a secure place with a trained caretaker for his or her small children. With conscious investment in the form of state support and public cofinancing, our goal of "full coverage" by the year 2000 is within reach. Looking back, I am proud of the results. At the end of the decade, having achieved 90 percent coverage for children below five, the Labor government could commit to make nursery-school access a right for every child, by law.

When conceiving the Labor Party program for 1989–93, we considered the importance of a strong economy and a strong export-oriented trade and industry sector in our ability to finance our reforms of the welfare state. It was also necessary to help Norwegian corporations in their search for new markets. To me it seems self-evident that the Prime Minister and the government should get involved in the work of building bridges to other countries and laying the groundwork for new contacts abroad for our trade and industry. Once Norway had voted to stay outside the European Union, it became even more important to build up lines of communication to, among others, the Asian countries.

When we set ourselves ambitious goals, we must never forget to ask a basic question of ourselves: Do the interests of the individual permeate every aspect of public and private activity?

Cooperation among trade and industry, the union movement, and the authorities was the sine qua non of our reform policy. In the earliest years there were large unofficial gatherings in the government's hospitality suite just behind the Royal Palace, at which the economy, trade and industry, and social reforms were the subjects of discussion. Later we organized the "Forum for the Creation of Wealth," which was chiefly the responsibility of the Ministries of Trade and Industry but which held meetings led by the Prime Minister in the cabinet's meeting room. Among the issues that concerned us were the development of tax reforms and higher education. People from trade and industry had ideas and experiences to share with us.

Social democracy offers us our model for a welfare state. The labor movement created the structure that is today the model for many others. We can be proud of a process that in an incredibly short time transformed a society of poverty into a welfare society. But pleasure in our achievements must not blind us to new problems that arise. What was yesterday a radical solution might today be a hindrance. We have to be careful that our own organization and our own party do not obstruct the processes of renewal. We have to be on guard against inertia and stiffness.

In certain quarters of the union movement, the old principle persisted that everything that was done as a joint effort should be paid for by the state or the municipality. We had, for instance, an ambitious program for both child care and the care of the elderly, one that found inventive and commonsense solutions to age-old problems. Yet we must never forget that we have to pay for our efforts. We won't manage to finance all the services and benefits that we're going to need in coming years just by building on the traditional public sector, and certainly not if the money spent on subsidizing trade and industry and social security keeps rising.

In spite of the fact that we have created a broader basis for common solutions and a "third sector" between the private and the public, there has been a steep growth in the services offered by the community. As a result of a broad program of reforms, one in every four persons at work in Norway is now working in the public sector, most of them in education and training, health care, and care of the elderly. This is how it has to be if a society is rooted in solidarity and its people intent on finding solutions together. We can use everyone, and we need to make room for everyone.

I'll never forget the impression it made on me as a young Deputy Leader to see how some of the leading women in the union movement considered it their primary task to agitate for full-time jobs for women. It was clear to me, however, that what many women wanted was more part-time jobs. The union women saw their fight as one to achieve equality between men and women, and that was why they fought for full-time jobs. Seen as a matter of principle it made sense. But for women struggling to achieve a balance in their lives, it was by no means the desired solution. We've come a long way when men, too, can take paternity leave, and when there seems nothing odd about men working shorter hours at certain times during the earliest years of a child's life.

The year 1996 marked a decade of great reform. We had conducted a policy that created results that truly mattered for most people. That makes political work worthwhile.

Leaving the Office

Friday, October 25, 1996, Thorbjørn came to my office and I gave him the keys. Journalists and photographers filled the room. I suppose it was a historic moment.

I took a last sweep around the offices. Political positions are positions of insecurity. Some could continue in their previous jobs, some would take different positions, others would simply be replaced. Some people will always be disappointed when there is a change of government.

Then I took the elevator from the Prime Minister's office for the last time. Mr. Singsaas accompanied me down. Olav was waiting in the car. He had filled it up with clothes, tools, and a case of light beer. Everything was open to view by the journalists and photographers, and every detail proved to be communicated to the readers and the viewers.

A few journalists attempted to ask me political questions. They got a smile only. We were now going to our winter cottage at Lake Mylla.

It was Olav's idea. Not for a weekend as usual, but for a whole week. I loved the idea. For what is most important in life beyond one's job? Family, and being outdoors with one's closest.

Friday night alone, just the two of us. Telephone calls from the family and from dispirited colleagues. But on Saturday the family comes, one by one; no invitation, it's automatic. The attraction of Lake Mylla is irresistible.

Sunday evening. Again there is quiet. We are looking forward to a number of days of peace and freedom. Olav is fixing a table for himself and one for me in adjacent rooms. Then he ambles toward me with a full package of blank paper. Five hundred sheets, which he gives me, saying: "Gro, you may now begin writing." I tear into the package, thinking about what the coming days had in store. How about this: time, without interruptions, alone with a pencil and clean sheets of paper?

My Way to the WHO

18

It is mid-morning, January 27, 1998. I am in the office of the Norwegian ambassador to the U.N. in Geneva, waiting for the outcome of the nomination for the new Director General of the World Health Organization (WHO). I am one of the candidates. The 32 members of the executive board are now casting their votes. The board is a miniature version of the 191-member organization. It meets in a closed session after having the day before listened to the five candidates present themselves one by one. The voting is secret. The first one to get seventeen votes out of thirty-two is nominated. The first rounds of voting were inconclusive, since many board members initially vote for their favorites or for candidates from their respective parts of the world even if that person's chances to win are very slim. The one who gets the least votes in each round is out.

Information trickles out. The first round is inconclusive. I had twelve votes. Number two had seven votes. Because two candidates had tied for fourth place, there had to be a new round with all five candidates. The whole process might take some time.

The next round, however, produced a loser. I kept my twelve votes, while my strongest competitor, Dr. George Alleyne of Barbados, the regional director for the WHO in the Americas, increased his to eight. Those who had thought that a former Prime Minister would automatically be selected over her competitors with less experience in elective office were sorely disappointed. Perhaps this would be a bust for those who wanted renewal in the WHO.

After the third round, there still were three candidates in the contest. I had increased my lead to fifteen votes while Dr. Alleyne now had nine. Leaks and rumors reached the media. Back home in Oslo, Olav was listening to the radio and checking the news. He was soon on the telephone: The Norwegian Broadcasting Corporation (NRK) said there was more competition than expected. How were things going?

I didn't know. Since April 1997, when I had made myself available for the WHO position, I had been busy campaigning and had traveled to many parts of the world. At this point, there was nothing more I could do to influence the outcome.

The Persuasiveness of Four Blue Eyes

While waiting, I had to think about how I had been persuaded by others to confirm my availability. I had not gone for the position for my own sake. I had more or less been pushed into entering the race.

In March two enthusiastic men had visited my office in the Norwegian Parliament. Both were my colleagues in the medical profession. One of them, Dr. Sverre Lie, came from my own class at the Medical Faculty of the University of Oslo. He had specialized in pediatrics and had worked for the WHO on projects in the Middle East. An idealist. A humanist. The other, Dr. Tore Godal, was a specialist in tropical medicine, also from the University of Oslo, who had long worked for the WHO in Ethiopia and as a director in Geneva.

They brought one message only: "Gro, you are the natural next Director General of the World Health Organization. We really need

you. Only you can make a difference. Norway has never had a better candidate for a U.N. position. You can surely win. Please do it.
Do it in order to put new life into the most important specialized
agency of the United Nations, the significance of which is on the
rise because of new and reemerging diseases."

It was not the first time someone had approached me. But these
two blue-eyed and idealistic doctors certainly managed to make an
impression on me. They hit a weak spot; they nearly created a feeling of guilt in me. I am a doctor, even though my life for twenty-
two years was dedicated to national politics and leadership. If these
colleagues were out in the forefront, why shouldn't I be there as
well? How could I say no to their appeal?

One among those who had tried to convince me earlier was the
Norwegian Minister of Health. I had myself recruited him during a
transatlantic flight in 1990 for the position of Minister of Education
when I served as Prime Minister and needed him for that important
position in the Norwegian cabinet. He had been on his way to enjoy a year as guest professor at Harvard University but was willing
to return at once.

He came to me before Christmas in 1996 and challenged me to
do for him what he had done for me: Respond to the call of duty.
Go for the job at the WHO. A seed had been sown. As a matter of
fact, even while I was serving as Prime Minister, my name had
been brought up in many a speculative discussion about positions
in international organizations, be it the WHO, the U.N., or NATO.
Boutros Boutros-Ghali writes in his book, *Unvanquished*, that Gorbachev had told him that he'd received a call from John Major to
collect support for me as the Secretary-General to follow Perez de
Cuellar. U.S. Defense Secretary William Perry had once asked my
Defense Minister whether I was available for NATO when Spanish
Foreign Minister Javier Solana eventually was picked as secretary-
general. I had never offered my candidacy, however, and had concentrated on taking care of my responsibilities as Prime Minister.

Since October 1996, however, I had enjoyed freedom from most
political responsibilities, though I was still a Member of Parliament.

My term would end next summer, so I had some time to think about what to do. Just before New Year's I sent the Oslo branch of the Labor Party a fax from Lake Mylla informing them that I was not willing to stand for renomination for a new four-year term in Parliament.

Then the speculation really started. What next? I had begun writing my memoirs and had more time to spend with my children and grandchildren. I explained this when asked by reporters, but they hardly believed me. The contrast of an active Prime Minister on the political center stage and a writing grandmother in seclusion in her winter home seemed too strange to them. They figured there must be something in the pipeline—perhaps something international in nature? Some inquired about the United Nations. Some anticipated that the position of Director General of the International Labor Office (ILO) would soon be vacant.

While considering Geneva, or for that matter any foreign post, I was pondering two questions: (1) Would my husband be willing to go along and prematurely leave his position at the Norwegian Institute of International Affairs? (2) Would I be able to persuade at least one of my best collaborators in the office of the Prime Minister to come along? Jonas Gahr Støre had continued as Director of International Relations when I had stepped down. After a short stint as State Secretary for the Minister of Oil and Energy, Morten Wetland had gone back to his career in the Norwegian Foreign Service. Morten was soon to become one of the youngest ambassadors to one of our most important allies, Germany.

During the winter, I tried to find out whether Jonas would be willing. He came one weekend with my eldest son Knut to our winter holiday home at Lake Mylla. He knew that I had met Secretary-General Kofi Annan a few weeks earlier. I was in New York and on my way home from a meeting of the Carnegie Commission on Preventing Deadly Conflict, which I had joined at the behest of Cyrus Vance, former U.S. Secretary of State and mediator in the Balkans.

Annan wanted me to consider the new position of Deputy Secretary-General, which he planned to establish as part of his drive for modernizing and streamlining the U.N. He wanted a woman to fill that position, and he saw my experience and background as particularly well suited for it. After my final choice of going to Geneva to seek the WHO position, he chose the former Canadian Deputy Minister of Defense and longtime ambassador to the U.N. Louise Frechette.

When contemplating whether to move away from Oslo and my family during the winter of 1997, it seemed that I would relocate to either New York or Geneva. I wanted time to think it over. Twenty-two years in top positions in Norwegian politics made me resistant to any demand that I take on another heavy responsibility. I still thought I had the right to be a grandmother. However, I had long ago made up my mind not to be a backseat driver in Norwegian politics after leaving Parliament. Avoiding comment on Norwegian politics would be easier if I had an international responsibility to take care of and was living abroad.

But I did not want to leave my family. Geneva was not that far away, but since direct flights had been discontinued, traveling time between Geneva and Oslo would amount to more than four hours. New York was six to seven hours away. Impromptu visits to Oslo to see my grandchildren would not be easy from either post.

The weekend with Jonas was too soon for me to make a decision. He was careful not to assert any of his preferences. But he indicated that I was not meant to be number two and that it was better to focus on world health and make sense of it. My husband, however, whispered a preference for New York, if I decided to move.

Rumors and speculations had started. Olav told me that during the annual meeting of the World Economic Forum at Davos in January 1997, he had been approached by an old friend who was now serving as the Slovenian ambassador to the U.N. His message was clear: We want her at the WHO, but we will not beg her to come kicking and screaming. If she is willing, she must campaign for it.

Well, the truth was that I still had not made up my mind if I was willing to take the job. In any case I outright hated the idea of any sort of personal campaign. In fact at the same Davos meeting, Secretary of Health and Human Services, Donna Shalala, had asked to see me. She raised the question of the important upcoming election of a new leader of the WHO, and asked me if I would be available as a candidate for the job. She conveyed her conviction that change was urgently needed to strengthen this key international institution. She would fight for it, and thought that I would be very well suited to make it happen. I told her I was reflecting on my next move and that Kofi Annan had already approached me.

In my political career, I had never campaigned for myself. Sure, I had promoted causes and the Labor Party platform, but not for personal enhancement. The concept of the Norwegian Labor Party had been that you willingly served in the positions given to you by "the movement," as we used to say.

I never asked positions for myself, and I never compromised in order to hold on to any position. Nor did I ever advance a cause by threatening resignation. Unlike many politicians, I always had a solid fallback position. At any time I could go back to working as a medical doctor. Had Kofi Annan asked me directly to come to New York, my upbringing and instincts might very well have told me to answer in the affirmative. But the Secretary-General was more considerate and soft-spoken, and he very well knew I was also being asked to run for the position at the WHO. I would have to make my own difficult decision.

In February 1997 Ambassador Bjørn Skogmo, who had served with me at the Prime Minister's office, invited me to an informal dinner with a number of ambassadors who had formed a group they called "friends of the WHO." Skogmo seated me between the Egyptian ambassador, Mounir Zahran, and the British ambassador, Nigel Williams, who was one of the group's leaders. Ambassador Williams went through a good number of arguments why a change in the WHO was important and why I would be the best candidate.

I listened but was not ready to give a clear answer. The British, however, did not give up. Ambassador Williams stayed in touch with Ambassador Skogmo, and when he left Geneva at the end of April to be succeeded by Roderick Lyne, Skogmo's very close ties with the British government continued.

Motions for renewal of the WHO came in from all sides. Most notable was a series of articles in the *British Medical Journal*. The

WHO was seen as unfocused, even corrupt, and overrun by middle-level management. Some of the countries with the most positive attitudes toward the U.N. had begun scaling back their contributions to the WHO, Sweden and Denmark among them. This did not bode well for the future, unless change was brought about. And it seemed as though change would not come easily. The state of affairs, however irreparable, actually stimulated me to step forward. But it would not be an easy job.

Why the WHO?

I had the feeling that Olav was still in favor of a foreign assignment. He used to say mischievously that I had too much energy left for staying at home. But I had frequently asked him to drop the issue. On our first day of skiing during Easter vacation, I wanted to tell him about my meeting with my two blue-eyed medical colleagues, but he showed no interest for talk and left me behind on the trails. It took hours to return to the cabin and talk in front of the fireplace. He then realized that I was considering the WHO for real. Certainly he stuck to his former promise of willingness to come along.

I thought of my life as being one of public service. Since childhood, I had heard the call to duty, the call to contribute.

I suddenly knew I would be the first woman leader of the WHO, as I had been the first woman Prime Minister in my country, and the first woman elected to lead a major U.N. commission. As a doctor, a constitutional requirement for the leader of the World Health Organization and as a national and international politician, I felt I could make a difference.

What My Availability Means

For my campaign to succeed, preparations would have to begin before the World Health Assembly in May. The Ministry of Foreign Affairs was informed right away that I had agreed to make myself available. In Geneva, Ambassador Skogmo had informed all those who had urged me to stand that I would indeed be available if there was a genuine wish that I should. Similar communications were made in various capitals through diplomatic channels.

The spontaneous reaction was identical nearly everywhere: "This is very good news. It would be a very good thing for the WHO." In the three weeks between Easter and the World Health Assembly, many countries indicated that they would actively support my candidacy. Not all those countries had representatives on the executive board, however, so the outpouring of support could not immediately be translated into votes in the body that would make the nomination. I felt personally it would be essential that support must come from developing countries. Important countries in Africa, Latin America, and Asia indicated that they welcomed my decision and supported my efforts to be a spokesperson for issues of the developing world.

Two weeks before the World Health Assembly, Dr. Hiroshi Nakajima announced to a group of Japanese journalists that he had decided not to run for a third term as the WHO's leader.

I decided to travel to the World Health Assembly in Geneva in early May 1997 to meet with some of the key people. There was very little time to prepare, but I decided that it would be useful to meet with representatives of key governments, to listen to their ideas, concerns, and advice.

A reception was arranged on short notice at Ambassador Skogmo's residence so that World Health Assembly delegates could meet me. The weather in Geneva in May can be fairly unpredictable, and a tent was set up in the garden to give added space for the guests, if necessary. It proved to be a wise precaution. There was a very large turnout in spite of the pouring rain. Many countries sent their entire World Health Assembly delegations to meet this person whose name many had heard of but whom they had never seen. I was happy to have a clearheaded if soft-spoken ambassador who knew me well and could correct any misconception that might surface, be it because of ignorance or competitive mischief.

I had the opportunity to exchange a few words with Dr. Nakajima. I also spoke with many Health Ministers, some from countries that would be on the executive board in January. At the time, I had more questions than answers about the WHO, but I heard many calls for reform and some concrete ideas for change.

Dr. Nakajima's withdrawal from the race had another effect in that several internal candidates who had felt unable to run against their boss now felt free to throw their hats in the ring. Dr. Ibrahim Samba of Gambia, who was the Regional Director for Africa, had already announced his candidacy that winter. Also in the field were Dr. Sir George Alleyne from Barbados, the Regional Director for the Americas; Dr. Rafei Uton of Indonesia, the Regional Director of the South Asian Region; Dr. Nafis Sadik, the leader of the United Nations Population Fund; and the former Health Minister of Jordan, Dr. Aref Batayneh.

Campaigning

Norway is among the top financial contributors to the U.N., but since the U.N.'s first Secretary-General, Trygve Lie, Norwegians had not actively sought positions in the U.N. system. Both from our delegation in Geneva and from the bureaucracy at home one message came loud and clear: This time Norway had to campaign for its candidate. An improvised attempt in 1987 to promote former Prime Minister Kåre Willoch as Secretary-General of NATO had been anything but successful. This time preparations were taken with much more organizational care.

An action group was established, made up of representatives from both the health and the foreign service specialties. This approach departed from the usual strategy to start with Nordic support and gradually to widen the circle. Instead, we followed a more global strategy, contacting like-minded countries in all regions, all those eager for a change at the WHO. As a matter of fact, we held off soliciting declarations of support from other European countries so as to dispel the impression that regions were competing against one another for the post.

Our approach reflected a reality. Many countries in Africa, Asia, and Latin America came to us and argued that the interests of world health would be best served if I were elected. They thought that my name and credibility would bring new awareness to global health issues and increase their importance on the world's economic and political agenda. They also reasoned that I would find success with my global approach, since all the other candidates sought to first obtain support from their own respective regions. In some cases—particularly in the Americas—the appeals for regional solidarity became so strong that countries that had indicated initial support for me later informed us that they had to vote for their regional candidate.

Canada, with whom we usually had the most comprehensive co-operation, was a natural ally. We soon learned that Canada had decided to offer support for George Alleyne, possibly in return for hemispheric support for Canada's membership in the U.N. Security Council. Their decision had been made early, by the Prime Minister himself. Regardless, Canadian diplomats were giving enthusiastic support for me as a political leader.

Other countries were signaling rather strongly that they would be happy to support a new candidate, particularly a well-qualified one. Among the strongest supporters for such a change was the United States, although Washington kept a rather low public profile.

In late August, the Norwegian Ministry of Foreign Affairs established a five-person campaign secretariat for our daily operations. The group took office in what Morten Wetland, its leader, called the "shabby" former archives in the Ministry of Foreign Affairs. An important aspect of our campaign was to arrange for visits to as many members of the executive board as was practically possible.

Setting up a travel plan was not easy. On short notice we had to approach countries with busy schedules and arrange time-consuming and complicated trips. These visits I could make partly in my capacity as former Prime Minister of Norway. Without breaking international protocol I could ask for meetings with heads of state or government, and not only with health officials. This gave me an opportunity for political discussions with a focus on U.N. reform.

On several of these trips I decided to bring "my decoration," Olav, who happened to be an academic specialist in international affairs. Men in similar situations would often bring their wives. Spouses are often invited on official visits. This was questioned in the Norwegian media. Why was Olav there? Who paid for his trip? Wetland answered that the campaign saw Olav's participation as important for its symbolic effect, for the atmosphere, and for the future in case I should win. Our international campaign was unquestionably worthwhile.

The Gulf States

Our first trip was to Oman, the United Arab Emirates, and Bahrain, all voting members of the executive board. This was a deliberate choice. Many observers believed that I would be met with reluctance in these countries because of my well-known pro-choice position and my role as an advocate for women's rights. My call in Cairo in 1994 for decriminalization of abortion had not been well received by either the mullahs or the Catholic hierarchy.

By taking our campaign to the Gulf States first, we wanted to send the message that we would be looking for support that other candidates in the region might perceive as rightfully theirs. We were drawing a wide circle to include those countries where we were hoping to build the needed majority. And we did it very publicly, putting the campaign message out into the press. Jack Freeman, a journalist of *The Earth Times*, a New York–based paper believed to be widely read by U.N. diplomats, was invited to make the trip with us in the Gulf.

Oman's Sultan Quabus was not in Muscat, but I met with the country's Crown Prince. Oman's Health Minister and his people gave us a rather optimistic picture: The standard of health services in Oman was high, and its people were healthy.

This was the situation in the other Gulf States as well. In the Emirates, important family business prevented the emir from receiving me, but we had a thorough discussion in the Health Ministry and a good working lunch hosted by the deputy of the Minister of Health. I also got the opportunity to speak to a joint Norwegian–United Arabic Emirate seminar on offshore safety and environmental issues.

When we left, somebody came up to our car and handed us a package. When we asked who sent it, we were told, simply, "the Highest." It turned out to be a wonderful example of the ceremonial silver dagger that they treasure so much in that part of the world. It is not exactly the deadliest of weapons, but it created a fuss in Bahrainan customs. Olav had packed it in his checked baggage, and the officials denied access to a bag containing a weapon. Explanations from the Health Ministry, however, solved the matter.

In Bahrain we had a meeting with the emir and his Prime Minister. I was struck by their outlook on the precariousness of their country's position in the volatile Gulf area. They treated me more like the Norwegian Prime Minister than as a candidate and wanted to strengthen ties with the outside world, Norway included. We happened to observe a visiting high-ranking U.S. Air Force general accompanied by a number of bodyguards moving about in the bazaars.

We had a most interesting inspection of health facilities, reflecting both general quality for all and special quality for the royal family. A female health worker efficiently used the opportunity of my visit to her ward to raise an important issue about sex education with the Health Minister.

Bahrain has the most wonderful religious and historic buildings. The House of the Qur'an and a many-centuries-old cemetery for the region were included in our program, and so was a visit to one of the present day's wonders, the bridge into Saudi Arabia.

Africa

In Angola, we saw a country virtually without any functioning health system at all, except in the major cities. The reason for this was apparent: the long-lasting civil war, of which we were acutely reminded when entering our hotel in the capital city, Luanda. Fresh bullet holes from that very morning marked the doors and walls. What a tragedy! Enormous wealth from oil and diamonds were spent by the two sides in a long and bitter fight for political power and with the obvious effect of breaking asunder civil society.

Botswana, next on our itinerary, has been a developmental success story. Norway had therefore recently decided to discontinue development aid and shift focus to less fortunate African countries and even to withdraw the Norwegian embassy from Botswana. We were met by a veritable shock: The AIDS pandemic was spiritually crippling this nation. Some 75 percent of all hospital beds were occupied by AIDS patients.

We surely were complicating the country's agenda by coming on short notice. The Deputy Minister due to meet us for lunch did not show up. The cabinet was in session examining the budget. We stood waiting in a Swiss-type restaurant while the rain poured. When the Minister eventually turned up, he directed most of his attention to the Swedish ambassador. We were not sure he had read his brief on an obviously busy day.

Attention was more focused in the Health Ministry and the Directorate of Health, and in particular with the President, a man I had met on former occasions as leaders of social-democratic parties convened in his country. The President looked like a man whose company was soon to face liquidation. He willingly admitted that, because of AIDS, the average life expectancy of Botswana would see a 50 percent reduction from seventy down to thirty-five years of age. The country had gone from success to tragedy. A major source of the AIDS pandemic was said to be "beer and prostitution" among migrant workers.

I felt sorry for this wonderful country while in the afternoon glorying in the mystique of the tropical natural park near the capital, Gabarone. Norway had helped finance this natural park. A special experience was to go behind a fence to actually touch a couple of cheetahs. The watchman, who regularly fed them, said there was no danger; these fastest creatures in the animal kingdom would not be hungry again for another two days.

In Zimbabwe, Health Minister Timothy Stamps took us around the wards of Harare General Hospital and to President Mugabe. The President and I met as old colleagues. He had visited Norway already in 1981 and I had flown with him to London afterward. Our conversation did not concentrate on health matters only but touched on the general international situation in Africa and in particular on the prospects for peace in Angola. The purpose of health policies should not be restricted to care for the casualties, but should rather extend to preventing and ending wars, we agreed.

Coming around to the topic of the WHO election, President Mugabe said that the Regional Director for Africa had had his country's solid support. Why then should he quit his current post and run for a new office? he asked, not entirely facetiously.

We discussed AIDS. Of particular importance was the research at the University of Harare on the loss to the national economy due to the AIDs pandemic. The reduction in productivity because of absenteeism due to funerals alone was estimated at 14 percent. The special traditional funerals in Africa regularly demand full participation of the entire extended family and are often time-consuming due to long travels and the custom of staying several days with the surviving relatives.

In Arusha, Tanzania, which was not an executive board member, there was an international conference of public health associations, to which I was asked to give the keynote address. The WHO Regional Director for Africa, Dr. Ibrahim Samba, was also present. The Health Minister who had been scheduled on the printed agenda never appeared. Room was made for a campaign speech by Dr. Samba. Who had made that decision?

Samba spoke exactly as long as I did. His speech was strong and colorful and focused on his African background and personal expe-

rience. We engaged one another in a somewhat heated debate on
the concept of aid and the need to acknowledge that support from
the industrialized countries is worthwhile. If donors were not convinced that their aid was acknowledged and well used, politicians
would find it hard to convince their parliaments and their people of
the need for continued aid. Most industrialized countries do not
fulfill the aim set by the United Nations of giving at least 0.7 percent of their GDP for development aid. One has to take seriously
what is called "donor fatigue."

At Kilimanjaro airport an old friend from the Beijing Conference
on Women, Gertrude Mongella, had come to meet me. She had a
leading function within the public health conference. It was a great
joy to see her again. We were both annoyed by the fact that people
in leading positions were so seldom prepared to face the AIDS epidemic. Considerations for tourism and arguments about the private
nature of AIDS made for an atmosphere of denial. In fact the Vice
President of Tanzania did not at all address the issue in his welcom-
ing speech. Other diseases, not least malaria, were also big killers.
But silence on AIDS, already a big and rapidly growing burden to
the economy, was destructive.

Egypt was not only a voting member of the Executive Board
(EB), but a country with substantial regional influence. I met President Mubarak and had conversations with both Foreign Minister
Amr Moussa and Health Minister Ismahil Shallam. Naturally we
discussed the broad outlook for peace in the Middle East to which
Norway was committed through the Oslo agreement. Little optimism was to be felt with regard to Israel's Prime Minister Netan-
yahu's commitment to the peace process.

At a splendid dinner table in one of the finer hotels in Cairo, I
heard my husband asking Mrs. Moussa jokingly to confirm that
the illuminated building on the hill across from us was not the
Acropolis. What he was pointing to was in fact the building of
the Egyptian Foreign Ministry.

Could we hope for Egyptian support? Our hosts took us to the
premises of the Arab League, apparently to demonstrate the wide

influence of Egypt. The League has members from northwest Africa to the Indian Ocean. Its Secretary-General made a statement to the press about the importance of the Arab dimension of Egyptian policy, including, he stressed, its votes in U.N. organizations. President Mubarak, however, once again remembered my speech to the U.N. Cairo Conference on Population in 1994, and was clear and outspoken about Egypt's support for me.

Asia

Korea honored us with access to its President, Foreign Minister, and Health Minister. Afterward we learned that President Kim Young Sam thought ours was one of the most extraordinary visits by any candidate. He liked that in my comments on the political, regional, and global issues I had refrained completely from even mentioning my candidacy. I have been several times to the "Blue House" in which the President resides. Always there is a word of gratitude for the Norwegian contribution during the Korean War, even if we had only helped establish a field hospital. When Kim Dae Jung, Kim Young Sam's successor, received his Nobel Peace Prize in Oslo in December 2000, I had the opportunity to discuss with him the role of health issues in further relaxation of tensions on the Korean peninsula.

I got the feeling that the Health Ministry people were perhaps more interested in how I could have been Prime Minister for ten years and leave voluntarily with the national economy in good shape. What was the political and economic secret? We were visiting at a time when Korea was deepest in its financial and economic crisis.

Japan was different. The Prime Minister sent his greetings on a photograph he himself had taken of his beautiful garden. And I saw the Health Minister and Ms. Takako Doi, who was a former Labor Party Leader and Speaker of the Diet. The Health Ministry people

turned out to be using their time during our long meeting in the
Norwegian Embassy to try to secure high-level positions in the
WHO for Japanese candidates. Japan is not alone in seeking U.N.
posts for its citizens, but it is more systematic in its approach than
most. In fact, Japan is the country at the low end of our so-called
"desired range of participation."

In Sri Lanka, we were shown examples of both Western and traditional indigenous medicine. Sri Lanka has had hospitals for more
than three thousand years. The Deputy Minister of Finance, upon
asking the names of the other candidates besides the former Norwegian Prime Minister, shrugged his shoulders as if to ask what the
agonizing was all about.

Bhutan was extremely different. Health services started there
with two doctors in the early 1960s. The country is very serious
about sustainable development. The planting of forests is considered important, and 72 percent of the territory is covered with
trees. The King was touring to promote the next national economic
plan. He took a break and spent many hours on the road to come
back to the capital to meet me and to reopen the Royal Guest
House for us. As it happened, friends of my daughter-in-law, Cecilie, were close friends of His Majesty and had communicated their
recommendations.

My feeling of support from Bhutan was distinct and overwhelming. Instead of a formal meeting with the health bureaucrat responsible for the WHO, the King put at our disposal riding horses
which took us several hundred feet up along a very small trail to
one of the Buddhist monasteries on a hilltop. The trail was a yard
wide at the most, and the abyss over the edge of the trail was hundreds of feet deep. What was in our karma? I was scared to death,
but I didn't bat an eye. We carried out our discussion about health
and monastic life with Mr. Ngedup, a top health official, drinking
the country's traditional buttery tea and listening to the afternoon

prayers of the monks. We saw museums and ancient fortresses which the Bhutanese had won in battle with the Tibetans, but we didn't see much in the way of modern medical facilities.

Elsewhere

The United States and India did not have seats on the executive board, but we kept in touch with both countries. In particular, the U.S. Secretary of Health and Human Services, Donna Shalala, was actively encouraging and supportive, as were many Americans, especially the people connected with the Harvard School of Public Health, my own alma mater.

While I was in Washington, D.C., Dr. Alleyne briefed me on the situation in the Americas. Olav reminded me later that he had also cited a famous remark made between U.S. candidates before an election: "We shall conduct ourselves in a way that recalls that, when the campaign is over, we shall again be eating our lunches in the same restaurant." A remark from Dr. David Hamburg of the Carnegie Corporation to my husband is on record. Dr. Hamburg is an old friend of Dr. Alleyne, but had told him directly: "OK, George, this is the time for Gro and not for you, old pal."

Indian support was clear as well. But I was also asked why I wanted the WHO post and not the more important job of Secretary-General of the U.N. itself. The Prime Minister meant well, but he had touched upon a sore subject. In India, as in other places, I was met with some suspicion that my willingness to take responsibility for the WHO was only to create a platform from which to reach for the U.N. leadership. Few at the top levels in member states were directly interested in the WHO and health matters. These were looked upon as secondary and often left to junior Ministers. I not only disagreed with this outlook but also made an effort to underline the importance of making health matters a top priority for heads of national governments worldwide. It strengthened my belief that a reform of the health sector in many countries was necessary to really make a difference. The Finance Minister and even the Prime Minister should be as much involved in health issues as the actual Health Minister.

Particularly in India, I sensed a general lack of confidence among journalists in their country's health system. We visited the Minister of Health and had a long and detailed discussion examining both the successes and the shortcomings in his country. At a press conference later that day in the Norwegian Embassy I was confronted with a barrage of negative questions amounting to a message of despair and lack of trust in the democratic system. I had to lift people's spirits and so I coined a phrase: "We will fight until we win!" At least the motto went down very well with Olav and has become a household slogan. On an international level, the widespread lack of belief in the democratic system is a great danger. But the system has to deliver.

Unclear Signals

I must say, we gathered a variety of impressions about health and development during our travels. We had to realize that many countries had overlapping and competing agendas. We also found that it could be difficult to identify the person who in reality controlled the country's vote. Was the Health Minister or National Director of Public Health in control, or was the real decision made at a lower administrative or a higher political level? Any single representative could have a personal agenda to look after. Promises of support were given in a variety of tones, but cards were always kept relatively close to the chest.

I felt confident of the support of Germany, the Netherlands, and Ireland, but I was far from assured of the Polish vote or the Croatian vote, since Croatia was flirting with nominating its own candidate. For a while, the new British vote looked a bit unsure as well. The British Minister of Development, Clare Short, favored Nafis Sadik whom she knew and respected. It took some time before the

British preference for me was finally made clear by Prime Minister Tony Blair. From the start, Clare and the United Kingdom have been great supporters.

I had long been sympathetic to secret voting, as it is the best way of obtaining the truest outcome. You cannot be punished for a vote that no one can attribute to you. On the other hand, secret voting can be open to manipulation. Kofi Annan has a telling story about secret ballots. Thirty-two African countries had once decided to vote for the same candidate. But after the election, it was clear that only eight votes could have come from Africa. At a subsequent "clean-up" meeting among the thirty-two, each and every one stood up and guaranteed that his delegation had been voting according to the agreement.

Somebody had obviously concocted the idea that as a former Prime Minister of Norway, I was traveling around in developing countries, promising an increase in Norwegian development aid as payment for the vote. Needless to say, this was not the case. Norway was in fact doing quite the contrary vis-à-vis Botswana, cutting down on assistance and moving the embassy out.

At home I enjoyed broad support, although the leader of the Progressive Party criticized the use of public money for my candidacy. He warned that it would be costly for Norway to have Gro Harlem Brundtland atop one of the U.N. organizations since her position would lead to increased Norwegian spending on the U.N.

But Morten Wetland felt sure that my candidacy would be better acknowledged abroad if it was openly supported at home. Consequently, he stimulated substantial Norwegian press coverage, strong enough to convince Oslo-based diplomats to write positive reports to their capitals about my "overwhelming campaign." We also had to handle the domestic nay-sayers who were grumpy about the cost of our successful campaign. When challenged, we answered that the cost of the campaign was roughly equal to a few hundred seconds of TV advertising for, let's say, detergents. It worked. None seriously questioned the campaign costs at home.

We were running a clean campaign. We did not make shady

promises or "dirty deals"; in fact we made no deals at all. Years later I learned that an Asian colleague had suggested that Norway should take from its "Official Development Assistance" (ODA) account to help alleviate the damage created by a cyclone over the Cook Islands. In his words, Norway should use its "ODA muscle" on this voting member of the EB. The suggestion, however, was turned down as soon as it reached the Ministry of Foreign Affairs in Oslo. A candidate is much better off if she is elected without strings and promises attached. Stories about corrupt practices are sadly quite frequent.

The Nomination

It was not until the fourth round of voting on January 27 that a majority was established. Eighteen votes were cast in my favor. I was the nominee of the Executive Board to be put forward to the Health Assembly in May. I was the first woman nominated through a broad electoral process to the top position of any U.N. agency. I felt a mixture of relief at this outcome and a tingling anticipation for the future.

There was no other nominee and the Health Assembly had always followed the recommendation from the EB, but formally I was only a nominee and I asked that this somewhat modest designation should be observed. I was in no rush to have anyone prematurely upgrading me. It would certainly invite criticism if a woman even inadvertently looked like she was craving status.

Olav took the first plane from Oslo to join us in a reception at Ambassador Skogmo's residence. It was time for joy, especially for the many who had worked on my campaign.

The Transition Team

The idea of creating a transition team had come up in the fall. We took our inspiration from the U.S. election practice. A month before the nomination, Jonas produced a memorandum on the organization of the team. I had wanted to have at least two or three new initiatives ready for implementation from Day One of my possible tenure. I wanted to demonstrate a dramatically different way of working from the very first day. We established our priorities: efforts to roll back malaria, vigorous opposition to the tobacco industry, and a serious look at mental health.

Morten and Jonas suggested that we ask the Norwegian government for a grant to support our transition team. They argued that having only one financial source was a great asset. With many donors we would only risk having "stakeholders" with notions of exclusive rights to the new administration. It had been my line from the beginning, as it had been during more than twenty years in Norwegian politics, to avoid giving lobbying groups any special rights.

Knut Vollebaek, the Foreign Minister of the new minority government by the parties of the Middle, agreed with our ideas. He had a long track record, as a civil servant and first-class diplomat, of supporting development policies. He saw the window of opportunity for world health and granted us $750,000 for the transition. We now had a real opportunity to prepare well.

The support from the Norwegian Ministry of Foreign Affairs meant that we were ready to hit the ground running after the nomination was secured. Jonas left the Prime Minister's office immediately and started our preparatory work. He moved into offices at the Ecumenical Center in Geneva, located in the immediate neighborhood of the WHO. Norway gave him the title of ambassador. He soon had a small team around him, one that represented a broad mix of health experience, Ministerial administrative experience, and internal WHO expertise. We recruited on a wide geographical basis. It was not a team that could be depicted as just another Scandinavian group. A photograph of the group would show its global composition.

I was paid no salary. It was not really important to me, but I realized that during the first half of 1998, for the first time in my professional life, I was without regular income. Economically, I was for the first time a housewife dependent on the income of my husband.

Dissatisfaction

Among member states there had been a growing dissatisfaction with the WHO's ability to deliver strategic advice and direction. This problem became more pressing as the need for a strong international source of expertise increased. The vast majority of countries are now undergoing profound changes in the organization of their health systems, due not only to economic factors, but also to the dramatic changes in international health conditions. Developing countries now face the double burden of disease. In addition to the traditional maternal and childhood ill health and the toll of infectious disease, they also face an aging population with newly emerging noncommunicable diseases.

There are many reasons why the WHO had failed to perform. New players had emerged on the scene of global development, including the World Bank; lack of credit and financial support for many countries had had an increasing impact, often resulting in conflicting advice to troubled countries from different parts of the U.N. system.

To continue to be a credible source of advice in health, the WHO needed to coordinate with others. It needed to take into account links between health and the economy, the priorities set in national budgets, and the financing systems for health. Improved management and prioritizing were big issues.

The problems were integral to the organization itself. The WHO had weak management. There was no formal senior management setting priorities in an organized manner. There were, so to speak, seven WHOs, meaning Geneva and the six regional offices; or perhaps there were two WHOs—the one financed by the regular budget and the one financed by "extrabudgetary contributions, donations by member countries as well as by public and private entities." There were more than fifty individual programs at the headquarters in Geneva. The WHO was gradually developing into what I would call a nonaligned organization as its different parts moved in different directions, each regional office operating in its own sphere.

The Formal Election

Support for me was overwhelming at the World Health Assembly, and I was soon Director General–elect two months before the formal takeover.

By using the model of the cabinet in a parliamentary system, we planned to create streamlining and a cabinet-style leadership that could act in a coordinated way. Any Executive Director in the cabinet would have two different responsibilities: to manage his or her "cluster" and to advance our whole general platform. The WHO needed renewal; a Geneva cabinet of executive directors would be one of its new features. Every new Executive Director would have to share general responsibility for the agency and defend the conclusions we all reached, just as any cabinet Minister in a parliamentary system would have to do. Terms would be two years to start with.

We were creating a small revolution. We put together a relatively small cabinet consisting of ten persons, including me. I was happy to see that six of our ten executives were women. My feeling has been that as new winds are blowing through the U.N. system, a specialized agency like the World Health Organization should certainly be able to widen its base to recruit its top management team with less of a straitjacket. The Security Council has the imprint of the major powers of the world in 1945. As we were moving into the next century, why not try a change?

The cabinet responsibilities were given to nationals from Mexico, Germany, South Africa, Tunisia, India, Australia, and Japan, as well as two citizens of permanent members of the Security Council, the United States and China. In choosing my senior policy advisers, we covered two more of the permanent five, the United Kingdom and France. In addition, there was room for staffers from Turkey, Ghana, and South Korea. The leadership's average age was lowered from fifty-nine to forty-nine.

My insistence on having the final word in the selection of executive directors might have come as a surprise to some. The Japanese Ministry of Health had brought forward three names for consideration. All three male. All very senior. I asked for women. I got no an-

swer. Eventually I chose Dr. Hiro Suzuki. He was not yet forty years
of age.

The former senior management team was asked to make their
positions available. They were not asked to leave. A few became my
close collaborators. Others left gradually as they reached retirement
age.

Before taking over in Geneva, I had family plans. Cecilie and
Knut had invited us to the baptism of their third child, Anders. At
the party with family and friends, we enjoyed the best summer
weather Norway offers.

Jonas and I returned to Geneva that same afternoon. He had participated in the family event as a longtime friend of Knut and Cecilie's. Jonas who so ably had managed my transition team, came
along to the WHO to be my *"chef du cabinet."*

I was especially saddened to leave my daughter Kaja and my sister Hanne, who were both sorry that I had begun working in a foreign country. I also had to leave my mother, who was aging and
would soon be unable to look after herself.

Sunday, July 19, 1998, on my way to Geneva, I flew over the
beautiful Oslo Fjord and its series of small islands along the coast; I
was thrilled to identify the area of our summer home. This was the
first time since 1965, when our little family returned from a year in
the United States, that we would be split. But I was not alone. As
Jonas and I began the detailed planning of the crucial days ahead,
my spirits lifted. We had a mission. Through systematic preparation
we had developed a vision for the WHO and a strategy for implementing it. I would be in for a long journey, one of working with
others to make a difference.

Day One

The departing Director General, Dr. Nakajima, was expecting me
on July 21 for the formal turnover of responsibility. As you enter

the WHO building's seventh floor, you see a reception area with large windows facing the Jura Mountains to the northwest. Geneva is a green city. Although far from home here, I would be close to nature. The Director General told me about the origins of some of the objets d'art on the shelves, tokens of appreciation from different member states over the decades. Now I was to be their caretaker. To him this was clearly symbolic.

On Day One, I announced my structural changes. I abolished the post of Deputy Director General, and installed my ten-member senior management team of Executive Directors to carry out real executive functions.

The day before the ten of us had met for the first time at the shining mahogany dinner table in the residence of the Norwegian Ambassador. We discussed why the WHO had gradually been moved aside, not only on the international development scene but also within the health field. I wrote out for my colleagues points of advice from my experience building cabinet teams. My cabinet would have regular meetings on a prepared agenda, with both the agenda and the meetings' conclusions circulated throughout the agency. All background papers on strategic issues would also be circulated throughout the agency for input.

Clusters

The WHO has been said to have the financial resources of a middle-sized university hospital. Relative to its task of helping to provide humanity with the highest possible level of human health, it is not a very wealthy institution. It might rather be thought of as a global Ministry of Health dedicated to serving the planet.

To integrate and consolidate the work we created nine clusters, which signaled our broad approach.

"Communicable Diseases" focuses, through global partnerships, on reducing the impact of malaria and tuberculosis and on monitoring health problems to enable effective responses to epidemics.

"Noncommunicable Diseases" develops and tests preventive strategies to address several major diseases through their common risk factors. A special focus is given to cancer, cardiovascular diseases, and tobacco-related illnesses.

"Sustainable Development and Healthy Environments" focuses on supporting countries and promoting policies that can address poverty as a major cause of ill health.

"Health Systems and Community Health" focuses on the delivery of high-quality health services and on developing the WHO's role in the international response to the global HIV/AIDS epidemic.

"Evidence and Information for Policy" develops methods, tools, and standards to collect data for health policy analysis. This cluster is expected to help develop methods for examining the effectiveness of different approaches to health-care financing.

"Health Technology and Drugs" focuses on clinical technology, assuring the safety, quality, and cost-effectiveness of blood transfusions, products, and services. Attention is also given to developing the WHO's role in immunization. The last stretch in a long march toward polio eradication is another important challenge.

"Social Change and Mental Health" focuses on the growing burden of mental illness.

"External Relations and Governing Bodies" reaches out to external partners—other U.N. agencies, the Bretton Woods institutions, the private sector, and NGOs.

"General Management" pursues reform with the overall aim of reducing administrative costs, strengthening our information technology base, and developing new policies for staff development and training.

The WHO has another important job: to be a focal point for the best research. We established three pathfinder projects: Roll Back Malaria, the Tobacco-Free Initiative, and Partnership for Health Sector Development.

My plans for the reorganization were already there by the time of the Health Assembly in May. The speech I gave to the assembly expressed my ambitions. When I read that speech today it seems a blueprint for what I have since tried to achieve.

I had been in Oslo, in daily contact with Jonas—but at a useful distance from all the pressures in Geneva. I did come to Geneva a few times for prepared brainstorming.

When I had met with Dr. Nakajima the day after my nomination, I raised the question of nominations to senior posts in the remaining six months. We agreed that I would be informed of all upcoming senior appointments. It all worked out as intended. Very few appointments were made, and the ones my predecessor put forward were first discussed with me.

Two days after the nomination, I met with Kofi Annan in Davos. He gave me firm support. Take the initiative, set concrete goals, keep the momentum, don't yield to pressure, he told me. This advice was nothing new to me, but it confirmed how the Secretary-General looked at things.

Throughout the transition months, Jonas kept close contact with the Secretary-General's office. Annan invited member states to support a renewal fund for the incoming Director General. I came in in the middle of a tight budget period. We raised close to $7 million, which allowed us to invest in new communication systems, extensive training programs, and the building of what we called the evidence base, the data for health policy analysis.

During the spring the Director General–elect of the International Labor Organization (ILO) came to see the offices of the transition team. Juan Samovia was in a similar situation, between winning his election and actually taking over the ILO. He liked the concept of a transition team and created his own, as did Mark Malloch Brown, Director General–elect of the United Nations Development Program (UNDP). I asked Jonas to open all books and share all our experience.

It was important to set the right tone from the very start. My central point in my address to staff was that serving in the WHO was a privilege. We could make a difference. We could help build healthy communities and populations. To do so, the WHO would have to work as one organization, as a team with a strong team spirit, turning our diversity into our strength.

I knew there would be many difficult challenges ahead. On my first day in office I felt in equal parts eagerness, inspiration, and anxious concern.

In my opening address, I said it was my prime responsibility to maintain and further develop the technical excellence of the WHO. But I was also convinced that I needed to bring a political dimension to the WHO's leadership, a greater awareness of a changing world, a better sense of interaction with the countries and populations we were there to serve, a better grasp of the key economic and technological issues that shape the global development agenda of which health is such a critical component.

Health and Globalization

19

Trends in Global Health: Our Challenge

My vision for the new WHO came in response to the health challenges of the world, which are in transition. In 1990, almost half of the global burden of disease was due to communicable diseases, problems of childhood and maternal health, and malnutrition. In 2020, it is expected that these conditions will account for less than one quarter of human ill health. Noncommunicable diseases and injuries will have gained in relative importance.

There are important achievements to build on. Child mortality is decreasing, but we must lower the rate further through increased immunization. Mental health needs to become a major public health concern, and we must push for better data and the best policy advice. I have made the decision to upgrade our work and prepare for a major, new effort and a World Health Report to focus solely on this burning issue.

Women are the primary caretakers. We must push for real change for women, children, and families. Unless the world starts acting much more effectively, the coming years will be dominated by poverty and underdevelopment, the persistence of infectious disease and malnutrition, unsafe conditions for motherhood and lack of prenatal care.

More than half of deaths due to acute respiratory infections and nearly 90 percent of deaths due to diarrhea, malaria, and measles occur among children under the age of five. Underpinning all these problems is poverty, which leads to ill health, which in turn breeds more poverty. Today, 90 percent of resources allocated for health are spent on 10 percent of the world's population, the wealthiest part. This clearly has to change.

In early 1999, preparing for my first World Health Report as Director General of the WHO, we focused on a few key points to show that combating poverty through better health is also sound economics. Because of the great health achievements of the twentieth century, living conditions improved dramatically for the large majority of human beings, and health care has grown into a vast industry absorbing more than 9 percent of the world's wealth—more than $2,000 billion.

Yet more than a billion people have been left behind. I see this as our single most important challenge—to help lift the poor out of poverty. It means making a special effort to ensure that the poorest one billion people in our world get the health services they need to prosper. It means addressing up front the many components of global health—reproductive health, immunization, environmental health, and nutrition. It means making sure that health systems around the world work well and respond in a fair way to poor people's needs.

Women and children suffer more than men. There is a need to invest more in reducing maternal mortality. No other health issue is more directly linked to poverty than the conditions related to pregnancy—around the world, every minute of every day, a woman dies during pregnancy. She dies because there is no skilled person to handle complications during delivery or because she has been referred to a hospital too late. She may even die in a hospital without the treatment she needs. Here the gap between rich and poor is at its most extreme. While the risk of death due to giving birth is one in four thousand in rich countries, it can be as high as one in fifteen in the most disadvantaged communities of African countries.

To widen the scope of our work and to help set the agenda for the World Health Assembly in 1999, I invited the new Nobel Laureate in Economic Science, Professor Amartya Sen, to share his visions, putting health into the broader context of poverty and its alleviation. Amartya Sen was now the husband of my friend and colleague Emma Rothschild, who worked with us on the Palme Commission.

There is mounting evidence that targeted health interventions aimed at improving the health of the poor can bring about real developmental gains. As in Europe at the end of the nineteenth and the beginning of the twentieth century, we have seen that developing countries investing relatively more in health, and investing well, are likely to achieve higher economic growth. As another example, in East Asia life expectancy increased by more than eighteen years in the two decades that preceded the most dramatic economic boom in history. A recent analysis by the Asian Development Bank concluded that one third of the phenomenal Asian economic growth between 1965 and 1997 resulted from investment in people's health.

I sensed a growing realization among decision makers that to reduce poverty, we must improve health. Healthy populations have better school attendance, higher incomes, and more rapid economic development. However, I knew there was a real need to gather more hard evidence and involve top economists, development experts, and key health experts in order to create a clarion call for action. A commission, like the one I chaired on environment and development, could have the potential to reach finance ministers, prime ministers, and heads of state.

In the fall of 1999, I asked leading economists and health experts from around the world, led by Harvard professor Jeffrey Sachs, to analyze the links between health and economic development, and the Commission on Macroeconomics and Health was born.

At the World Health Assembly in May 2000 I could confidently say that health was no longer an issue of exclusive concern to health professionals. Health issues had now become prominent on the agendas of heads of state debating the major political issues facing our world. Health was seen as a key component of human security, a view that brings together human development and national security as the basis of foreign policy. For the first time in its history a health issue—HIV/AIDS in Africa—was discussed by the U.N. Security Council. Health was also a key theme of the Millennium Report presented by the United Nations Secretary-General.

As momentum grew, we in the WHO started to talk about the need for the world to rise to the challenge of saving people's lives and addressing the forgotten, but preventable or treatable disease burden of the poor. As I traveled to the Regional Committees of the WHO in September 2000, I addressed the key diseases of poverty—malaria, HIV/AIDS, tuberculosis, and childhood diseases. I summed up the key role they play in sustaining poverty and declared that what we now needed was a "massive effort."

I had asked the question in the WHO—what will be the main sources of the global burden of disease into the twenty-first century? It was necessary to focus the world's attention where it would make the most impact. The following issues are especially important:

Malaria

Partly inspired by our steadfast push and attention, the G-8, the seven most industrialized countries, supplemented by Russia, were focusing more clearly on global health and development issues. More than thirty heads of state met at the Abuja Summit in Nigeria to focus on malaria. As Professor Sachs presented the alarming economic effects of malaria, I was struck by the enormous damage caused by this ancient disease—a loss of economic growth of more

than one percentage point per year, amounting to a 20 percent reduction in GNP after fifteen years. Short-term economic benefits
from malaria control can be up to $12 billion each year. These are
staggering numbers and there is no doubt that malaria is taking a
big bite out of Africa's economic growth.

With Olav I visited Mozambique, Zimbabwe, and Ivory Coast in
the spring. Flowers from the Norwegian King and the Prime Minister surprised me in our room that morning! During my visit with
Gracha Machel, the child activist now married to Nelson Mandela,
she tracked mosquitoes, uninvited guests in her living room, as we
spoke on the health of Africa. She swatted hard to prevent the Director General of the WHO from coming down with malaria as a
result of a visit to Mozambique and her home.

When I had traveled to African countries in the Fall of 1997, visiting patients' wards and talking with health professionals, health
ministers, and heads of state, I was sure to always ask the question,
"What in your view is the biggest burden for Africa—malaria or
HIV/AIDS?" Somewhat surprisingly, everyone gave the same answer: malaria. The spread of the disease was terrifying, the projections of its influence on future life expectancy shocking. Every
day, three thousand children die from malaria. Every year, there are
three to five hundred million cases among children and adults.

But malaria is not just an African issue. Malaria and its economic
impact threaten our stability as a global community and the future
of our increasingly global economy. With the African governments,
we had developed a program of key interventions called Roll Back
Malaria: insecticide-treated nets in the home to reduce transmis-
sion and prevent infection; indoor spraying with safe insecticides;
malaria treatment during pregnancy to protect the mother's health
and improve the birth rate; rapid diagnosis and early treatment to
shorten the illness time and reduce death rates.

Tobacco

At the World Health Assembly in 1998, I had called the audience to
confront an emerging global threat: "Tobacco should not be adver-

tised, subsidized, or glamorized." The WHO launched the Tobacco Free Initiative, calling on a wide range of partners to hold back the relentless increase in global tobacco consumption and to confront powerful vested interests. This is a global health challenge, but also a cultural challenge.

The fact is that four million people die each year from tobacco-related diseases. Tobacco is ranked second on the list of the world's killers, responsible for 6 percent of the causes of fatal disease. But the future predictions were what really caught my attention: if people continue smoking the way they do today, by 2020 tobacco will be the leading cause of death and disability, killing more than ten million people each year. Some 70 percent of the tobacco deaths will be in the developing world, which cannot afford this added burden.

A year later I appointed a committee of experts to study the tobacco's industry's secret and subversive actions, revealed through court cases in the United States. We needed to know whether undue industry influence was at play within the WHO. The report confirmed that the tobacco industry saw itself as being embattled with the WHO and fighting our agenda, staging events to divert attention from this public health issue, attempting to reduce national budgets for tobacco control, and discrediting the WHO as an institution. We advised our member states to be vigilant, and to seek to avoid and reveal such infiltration as it occurred. Not surprisingly, we found that the industry's internal documents also made reference to a rising figure, the former Prime Minister of Norway, as a major force to look out for. They had followed my actions and statements in the 1980s and 1990s—such as a speech I gave at an international meeting on cardiovascular diseases in Oslo, where I presented the evidence that, though emphysema and lung cancer are its more well-known effects, there is a shocking toll of heart and other circulatory system deaths due to tobacco.

Tuberculosis

In the fall of 1998, the WHO launched the Stop TB Initiative at the Global Conference on Lung Health and called for partners to join.

Some 98 percent of the deaths due to TB, and 95 percent of eight million new cases every year, are in developing countries, making the poor poorer.

On average, a TB patient loses three to four months of work time—equivalent to 20–30 percent of annual household income. Whole economies are also affected, as 75 percent of TB patients are men and women in the most economically active age group. Treatment is available and effective, but it is quite costly and it takes months of directly observed treatment.

If not adequately monitored, the risk of drug-resistant tuberculosis increases enormously and becomes a threat to everyone. My visit to Russia in November 2000 provided me with a dramatic illustration of how difficult life situations contribute to the spread of this terrible disease. As we planned our visit to Butyrskaya Prison Hospital in Moscow, our WHO medical service searched for the safest possible face masks to prevent us from acquiring multi-drug-resistant TB.

In my speech to the WHO's Executive Board in January 2001, I described the plight of a very thin man, perhaps in his early forties, standing in his bare cell and telling me about his personal struggle: despite his TB medication, he concluded, he would never survive his nine-year sentence, since he was also HIV positive. Around him stood several cellmates, all of them with TB they had contracted in prison. Both the health and justice ministers are going to great lengths to put Russia's limited resources to their best use. But TB is not only a Russian problem. That prison cell could have been in any of a number of countries. We need to make sure that people can get treatment, regardless of whether they can pay for it.

Vaccines and Immunization

The WHO's goal is the vaccination of every child. The success of national vaccination programs depends on many local factors, but also on international policies that influence the price of essential pharmaceuticals and on the incentives that govern research and development worldwide. Through an exceptionally generous grant from the Bill and Melinda Gates foundation—$750 million—we founded the Global Alliance for Vaccines and Immunization (GAVI) to vaccinate the poor children of the world. This donation stimulated collaboration between key institutions such as the WHO, UNICEF, the World Bank, and a number of other private donors.

Immunization coverage has slipped to dismal levels in many countries—in parts of Africa, coverage is now well below 50 percent. We need to expand the number of existing vaccines that are part of routine immunization. GAVI helps governments and communities address these challenges. In less than two years, GAVI has responded to 36 countries, committing more than $600 million for upgrading immunization programs.

Lifting Health to the Top Political Level

I had already defined the need for the WHO to become more political. There was no way to effect change without influencing the thinking of others, to reach the minds and hearts of key decision-makers worldwide. This aspect was key to the developments from the very beginning of my term.

Nigerian President–elect Olusegun Obasanjo, a friend of mine from the Palme Commission, traveled to Geneva and New York in preparation for his accession to office in his country. He had asked to see me, and with my staff we discussed health problems in Nigeria but also in Africa in general. As I listened to Olusegun's briefings, I sensed that his primary concerns were not really focused on health. But his mind was open—he listened as I brought him through the problems of malaria and HIV/AIDS, and shared with him the key role that Nigeria itself could play in the eradication of polio in Africa.

We agreed to work together, and as our meeting came to an end, he had been inspired by the challenge of Roll Back Malaria and wanted to host a summit to help create the necessary political momentum in Africa. We worked in partnership to make African leaders commit to Roll Back Malaria as well as to combat HIV/AIDS and tuberculosis.

In July 2000 we met again, in Tokyo. I was addressing the G-8—the seven most industrialized countries, plus Russia—on poverty and disease, while President Obasanjo spoke on urgent issues for the development agenda, such as debt relief and the key importance of health in development. He was invited as the present chair of the so-called Group of 77, which comprises developing countries worldwide.

Japanese Prime Minister Obuchi had invited me to Tokyo, where I found myself addressing, among others, President Jacques Chirac, Prime Minister Tony Blair, and Commission President Romano Prodi of the EU. Because I had met and worked with these leaders before, I sharpened my message: people in developing countries die young, half of them as a result of infectious disease, and at least half of these deaths are due to HIV, TB, and malaria. Each death could be avoided with technologies available today. Although intervention is inexpensive and cost-effective, their cost cannot be met by governments working with health-care budgets of less than $10 per capita.

To make a real change in this picture, we needed to create new international commitment—especially in the US, Europe, Canada, and Japan.

The European Union is a key player in global political issues, in trade, in the environment, in other issues affecting global health, and, of course, in development cooperation. When Romano Prodi assumed EU Commission leadership it meant that once again a European politician who I had known before was at the helm of the Commission. Pascal Lamy, the EU Commissioner for Trade and Economy, had been a key ally as Norway negotiated and participated in creating the European Economic Area. Pascal Lamy had been "chef de cabinet" under Jacques Delors, a friend and colleague of mine for many years. Poul Nielsen, the Danish commissioner responsible for development cooperation in the EU, was also an old political colleague from the Nordic Council. The young, enthusiastic Commissioner for the Environment, Margot Wallstrøm, belonged to a new generation of Swedish politicians.

I visited Brussels once again under the new Commission. A new era of cooperation was evolving among Commissioners inside the

Prodi Commission, linking development, trade, environment, and health issues in an unprecedented manner. It was terrifically encouraging. After all, not only did the European Commission represent key donors and supporters of the United Nations system, including the Nordic countries, it also included four of the G-8—the United Kingdom, France, Italy, and Germany. The policies evolving within the European Union would clearly have an impact on the policies pursued by the G-8.

New Ideas

The July 2001 G-8 meeting in Genoa will be remembered for its very tight security measures, which brought part of the city to a complete standstill. I will remember my first meeting with President George W. Bush, who greeted me cheerily and warmly, applauding the work my staff and I do in the WHO. Health was firmly on the agenda. President Bush had already announced the first contribution to the Global Fund in May. We had had the honor to receive the Secretary-General of the United Nations, who addressed the World Health Assembly on global health and the new fund—the first address ever by a UN Secretary-General to that important ministerial gathering.

By 2002, the Global Fund had mobilized around $2 billion in additional resources for key health interventions. The new fund was a natural alliance of positive forces mobilizing for equitable, measurable real health outcomes in scaled-up efforts to take on HIV/AIDS, TB, and malaria. As we had seen with GAVI, the Global Fund would provide momentum, inspiration, and renewed conviction that a massive effort is both essential and indeed possible. This was high on the agenda by the time of the second Abuja Summit called by President Obasanjo, which focused on the dramatically increasing burden of AIDS. The silence had been broken. The Secretary-General of the UN addressed the issue very forcefully and called for a New Global Fund to fight AIDS, tuberculosis, and malaria.

I was optimistic as we moved into 2002. In London, I received the Commission on Macroeconomics and Health report together with Clare Short, a staunch supporter of global health and development action. The Commission's report convincingly demonstrated that just a few health conditions are responsible for a high proportion of the avoidable deaths in poor countries. It also illustrated how well-targeted measures, using existing technologies, could save the lives of around 8 million people per year and generate yearly economic benefits of more than $360 billion by the year 2015. On average, the price tag for the essential interventions per person per year in low- and middle-income countries will be $34 by 2007, compared to an average $2000 per person today in industrialized countries. The economic benefits would vastly outstrip the costs of the program. As Jeffrey Sachs effectively put it, this is asking for no more than a penny out of every $10 from the richer countries.

This report was a turning point. We now had solid scientific basis for action and measurable ways to save the lives of millions of people, who will gain freedom from disease and create, produce, and participate in building stronger and better communities and nations.

This was the groundbreaking idea of the Marshall Plan in the aftermath of World War II. Billions and billions of dollars, invested over a number of years in the peoples and futures of a war-torn Europe, solidified democracy, rebuilt the strength of new generations, and created new and lasting prosperity—to the benefit of all, including the country that donated these crucial investments: it boosted economic growth in the United States more than anywhere else, and it inspired hope and prosperity around the globe. A penny for every ten dollars means this costs far less than that visionary policy of the mid last century.

A Global Agenda

In the years approaching the turn of the last century, there were great hopes and expectations for a brighter, more peaceful new millennium. It was a decade of major United Nations conferences, with governments, research institutions, nongovernmental organizations, and the whole of the United Nations family of institutions coming together to follow up key challenges to our common future.

In the biggest global summit ever, the September 2000 Millennium Summit at the General Assembly in New York, world leaders and heads of state and government declared the Millennium Development Goals: Income, Poverty, Food Security and Nutrition, Health and Mortality, Reproductive Health, Education, Gender Equality and Women's Empowerment, and the Environment. I felt it covered the keys to our common future, all the crucial concerns to be addressed in helping to fulfill the rights of people wherever they live. And health figured prominently to build sustainable development.

A year later, the Norwegian Nobel Committee awarded, in equal parts, the Nobel Peace Prize to the United Nations and to its Secretary-General, Kofi Annan. It was a sign of hope and trust, a demonstration of support to an institution that we all own and must use to its fullest capacity. It was an expression of respect, love, and gratitude to the man who has been at its helm and helped inspire common causes and actions for humanity. Kofi Annan's determined efforts and success in helping bring the AIDS crisis fully onto the global and African agenda had illustrated his commitment.

New Response

I was in the Singapore airport, on my return trip from Brunei, the host country for our annual committee meeting of the Western Pacific region, when I watched the destruction of the World Trade Center on September 11, 2001. Like hundreds of other organizations, we at the WHO suddenly perceived our mission in new and urgent terms. Emerging threats and the prospect of hundreds of thousands of refugees in central Asia was a reminder that basic issues of human health, too, had been globalized, and that the strike on buildings in New York could lead people to go hungry in Peshawar.

It took less than a week after the attack before the WHO was deeply involved in its immediate consequences. In the industrialized world there was now a new sense of emergency and fear—risks of bioterrorism, exemplified through anthrax scares, were suddenly much more relevant. With the emergence of biological weapons, which few if anyone had fully imagined could be used, we found ourselves asking, Could smallpox or chemical weapons be the next shock to humanity?

We started getting questions from capitals all over the world. From a Prime Minister's office came a call to me: What are the risks? What should be done? We advised governments in general that knowledge, preparedness, and contingency plans were the proper defense. We quickly updated our 1970 manual on biological and chemical weapons and posted it on the WHO website so that governments and public health professionals would have immediate access to it. I was due to address our American regional committee in Washington, D.C., just 10 days after the attacks. My message would illustrate our interdependence in this world and would stress vigilance, preparedness, and the need to mobilize our combined resources in order to protect public health. Reliable health intelligence is a critical element of the public health response to all outbreaks, whatever the cause.

The national disease surveillance and response system is a global network, backed by the WHO, with expertise, prepositioned resources and support from more than 250 laboratories. The global network is linked to the International Health Regulations—the legally binding instrument that governs the reporting of epidemic-prone diseases and the application of measures to prevent their spread. The global network also has capacity to work with countries to investigate dangerous pathogens and confirm case diagnoses.

In the first weeks following the attacks, shock, fear, anger, and denial dominated many people's perspectives. Focus was on retaliation, on how to bring justice to the perpetrators. A coalition of new determinism to fight terrorism was emerging. Nothing could be more compelling to convince individuals and societies that we have become intrinsically dependent on one another as a global community.

If many Americans once thought there was no connection between the United States and a place as seemingly remote as Afghanistan, that illusion has been forever shattered. And if the impact of endangered lives runs so far and so deeply, then surely the impact of lives lived in the leper colonies of India and the malaria swamps of Africa has reach as well.

Before September 11, world leaders had started making commitments to attack the major diseases associated with poverty. We were determined that we would not lose track of the broader picture. In the face of security threats of a new dimension, we needed renewed collaboration. A sense of global community would have to prevail to promote sustainable development and a decent life for all peoples.

Doctor or Politician?

I have had to ask myself this question again and again: Am I a doctor or a politician?

As I entered the World Health Organization in 1998, my leadership role had a precise requirement. It says in the constitution that the leader must be a doctor. Now clearly I was both doctor and politician. My life had in many ways been a preparation for this.

My training in public health has guided me as a politician. And I chose public health because I had values to pursue. As a doctor and as a politician, you have to first ask: What is the problem? Then, how can we prevent and cure this problem? Who needs to become involved? How shall we act together to reach common goals?

Answering those questions is what I have done all my life. This is my philosophical and practical approach. I come from a political background where "solidarity" is an honorable word. We stand to gain if we as people and societies are able to harness everyone's resources, regardless of nationality, economic position, heritage, religion, race, or gender.

This outlook is the one that will help us rise to the challenges of the twenty-first century.

Index